ALEXANDER THE GREAT

J. F. C. FULLER

DA CAPO PRESS

Library of Congress Cataloging in Publication Data

Fuller, J.F.C. (John Frederick Charles), 1878-1966.
  The Generalship of Alexander the Great.

(A Da Capo paperback)
  Reprint. Originally published: New Brunswick, N.J.: Rutgers
University Press, 1960.
  Includes bibliographical references and index.
  1. Alexander, The Great, 356-323 B.C.—Military leadership. 2.
Greece—History—Macedonian Expansion, 359-323 B.C. I. Title.
DF234.2.F85   1989   355'0092 [B]   89-11796
ISBN 0-306-80371-3

This Da Capo Press paperback edition of
The Generalship of Alexander the Great
is an unabridged republication of the
edition published in New Brunswick, New Jersey
in 1960. It is reprinted by arrangement
with Rutgers University Press.

3 4 5 6 7 8 9 10   02 01 00 99

Published by Da Capo Press, Inc.
A member of the Perseus Books Group

PREFACE

✯✯✯✯

Alexander the Great first aroused my interest in 1917, when I read Colonel Theodore A. Dodge's two volumes on Alexander in his *Great Captains* series while in France on the Headquarters Staff of the recently raised Tank Corps. It struck me how modern were Alexander's campaigns, and how much could be learnt from his battles which might be applied to tank warfare. When I became an instructor at the Camberley Staff College in 1923, as one of my duties was to lecture on military history, instead of selecting the last war, or Stonewall Jackson's campaigns, which had been the stock subject since about 1900, I decided that were my students to be taught anything of historical value to them in the next war, I could not do better than select Alexander's campaigns. The result was a series of some twenty lectures, very amateurish I am afraid, because my other duties did not permit me to do more than base them on Dodge and Arrian's *Anabasis of Alexander*. I found my subject so interesting, and so extraordinarily modern, that in 1925 I made up my mind, after further study, to write, not a new life of Alexander, of which there were many, but an analysis of his generalship, on which, so far as I was then aware – and still am – no single work had been devoted. Fortunately I was unable to undertake the task until recently, because since 1925 much literature of a highly critical nature has appeared on Alexander.

Whether the reader is a classical scholar or, like myself, merely a student of history, a point which is likely to strike him is that, unlike Julius Caesar, who is intimately known to us from his *Commentaries* and the writings of Cicero and others, we have practically no first-hand contemporary evidence on Alexander. We have a multitude of his alleged sayings and a number of his letters, some judged genuine and others spurious, but except for a few comments and fragments, we have nothing written of him within 300 years of his lifetime until he came into fashion during the late Roman Republic and early Roman Empire. Then we have the histories of Diodorus Siculus (first century B.C.),

5

Plutarch (second century A.D.), Curtius Rufus (first and second centuries A.D.), and Arrian (second century A.D.), of which the last is outstanding because it is based on the now lost histories of Ptolemy – one
of Alexander's most noted generals, who made use of his *Ephemerides*
(Official Journal) – and of Aristobulus the geographer – one of his
leading technicians.

Long before these late histories, besides those of Ptolemy and Aristobulus, others had appeared, none of which, except in fragments, is
extant. Most of them would seem to have been written by writers of
either the Peripatetic (Aristotle's) school or of Stoic persuasions: the
former hated Alexander because he had put to death his official historian (Callisthenes), a nephew of Aristotle; the latter hated his type –
'the tyrannical man' – as opposed to their ideal of the wise and virtuous
ruler. These prejudiced histories for ages shrouded Alexander's reputation in a fog of falsehood and fictions, and only recently, thanks largely
to Sir William Tarn, has this fog been dissipated. It seems to me that
Tarn has most thoroughly examined the sources of Alexander's history,
and, supported by the classical scholars I have consulted, I have accepted
him as my guide. I am well aware that not all scholars agree with some
of his conclusions; but I am not a scholar, and as scholars are apt to disagree, as a student of history it seems wiser to restrict myself to one
guide than to get involved in the arguments of several, of which I can
be no judge.

Related to this is the question of the reliability of contemporary
documentary evidence. As every subaltern knows, frequently the news-
paper report of an action he has taken part in bears little or no resemblance to what happened. Much the same may be said of Blue Books
and official histories which by careful selection and omission can completely obscure the truth. As so often it is difficult enough to winnow
truth from contemporary documents, how much more difficult must it
be for a scholar, however honest and erudite, to do so from copied and
re-copied records of events which took place 2,000 years before he was
born. This does not mean that frequently he cannot prove that a certain statement is erroneous, highly improbable, impossible, a latter-day
interpolation or propaganda; but it does mean that when a reliable historian, such as Arrian, writes that Alexander did so and so, or said so
and so, which may seem improbable, it is safer to check it against what
is known of Alexander's character and activities than to try to discover
whether it was derived from a reliable or unreliable source. At times,
even unreliable historians hit the nail on the head. As regards this, I
cannot forbear to refer the reader to what Professor T. Rice Holmes

has to say on 'The Authorities of our Authorities' in volume I of his *Roman Republic and the Founder of the Empire.*

Happily, in this study of Alexander's generalship I am not called upon to be a *Quellenforscher*, because the art of war – certainly in its essentials – was the same in Alexander's day as it is now, and this, I hope, will become clearly apparent in Chapter 10. If I am unable to test the credibility of my classical authorities, I am, or should be, able by reference to this art to test the military abilities of Alexander, and by relying on what has been called the method of inherent probabilities in part to make good the frequent omission of tactical and other detail in the classical histories, due to their writers' lack of maps, operation orders and battle reports. This does not mean that exactness can be guaranteed; but it does mean, so I hold, that once the character and talents of a general have been assessed, his aim and problem fathomed, and the conditions in which he was called upon to wage war appraised, it is possible to arrive at a highly probable picture of what happened in a given set of circumstances, even should the date be 2000 B.C.

I have divided this book into two parts, The Record and The Analysis, although this is responsible for a few unavoidable repetitions. Part I provides a condensed history of Alexander's career as statesman and soldier, together with its background; Part II examines Alexander's great battles, sieges and small wars in considerable detail. Finally, his worth as a statesman and a general is assessed. I believe that if books on somewhat similar lines were written on half a dozen or more of the leading generals in history, and the whole then condensed into a single volume, an invaluable manual on generalship could be produced. It is perplexing that this has not been done long ago, if only because as far back as the opening of the last century, Napoleon bade all soldiers who aspired to become successful generals to read and re-read, and model themselves on the eighty-three campaigns of Alexander, Hannibal, Caesar, Gustavus Adolphus, Turenne, Eugene, and Frederick. This, he said, 'is the only way to become a great captain and fathom the secrets of the art'. To accentuate the importance of this, the book has a brief epilogue on the value of history in which I have tried to show that had statesmen and generals-in-chief been acquainted with the history of Greece in the fourth century B.C., they might have avoided many of the colossal blunders perpetrated by them in the Second World War.

Two additional points need mentioning. The first is that, according to wording, I have made use of two English translations of Arrian's *Anabasis of Alexander*; one by Edward James Chinnock in Bohn's

Classical Library, and a more recent translation by the Reverend E. Iliff Robson in the Loeb Classical Library. As the latter library has not yet published a translation of the XVIIth Book of Diodorus Siculus, when referring to this I have relied on the 1814 edition of G. Booth's translation of 1700, which I understand is reliable. The second point is that when I have considered it necessary to convert classical money values into English pounds, I have quoted its 1913 sterling value, when the sovereign was rigidly tied to gold. What its value is today is speculative, and what it may be tomorrow is any man's guess. Again, I would refer the reader to what Rice Holmes has to say on 'The equivalents in our money of the sesterce, the denarius, and the talent' in Volume I of his history.

Finally, my thanks are due to Mr J. P. V. D. Balsdon, M.A., Fellow of Exeter College, Oxford, who most kindly read through the manuscript and made many most valuable suggestions, for which I am greatly indebted; to Mr Anthony S. F. Rippon for his unstinting care in preparing the typescript for the press; to Brigadier J. G. Browne, C.M.G., C.B.E., D.S.O., who in 1928, when Commandant of the Iraq Levies, most kindly arranged for aerial photographs of the village and mound of Keramlais to be taken; to Brigadier Nazeer Ali Shar and his nephew Brigadier Waheed Haidar, both of the Pakistani Army, for obtaining for me the aerial photographs of Pir-sar, for which I am most grateful; and lastly to the Council of the Hellenic Society for their kind permission to reproduce from a silver tetradrachm of Lysimachus (c. 355–281 B.C.) the head of Alexander as frontispiece. The profile is supposed to have been taken from a statue-portrait by Lysippus, or a gem-portrait by Pyrgoteles.

J. F. C. FULLER.

Crowborough.
October, 1957.

CONTENTS

❊❊❊❊

Part I

THE RECORD

Part II

THE ANALYSIS

ILLUSTRATIONS

Part I

THE RECORD

THE BACKGROUND

❧❧❧

Decay of the City-States

When, as is conjectured, those tribes of Indo-European stock to become known to history as the Greeks percolated into the mountain-tangle of the Balkans to settle in its more fertile valleys, they formed pockets of agricultural communities, each cut off from the other. At first each tribal group of villages was congregated closely around its leader's stockaded stronghold, or acropolis; but later, to enhance their protection, the villages were walled in and together with the acropolis became a fortified town. Thus originated the city-state or *polis*, each a minute nation[1] in which citizenship was commonly based on descent from the original conquerors: the citizens possessed all real property, exercised all political rights and performed all military duties. The key to society throughout the heroic age was the tribe and its clans: 'Separate thy men by tribes, by clans', says Nestor to Agamemnon, 'that clan may bear aid to clan and tribe to tribe.' [2]

Each city was a sovereign power with its own king, laws, army, and gods, and each citizen owed allegiance to his city and to no other. The exceptions to this general rule were four regions, each roughly a geographical unit; the kingdoms of Sparta and Argos, which together occupied a considerable part of the Peloponnese; the Attic peninsula, in which Athens absorbed its little city kingdoms; and Boeotia, where the city-states, though not absorbed, fell under the leadership of Thebes.

The political institutions of Homeric times show that the king, as leader of his tribe, was guided by a council of his chiefs, and that his decisions were brought before the Assembly, or gathering of the folk,

---

[1] On the island of Crete alone there were more than fifty small city-states.
[2] *The Iliad*, II, 362.

for ratification. The king was chief priest, chief judge, and supreme war lord; he claimed descent from the gods, and was protected by a body-guard of his companions, as in after times Danish and Saxon kings were by their housecarls.

The political life of the Greek cities was one of nearly endless inter-city war, or of civil discord (*stasis*) within their walls. Plato points out that these inter-city wars were largely caused by over-population,[1] at times relieved by emigration. It was a life of restless ambitions, personal jealousies, party factions and endless cattle raiding; maritime commercial rivals were in a state of constant war. In the seventh century B.C., the poet Archilochus described the free-booter's life at sea: 'In my spear is kneaded bread, in my spear is the wine of Asmarus and I lie upon my spear as I drink.'[2]

Because the citizens lived for war,[3] they had no time for peaceful occupations, which were relegated to serfs, slaves, and metics (aliens). The division between the citizen-soldier and the agricultural labourer formed two main classes, the nobles and the peasants, and the struggle between them became the decisive problem in city politics. After the eighth century B.C., as republics replaced the vanishing clan monarchies, there emerged from the class struggle the forms of government commonly identified with the Greek city-states – aristocracy, oligarchy, democracy, and tyranny; and a point to note is that with the exception of Sparta where a dual monarchy was adopted,[4] no Hellenic city developed a stable form of government.

There were no bonds between the cities except the common language and the great athletic festivals, held under religious auspices and open to all Hellenes. Of these the most noted were the Olympic Games, founded traditionally in the eighth century B.C. and held every fourth year in honour of Olympian Zeus, and the Pythian Games in honour of Apollo of Delphi, which early in the sixth century B.C. were placed under the management of the Amphictyonic Council.[5] Only the

[1] *The Republic of Plato*, trans. A. D. Lindsay (1935), II, 372-3. Compare Hobbes in *Leviathan* (pt. 2, chap. 30): 'And when all the world is overcharged with inhabitants, then the last remedy of all is Warre; which provideth for everyman, by Victory or Death.'
[2] Cited by William Reginald Halliday in *The Growth of the City State* (1923), p. 47.
[3] Again compare Hobbes: 'During the time men live without a common power to keep them all in one they are in that condition which is called Warre' (*Leviathan*, pt. 1, chap. 13).
[4] Artistotle (Politics, 1285a) describes the kings as hereditary generals.
[5] The Delphic Amphictyony was originally a league of twelve ancient Greek tribes inhabiting the country around Thermopylae.

dire threat to all city-states by the Persians, under Xerxes (485–465 B.C.) which was brought to naught at Salamis and Plataea in 480 and 479 B.C., produced some semblance of common patriotism and caused the rise of the Athenian empire with its Periclean dream of union. In the Peloponnesian War (431–404 B.C.) that empire was destroyed, and its policy of union failed because, as Sir Ernest Barker points out, both Athens and her allies, 'equally trammelled by the thought of the city-state, could not arise to the conception of a great non-civic state united in a common citizenship . . . because her citizenship meant – and could only mean – Athenian birth and a full participation in Athenian local life and ways and temper: on their side they could not have accepted the gift if it had been offered, because their citizenship of their cities meant just as much to them'.[1]

The Peloponnesian War, which involved nearly all the city-states, was disastrous to Hellenic polity. By destroying the Athenian empire it upset the balance of power between Greece and Persia, and in 386 B.C. the Sparto-Persian alliance caused the shameful King's Peace, or Peace of Antalcidas, dictated to the Greek states by Artaxerxes II (404–358 B.C.). By its terms the Asiatic Greek cities and Cyprus were abandoned to Persia, the leadership of Sparta within Greece was acknowledged, and any state which did not accept the peace was to be compelled by Persia to do so. Thus the Great King became the arbiter of Greece with the right of perpetual interference.

Equally momentous, this 'Thirty Years War' of the Hellenic age sowed seeds of decay within the cities. Not only did it ruin the agricultural industry of Attica and throw thousands of her peasant farmers into the ranks of the unemployed, but during the long struggle the old militias, the backbone of the city system, through constant service became increasingly professionalized. Although adventurous Greek soldiers and freebooters had hired themselves to foreign princes long before the Persian invasion,[2] and early Greek tyrants had used mercenaries as body-guards, not until the Peloponnesian War did the opportunity arise for their employment on a large scale. By the opening of the fourth

---

[1] *The Cambridge Ancient History*, vol. VI, p. 506. In a footnote Sir Ernest adds: 'A common citizenship would have been to the religious consciousness of all concerned (for the cult of the city-state was in effect a religion) "an intolerable monotheism". Political polytheism was the Greek creed; and that creed overthrew the Athenian Empire. It is curious to reflect that as religion (the religion of the city) was the ruin of the Athenian Empire, so religion (in the sense of a common worship by all cities of a deified ruler) was the basis of the Empire of Alexander among the Greeks.'

[2] See Herodotus (trans. George Rawlinson, edit. 1920, II, 152, 154) for those hired by Psammeticus, king of Egypt (671–617 B.C.).

century B.C. the ordinary Greek citizen militias were so completely outclassed by professional mercenaries that the latter became a typical feature in Greek warfare. There were two results of this: the first was that as mercenaries were not bound by allegiance to any city-state they sold their services to the highest bidder and so became the means whereby democracy could be violently subdued by autocracy; the second was that their services became so eagerly sought after that in the fourth century most of the Persian army infantry was composed of Greek mercenaries. For his expedition against his elder brother Artaxerxes II, in 401 B.C., Cyrus the Younger recruited some 13,000 Greek mercenaries, of whom more than half were poverty-stricken Arcadians and Achaeans.[1] After his defeat at Cunaxa, the remnants of this army retired to the Troad under Xenophon and turned professionals, 'and from them', writes Sir William Tarn, 'dates the growth in Greek history of a world separate from the city-state, the world of mercenaries'.[2]

Thucydides tells us that when the Peloponnesian War broke out the Athenian citizens were ever-ready to brave danger and suffer fatigue and privations for the glory of Athens. He makes the Corinthians say of them: '. . . their only idea of a holiday is to do what the occasion demands, and to them laborious occupation is less of a misfortune than the peace of a quiet life. To describe their character in a word, one might truly say that they were born into the world to take no rest themselves and give none to others.'[3] But as the defence of the cities became more and more dependent upon mercenaries, the ordinary citizen felt military service a burden; he became increasingly pacific and immersed himself in industrial and professional pursuits – in money-making. So pronounced was this change that in order to guarantee a quorum at the meetings of the Athenian Assembly payment of each citizen attending was introduced, and to maintain the unemployed tranquil they were given free seats at the theatre. 'The city was ceasing to be', writes Sir Ernest Barker, 'a partnership in high achievement and noble living: it was becoming a commercial association for the distribution among its members of dividends which they had not earned.'[4]

---

[1] Xenophon's *Anabasis*, vi, 2, 10.
[2] *Hellenistic Military and Naval Developments* (1930), p. 10. See also Grote's *History of Greece* (edit. 1905), vol. IX, p. 274.
[3] *The History of the Peloponnesian War*, trans. Richard Crawley (1874), I, 70.
[4] *The Cambridge Ancient History*, vol. VI, p. 511. See also Grote, vol. IX, pp. 272–274. In *The Ecclesiazusae* (204–5) Aristophanes writes of the Athenians in 393 B.C.: 'Ye draw your wages from the public purse, yet each man seeks his private gain alone.' In 383 B.C. Sparta found her allies so reluctant to serve as soldiers that she was

Reforms of the Philosophers

The decline in morale of the city-state, coupled with the devastation resulting from endless inter-city warfare, shocked the Greek conscience and was rendered vocal by the philosophers, whose speculations, like those of Voltaire, Rousseau, Kant, and others in eighteenth-century Europe, initiated a period of enlightenment which did not reinvigorate but rotted what remained of the crumbling polity of the city-state. The more outstanding of these would-be reformers were Socrates (469–399 B.C.), Plato (429–347 B.C.), and Aristotle (384–322 B.C.).

What these philosophers were unable to understand was that the problem was not the reform of the constitution of the city in accordance with an ideal archetypal *polis* but to expand the circumference of the city until it included all the Hellenic states in Greece, and thereby to create an Hellenic unity and brotherhood. Of Socrates, the earliest in date of the three, all we know of him, as he left nothing in writing, is what has been recorded by Plato, Xenophon, and Aristophanes. He conceived that he had a heavenly mission to educate all and sundry, and Xenophon tells us that – like Joan of Arc – he was directed by divine voices.[1] His tedious dialectics of question and answer must have confused the minds of many of his hearers, and should Plato's dialogues represent his views correctly, then there would seem to have been adequate reason why the conservative Athenians looked upon him as a dangerous visionary and corrupter of youth.[2]

This becomes apparent when we turn to Plato's *Republic* and *Laws*, in which are described the Socratic constitution of the archetypal city-state, the heavenly pattern toward which all reforms were to be directed. The proposals made in these books may be compared with a mixture of the ideas of Calvin, Robespierre, Marx, and Lenin, and the whole summed up as 'Transcendental Bolshevism', which must have been as repellent to Athenian democrats of the fifth and fourth centuries B.C. as Marxian Bolshevism is to Western democrats today.

In this supernal, self-contained, self-sufficient, and self-controlling city-state, the citizens were divided into two classes, the governors and the governed. The former, called 'Guardians', were philosopher

compelled to agree to their commuting their service by paying 3 obols for each foot soldier and 12 for each horse soldier (Xenophon's *Hellenics*, v. ii. 20).

[1] *Memorabilia of Socrates*, I, i, 2 and I, iii, 4.

[2] Although in *Clouds* Aristophanes gives us a distorted caricature of Socrates, it probably voices a considerable section of popular opinion.

soldiers, female[1] as well as male; the latter, the proletariat, craftsmen and menial labourers, who were disenfranchised. So that they might devote all their time to righteousness, the Guardians were deprived of all property, lived in common, fed at the public tables, possessed no money, and were supported by the proletariat. Their wives and children were also held in common; the marriages were regulated, no child knew his father or mother, and all this in order that the state might be one family.[2]

Among the common people, nothing was left to the caprice of individuals; their marriages, fixed between thirty and thirty-five years of age for men and between sixteen and twenty for girls, were controlled by a board of women so that the population might be kept at a uniform level, and all promiscuous unions were strictly forbidden. A Nocturnal Council was established as a Committee of Public Safety, as well as Curators of the Law – a species of secret police – whose task was to hound down heretics. Spying was universal and all wrong-doing reported to the authorities. Also, we read, he who endeavoured 'to second the authorities in their work of repression, he is the great and perfect citizen'.[3]

Other regulations were that all foreign travel was forbidden to citizens under forty years of age, and then only under licence; on their return they 'shall explain to their juniors how inferior are the ways of other nations to the institutions of their own land'.[4] Drinking of wine was prohibited; poets were forbidden to circulate any verses that had not been censored by the Curators, no lending on usury was allowed, no internal currency was to be exported, no citizen was to possess a private shrine in his dwelling and erroneous beliefs about God and the unseen world were to be dealt with as crimes and those who held them were prosecuted.

Plato's aim was ruthless – it was to make all men good, as he conceived goodness. The end justified the means; the end was

---

[1] Plato's views on women were peculiar. He writes that the difference between women and men was 'that the female conceives and the male begets'; then he adds, 'we shall not allow that that goes any way to prove that a woman differs from a man . . . and we shall still consider that our guardians and their wives ought to follow the same pursuits. . . . Then for the purpose of guarding the city the nature of men and women is the same' (*The Republic*, V, 454 and 456). His views on children are equally peculiar: They 'should see war' and should be mounted on horseback, but 'not on spirited chargers', so that when in danger they may escape, 'for in this way they will get the best view of the work for which they are destined' (Ibid., V. 467).

[2] These communistic arrangements are parodied by Aristophanes in his *Ecclesiazusae*.

[3] *The Laws of Plato*, trans. A. E. Taylor (1934), V, 730.   [4] Ibid., XII, 951.

sovereign; the state existed solely to convert each city into a divine ant-hill.

Only when Plato considers the barbarians does he recognize the existence of a common society of Greek states:

> I declare [he writes] the Greek race to be akin and related to them-selves, but foreign and alien to the barbarians . . . Then when Greeks and barbarians fight, we shall say that they are natural enemies, war-ring against one another, and this enmity is to be called war; but when Greeks fight with Greeks, we shall declare that naturally they are friends . . . they should behave to barbarians as Greeks now be-have to one another.[1]

Aristotle is more moderate. A firm believer in Greek life as em-bodied in the city-state, he set out to reform and not to revolutionize. He rejected Plato's communism as impracticable, but nevertheless held that no citizen 'should be permitted to exercise any mechanic employ-ment or follow merchandise, as being ignoble and destructive of virtue; neither should they be husbandmen, that they may be at leisure and perform the duty they owe to the state . . . husbandmen should by all means be slaves'.[2] Like Plato, he considered that barbarians were natural slaves and writes: '. . . it is proper for the Greeks to govern the barbarians as if a barbarian and a slave were by nature one',[3] and 'what we gain in war is in a certain degree a natural acquisition; for hunting is a part of it, which it is necessary for us to employ against wild beasts; and those men who being intended by nature for slavery are unwilling to submit to it, on which occasion such a war is by nature just'.[4]

Neither Plato nor Aristotle was cosmopolitan-minded, and it was left to Isocrates (436–338 B.C.), an Athenian pamphleteer, to point the way toward a better polity than that of the city-state. In 380 B.C., prob-ably a few years after Plato wrote his *Republic*, Isocrates, who desired unity in politics though not in constitution, proclaimed in his *Panegyri-cus* that the Greek world should seek unity less in blood than in a common type of mind. He urged Athens and Sparta to lay aside their animosity and make common cause against Persia.

> I am here to advise you [he said] concerning war against barbarians and harmony among ourselves . . . And it makes a nobler thing to

---

[1] *The Republic*, V, 470–1. This is in contradiction to Socrates' objection to Simonides' definition of justice as 'doing good to friends and evil to enemies' (Ibid., II, 332–4).
[2] *The Politics of Aristotle*, trans. William Ellis (1952), VII, 1328b and 1330a.
[3] Ibid., I, 1252b.   [4] Ibid., I, 1256b.

fight with him [the King of Persia] for his kingdom than to wrangle among ourselves for the leadership of Hellas . . . We cannot enjoy a sure peace unless we make war in common against the barbarians, nor can Hellas be made of one mind until we secure advantages from the same enemies [i.e. the Persians] and meet our perils in the face of the same foes.[1]

These words fell upon sterile soil, because he urged that the leadership against Persia should go to Athens, and to this Sparta most emphatically would not agree.

Philip II of Macedon

Once the King's Peace had freed Sparta from complications in Asia, she returned to her policy of establishing a hegemony over Greece. In 378 B.C. this caused war with Thebes in which Thebes was supported by Athens, and desultory operations followed until 371 B.C., when a mutual agreement was arrived at to discuss peace. But as the Spartans refused to agree that Thebes should represent the whole of Boeotia, the Thebans decided to carry on the war single-handed, and had it not been for their commander, Epaminondas, undoubtedly they would have succumbed.

He was a tactician of genius, and the first Greek general in history to grasp the importance of concentrating superiority of force against a selected point in the enemy's front. He realized that the Spartans were too conservative to change their traditional tactics, the success of which depended on an advance in parallel order, all spears of the phalanx striking the enemy's front simultaneously, and he devised a system of tactics which would prevent this and throw the phalanx into confusion. It was the simplest of ideas; instead of drawing up his troops in line parallel with the Spartan army, he formed them into oblique order to it with his left leading and his right refused. And on his left wing he massed a deep column of troops which could meet shock by super-shock and possessed sufficient reserve force to lap round the enemy's right wing and drive it on to his centre. In July, 371 B.C., he used these tactics when he met and decisively defeated the Spartan army and killed their leader, King Cleombrotus, at Leuctra, in southern Boeotia. This battle broke the charm of Spartan prestige, and ended Sparta's short-lived hegemony.

[1] *The Orations of Isocrates*, trans. J. H. Freese (edit. 1894), 'Panegyricus', III, 166 and 173.

Until 362 B.C. Thebes had the chance to do what both Athens and Sparta had failed to do: to weld the Greek city-states into a federated nation. She built a fleet and weakened Athens at sea, and under Epaminondas and Pelopidas gained the leadership of Greece. But her supremacy hung on the life of one man – Epaminondas. In the summer of 362 B.C., at Mantinea, in Arcadia, he again defeated the Spartans with the same tactics he had used at Leuctra. But the Theban victory was the death-blow to their supremacy, for toward the close of the battle Epaminondas was killed; the light that had guided the Thebans was extinguished, their power by land and sea collapsed. Thus three great city-states, Athens, Sparta, and Thebes, had each failed in turn to establish a federated Hellenic world and Hellas was ready to fall before a conqueror from outside. His name was Philip of Macedon.

Macedonia proper comprised the coastal plain along the Thermaic Gulf (Gulf of Thessalonica) between the Haliacmon (Vistriza) and Axius (Vardar) rivers. According to Herodotus,[1] a Dorian tribe, known as the Macedni, occupied this region, which was inhabited by Illyrian and Thracian tribes, intermarried with them, became barbarized and ceased to be regarded as genuine Greeks by the Hellenes. They had a landed aristocracy and a free peasantry and were governed by a primitive, hereditary patriarchal monarchy. Though the restrictions of the city-state were unknown to them, their institutions were similar to those which existed in Greece in the Heroic Age. They were a turbulent and warlike people and it was the exception for their kings to die in their beds.

In 364 B.C. Perdiccas III ascended the throne of Macedon, and in 359 B.C. he was defeated and slain by the Illyrians in one of the frequent frontier wars. Because his son, Amyntas, was an infant, Perdiccas' brother, Philip, born in 382 B.C., was appointed regent. Perdiccas' death threw Macedonia into turmoil; there were five possible claimants to the throne, and the barbaric Paeonians and Illyrians at once ravaged the Macedonian frontiers. So energetically did Philip deal with this desperate situation that soon after he assumed the Regency the Macedonian army set Amyntas aside and acclaimed him king.

When Philip was fifteen years old he had been sent to Thebes as a hostage where, according to Diodorus,[2] he learnt to appreciate Hellenic culture under the tutorship of a Pythagorean in the household of Epaminondas. More important, during his three years in Thebes, through

[1] I, 56.

[2] *Diodorus of Sicily*, XVI, 2, 2–3. Plutarch ('Pelopidas', xxvi) says that he lived in Thebes with Pammenes.

his acquaintance with Epaminondas and Pelopidas, he became grounded in the Theban art of war.

Philip was a man of outstanding character; practical, long-sighted and unscrupulous. He was a master diplomatist and an astute opportunist to whom success justified everything. He was recklessly brave,[1] yet unlike so many brave generals he would at once set force aside should he consider that bribery[2] or liberality or feigned friendship was more likely to secure his end. He possessed in marked degree the gift of divining what was in his enemy's mind, and when beaten in the field would accept defeat and prepare for victory. Throughout his life he never lost sight of his aim – to bring the whole of Greece under his dominion. As Hogarth writes of him: 'Fraud before force, but force at the last'[3] was his principle of empire. After his death his great opponent Demosthenes said:

> In the first place, he was the despotic commander of his adherents: and in war that is the most important of all advantages. Secondly, they had their weapons constantly in their hands. Then he was well provided with money: he did whatever he chose, without giving notice by publishing decrees, or deliberating in public, without fear of prosecution by informers and indictment for illegal measures. He was responsible to nobody: he was the absolute autocrat, commander, and master of everybody and everything. And I, his chosen adversary – it is fair inquiry – of what was I master? Of nothing at all![4]

Although we do not know what was in Philip's mind in the year 359 B.C., when we look back on his reign it becomes apparent that from the start his intentions were to master the Balkan Peninsula and simultaneously to introduce Greek culture into Macedonia so that his native land might be worthy of his empire. He discerned, as history shows, that in spite of the paucity of his means, because of their political limitations no likely combination of city-states could stand against him. He also recognized that his people, who despised the Hellenes, would never voluntarily adopt Hellenic ways, and that he could not incorporate Greeks, as he could Thracians and Illyrians, into his empire. Therefore he adopted a formula of association, which would save the face of

---

[1] After his death Demosthenes said of him that in 'contending for empire & supremacy he had endured the loss of an eye, the fracture of his collar-bone, the mutilations of his hand and his leg, and was ready to sacrifice to the future of war any and every part of his body, if only the life of the shattered remnants should be a life of honour and renown' (*On the Crown*, trans. C. A. and J. H. Vince (1936), 67).

[2] Diodorus (xvi, 53, 3), writes: 'Indeed he was wont to declare that it was far more by the use of gold than of arms that he had enlarged his kingdom.'

[3] *Philip and Alexander of Macedon* (1897), p. 64.   [4] *On the Crown*, 235.

the city-states and guarantee his supremacy over them. Because this would violate the terms of the King's Peace of 386 B.C. and involve him in a conflict with Persia, the association he had in mind was a combination of all Hellenic states under the aegis of Macedonia in a crusade against Persia. This, he considered, would arouse a feeling of national patriotism and bind the Hellenes together. In order to civilize Macedonia – looked upon by the Hellenes as a barbarous country – and to make her a respected head of the association, he attracted many Greeks to his court and compelled his courtiers and nobles to speak the Athenian language. Two things were imperative. Athens was still the greatest naval power in Greece and were she to throw in her lot with Persia his hegemony would become impossible. She had to be neutralized. Also, he must win her good-will, for she was the centre of Hellenic culture and it was by means of her culture that he hoped to cement the fractions of his empire into one whole. Athens was the kernel of his problem.

The increasing use of mercenaries during and following the Peloponnesian War undermined the city-states by demilitarizing their citizens and by placing their security in the hands of men who owed no allegiance to the cities. Another result of constant warfare was the creation of a city plutocracy and proletariat – antagonistic factions which undermined the unity of the city as a state. In Athens, the effects of these changes, coupled with her democratic government, are clearly described by Plato:

> In this city there is no necessity to rule even if you are capable of ruling, or to be ruled if you do not want to be, or to be at war because the rest of the city is, or when the rest of the city is at peace, to observe peace if you don't wish to; if there is a law forbidding you to be a magistrate or a judge, that is no reason why you should not be both magistrate and judge if you have the mind to.[1]

This was his view of the democratic Athenian:

> Day after day he gratifies the pleasures as they come – now fluting down the primrose path of wine, now given over to teetotalism and banting; one day in hard training, the next slacking and idling, and the third playing the philosopher. Often he will take to politics, leap to his feet and do or say whatever comes into his head; or he conceives an admiration for a general, and his interests are in war; or for a man of business, and straightway that is his line. . . .[2]

[1] *The Republic*, VIII, 557.   [2] Ibid., VIII, 561.

Demosthenes is equally scathing. He says:

> Formerly when the people of Athens had the courage to act and
> fight, they controlled the politicians. Now, on the contrary, the poli-
> ticians hold the purse-strings and manage everything, while you, the
> people, robbed of nerve and sinew, stripped of wealth and of allies,
> have sunk to the level of lackeys and hangers-on, content if the poli-
> ticians gratify you with a dole from the Theoric Fund or a proces-
> sion at the Boëdromia, and your manliness reaches its climax when
> you add your thanks for what you own.[1]

It was as much due to the political instability of Athens – which
should have assumed the leadership of the Hellenes against Macedonia – as to Philip's military genius, that Philip was able to implement
his policy and achieve his aim. Democracy went down before autocracy
because, like the Hydra, democracy was many-headed.

Amphipolis and the First Sacred War

Philip's masterly diplomacy between 359 and 357 B.C. proves that
from the opening of his reign he took advantage of the political discord
within Athens. Beset on all sides, he first dealt with those claimants of
his throne who were within his reach, bought off the Paeonians with a
heavy bribe, and then marched against the Pretender Argaeus, who
was supported by a strong Athenian fleet, and defeated him. Next, to
propitiate Athens and throw her off-guard, he released without ransom
the Athenian prisoners he had captured, and at the same time re-
nounced his claim to Amphipolis,[2] which his brother Perdiccas had
occupied and garrisoned. He then reorganized the Macedonian army
and recruited it to a strength of 600 cavalry and 10,000 infantry;[3] set
out with it to secure his northern and western frontiers and in two
swift campaigns drove the Paeonians and Illyrians from Macedonia
and reduced them to temporary subjection.

---

[1] *Third Olynthiac*, trans. J. H. Vince (1930), 30–1. The Theoric Funds were state
allowances made to the poorer citizens of Athens to enable them to visit the theatres.
They 'symbolized the democratic principle that all alike were entitled to a share in
the profits of state-management; they were, as Demades called them, the "cement of
the democracy" ' (*The Cambridge Ancient History*, vol. VI, p. 222). The Boëdromia
was a festival in honour of Apollo, celebrated in the third Attic month.

[2] Amphipolis had been colonized by Athens in 437 B.C., but lost to the Spartan
Brasidas in the Peloponnesian War (424 B.C.); since then, though the Athenians had
never relinquished their claim to it, it had become an independent city.

[3] Diodorus, XVI, 4, 4. It would appear that the task of reorganizing the army was
taken in hand soon after Philip's return from Thebes in 364 B.C.

1 GREECE

When Philip bought off the Athenians by relinquishing his claim to Amphipolis, he simultaneously entered into a secret pact with them: if they agreed that he should seize Pydna – a free city and not in their gift – he would conquer Amphipolis for them. Foolishly they stepped into the trap. He had no intention of permanently relinquishing Amphipolis; it guarded the gold mines of Mount Pangaeus and their bullion was essential for the financing of his projects. So it came about that once he had settled with the Paeonians and Illyrians he marched against Amphipolis in which, before his withdrawal of Perdiccas' garrison, he had taken the precaution to plant a pro-Macedonian faction – a 'fifth column' – which, in spite of the brave resistance of the Amphipolitans, betrayed the fortress to him. He then seized Pydna and Potidaea and to persuade the Olynthians not to call Athens to their aid, he handed Potidaea over to them. Thus by means as dubious as they were masterful, he secured the gold mines, which brought him a steady revenue of 1,000 talents yearly;[1] gained the forests of Mount Pangaeus, which supplied him with timber for his fleet; isolated Olynthus, which he intended to devour at a later date – and, with the exception of Methone, left the Athenians with no foothold on the coast of the Thermaic Gulf. Also, in 357 B.C., to propitiate Neoptolemus of Epirus and thereby to secure the south-western flank of Macedonia, he married his daughter Olympias. In the summer of 356 B.C. she presented him with a son, whom he named Alexander.

The Thebans had gained control of the Amphictyony during their brief hegemony and to avenge themselves on the Phocians, who had assisted the Spartans in the Leuctra campaign, they passed through the Council a threat that unless the Phocians, then led by Philomelus, paid a crushing fine in penalty for cultivating land near Delphi, which was sacred to Apollo, war would be declared on them. The Phocians refused to pay and in the autumn of 355 B.C., when the Thebans obtained a declaration of war from the Amphictyony, Philomelus, supported by the good-will of Athens, Sparta and Achaea, in face of a coalition of Boeotia, Locris, and Thessaly, occupied Delphi, seized the treasure stored there and with it raised a force of mercenaries. Thus opened the First Sacred War of the fourth century which, through Philip's astuteness, was destined to win for him the balance of power in Greece.

Philomelus defeated the Thessalians but was cut to pieces by the Boeotians and succeeded by Onomarchus. Philip was not idle; with an

---

[1] Philip's gold staters were the first regular gold coins to be struck on the European side of the Aegean.

eye on Thessaly he took advantage of the turmoil to foster the division existing among the Thessalians. Lycophron, the Thessalian tyrant, appealed to Onomarchus, who sent an army under his brother Phayllus to his help. When Philip defeated Phayllus, Onomarchus led his whole army to the support of Lycophron and defeated Philip in two battles. Philip then withdrew to Macedonia, as he said, 'Like a ram to butt the harder next time.'[1] While Philip was out of the way, Onomarchus invaded Boeotia in the spring of 352 B.C., but soon after was called back to Thessaly to oppose Philip, who in the interval had persuaded the Thessalians to abandon their mutual hostilities and to make common cause with him against the temple robbers. A battle followed in which Onomarchus was defeated and killed. Philip then occupied Pherae and established his control over Thessaly. But when in the summer of 352 B.C. he advanced on Thermopylae to seize the gateway into central Greece he found that the Athenians, at last aroused, had sent out an expedition to hold it. Philip, who did not wish to become directly involved with Athens, returned to Macedonia. In the autumn he set out for the Thracian coast and fell ill.

It was during this war that Philip's great antagonist Demosthenes (384–322 B.C.) first appeared on the political stage. An orator of remarkable eloquence, a tricky politician who twisted facts to suit his ends, he was also an irascible demagogue who, when aroused, smeared his opponents in the vilest ways. He called his rival Aeschines: 'This monkey of melodrama, this bumpkin tragedy-king, this pinchbeck orator', and to blacken him in the eyes of the people, he declared that his mother 'practised daylight-nuptials in an outhouse next door to Heros the bone-setter'.[2] On the other hand he was a great patriot and his faith in Athens as the champion of freedom was unbounded; he looked upon Macedonia as a land of barbarians.[3] He was the advocate of civic autonomy against Philip's autocracy; but although he lived in fourth-century Athens, he thought and spoke as if it were still the Athens of Pericles.

In his unending duel with Philip his aim was to rouse the Athenians to face the danger and to induce them to raise a standing army ready to fight wherever needed. He thundered against them because they would neither risk their skins in war nor open their purses to hire mercenaries

[1] *The Cambridge Ancient History*, vol. VI, p. 220.
[2] *On the Crown*, 242, 129. Other epithets were: 'bribe-taker', 'unclean scoundrel', 'slave of filthy lucre', 'impudent blackguard', and 'idiot'.
[3] *Third Olynthiac*, 24. Polybius (XVIII, 14) writes of him: 'The man who measures everything by the interests of his own particular state, and imagines that all Greeks ought to have their eyes fixed upon Athens.'

to fight for them. In 351 B.C. he lashed them with these scathing words:

> So you, if you hear of Philip in the Chersonese, vote an expedition there, if at Thermopylae, you vote one there; if somewhere else, you still keep pace with him to and fro. You take your marching orders from him; you have never formed any plan of campaign for your-selves, never foreseen any event, until you learn that something has happened or is happening . . . So scandalous is our present system that every general is tried two or three times for his life in your courts, but not one of them dares to risk death in battle against the enemy . . . Our business is not to speculate on what the future may bring forth, but to be certain that it will bring disaster, unless you face the facts and consent to do your duty.[1]

Meanwhile the Sacred War meandered on. In 350 B.C. the Thebans, now in financial straits, appealed to Artaxerxes III (358–338 B.C.) for funds; he gladly responded and sent them 300 talents. Then, in the following year, the Olynthians, although they had agreed not to ally themselves with the Athenians apart from Philip, appealed to Athens and Demosthenes urged the Athenians to face up to Philip. The appeal was renewed, an alliance with the Olynthians was agreed, and an in-adequate force sent to their aid. Next, apparently through the intrigues of Philip, the Athenians got involved in Euboea. While they were en-tangled there Philip moved on Olynthus and in the summer of 348 B.C. the city was betrayed to him by traitors he had planted within its walls. After this, so that he might tighten his grip on Thrace before he plunged into central Greece, he professed his desire for peace and ex-pressed such friendly feelings toward Athens that the Athenian Assem-bly welcomed his approach, opened negotiations with him, and in 346 B.C., on the motion of Philocrates, an embassy was sent to Pella, where it was graciously received by Philip. By the terms of the Peace of Philocrates it was agreed that Philip should keep Amphipolis and that he should not interfere in the Chersonese, but Cardia was to be ex-cluded as a Macedonian ally, and though the ambassadors were anxious to save the Phocians, Philip set their plea aside as he had made up his mind how to deal with them. The embassy then returned to Athens, and the terms were submitted to the Assembly. As there was no alter-native between their acceptance and continuation of the war, peace was sworn by the Athenians and their allies. The ambassadors were then sent back to Pella to receive the oaths of Philip and his allies, and when

---

[1] *First Philippic*, trans. J. H. Vince (1930), 41, 47, and 50.

they had been taken they set out on their return. But before they reached Athens news was received that Philip was at Thermopylae. The Assembly, little perturbed by this, thanked Philip for the part he had played and called upon the Phocians to surrender the temple of Apollo to the Amphictyons and to lay down their arms. No sooner was this request dispatched than the startling news came in that Phalaecus, in command of the Phocian forces at Thermopylae, had surrendered the pass to Philip. This threw Athens into panic and for a third time the ambassadors hurried to Pella to propitiate Philip by every means possible. It seems that either Phalaecus had exhausted his funds and could no longer hold his mercenaries to their post or, more probable, Philip had bought him over.

The fate of the Phocians was determined by the Amphictyonic Council. Their cities were dismantled, they were ordered to pay back in yearly instalments the temple treasure they had seized, and their votes in the Amphictyonic Council were transferred to Philip who was honoured by being appointed to preside over the forthcoming Pythian Games.

Isocrates' Panhellenic Programme

It was because the city-states were torn by factions and their foreign policies decided by emotional Assemblies that Philip, supreme war lord and sole conductor of foreign policy, raised Macedonia from an obscure barbaric kingdom to be the leading power in Greece. So enormous was his achievement that in the year of his triumph, Isocrates, now ninety years of age, returned to the thesis of his *Panegyricus* of 380 B.C., and in his *Philippus*[1] commended to Philip a Panhellenic programme.

'We are fighting one another about trifles', he wrote to Philip and added that there was no other way for Hellas to live in peace 'except by the determination of the leading states to make up their mutual quarrels and carry the war into Asia'. Therefore, he continued, 'my intention is to advise you to take the lead both in securing the harmony of Hellas[2] and in conducting the expedition against the barbarians [i.e. the Persians]. Use persuasion towards the one and force towards the other; but those who would counsel aright ought not to carry the war

[1] *The Orations of Isocrates*, trans. J. H. Freese; vol. I.
[2] It should be borne in mind that Isocrates never thought in terms of a politically unified Greece under Philip. The type of unity he advocated was that of *Homonoia* ('concord') between the states, which demanded the elimination of their mutual antagonisms.

into the King's country until someone has reconciled the Hellenes and made them desist from their present folly.'

He urged Philip to pay no attention to 'those who rave on the platforms [i.e. the orators]' and 'who regard peace, which is for the public advantage, as a war against their own private interests', but instead to act in a manner 'whereby you will both gain the confidence of the Hellenes and inspire the barbarians with fear'. He suggested that if a reconciliation of Argos, Sparta, Thebes, and Athens were brought about, the smaller states would be compelled to follow suit.

He scoffed at Persia's apparent strength and wrote of the expedition of Cyrus and Clearchus: 'It is agreed that they gained a complete victory over the whole of the King's forces as if they had fought against the Persian women.' And he reminded Philip that he would be able to find all the soldiers he needed; 'for such is the condition of Hellas, that it is easier to get together a larger and better force from wanderers than from settled inhabitants'.

He appealed to Philip's racial vanity by introducing Heracles; he accentuated his 'intellectual excellence' and pointed out that he was 'distinguished above all his predecessors by his wisdom, honourable ambitions and justice, rather than by his strength'. Endeavour, he wrote, to become like him, and he added, there was no necessity for him to seek foreign examples, since he had one ready at hand in his own family. Therefore he urged him to make himself like his ancestor 'in intellectual character, love of mankind, and good will, such as he showed towards the Hellenes'.

He suggested that in order to conquer Persia Philip should first free the subjugated Ionic cities; 'promise them freedom, and scatter the word broadcast in Asia, which, falling on the soil of Hellas, has broken up our empire as well as that of the Lacedaemonians'. This done, he urged Philip 'to destroy the whole kingdom, or, if not, to take away from it as much territory as possible'; to 'build cities throughout' the conquered territories 'and send thither as colonists those who are now wanderers from want of their daily bread, and who harass all whom they meet. For if we do not put a stop to their massing together by providing them with sufficient to live upon, they will imperceptibly become so numerous that they will be as great a cause for alarm to the Hellenes as the barbarians . . . form communities out of them, and make these the boundaries of Hellas, and set them in front of us like a bulwark.'

He urged Philip to look upon the whole of Hellas as his fatherland, in the same manner as had Heracles – the father of his race. Finally, he counselled him to rule with moderation, because 'harshness is equally grievous to those who show it and to those who experience it'; and to bear in mind that although our bodies are mortal, fame partakes of immortality, and 'those men of the greatest renown . . . are looked upon as demi-gods'.

Byzantium and the Second Sacred War

No sooner were the Athenians free from war than violent dissensions swept Athens; Philocrates was indicted for treason and Demosthenes hurled charges of corruption against Aeschines. Later, when speaking on this period,[1] Demosthenes accused Philip of playing off one faction against the other; but what he failed to understand was that it was he and his like who were so largely responsible for the discord. By now political unrest had made every city insecure and, as Parke points out,[2] the presence of mercenaries and their readiness to sell themselves for pay facilitated every form of revolution. Philip was thus aided in establishing pro-Macedonian parties in the cities hostile to him, an internal danger clearly mirrored by Aeneas Tacticus, a contemporary writer, in his *Military Manual*.[3] More than half of it is directed toward the prevention of treachery and the forestalling of revolutions within a city; from a present-day point of view it might aptly be described as an anti-cold war text-book.

While the Athenian orators hurled insulting epithets at each other, Philip spent the three years following the peace in enforcing his will on the tribes on his frontiers so that he might be free when the moment was opportune to concentrate everything on his grand design. His greatest success was, however, in Thessaly; there in 344 B.C., with the good-will of the Thessalians, he was appointed their *tagus*, or ruler, for life. This gave him the finest cavalry in Greece.

Once Thessaly was his, he turned his attention to the Thracian hinterland, and in this the Athenians rightly saw a threat to their Hellespontine corn route.[4] Further to secure it, in 343 B.C. Athenian settlers were sent to the Chersonese; but soon after their arrival they

---

[1] *On the Crown*, 61.

[2] *The Greek Mercenary Soldiers from the Earliest Times to the Battle of Issus*, H. W. Parke (1933), p. 95.

[3] Trans. by the Illinois Greek Club (Loeb Classical Library, 1933). See more particularly II, 2; III, 3; X, 6 and 20.

[4] Demosthenes says in *On the Crown*, 87: '. . . he cast about for a second plan of attack against Athens; and observing that we consume more imported corn than any other nation, he proposed to get control of the carrying trade in corn.'

quarrelled with the people of Cardia, a pro-Macedonian city which was expressly excluded from the Athenians by the Peace of Philocrates. In 341 B.C., Demosthenes, who was largely responsible for the quarrel, in his *Third Philippic* launched a violent verbal crusade against Philip, and what was more effective, he visited Byzantium and won over its citizens.

Philip was roused by this demonstration of hostility and called upon Perinthus and Byzantium – nominal allies – to help him, and when they refused he laid siege to Perinthus. As this was a threat to the Bosporus, and consequently to Asia Minor, Artaxerxes ordered Arsites, Satrap of Hellespontine-Phrygia, to support the Perinthans, and a large force of mercenaries, commanded by the Athenian Apollodorus, was sent to their aid: thus Persia declared openly against Philip. When he found Perinthus too hard a nut to crack Philip suddenly withdrew his troops and laid siege to Byzantium; but because two Athenian squadrons were sent to its support he was unable to invest it on its seaward side and after a long siege was compelled to abandon his attempt to take it. To make good this loss of face he carried out a punitive expedition against the Scythian tribes in the Dobrudja, and early in 339 B.C. set out on his return to Macedonia.

Philip had not long to wait for an opportunity to make good his double failure in the Propontis, for on his way home another Sacred War broke out; this time the Locrians of Amphissa were accused of cultivating land sacred to Apollo. At first the Amphictyonic Council appealed to Thebes and Athens, but when it failed to gain their support it turned to Philip and invited him to punish the Locrians. This was such a god-sent opportunity that more than one historian has suspected the invitation was prompted by Philip himself. He immediately answered the call; but instead of marching on Amphissa he occupied the ruined fortress of Elatea, which commanded the main road into western Boeotia, and from there sent an embassy to propose to the Thebans a joint invasion of Attica.

When the news of Philip's occupation of Elatea reached Athens her citizens were so terrified that, on the advice of Demosthenes, they sent a delegation to Thebes to offer a military alliance against Philip. It was successful in its mission and a body of Athenian mercenaries, under Chares, was hurried forward to reinforce the Thebans who held the passes from Boeotia into Phocis. Philip made no serious effort until the summer of 338 B.C. when he carried out a lightning campaign against Amphissa, defeated Chares, and then seized Naupactus (Lepanto) on the Gulf of Corinth. As this advance threatened the southern flank of the allied army it was withdrawn from the passes and massed at Chaeronea. Philip then returned to Elatea, advanced through the pass of Parapotamii (seven miles south of Elatea) and, probably on August 2 or September 1, he came up with his enemy. He had with him 30,000 foot and 2,000 horse; what the allied strength was is unknown.

In the allied order of battle the Thebans were on the right, the lesser allies in the centre, and the Athenians on the left. On the Macedonian side, Philip took command of the right wing of his army, and allotted the left wing to his son Alexander, now eighteen years of age. Little has been recorded of the battle, but it would appear that Philip's tactics, in idea at least, resembled those of Leuctra. We are told that at first Philip deliberately gave way in order to draw the Athenians forward of the allied centre, a manœuvre which so elated their general that he set out to pursue Philip's wing.[1] At the same time Alexander violently attacked the Theban wing and, after a fierce struggle, he burst through it. Then Philip advanced, broke through the Athenians, wheeled to his left while Alexander wheeled to his right, and between them they crushed the allied centre out of existence. Panic seized the allied army, among whose fugitives was Demosthenes.

The battle of Chaeronea was decisive; on its fateful field – still marked by the mound beneath which lie the Macedonian dead – was sounded the death-knell of the independent *polis*.

Athens was rocked by panic when the news of the allied disaster was brought by fugitives, but the terror of her citizens was unfounded because Philip's projected war against Persia demanded their good-will and, above all, the support of their fleet. Philip was lenient, not to say generous.[2] His terms were that he would guarantee not to invade Attica and would leave to Athens her Aegean islands; but he required from her the surrender of the Chersonese, for which she would receive Oropus, a Boeotian city, in compensation. The Athenian League was to be dissolved, and Athens was to become a Macedonian ally. Further

---

[1] That Philip was able to carry out this manœuvre shows how superlatively well he had disciplined and trained his troops; with hoplites few things could be more difficult than to retire in face of an advancing enemy, turn about and launch an attack.

[2] 'The success which he [Philip] obtained, after his victory over the Athenians at Chaeronea, was not due so much to his superiority in arms, as to his justice and humanity. His victory in the field gave him the mastery only over those immediately engaged against him; while his equity and moderation secured his hold upon the entire Athenian people and their city. For he did not allow his measures to be dictated by vindictive passion; but laid aside his arms and warlike measures, as soon as he found himself in a position to display the mildness of his temper and the uprightness of his motives' (*The Histories of Polybius*, trans. Evelyn S. Shuckburgh, 1889, V, 10).

to propitiate Athens, Philip released free of ransom the Athenian prisoners he had captured and sent a delegation, headed by Alexander and Parmenion, to Athens, bearing with them the ashes of the Athenian soldiers who had fallen at Chaeronea. This leniency so surprised the Athenians that in gratitude they granted Attic citizenship to Philip and his son and erected a statue of Philip in their *agora*. But to Thebes Philip showed little mercy: her anti-Macedonian leaders were either executed or banished, her captured soldiers sold into slavery, her hegemony over Boeotia was annulled and the Cadmea (citadel) of Thebes was occupied by a Macedonian garrison.

The Congress of Corinth

For twenty years Philip's primary aim had been to extend his power over Greece, but unlike so many conquerors he was wise enough to understand that unless he could win over the good-will of the conquered peoples his empire would be no more than ephemeral. In order to achieve this secondary aim he struck a compromise between his own policy of power and Isocrates' Panhellenic programme,[1] and to clothe his power in legal form he called on all the Greek states to send envoys to Corinth to consult with him on his New Order. All except Sparta agreed to do so.

At the close of 338 B.C., the Congress of Corinth, the crowning achievement of Philip's statecraft, assembled. Its importance was indeed great, because its decisions were to form the foundation of Alexander's relations towards Greece. When the conference opened, Philip laid his proposals before it, not in the form of a dictate, but as a basis for general discussion. He adopted this tactful course because he was anxious to win the sympathy of the Greeks. The chief points agreed were:

An offensive and defensive alliance in perpetuity was to be concluded between the Greek states and Macedonia. The former were to be constituted into an Hellenic League, represented by a *Synhedrion*, or Federal Council, to which individual states were to be instructed to send deputies in number according to their military strength. The

---

[1] When ninety-eight years of age and shortly before his death, Isocrates addressed a letter to Philip (see *Isocrates*, trans. Larue van Hook, Loeb edit., 1945, vol. III, pp. 403–7), in which he exhorted him to hold fast to a war against Persia, and 'force the king who is now called Great to do whatever you command. For then will naught be left for you except to become a god' (i.e. like Heracles, to be worshipped as a godlike hero). He ended his letter by saying that he was grateful to have lived to see the dreams of his youth approaching fulfilment through Philip's achievements.

sessions of the Federal Council were to be held either at Corinth or at the localities of the great panhellenic festivals. The permanent business of the Council was to be entrusted to a directorate of five members; because Macedonia was not a member of the League Philip was to be excluded from them. His position was to be that of generalissimo of the League forces, and as such he was to be elected hegemon for life. Each member of the League was to be protected by the combined forces of the League. Existing constitutions were to remain undisturbed and no tribute was to be exacted. The Federal Council was to act as the supreme tribunal, empowered to take what action it thought fit against a transgressor of the treaty; and should war be declared, the hegemon was to decide the contingents each member should furnish, and conduct the war on the part of the League.

Provisions for a universal peace were included in the treaty. They were:

(1) Peace between the League and Philip was established by each member state binding itself by oath not to attempt to overthrow the monarchy of Philip or that of his descendants.

(2) Internal peace between states was secured by all members swearing to keep perpetual peace between themselves. Piracy was forbidden them, and the freedom and security of the sea were placed under the protection of the League.

(3) Internal peace within each state was guaranteed by each member swearing that he would not subvert the constitution of his state, and severe penalties were ordained against any citizen who attempted to do so, or to conspire with or to take service with a foreign power against the League or Philip.[1]

Thus, through Philip's statesmanship – seldom paralleled in history – all the Hellenes in Greece, except the Spartans, were united into a single Greek federation.

After the unanimous adoption of the treaty, the envoys returned to their cities, elections were held and early in the summer of 337 B.C. the Federal Council met at Corinth for its first session. Philip then placed before it his final project – war against Persia. Though in his own mind it may have been a war of aggrandizement, he knew that such an aim would not appeal to the members of the League so he proclaimed it to be a war of revenge to wipe out the crimes perpetrated by Xerxes on the temples and sanctuaries of the Greek gods; a religious war, or crusade, which he felt would unite the Greeks in common

---

[1] These regulations were specifically framed to put an end to internal city discords and to stop the enlistment of Greek mercenaries in the service of Persia.

cause. Nor was he mistaken; the representatives voted for war and appointed Philip supreme commander with unlimited powers. Philip then returned to Macedonia and in the spring of 336 B.C. sent across the Hellespont an advanced guard of 10,000 men, under Parmenion and Attalus, to establish a bridgehead in Asia and promote the secession of the Asiatic Greeks from Persia. This was his declaration of war. Fate decided that he should never wage it.

Seized by a passion for Cleopatra, the niece of Attalus, he set Olympias aside and made Cleopatra his lawful wife. As this endangered Alexander's claim to succession a violent family quarrel resulted. Olympias retired to her brother, Alexander of Epirus and, possibly to rouse the Illyrians against Philip, Alexander went to Illyria. As it would have been inexpedient for Philip to leave on his flank a dis-affected Epirus and Illyria, a family reconciliation was arranged through the mediation of Demaratus of Corinth. Alexander then re-turned to Pella, and Philip's daughter by Olympias, also named Cleopatra, was offered in marriage to her uncle, Alexander of Epirus. Then in mid-summer 336 B.C., when Philip attended her marriage, he was stabbed to death by Pausanias, a young Macedonian noble who had a personal grievance against Attalus, which Philip had refused to inquire into. Others were involved in the plot and, because of what had happened, suspicion fell on Olympias. But whether she was privy to the assassination is unknown and it is generally held that Alexander was in no way implicated, as his enemies declared him to be.

2

THE MACEDONIAN ARMY

Greek Warfare before Philip

Alexander inherited from his father the most perfectly organized, trained, and equipped army of classical times. It was Philip's master-piece and the genius he displayed in its creation can best be measured by contrasting it with the slow and haphazard progress in military organization before his day.

In the heroic period of Greek warfare the nobles were the warriors. They drove on to the battlefield in their chariots, dismounted, and engaged each other in hand-to-hand combat while their ill-armed re-tainers stood apart and cheered them on; battles were little more than displays of personal valour. This mode of fighting demanded an agile fighter, lightly armed and armoured. For his protection the warrior relied mainly on a round shield provided with a single hand-grip in its centre; to it was attached a thong which was fastened round the warrior's neck, so that should he have to retire, he could sling the shield round to protect his back. His offensive weapons were one or two light spears and a sword; he frequently hurled the spears at his adversary, and should they fail to bring him down, he engaged him with the sword. The bow was looked upon as a cowardly weapon and seldom used.

Early in the seventh century these hand-to-hand encounters gave way to group fighting. Increasing prosperity and improvement in smelting, which cheapened armour, enabled more and more com-moners to arm themselves like nobles with a complete panoply, which consisted of a metal helmet, a breast-plate, greaves, thigh-pieces, shield, spear and sword. This transformation, both levelling and democratic,[1]

---

[1] See Aristotle's *Politics*, 1297b. 'It is significant', writes Bury, 'that in Thessaly, where the system of hoplites was not introduced and cavalry was always the kernel of

placed the wealthy commoner and the noble on equal footing on the battlefield. Both now became hoplites (heavy infantry spearmen) who fought in rank instead of individually. The spear ceased to be a missile and was used for thrusting; the shield was enlarged and held on the left forearm by an arm-band, through which the arm was thrust, and a grip on the rim was provided for the hand. The neck thong was abandoned, obviously because in a line of men it would be fatal should one or more try to retire.

With this increase in the number of warriors the city-state army may be said to have been born, and from then two factors determined its tactics and organization – the city walls and the field lands surrounding them.

Before siege engines were introduced, walled cities were virtually impregnable to assault and the normal means of reducing them were through starvation or treason. The former meant blockade, and because the means of supplying the besieging army were rudimentary, except in sieges of coastal cities, when the besiegers could be supplied by ship, sieges were generally brief. Also, until the advent of the mercenary soldier, betrayal through subversion of the garrison was far more difficult. But the cities' field lands were always attackable and the most effective method to force an enemy to abandon his walls and settle the argument in the field was either to destroy his crops and herds or to appropriate them. This meant that warfare was restricted to the summer months, when crops grew and cattle grazed.

Because the winter months were free from war, a standing army was not needed, and as soldiers were seldom more than militiamen required to fight on the level fields the simplest organization was that of the phalanx,[1] a line of spearmen marshalled in eight to ten ranks whose tactics were restricted to push of pikes. Phalanx met phalanx in parallel order and the victor, after he had set up a trophy on the battlefield, either destroyed his enemy's crops and herds or, what was more profitable, appropriated them.

As long as the phalanx maintained its alignment, which it could only do at a slow pace over level ground, it was, as Polybius says,

the army, democratic ideas never made way' (*A History of Greece*, 1951 edit., p. 129). Like the pike of the hoplite, the musket was also a 'democratic' weapon; this was noted by Condorcet who, in his *Tableau historique des progrès de l'esprit humain*, connects the rise of democracy with the rise of modern infantry.

[1] Professor A. Andrewes' opinion is that probably Pheidon of Argos, soon after 675 B.C., was the first successful exponent of the new hoplite tactics of fighting in phalanx. (*The Greek Tyrants*, 1956, pp. 40–1.) In Asia the phalanx was a very old battle formation, and is depicted on a Sumerian stele of the early third millennium B.C. found at Lagash.

'irresistible in face-to-face battles'.[1] But over broken ground it rapidly lost its dressing and became disorganized. To this limitation must be added its incapacity either to change front to a flank rapidly or to maintain an orderly pursuit. Like a battering-ram, it was designed for a single purpose – to rupture its enemy's front.

Of all the city-states Sparta was the best organized for war, and there were two reasons for this. The first was that she remained a monarchy, under a dual kingship, and was therefore less subject to civil discord than were the Hellenic democracies and oligarchies; and the second, that by law she was established on a wholly military footing, as the exiled Spartan king Demaratus explained to Xerxes. Though my people are freemen, he said, they 'are not in all respects free; Law is the master whom they own . . . whatever he commands they do; and his commandment is always the same: it forbids them to flee in battle, whatever the number of their foes, and requires them to stand firm and either conquer or die'.[2]

Because the Spartans relied on the superiority of their hoplites, Sparta was left unwalled until the second century. The original inhabitants were reduced either to helots (serfs) or to *perioeci* (provincials), and though the latter maintained a partial independence they were obliged to serve Sparta in war. This meant that the highly trained Spartan army was supplemented by a militia. At the battle of Plataea, in 479 B.C., the Spartan phalanx, 5,000 hoplites organized in five territorial regiments, was supported by 5,000 *perioeci*. Before the advent of Philip Sparta was the only example in Hellas of a nation-in-arms.

Because the pace of the phalanx could not be increased without loss of dressing, and because maintenance of alignment was the essence of shock, mobile operations were prohibited, and though this restriction could in part be mitigated by combining cavalry and light-armed troops with the hoplites, for long these arms were sparingly used. The reasons for this were the traditional conservativism of armies and the hoplites' contempt for the light-armed. Also, as Aristotle points out, because only the wealthy citizens could afford to keep a horse, cavalry favoured the establishment of oligarchies, and in a lesser degree this held good for the heavy-armed, 'but that the light-armed and the sailors always contribute to support a democracy', and 'when the

---

[1] For Polybius' views on the phalanx, see XVIII, 29–31.

[2] Herodotus, VII, 104. Except for Sparta, the Greek citizen-armies were governed by civil discipline, which made it difficult for a general to exercise his authority, and as he was an official elected by his subordinates in their capacity as citizens he was reluctant to make himself unpopular by being too strict.

number of these is very great and a sedition arises, the other parts of the community fight at a disadvantage'.[1]

In spite of these restrictions, small numbers of light cavalry and light infantry were employed from early times as scouts and marauders. At Marathon, in 490 B.C., no Greek cavalry took the field, and eleven years later, in the Plataea campaign, the only cavalry on the Greek side was the Thessalian, and it was completely outclassed by the Persian. For the siege of Syracuse, in 415 B.C., Nicias, the Athenian commander-in-chief, took with him no more than thirty horses,[2] but soon after, in order to protect his foragers, he found the need of cavalry so great that he sent back to Athens for an additional 250 troopers and raised 400 local cavalry in Sicily.[3] This lack of appreciation of cavalry is all the more remarkable since a century earlier 1,000 Thessalian cavalry had stormed a Spartan bridgehead at Phalerum, in an attempted invasion of Attica.[4] Within twenty years of the siege of Syracuse this situation was reversed when, in 394 B.C., Agesilaus, king of Sparta, raised a very efficient body of cavalry and with it defeated a body of Thessalian cavalry. Xenophon writes that Agesilaus was 'greatly delighted with his exploit, in having defeated, with cavalry, which he himself had formed, a people who prided themselves on their equestrian skill'.[5]

When after the Peloponnesian wars the mercenary soldier began to dominate warfare, the low cost of raising light-armed mercenary troops caused their steadily increasing use and efficiency. The Athenian mercenary general Iphicrates (415–353 B.C.) was one of the first to grasp how formidable they might be made. He raised a force of light infantry, modelled on the Thracian javelin-men – known as peltasts from the small round shields (*pelta*) they carried – and trained his men in rapid co-ordinated advances and retirements over every type of ground, both for missile and hand-to-hand attack. He lengthened by a half both the light Thracian javelin and short sword and introduced a species of leggings known as '*Iphicratides*'. In 300 B.C., with his light troops he annihilated a body of 600 Spartan hoplites near Corinth[6] and from that day the trained peltast became an essential auxiliary to the hoplite, especially in broken and mountainous country, where they could reduplicate the functions of cavalry on the plains.

Little progress in siegecraft was made until the fourth century, and though city walls were largely or wholly built of sun-baked bricks and wood, it remained rare for a city to be taken by assault. Tunnelling

---

[1] *Politics*, XI, vii, 1321a.　　[2] Thucydides, VI, 43.　　[3] Ibid., VI, 95 and 98.
[4] Herodotus, V, 63.　　[5] *Hellenics*, IV, iii, 6.　　[6] Ibid., IV, v, 11–17.

under a city wall was at times resorted to, and mounds of earth were raised, from the summits of which command of the wall could be gained. Battering-rams are mentioned by Thucydides, also scaling-ladders and fire-throwing and fire-resisting devices. He records that at the siege of Plataea, in 429 B.C., the Plataeans covered their walls with skins and hides to protect their woodwork against burning missiles,[1] and that at the siege of Syracuse, in 413 B.C., the Syracusans defended their walls by burning the Athenian rams with liquid fire.[2] In the same year an ingenious engine was used by the Megarians in their siege of Delium.

> They sawed in two and scooped out a great beam from end to end, and fitting it nicely together again like a pipe, hung by chains a cauldron at one extremity, with which communicated an iron tube projecting from the beam, which was itself a great part plated with iron. This they brought up from a distance upon their carts to the part of the wall principally composed of vines and timber, and when it was near, inserted huge bellows into their end of the beam and blew with them. The blast passing closely confined into the cauldron, which was filled with lighted coals, sulphur and pitch, made a great blaze and set fire to the wall, which soon became untenable for its defenders, who left it and fled; in this way the fort was taken.[3]

Another ingenious means was adopted by Agesipolis, king of Sparta, in 385 B.C. at the siege of Mantinea. He dammed up the river which flowed through the city, and caused its water to rise above the foundations of the city wall, which were built of sun-baked brick. The bricks soon began to dissolve, and when the superstructure was about to collapse, the Mantineans surrendered their city to him.[4]

The first real advance in siegecraft was made by Dionysius I, tyrant of Syracuse (430–367 B.C.) in his wars with the Carthaginians, and notably at the siege of Motya in 398 B.C. It was a fortress-city built on a small island, separated from the mainland by a narrow channel. Dionysius built a mole across the channel and at the island end of the mole erected six-storied wooden towers moved on wheels. He installed powerful battering-rams on their ground floors and arrow-firing catapults in their stories. While the rams battered the enemy's wall from below, the catapults swept its summit and he gained

---

[1] Thucydides, II, 75.   [2] Ibid., VII, 43.

[3] Ibid., IV, 100. In the following century Aeneas Tacticus (XXXV) describes an incendiary mixture which, so he says, was impossible to extinguish. It was composed of pitch, sulphur, tow, pounded gum of frankincense and pine sawdust.

[4] Xenophon, *Hellenics*, V, ii, 5.

an entrance into the city. Next, he wheeled his towers within the city walls and, according to Diodorus, from their top stories he let down bridges on to the houses. His men passed over these, broke through the roofs, descended into the streets and took the city by storm.[1]

The introduction of the movable siege tower and the catapult radically changed siege warfare. The former was an old invention dating

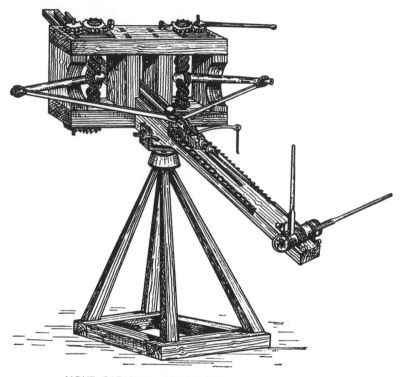

LIGHT CATAPULT, ACCORDING TO PAYNE-GALLWEY

back to the Assyrians in the ninth century, and is depicted on bas-reliefs of the palace of Ashur-Nazir-Pal III, in which the battering-ram is shown in operation on the ground floor while archers on the summit of the tower clear the top of the enemy's wall with their arrows. It was known to Xenophon, who also describes a field battering-ram – real or imaginary – worked from a wooden tower mounted on a wagon with eight poles and drawn by eight yoke of oxen. Of this machine he writes: 'Cyrus felt that if he had a series of such towers brought into the field at a fair pace they would be of immense service

[1] *Diodorus*, XIV, 48–54.

to him . . . The towers were built with galleries and parapets, and each of them could carry twenty men.'[1] In idea they were a species of tank.

It would appear that the torsion catapult[2] was invented by the Phoenicians.[3] There were two types, varying mainly in size, the light and the heavy; the former, the *Katapeltes* – a machine that could pierce a shield (*pelta*) – threw arrows, javelins, pebbles or small lead shot, and the latter, the *Petrobolos*, threw stones up to 50 or 60 lb. in weight. The motive power was provided by two tightly twisted skeins of sinews or of human hair, and with an 8 lb. shot the maximum range of the lighter type was about 450 yards. Later, in Hellenistic or Roman times, a more powerful stone-thrower, the *Ballista* or *Onager* (a type of howitzer) was invented. An excellent description of both the catapult and *ballista* is given by Ammianus Marcellinus, a Roman historian of the fourth century A.D.[4]

When the catapult was first introduced into Greece is not known. In about 350 B.C., it is mentioned with other siege-devices by Aeneas Tacticus,[5] and in 341 B.C. Philip of Macedon made use of arrow-discharging catapults as well as movable towers, said by Diodorus to have been 120 feet high, during his siege of Perinthus.

The development of individual arms inevitably raised the problem of how best to combine them in an army of professional soldiers.[6] Although this problem was not fully solved until Philip reorganized the Macedonian army, two great forerunners set the pace for him; they were the two tyrants Dionysius I of Syracuse and Jason of Pherae (*c.* 380–370 B.C.).

[1] *Cyropaedia*, VI, i, 53–5.
[2] According to Tarn (*Hellenistic Military and Naval Developments*, p. 104), in Europe the torsion catapult was preceded by the Greek crossbow (a small tension catapult) invented by Zopyrus of Tarentum, but it is never mentioned by historians.
[3] Though Pliny, in his *Natural History*, VII, LVI, 201, says Cretans.
[4] *The Roman History of Ammianus Marcellinus*, XXIII, iv, 1–7. See also *The Projectile-Throwing Engines of the Ancients*, Sir Ralph Payne-Gallwey (1907).
[5] XXII, 8–10.
[6] The need for professional opposed to part-time soldiers was argued by Socrates (Plato's *Republic*, II, 374), and though in his day the nearest approach to a professional army was the Spartan, because it was in part composed of *perioeci* and helots it was not strictly speaking a professional one. In 424 B.C. hoplite regiments of helots were raised in Sparta (Thucydides, IV, xiv, 80), and in 396 B.C. 6,000 helots were enlisted (Xenophon, *Hellenics*, VI, 5, 29). It would appear that the earliest professional *corps d'élite* – a picked body of 1,000 men – was formed in Argos in 418 B.C. (Thucydides, V, xvi, 72). The Theban 'Sacred Band' formed by Gorgidas, a battalion of shock troops 300 strong, was of similar character. It was raised shortly before the battle of Leuctra; its men were not recruited on a tribal basis, which hitherto had been customary, but from mutual friends devoted to one another (*Plutarch's Lives*, 'Pelopidas', XVIII).

Dionysius raised an army of all arms, which is said to have included 80,000 infantry. Professor Bury writes of him:

> In military innovations he is the forerunner of the great Macedonians and the originator of the methods which they employed. He first thought out and taught how the heterogeneous parts of a military armament—the army and the navy, the cavalry and the infantry, the heavy and the light troops – might be closely and systematically co-ordinated so as to act as if they were a single organized body.[1]

Or as Plutarch makes Iphicrates say: 'The light-armed troops are like the hands, the cavalry like the feet, the line of men-at-arms itself like chest and breast-plate, and the general like the head.' [2]

Jason of Pherae, who in disposition and character closely resembled Philip, first appears in history in 380 B.C. Polydamas of Pharsalus says of him:

> He is able to take advantage of the night as well as of the day; and, when he is hurried, can attend to business while he takes his dinner or supper. Rest he thinks he ought to take only when he has arrived at the place to which he is going, or has accomplished the object which he had in view; and he has accustomed all about him to act like himself . . . whatever he attempts, either by secret machinations, or in anticipation of the schemes of others, or by open force, he is by no means likely to fail.[3]

This might equally well be a description of Philip.

When Jason made himself tagus of Thessaly, he had at his disposal 20,000 hoplites, 8,000 cavalry, 6,000 mercenaries and 'enough peltasts to fight the whole world'.[4] It was a highly paid and well-disciplined army, and it would appear that his intention was to use it against Persia. After their victory over the Spartans at Leuctra in 371 B.C., because the Spartans had decided to continue the war, the Thebans appealed to Jason for aid. He set out at once with 1,500 infantry and 500 cavalry and rushed through the territory of Phocis with such speed that 'in many towns he was seen before news came that he was on the march'.[5] But as his intention apparently was to make himself hegemon of all Greece and lead the Greeks against the Persians, he patched up a truce and the Spartans abandoned the cam-

[1] *A History of Greece*, p. 648.   [2] 'Pelopidas', II.
[3] Xenophon, *Hellenics*, VI, i, 15.   [4] Ibid., VI, i, 5 and 19.
[5] Ibid., VI, iv, 21.

paign. In the ensuing year his intention was to visit Delphi, where he proposed to preside over the Pythian Games, and – presumably – announce his war on Persia. But before he could set out he was assassinated.

Philip's New Model Army

Since early times the Macedonian army had consisted of three forces; the king's retinue of mounted nobles, known as the *Hetairoi*, or Companions, to which was added the Royal Squadron, recruited from the lesser nobles, whose duty it was to protect the king's person in battle; a small foot-guard of household troops called the *agema*, who guarded him at all times other than in battle; and the tribal levies of infantry recruited from the peasants and mountain shepherds. The Companions, like the Thessalian cavalry, were a well-mounted force armed with cuirass and the short thrusting spear (*xyston*) for close combat:[1] the *agema* was a standing professional force, and the tribal levies were an untrained rabble armed with sword or spear and a wicker shield. When, in 429 B.C., the Thracians, under Sitalces, invaded Macedonia, Thucydides writes that Perdiccas II considered his levies of so little value that he 'never thought of meeting him with his infantry'; but that his cavalry were 'excellent horsemen' who, wherever they charged, 'overthrew all before them'.[2] It was out of these small beginnings that Philip created his army; but before discussing how he did so, it is as well to look at his problem in the whole.

He was a far-sighted man who realized that the warfare of his day was increasingly becoming the business of specialists, and because of the untrustworthiness of the mercenary a more reliable soldier was needed. He determined to combine the skill of the mercenary with the loyalty of the city militiaman and to convert his tribal levies into a professional army imbued with a national spirit. Further, as his political aim was to expand his dominion over the whole of Greece, this demanded that, unlike the city militias, his army had to be a force

[1] It should be remembered that the Greeks rode bare-back without saddles and stirrups, as Alexander is depicted on the Sidon sarcophagus; horses were small, little more than sturdy ponies, and mounting was by vaulting. The first saddle proper (other than saddle cloth) was not introduced until the fourth century A.D., and the earliest evidence in Europe of the use of stirrups is mentioned in the *Art of War* of the emperor Maurice (A.D. 582–602). Without saddle and stirrups the lance-charge of the medieval knight was impossible; the classical charge took the form of a thrusting mêlée, hence the *xyston*. Further, horse-shoes were not introduced until the second century B.C., and did not become commonly known until the fifth century A.D. [2] II, 100.

of all arms: it must include heavy cavalry and heavy infantry for close-order field battles; light cavalry and light infantry for protective and loose-order operations, and artillery and engineers for sieges. Because he already had at his disposal an efficient body of horsemen who had proved their value in war, he decided to make his cavalry his decisive arm; that is, it would replace the phalanx as the instrument of shock, while the phalanx he intended to form would constitute the base of cavalry action. Instead of assaulting, normally the phalanx would threaten to do so, and through the terror its advance always instilled[1] it would immobilize the enemy and morally prepare the way for the decisive charge. Scouting, skirmishing, covering the front and flanks of the heavy striking force, as well as mountain warfare and guerrilla operations, were to be the tasks of the light cavalry and light-armed infantry, and the artillery with its ammunition train was to form an integral part of the army. This army was to be a combined force of all arms ever-ready to fight both in winter and summer over all types of country.

When in his *Third Philippic* (48–51) Demosthenes compares the warfare Philip introduced with the traditional method, he says:

> ... I consider that nothing has been more revolutionized and improved than the art of war. For in the first place I am informed that in those days the Lacedaemonians, like everyone else, would spend the four or five months in the summer 'season' in invading and laying waste the enemy's territory with heavy infantry and levies of citizens, and would retire home again; and they were so old fashioned, or rather such good citizens [i.e. true to the spirit of a free, constitutional state] that they never used money to buy an advantage from anyone, but their fighting was of the fair and open kind ... on the other hand you hear of Philip marching unchecked, not because he leads a phalanx of heavy infantry, but because he is accompanied by skirmishers, cavalry, archers, mercenaries, and similar troops. When relying on this force, he attacks some people that is at variance with itself, and when through distrust no one goes forth to fight for his country, then he brings up his artillery and lays siege. I need hardly tell you that he makes no difference between summer and winter and has no season set apart for inaction.

---

[1] The power of the phalanx lay largely in its moral effect. At the sight of 'the bristling rampart of outstretched pikes', says Aemilius Paullus at the battle of Pydna, in 168 B.C., he 'was smitten at once with astonishment and terror'; never before had he seen so fearful a spectacle (*Plutarch's Lives*, 'Aemilius Paullus', XLIV. See also Polybius, XXIX, 17).

As nothing is known of Philip's military reforms other than their results, all we can do is to consider these results and then by an inverse process arrive at the steps he probably took to achieve them.

He was a practical man and did not invent a new army; instead he converted what he had into two armies. He turned his feudal cavalry and body-guard into a Royal Army, under his personal command, and his levies into a Territorial Army. He adopted this course not only because it was the simplest thing to do, but because the two armies would act as a counterpoise to each other and together would prevent too much power passing either into the hands of the nobility or of the peasantry. A balance of power would be established between the two main social divisions of his people that would guarantee the reliability of the whole.

The Royal Army consisted of two forces, the Royal Companion Cavalry and the Royal Hypaspists. The former Philip formed out of the Royal Squadron of the Companions by expanding it to eight squadrons or *ilai*; each *ile* numbered from 200 to 300 horsemen armed with the *xyston*, and the whole was placed under the command of a cavalry leader. In this expansion the original squadron was not deprived of its duty of protecting the king in battle and remained his mounted body-guard; it is sometimes referred to as the *agema* of the Companions.

The Royal Hypaspists, or Hypaspists of the Companions, frequently referred to by Arrian as the 'Shield-Bearing Guard', was a force of infantry Philip formed out of his original foot-guards by increasing their strength to three battalions, each of 1,000 men. Again he did not deprive the original *agema* of its special duties, and this particular battalion is generally referred to as the *agema* of the hypaspists. Thus the King's Army consisted in all of eight squadrons of Companion cavalry, one of which was a squadron of Royal Horse Guards, and three battalions of hypaspists, of which one was a battalion of Royal Foot Guards.

How the hypaspists were armed and equipped is not known. Sir William Tarn is of opinion that 'they were heavy infantry, as heavily armed as the phalanx', and that their difference from hoplites 'was one of history, recruitment, and standing, not of armament'.[1] Wilcken considers that they were light-armed infantry, 'whose battle-role was to hasten forward at quick march or the double and make connection between the cavalry and the phalanx'.[2] And Grote suggests that 'they were hoplites, keeping regular array and intended for close combat, but

---

[1] *Alexander the Great* (1948), vol. II, p. 153.
[2] *Alexander the Great* (English trans. 1932), p. 32.

more lightly armed, and more fit for diversities of circumstance and position than the phalanx... They occupied a sort of intermediate place between the heavy infantry of the phalanx properly so called, and the peltasts and light troops generally.'[1] Because Arrian records that Alexander made use of them to follow up cavalry, storm walled places, execute rapid night marches and other mobile operations, it would seem probable that they were more lightly armed and equipped than hoplites.

The purpose of the Territorial Army was to provide the Royal Army with a pivot of manœuvre – a tactical base of action. As mentioned, its task was to pin down the enemy's phalanx while the Royal Army assaulted. Philip created it by transforming the old Macedonian tribal levies into a standing force of six *taxeis*,[2] or battalions, of hoplites, known as *Pezetairoi* (Foot Companions), and historically referred to as the phalanx. Each *taxis* consisted of 1,536 men and was divided into three pentacosiarchies of 512 men each, which in their turn were subdivided into smaller units down to the file of sixteen men, which was the basic unit.[3] Each *taxis* had its own commander; there was no over-all phalanx commander, and the leader of each file was called a *decadarches*.[4] The two men immediately behind him were selected for their courage and skill, and the rearmost man, also a picked soldier, was the file-closer. Asclepiodotus, a writer of the first century B.C., says that the file-leader and file-closer were the most efficient soldiers in each file, and that 'this line of file-leaders builds the phalanx together and is like the cutting edge of the sword'.[5]

The outstanding difference between the Macedonian and Greek hoplites was that, while the latter were armed with a nine-foot spear held in the right hand, Philip armed his hoplites with the *sarissa*,[6] a spear – better called a pike – of 13 to 14 feet in length, held in both hands, with shield slung on the left shoulder. The lengthening by a half of the hoplite's main offensive weapon gave his phalanx a decisive advantage over the traditional phalanx armed with the shorter weapon, an advantage which in battle may be compared to a 50 per cent.

---

[1] *A History of Greece* (edit. 1906), vol. X, p. 12.

[2] *Taxis* means a 'formation', see Tarn, II, p. 136.

[3] Xenophon (*Hellenics*, IV, 2, 18) mentions the sixteen-deep file as customary in his day.

[4] Arrian's *Anabasis*, trans. Edward James Chinnock (1893), VII, 23, 3. This shows that originally a file consisted of ten men.

[5] *Outline of Tactics*, trans. the Illinois Greek Club (1933), III, 5.

[6] For the length of the *sarissa*, see Tarn's *Alexander the Great*, vol. II, pp. 169–71. J. G. Droysen in his *Alexander the Great* (French edit. 1935, p. 127) estimates its length at from 14 to 16 feet.

increase of range of the musket, because in the clinch between two phalanxes, the one armed with the longer weapon could at the same time engage its enemy and keep out of effective range. It is strange that this innovation had not been adopted before; a possible reason is that the Greeks were loth to reduce the size and weight of their large shield, which required the full use of one arm.

Besides the *sarissa*, the Macedonian hoplite was armed with a short sword; he carried a light circular shield; wore a breast-plate, leggings and helmet, and at times the *causia*, a broad-brimmed hat. In addition to possession of the *sarissa*, the superiority of Philip's Territorial Army lay in that it was a standing force of men recruited on a national footing, whose morale was in every respect superior to that of the professional mercenary. Further, its men were in constant training and so true professional soldiers.

Before the end of his reign Philip also raised large contingents of troops from his subject and allied peoples. The Thessalians furnished him with a body of some 2,000 heavy cavalry, armed like the Companion cavalry, and little inferior to it. For his light cavalry he recruited 1,200 Thracian, Paeonian and Odrysian horse, as well as a body of Greek mercenary cavalry. The Thracian contingent included a regiment of lancers, known as *Sarissophori*,[1] because they were armed with the *sarissa*; these men usually operated like Cossacks. In battle the light cavalry covered the flanks of the phalanx and Companion cavalry – sometimes their front – and on the line of march their task was to scout ahead and reconnoitre. All these auxiliary bodies of cavalry were, like the Macedonian, divided into *ilai* and commanded by Macedonian officers.

Of auxiliary infantry, the League of Corinth placed at Philip's disposal 7,000 hoplites armed in the Greek fashion, and 5,000 Greek mercenaries – part hoplites, part peltasts. And from the Thracians, Paeonians, Illyrians and other warlike tribes bordering Macedonia, Philip raised some 6,000 light-armed infantry, the most noted of whom were the Agrianians – a Paeonian tribe – who were superb javelin-men. Besides these troops he recruited two bodies of archers, one Macedonian and the other Cretan; the latter were the most skilled bowmen of their day.

Little is known of his artillery park and siege train; they were probably modelled on those of Dionysius I, and when judged from the use Alexander made of them, both were highly organized and extremely efficient. The siege train consisted of towers, rams, pent-houses, of

[1] Also called '*prodromoi*' – scouts.

which only the essential parts were carried in the field, the woodwork was constructed when needed. Even in Alexander's most exacting marches his field artillery accompanied him; it must have been transported in sections on pack horses like modern mountain artillery.

There is not much known of Philip's system of command, staff and services, and it is not possible to differentiate between what is attributable to him and what to his son. Both held a threefold command; they were simultaneously commanders-in-chief of all their forces, general officers in personal command of the Macedonian Royal Army, and generalissimos of the forces raised by the League. Parmenion was second in command to both kings. To assist the king, he had at his disposal a Personal Staff, and also a small company of selected officers of high position who, to quote Sir William Tarn, 'acted as an informal council, and formed his general reserve both for special duties and for filling all high offices, whether military or administrative'.[1]

Of Alexander's technical services, most if not the whole of which must be credited to Philip, Sir William writes:

> ... Alexander had with him a number of Greek technicians, of whom too little is known. He had a siege train, with engineers for constructing siege machines, the chief engineer being the Thessalian Diades, 'the man who took Tyre with Alexander' ... There were sappers for siege works and making pontoons, water and mining engineers, and architects like Deinocrates, who laid out Alexandria; to this company belonged the historian Aristobulus, architect and geographer. There was a surveying section (the bematists), who collected information about routes and camping grounds and recorded the distances marched; their records, which were checked by Alexander, for long formed the basis of the geography of Asia. There was a baggage train; as for commissariat, supplies were collected in each district as conquered and used for the next advance. The secretarial department was under Eumenes of Cardia, who wrote the Journal, the daily official record of the expedition ...[2]

Also there were physicians, such as Philip the Acarnanian, who attended the king, naval experts and scientists, and the official historian was Callisthenes of Olynthus, a nephew of Aristotle.

Because supply is the basis of strategy and tactics it is exasperating that no information is forthcoming on how the Macedonian army was supplied in the field. To write off this question by stating that it lived

[1] *Alexander the Great*, vol. I, p. 12, and vol. II, p. 141.
[2] Ibid., vol. I, pp. 12–13, and vol. II, p. 39.

on the country it traversed is to burke it, because even then supplies had to be collected; an army of between 30,000 and 50,000 men, without counting followers, can seldom be adequately supplied by foraging. Without an extensive and highly efficient supply train it would have been totally impossible for Alexander to have carried out his many rapid marches, to have crossed the sparsely inhabited plains of Persia, to have led his army over the Hindu-Kush, to have operated for months on end in the mountain fastness of the North-West Frontier of India, and to have traversed the deserts of Makran. Further, he could never have maintained in the field his large force of cavalry by grazing alone.

It was not that this problem went unrecognized – save by military historians who throughout history have paid little attention to it—for Xenophon in his *Cyropaedia*, largely a textbook on generalship, is fully aware of its importance. He makes Cambyses say to his son Cyrus: 'Soldiers, no less than servants in a house, are dependent on supplies ... And pray what will be the use of tactics to an army without supplies ...?' Cyrus observes: 'I was forced to tell the truth and admit that not a syllable had been mentioned on that score' by the teacher who had professed to instruct him in generalship.[1]

Another organization peculiar to the Macedonian army was the Corps of Royal Pages, recruited from the sons of the leading Macedonian nobles. These youths were kept in permanent residence around the king and 'were entrusted', Arrian writes, 'with the general attendance on the king's person and the protection of his body while he was asleep. Whenever the king rode out, some of them received the horses from the grooms, and brought them to him, and others assisted him to mount ... They were also companions of the king in the emulation of the chase.'[2] These youths also constituted a pool of officers from which many of Alexander's commanders were selected. It may be suspected that they were also a hostage for the good behaviour of their fathers when the king campaigned away from Macedonia.

Lastly, although Macedonia was not, like Athens or Persia, a maritime power, Philip raised a not inconsiderable fleet of undecked galleys of light structure of about 120 feet in length and 20 feet beam. Their crews numbered about 200 men a galley, and they were propelled by a square-rigged sail and by a single row of oars on each side, with three rowers to each oar. Larger vessels of a similar build but decked, known as quadriremes and quinqueremes (four and five rowers to an oar), and manned by Cypriots and Phoenicians, were at this

[1] I, 6, 12–14. [2] Arrian, IV, xiii, 1.

time to be found in the Persian service. It is as well to mention here that the galley, *par excellence* the war-ship of the classical age and for long after,[1] was a vessel of very limited powers. She could not safely operate in rough weather and therefore seldom sailed out of sight of land, and for fear of sudden storms was incapable of maintaining a close blockade. These limitations should be borne in mind when we come to the ineffective part played by the Persian fleet during the invasion of Asia by Alexander.

[1] The last great galley battle was that of Lepanto in 1571.

3

ALEXANDER

ᚦᚦᚦ

His Youth and Education

According to Plutarch, Alexander was born on the 6th of Hecatombaeon (July-August) 356 B.C.,[1] the day on which the temple of Artemis at Ephesus was burnt to the ground; a calamity, so the soothsayers announced, which indicated that in some part of the world a torch had been kindled that one day would consume all Asia.

Though this 'prophecy' can be no other than an after-thought, were it to be accepted as true, at that moment there was only one being in the world who could have related the torch to the newly born Macedonian prince, and that was his mother Olympias – an Epiriot princess who traced her descent from Achilles. From all accounts she was a savage, mystical and domineering woman, who from girlhood had been a partaker in the orgiastic rites of Dionysus,[2] son of Zeus and Semele, the daughter of Cadmus, king of Thebes. Nursed by the nymphs of Nysa, so the legend runs, when grown to manhood Dionysus visited Egypt, journeyed through Syria, traversed all Asia and penetrated into India, teaching as he went the cultivation of the vine and introducing the elements of civilization.

The story told by Plutarch that on the night before the consummation of her marriage with Philip, Olympias dreamt that a thunderbolt fell upon her body which kindled a great fire, the flames of which spread far and wide and then were extinguished, though clearly apocryphal, equally clearly fits her character. Nor does it seem improbable that she told her son that, like Dionysus, his spiritual father was

---

[1] *Plutarch's Lives*, 'Alexander', III. Tarn (*Alexander the Great*, vol. I, p. 1) places his birth in the summer of 356 B.C., and Hogarth (*Philip and Alexander of Macedon*, p. 66) in October of that year.

[2] According to Herodotus (V, 7), the Thracians worshipped Ares, Dionysus and Artemis.

Zeus, for Plutarch relates that Eratosthenes said that when she sent her son forth on his great expedition she revealed to him the secret of his birth and bade him behave himself with courage suitable to his divine origin.[1]

Although Alexander was not so credulous as to believe himself to be the son of a god – the ichor story about his blood indicates this[2] – the influence of his mother on him was profound.[3] He inherited from her his passionate, mystical nature; from his father he inherited his energy and practical sense. He venerated Achilles, but it was Heracles, his father's ancestor, the hero who laboured for the good of mankind, whom Isocrates had urged Philip to emulate, whom he chose as his prototype – not the man of moods but the man of deeds – and this is corroborated by the many occasions on which he honoured him, and represented him on his coinage.

Alexander was of middle height, his body as perfectly proportioned as an Olympic athlete, his face of remarkable beauty, his skin clear and white, his eyes large and liquid, his hair golden, and he is always represented as clean shaven. Lysippus, the sculptor, portrayed him in bronze; Apelles, the painter, in colour, and Pyrgoteles engraved his head on gems. Although all their representations of him have perished, copies and imitations of them were passed on to succeeding generations, and of those which have survived probably the most life-like appear on the coinage of Lysimachus (c. 355–281 B.C.), one of his companions and successors.

In early childhood he was entrusted to the care of his nurse Lanice, whom he grew to love as a second mother. Later all her sons gave their lives for him in battle, and her brother Cleitus, surnamed the Black, who in command of the Royal Squadron saved his life at the battle of the Granicus, was until his tragic death at Alexander's own hands one of his most cherished companions. When grown to boyhood, he was entrusted to Leonidas, a near kinsman of Olympias, a man of austere temper, and to an Acarnanian, Lysimachus, who was appointed to be his tutor. He would appear to have been somewhat of a flatterer, for Plutarch records that he was wont to call Philip Peleus and himself Phoenix, because in the *Iliad* Peleus had selected Phoenix to be tutor of Achilles, whose name he conferred on Alexander.

When his son was thirteen, Philip entrusted him to Aristotle, the

---

[1] Plutarch's 'Alexander', III.   [2] Ibid., XXVIII.

[3] On one occasion when Alexander read a letter from Antipater full of accusations against Olympias he said: 'Antipater knew not that one tear of a mother effaced ten thousand letters' (Ibid., XXXIX).

most renowned of Plato's pupils. His father, Nicomachus, for a time had held the appointment of physician to the court of Philip's father Amyntas II, and it was then, when still a child, that Philip first became acquainted with Aristotle. At the time of his appointment Aristotle was forty years of age, and it was in the village of Mieza that for three years he instilled into his youthful charge that insatiable curiosity and love of knowledge which as a man Alexander so conspicuously displayed. He instructed him in philosophy, in scientific inquiry, in medicine,[1] botany, zoology[2] and geography, and inspired him with a deep love of poetry and Greek culture; he annotated for him a copy of the *Iliad* which, it is said, was Alexander's constant companion in all his many campaigns. Further, he must have inspired the young prince with his own detestation of the Persians and lighted him on his path of conquest; for they had put to a cruel death Aristotle's close friend, Hermias of Atarneus.

It was during the three years under Aristotle that Alexander became, as Plutarch writes: 'a lover of learning and a lover of reading', so much so that, 'when he could find no other books (except the *Iliad*) in the interior of Asia, he ordered Harpalus to send him some. So Harpalus sent him the books of Philistus, a great many of the tragedies of Euripides, Sophocles, and Aeschylus, and the dithyrambic poems of Telestes and Philoxenus.' Further, Plutarch adds that his thirst and passion for learning, once implanted, never decayed.[3]

Whether Alexander ever read the histories of Herodotus, Thucydides and Xenophon is unknown, but as Xenophon was a close contemporary and a noted cavalry tactician it would seem probable that he was acquainted with his *Anabasis* and *Cyropaedia*, both of which are devoted to war in Persia. Another writer who must certainly have influenced him was Isocrates, who shortly before his death wrote a letter to Alexander.[4] It is nearly certain that he was acquainted with his *Philippus*, which, as we shall see, coincided closely with Alexander's policy towards both Greeks and Persians.

[1] According to Nearchus, when the Greek physicians were unable to cure the bites of Indian serpents, 'Alexander had collected around him all the Indians who were the cleverest in the medical art, and had it proclaimed through the camp that whoever was bitten should come to the king's tent' (Arrian, *The Indica*, XV, 11).

[2] It is recorded of Alexander 'that he reckoned new lore of plants and animals among the prizes of victory' (*The Ancient Explorers*, M. Cary and E. H. Warmington, 1926, p. 2).

[3] 'Alexander', VIII, 2–3.

[4] Letter No. 5, written probably in 342–341 B.C. (Pauly-Wissowa, IX, col. 2216).

His Genius and Personality

When in 336 B.C. Alexander succeeded to the throne of Macedonia he was in his twenty-first year, and twelve years later, when he died[1] at an age at which most great men are still on the threshold of their careers, he had not only conquered the ancient world of his day, but had set it revolving on a new axis. Ulrich Wilcken writes: 'The whole subsequent course of history, the political, economic and cultural life of after times, cannot be understood apart from the career of Alexander.' [2] Centuries after his death Appian of Alexandria compared his short reign to 'a brilliant flash of lightning',[3] so dazzling that only in recent times have historians appreciated its full significance.[4]

He was a man entirely wrapped up in his destiny and completely devoted to his task. He cared little for any physical pleasures except hunting. Save the love he bore his mother and nurse, he was never enthralled by any woman, and though twice he took to himself a wife, both his marriages were of a political and not of a romantic nature. He never had a mistress, nor was he impotent or a homosexual as his detractors put about in order to defame him.[5] This subordination of his bodily instincts to his task set him apart from the common ruck of men and placed him in that small company of rare and exalted individuals whose iron will, self-control and devotion to their life's task magnetize all who come into contact with them. As Carlyle wrote of Napoleon: 'There was an eye to see in this man, and a soul to dare and do. He rose naturally to be King. All men saw that he *was* such.'

His innate sense of royalty, of kingship based not on power but on nobleness of bearing, on chivalrous conduct and of living as a king should, overshadowed every action of his astonishing career. He thought it more kingly, writes Plutarch, to conquer himself than to conquer others, and while still a youth, when some of his friends who knew that he was fleet of foot urged him to run a race in the Olympic Games, his answer was that he would only do so if he might have kings to run with him. The reason is not in doubt: to place himself on a level with a professional athlete – a type of man he disliked – would be to demean his kingship in the eyes of the people.

[1] Arrian (VII, xxviii, 1) says he reigned 12 years and 8 months.
[2] *Alexander the Great* (English tr. 1932), p. 265.
[3] Preface to his *Roman History*.
[4] Except for Montaigne, the first to do so was Johann Gustav Droysen in his *Geschichte Alexanders des Grossen*, first published in 1833. He wrote: 'The name Alexander betokens the end of one world epoch, and the beginning of another.'
[5] See Tarn's *Alexander the Great*, vol. II, appx. 18.

Of the many instances of his sense of royalty and of his chivalrous bearing toward his enemies, the following are outstanding: When after his victory at Issus he learnt that Sisygambis, mother of Darius, and his wife and children had been captured and were lamenting his assumed death, he sent Leonnatus to inform them that Darius was still alive and that they were 'to retain the state and retinue befitting their royal rank, as well as the title of queens, for he had not undertaken the war against Darius from a feeling of hatred'. And on the following day, when with Hephaestion, his dearest friend, Alexander visited Sisygambis and she, mistaking the former for the king, prostrated herself before Hephaestion and was much abashed when she discovered her mistake, Alexander at once set her at her ease. He took her by the hand and raising her to her feet said to her: 'You were not mistaken, mother, for this man too is Alexander.' [1] Later when he found the murdered body of Darius, he had it sent to Persepolis 'with orders that it should be buried in the royal sepulchre as had all the other Persian kings'.[2] He showed the same respect for royalty when on his return from India he found that during his absence the tomb of Cyrus, founder of the Persian Empire, had been rifled. He at once ordered Aristobulus, the historian, to repair the damage done, to have the stolen treasures replaced by facsimilies, to block up the entrance of the tomb and to set the royal seal on the cement.[3] Of all his acts of royalty, the most typical is his treatment of Porus, whom he defeated on the banks of the Hydaspes (Jhelum). Struck by his kingly bearing, he asked him what treatment he wished to receive. Arrian relates that Porus replied:

'Treat me, O Alexander, in a kingly way!' Alexander being pleased at the expression, said: 'For my own sake, O Porus, thou shalt be thus treated; but for thy own sake do thou demand what is pleasing to thee?' But Porus said that everything was included in that. Alexander, being still more pleased at this remark, not only granted him the rule over his own Indians, but also added another country to that which he had before, of larger extent than the former. Thus he treated the brave man in a kingly way, and from that time found him faithful in all things.[4]

This sense of royalty sprang naturally from the romantic and mystical side of his nature and his living faith in his descent from

[1] Arrian, II, xii, 7.   [2] Ibid., III, xxii, i.
[3] Ibid., VI, xxix, 10, and Strabo, XV, iii, 9.   [4] Arrian, V, xix, 2-3.

Heracles and Achilles. Not only was his belief in the Homeric pan-
theon beyond question, but he felt himself overshadowed by the super-
natural and he stood in awe of the unseen. His motives are never in
doubt; he was never the victim of his own glory, and though his task
was to conquer he subdued his enemies by persuasion as much as by
force of arms. He revered the religion of his opponents, worshipped in
their temples and sacrificed to their gods, for they, like the gods of
Greece, were the Kings of kings.

The moral quality that distinguished him the most clearly from his
fellow-men was his compassion toward others. 'It is difficult to realize',
writes Tarn, 'how strange this trait of compassion in Alexander must
have seemed to his contemporaries, anyhow to Greeks; no public man
throughout Greek history is, I think, recorded to have shown pity: it
was unmanly, and best left to poets and philosophers.' [1] At Ephesus he
stopped the Ephesians slaughtering the oligarchs because he knew that
were the people not checked they 'would put to death, together with
the guilty, certain others, some from hatred, and some for plunder of
their goods'.[2] At the siege of Miletus, when some of the besieged had
sought refuge on an island and Alexander saw that they were going to
fight to the death, he felt compassion for them, 'because they appeared
to him both brave and loyal', and made a truce with them on the condition that they would serve as his soldiers.[3] After the battle of Issus he
showed compassion toward the Theban ambassadors, partly out of
pity for Thebes, the destruction of which he regretted.[4] And when on
his return from India, during the march through the desert of Gedrosia
(Makran) some of the famishing soldiers who had been placed on
guard over the magazines of corn, pilfered from them, when he learnt
of 'the necessity which constrained them so to act, he pardoned those
who had done the deed'.[5]

But it is in his behaviour towards women, who in nearly all ages
have been considered the legitimate spoil of the soldier, that his compassion is most clearly mirrored. Not only did he treat the captive wife

---

[1] *Alexander the Great*, vol. II, pp. 65–6. Plutarch in his 'On the Fortune of
Alexander', 334, 1 (Loeb edit. of the *Moralia*, 1936, vol. iv) records that Alexander,
tyrant of Pherae, on being moved to pity when watching a tragic actor, 'jumped up
and left the theatre at a rapid pace, exclaiming that it would be a dreadful thing, if,
when he was slaughtering so many citizens, he should be seen to weep over the
sufferings of Hecuba and Polyxena. And he came near visiting punishment upon the
actor because the man had softened his heart, as iron in the fire.'

[2] Arrian, I, xvii, 12–13.   [3] Ibid., I, xix, 6.   [4] Ibid., II, xv, 2.

[5] Ibid., VI, xxiii, 5. Of him, in 'On the Fortune of Alexander' (332, 11), Plutarch
writes: 'Who was ever more hostile to wrong doers or kinder to the unfortunate? Who
more stern to his opponents or more indulgent to petitioners?'

and daughters of Darius with a royal respect, but he held in abhorrence rape and violence, which in his day were the universal concomitants of war. On one occasion, when he heard that two Macedonians of Parmenion's command had outraged the wives of some of the mercenary soldiers, he wrote to Parmenion ordering him, 'in case the men were convicted, to punish them and put them to death as wild beasts born for the destruction of mankind'.[1] On another occasion, when Atropates, viceroy of Media, presented him with a hundred girls equipped and armed like horsemen, 'Alexander dismissed them from the army, that no attempt to violate them might be made by the Macedonians or barbarians'.[2] And at the alleged sack of Persepolis he ordered 'his men to spare the persons and the ornaments of the women'.[3] This compassion towards women, as Tarn points out, was the first-fruit of his self-control. 'It was the first time', he writes, 'that such a thing had happened publicly on the world's stage; and the world could not understand it, and it may have been one, though only one, of the reasons which made Arrian, in the great summing-up which ends his book, say that Alexander was like no other man.'[4]

Though in Part II of this book Alexander's generalship will be closely examined, as a preface to what is to come it is opportune to quote here what Arrian has to say of him as man and soldier:

He was very handsome in person [he writes] and much devoted to exertion, very active in mind, very heroic in courage, very tenacious of honour, exceedingly fond of incurring danger, and strictly observant of his duty to the deity. In regard to the pleasures of the body, he had perfect self-control; and of those of the mind, praise was the only one of which he was insatiable. He was very clever in recognizing what was necessary to be done, when others were still in a state of uncertainty; and very successful in conjecturing from the observation of facts what was likely to occur. In marshalling, arming and ruling an army, he was exceedingly skilful; and very renowned for rousing the courage of his soldiers, filling them with hopes of success, and dispelling their fear in the midst of danger by his own freedom from fear. Therefore even what he had to do in uncertainty of the result he did with the greatest boldness. He was also very clever in getting the start of his enemies, and snatching

---

[1] Plutarch, 'Alexander', XXII.   [2] Arrian, VII, xiii, 3.
[3] Curtius, V, vi, 8. '. . . neither, though the sack of Persepolis in Curtius is an invention, could any one have invented Alexander's order that the women were not to be touched; that order was given somewhere' (Tarn's *Alexander the Great*, vol. II, p. 325).   [4] *Alexander the Great*, vol. II, p. 326.

from them their advantages by secretly forestalling them, before any one even feared what was about to happen. He was likewise very steadfast in keeping the agreements and settlements which he made, as well as very sparing in the expenditure of money for the gratification of his own pleasures; but he was exceedingly bountiful in spending it for the benefit of his associates.[1]

Plutarch supplies us with the following description of his everyday life when not on campaign:

> In his times of leisure . . . after rising and sacrificing to the gods, he immediately took breakfast sitting; then he would spend the day in hunting or administering justice, or arranging his military affairs, or reading. If he were making a march which was not very urgent, he would practise, as he went along, either archery or mounting and dismounting from a chariot that was under way. Often, too, for diversion, he would hunt foxes or birds, as may be gathered from his journals. After he had taken quarters for the night, and while he was enjoying bath or anointing, he would enquire of his chief cooks and bakers whether the arrangements for his supper were duly made. When it was late and already dark, he would begin his supper, reclining on a couch, and marvellous was his care and circumspection at table, in order that everything might be served impartially and without stint: but over the wine . . . he would sit long for conversation's sake.[2]

His Misdeeds

When the moral standards of the fourth century are borne in mind, as well as Alexander's youth and the immensity of his task, its dangers and its difficulties, his misdeeds, when compared with those of other great conquerors, are remarkably few. Thanks to Sir William Tarn, the good Alexandrian tradition has been sifted from the bad,[3] and so far as it is possible he has winnowed facts from falsehoods so that it is unnecessary here to discuss the malicious inventions and gross misrepresentations of the Peripatetic and Stoic sources of Alexander's alleged misdeeds. Even were they true, most of them would not seriously detract from his generalship.

Those misdeeds which are undoubted are recorded by Arrian, who

[1] Arrian, VII, xxviii, 1–3.
[2] 'Alexander', XXIII. 'Aristobulus asserts that Alexander used to have long drinking parties, not for the purpose of enjoying wine, as he was not a great wine-drinker, but in order to exhibit his sociality and friendly feeling to his Companions' (Arrian, VII, xxix, 4).   [3] See *Alexander the Great*, vol. II, pt. i.

in his preface to the *Anabasis of Alexander* informs his readers that he has based his history on the now lost histories of Ptolemy and Aristobulus, because their narratives seemed to him to be 'more trustworthy than the rest'. Also because both accompanied Alexander throughout his campaigns, and as the former became a king, 'the falsification of facts would have been more disgraceful to him than to any other man'.[1] Further, he adds that their histories were written after Alexander's death, 'when neither compulsion was used nor reward offered them to write anything different from what really occurred'. Whatever may be Arrian's defects as an historian, he is patently an honest writer, a soldier who in A.D. 134 beat back the great Alan invasion, and understood war; also he was a pupil of Epictetus, who taught that nothing should be valued more than truth.

The misdeeds recorded in Arrian's history may be classified under two headings: unnecessary ruthlessness in waging war and personal crimes. As regards the first, the treatment meted out by Alexander to the Thebans, Tyrians and Gazans, as well as his slaughtering of the Sogdians and the Malli[2] have most frequently been condemned. Yet, when these alleged crimes are brought into focus with war as it was waged in the classical age, they are in no way exceptional. War between Greek and barbarian, writes Professor Freeman, 'was looked upon as the regular order of things. And war, it should be remembered, even when waged by Greek against Greek, carried with it utter havoc and devastation. Fruit-trees were cut down, cornfields were trampled, houses were burned, every kind of wanton ravage was brought ... Nothing but a special capitulation could even secure the life and freedom of the prisoner. To slaughter the men and sell the women and children of a captured town was looked on indeed as harshness, but as harshness which occasion might justify, and which was no breach of the received laws of war. If we look at it by these principles, we shall hardly pronounce Alexander's attack on the Persian Empire to have been unjust in itself; we shall certainly not pronounce it to have been carried out with wanton harshness in detail.'[3]

[1] Though in his *From Alexander to Constantine* (1956), p. 4, Sir Ernest Barker points out that 'this remark seems humorous, and even naïve', Mr Griffith of Caius College suggested to him, 'it would seem much less curious in those days of solemn treatises "On Kingship" than it does today'.

[2] Of the massacre of the Malli, Tarn (*Alexander the Great*, vol. I, p. 103) writes: 'Among Alexander's campaigns this is unique in its dreadful record of mere slaughter. The explanation probably is that the army hated it; they had no wish to fight, but as they had to, they gave no quarter, they did not mean to be turned back from their way home to quell a fresh rising.'

[3] *Historical Essays*, Second Series (1873), pp. 173-4.

The personal misdeeds include the murders of Parmenion and of Cleitus the Black, and the execution of Callisthenes, and the events which led up to them were as follows:

Parmenion was Philip's most noted general and it may be assumed that when Alexander set out on his war with Persia, because of his youth and inexperience the Macedonians relied more on Parmenion than on him. Also in their eyes Parmenion's importance may have been magnified by the latitude Alexander allowed his leading generals, which on one occasion caused his mother to rebuke him 'for making them the equals of kings'.[1] Yet in spite of Parmenion's undoubted experience, up to the battle of Arbela Alexander almost consistently set his advice aside, and as by then Parmenion was about seventy years old and had not done particularly well in that battle, soon after it Alexander removed him from his post of second in command and left him at Ecbatana (Hamadan) with a body of Thracian mercenaries to guard the treasure stored there and to protect the army's communications. Then in mid-summer 330 B.C., Alexander set out to pursue Darius. When he found him murdered, by right of conquest he became Lord of Asia. As king of Persia, it became as much a military as a political necessity to place his Persian subjects on equal footing with his Macedonians, who violently resented it and who never ceased to regard the Persians as a race of slaves. It is not improbable some looked toward Parmenion and his son Philotas – in command of the Companion cavalry – to right what they felt to be an insult to them.

Whether this was so can only be surmised, but what is known is that when Alexander reached Phrada (probably Nad-i-Ali) deep in Drangiana (Seistan), a plot against his life was discovered in which Philotas was involved. Arrian mentions that, according to Aristobulus and Ptolemy, when in Egypt Philotas had been implicated in a similar conspiracy, but that Alexander did not believe it to be possible, 'both on account of the long-existing friendship between them . . . and the confidence he reposed in Philotas himself'.[2] As custom demanded, Philotas and those alleged to be implicated, including Amyntas, a phalanx battalion leader, and his two brothers, were brought before the army for trial. When Philotas 'confessed that he had heard of a certain conspiracy which was being formed against Alexander',[3] because of his failure to report it he was convicted and executed; Amyntas and his brothers were acquitted.

Though there is little doubt that Philotas was fairly tried, it prob-

---

[1] Plutarch's 'Alexander', XXXIX.   [2] Arrian, III, xxvi, 1.
[3] Ibid. Strabo (XV, ii, 10), a sober historian, accepts Philotas as guilty.

ably would have been wiser had Alexander removed him from his command and hushed up the scandal; for now he was faced with a dilemma of quite exceptional magnitude. At Phrada, as the crow flies, he was over 800 miles from Ecbatana and was separated from it by the Salt Desert. If Parmenion in revenge for the death of his son were to use the imperial treasure to raise a rebellion in Hither Asia, Alexander's communications would be cut, the army stranded and the great campaign ruined. In any case the army would have to return – if it could – to quash the rebellion. As there was no evidence that Parmenion was implicated in the plot, Alexander could not arrest him and bring him to trial;[1] nor could he remove him from his great position without further antagonizing him. Rather than risk the ruin of his campaign, he decided to have him assassinated, and as soon as Philotas was dead he sent Polydamus by swift dromedaries across the desert with letters ordering the generals in Media to put Parmenion to death. This was done, and as Tarn points out, though 'Philotas' execution had been perfectly judicial, Parmenion's was 'plain murder'. But he adds that Alexander 'had shown his generals that he was master; he struck . . . with terrible effect, and the lesson went home; six years passed before he had to strike again'.[2]

Although the murder of Cleitus[3] bears no resemblance to that of Parmenion, it stemmed from the same root – Macedonian opposition to Alexander's Persian policy. It occurred at Maracanda (Samarkand) in Sogdiana at a banquet to which Alexander had invited Cleitus, Ptolemy, Perdiccas and other close companions. The subject of bravery cropped up, and to flatter Alexander some of those present compared him with Heracles and lauded his deeds over those of his father Philip. Cleitus, one of Philip's old soldiers, who was vexed with Alexander because he had adopted certain Persian customs, angrily replied that Alexander's deeds were solely to be credited to his Macedonians and vehemently reproached him with the murders of Attalus and Parmenion. Alexander sprang to his feet in fury and shouted for his hypaspists, but was restrained by those near him from hurling himself on Cleitus. At the same time Ptolemy hustled Cleitus out of the room, but a moment later he broke away from those holding him and rushed back. At sight of him, Alexander, no longer able to control himself,

[1] This has been questioned, because Curtius (VI, xi, 20) mentions that, according to the law of the Macedonians, 'the relatives of those who had plotted against the king should be put to death with the guilty parties'.
[2] *Alexander the Great,* vol. I, p. 64. See vol. II, appx. 12, for a full analysis.
[3] Recorded by Arrian in IV, viii and ix, and at greater length by Curtius in VIII, i, 22 to ii, 12.

snatched a pike from one of his body-guard, shouted, 'Go now to Philip, and Parmenion and Attalus!' [1] and ran him through. Then he realized the horror of his deed; he had killed the man who had saved his life on the Granicus, the brother of his nurse Lanice. He threw himself in an agony of contrition on his bed and for three days refused food and drink.

The only mitigating factor was that both Cleitus and Alexander were overcome by drink. It is the sole occasion on which Alexander is correctly recorded to have been drunk, and to have lost control of his passionate temper. Of his contrition Arrian writes: 'I think Alexander deserves great praise . . . that he did not obstinately persevere in evil, or still worse become a defender and advocate of the wrong which had been done, but confessed that he had committed a crime, being a man (and therefore liable to err).' [2] And in his 'Apology for Alexander's Errors' he writes: 'However I am certain that Alexander was the only one of the ancient kings who, from nobility of character, repented of the errors which he had committed.' [3]

Though the third misdeed attributed to Alexander bears no resemblance to these murders, again its roots went back to his pro-Persian policy. In 327 B.C., when in Bactra (Balkh), to further this policy he decided to introduce the Persian court practice of *proskynesis* ('prostration').[4] It was an age-old Oriental expression of deep reverence paid by the subject to his overlord, and had nothing to do with his worship as a god. But the Greeks and Macedonians so considered it and when performed before a man they looked upon it as a slave-like act.[5] It would appear that Alexander expected Callisthenes to support him in its introduction because he had consistently flattered him by calling him the son of Zeus and in his history he had gone so far as to write that when the army skirted the seashore at the foot of Mount Climax, in Lycia, the waves had prostrated themselves before Alexander as if he were a god. But when at a banquet *proskynesis* was introduced, Callisthenes opposed it, apparently to win favour in the eyes of the Macedonians. He urged Alexander to 'distinguish between the honours paid to

---

[1] Curtius, VIII, i, 52.   [2] Arrian, IV, ix, 6.   [3] Ibid., VII, xxix, 2.
[4] See Tarn's *Alexander the Great*, vol. I, pp. 77–81, and vol. II, appx. 22, II.
[5] A modern parallel is to be found in Robert Ford's *Captured in Tibet* (London, 1957, p. 21) where the ceremony in which he received the blessing of the Dalai Lama as a Tibetan official is described. 'There was one part of the prescribed ritual', he writes, 'that I did not perform myself. Had I been a Tibetan, I should have been required to prostrate myself three times before the throne. It was impossible for me to do this sincerely not because I was a European, but because I was not a Buddhist; and my own religion forbade it . . . This was therefore done for me by another official.'

him by his Greeks and Macedonians and those by his Persian subjects'.[1] This so vexed Alexander that he refused Callisthenes the customary kiss, on which Callisthenes insolently remarked: 'Well, then
I'll go away the poorer by a kiss.'[2]

Though Alexander was greatly annoyed, he realized that Callisthenes had voiced the sentiments of the army and, according to Arrian,
'he sent to prevent the Macedonians from making any further mention
of the ceremony of prostration', and then, after a period of silence,
allowed the most honourable of the Persians to prostrate their bodies
before him,[3] which implies that though he dropped prostration so far
as his soldiers were concerned, he maintained it for his Persian subjects. But he was furious that his flatterer had made a fool of him. Soon
came the Pages' conspiracy in which Callisthenes is said to have been
implicated.

Among their duties the Pages had to guard the king during the
night and attend him when hunting. One of them, Hermolaus, a
pupil of Callisthenes, was punished for a breach of etiquette while out
hunting and so deeply resented it that he determined to assassinate
Alexander while he slept. He won the support of some of his companions, but one of them, shocked at the suggestion, divulged the plot
to a friend and it was reported to Ptolemy. The conspirators were
arrested and, according to Arrian who quotes both Ptolemy and Aristobulus, the youths asserted that it was Callisthenes who instigated
them to make the attempt, but Arrian adds: 'Most writers, however,
do not agree with this, but represent that Alexander readily believed
the worst about Callisthenes, from the hatred he already felt towards
him, and because Hermolaus was known to be exceedingly intimate
with him.'[4] Those of the pages who were convicted were stoned to
death and Callisthenes was executed for conspiracy.

The truth would appear to be that Callisthenes was a talkative
busybody and a time-server who had an exaggerated opinion of his own
importance,[5] who flattered Alexander to his face and criticized him
behind his back for doing the very things his flattery suggested.
According to Timaeus (c. 356–260 B.C.), 'Callisthenes was a mere
sycophant . . . and acted in a manner utterly unworthy of his philosophy . . . and richly deserved the punishment which he met with at

---

[1] Arrian, IV, xi, 8.   [2] Plutarch's 'Alexander', LIV, and Arrian, IV, xii, 5.
[3] Arrian, IV, xii, 1.   [4] Ibid., IV, xiv, 1.
[5] According to Ammianus Marcellinus, when Aristotle sent Callisthenes to
Alexander, he warned him 'to say as little as he could, and that only of a pleasant
kind, before a man who carried the power of life & death on the tip of his tongue'
(XVIII, iii, 7).

the hands of Alexander, for having corrupted the mind of that monarch as far as he could.' [1] Yet, whether guilty or not, as Tarn points out, Callisthenes had his revenge because it was from the Peripatetic school, of which he had been a member, that the debased portrait of Alexander was painted. [2]

At the end of his history, Arrian looks back on Alexander's misdeeds, thus:

> Whoever therefore reproaches Alexander as a bad man, let him do so; but let him first not only bring before his mind all his actions deserving reproach, but also gather into one view all his deeds of every kind. Then, indeed, let him reflect who he is himself, and what kind of fortune he has experienced; and then consider who that man was whom he reproaches as bad, and to what a height of human success he attained, becoming without any dispute king of both continents [Europe and Asia] and reaching every place by his fame; while he himself who reproaches him is of small account, spending his labour on petty objects which, however, he does not succeed in effecting, petty as they are. For my own part, I think there was at that time no race of men, no city, nor even a single individual to whom Alexander's name and fame had not penetrated. For this reason it seems to me that a hero totally unlike any other human being could not have been born without the agency of the deity. [3]

[1] Quoted by Polybius, XII, 12.

[2] *Alexander the Great*, vol. I, p. 82. The medieval picture of Alexander was largely based on the works of those historians who drew upon this school. See *The Medieval Alexander*, George Cary, 1956.

[3] Arrian, VII, xxx, 1–2. In his essay on 'The worthiest and most excellent men' Montaigne selects Homer, Alexander and Epaminondas as his three outstanding examples, and of the second he writes: 'So infinite, rare and excellent virtues that were in him, as justice, temperance, liberalitie, integritie in words, love towards his [own people] and humanitie towards the conquered. For in truth, his maners seeme to admit no just cause of reproach: indeed some of his particular, rare and extraordinary actions, may in some sort be taxed. For it is impossible to conduct so great, and direct so violent motions with the strict rules of justice. Such men ought to be judged in grose, by the mistris end of their actions' (trans. John Florio, *The Temple Classics* (1897), vol. II, pp. 332–3). With this may be bracketed what Plutarch said of him in 'On the Fortune of Alexander' (340–8): 'And even though he became great through Fortune, he is even greater in that he made good use of his Fortune. And the more we praise his Fortune the more shall we exalt his Virtue by reason of which he became worthy of his Fortune.'

4

THE THEATRE OF WAR

꙳꙳꙳

Geography in the Fourth Century B.C.

Today it is difficult to picture any large-scale military operation with
out accurate maps to guide the strategist or tactician, yet only in recent
times has this become possible. In order to appreciate the difficulties
and hazards that faced Alexander when he set out on his conquests, it
is as well briefly to outline what was known of the world of his day,
and what it was possible for him to know of the theatre of war.

Geographically, the world as conceived in the fourth century was
but a fraction of its actual size. Anaximander of Miletus, born in 610
B.C., is the first Greek recorded to have drawn a map of it, which a
century later was adopted by the first Greek historian, Hecataeus, also
of Miletus, who took part in the Ionic revolt of 500–494 B.C.[1] On it
the world was shaped like a disk consisting of two half-moons of land,
the one to the north represented Europe and the southern combined
Asia and Africa; together they enclosed an inland sea – the Mediterranean. The centre of this world was the Bosporus, which linked Europe
with Asia, and around the whole flowed the Ocean Stream. It swept
northward from the western entrance of the Mediterranean (the
Pillars of Hercules), and then eastward to the Caspian (Hyrcanian)
Sea, which was believed to be a gulf on the extreme eastern flank of
Europe. The Mediterranean Sea was fairly accurately defined, as were
the Black Sea (Euxine) and Sea of Azov (Palus Maeotis). The Danube
(Ister) flowed south-eastward from somewhere in the north of modern
France into the Black Sea, and the sources of the Nile were thought to
be in India. India was placed immediately south of the Caspian Sea,

---

[1] Herodotus (V, 49) mentions that Aristagoras, one of the leaders in this revolt,
made use of a tablet on which was engraved the map of the world, and we are told
that he used it to point out where the Ionians, Lydians and Phrygians lived.

and the Nile flowed for a great distance south-west before it turned sharply north through Egypt to the Mediterranean.

After Hecataeus came Herodotus, born about 484 B.C. His geographical knowledge was largely based on extensive travelling and the information he picked up on his way; it was an immense advance on that of the Ionian cartographers. For a circular world he substituted an oblong, its longer extension running from east to west. He divided it into three continents – Europe, Asia and Libya – instead of two, and Libya, he states, was known to be washed on all sides by the sea, except where it was attached to Asia by the isthmus of Suez. Further, he records that it had been circumnavigated by Phoenicians sent out by Neco, king of Egypt (617–601 B.C.), who had sailed from the Red Sea and returned by way of the Pillars of Hercules. He, however, doubted the truth of this story because, when 'sailing round Libya' – that is, on its western flank – 'they had the [rising] sun upon their right hand',[1] which, should the story be other than an invention, is a proof that the circumnavigation was actually made.

He states that the boundaries of Europe were quite unknown, and 'there is not a man who can say whether any sea girds it round either to the north or to the east, while in length it undoubtedly extends as far as both the other two [continents]'.[2] He mentions that amber came from the north of Europe; repudiates all knowledge of the Cassiterides (Tin Islands), and has much to say on the region north of the Black Sea, particularly Scythia, which lay between the Danube and the Sea of Azov. Among a number of rivers, he mentions the Ister, Borysthenes (Dneiper), and Tanais (Don).

In advance of the geographers who preceded him, and of many who followed him, Herodotus correctly states that the Caspian Sea is a lake and not a gulf;[3] that on its western side it is bounded by the Caucasus, and on its eastern by a vast plain 'stretching out interminably before the eye', most of which was inhabited by the Massagetae. During his extensive travels in Egypt he learnt that there was a narrow gulf (the Red Sea) that ran inland from the Erythraean Sea (Indian Ocean) between Arabia and Egypt, and which in length was '40 row boat days'. 'In this sea', he adds, 'there is an ebb and flow of the tide every day.'[4] According to him, Arabia was the last of inhabitable land toward the south of Asia[5] and Ethiopia the last inhabited land in Libya.[6]

His knowledge of Asia was confined to the Persian Empire, through the western regions of which he travelled extensively, and in spite of the remoteness of India, he has much to say about that country.

[1] IV, 42.   [2] IV, 45.   [3] I, 203.   [4] II, 11.   [5] III, 107.   [6] III, 107.

His India was, however, confined to the Punjab, which he believed to be the furthest inhabited region of the world toward the east.[1] Beyond it there was nothing but sandy desert, and he knew nothing of its great southern peninsula. He mentions that it was thickly populated, that its tribes were numerous and did not speak the same language, that some were nomadic and others not, and that they refused to kill animals and lived on vegetables.[2] He mentions the city of Caspatyrus (*Kaspáturos*)[3] and the country of Pactyica (*Paktuike*), and that crocodiles were to be found in the Indus as in the Nile.

The last of the geographers to be considered here is Aristotle. He held that the earth was a sphere, in the centre of the universe, 'far smaller even than some of the stars'.[4] It was surrounded with water, and beyond India and the Pillars of Hercules there was nothing but Ocean.[5] He mentions two inland seas, the Hyrcanian and the Caspian, which 'have no connection with the outer ocean'.[6] This has led to the assumption that the two seas are the Caspian and the Sea of Aral. Of the rivers of Asia he writes:

> . . . most of the rivers in Asia and the largest of them flow from the mountain range called Parnassus (Paropamisus: Hindu-Kush) which is commonly regarded as the highest mountain towards the winter dawn (south-east; the direction in which the sun rises at the winter solstice). For when you have crossed it, the outer ocean, whose farther limit is unknown to the inhabitants of our part of the world, is already in sight. There flow from this mountain among other rivers the Bactrus (Oxus) the Choaspes (Karun), and the Araxes (Jaxartes); from the last of which the Tanais (Don) branches off and flows into Lake Maeotis (Sea of Azov). From it also flows the Indus, the greatest of all rivers. From the Caucasus there flow many

[1] III, 106.   [2] III, 98–100.

[3] III, 102. Sir Olaf Caroe, in his *The Pathans 550 B.C.–A.D. 1957* (1958), 32, points out that, because in a fragment of Hecateus of Miletus Kaspapuros (his spelling) is stated to be in Gandhara, the probability is that Paktuike is another name for that country. Further, that Kaspapuros is probably a scribal error for Paskapuros, and that Paskapuros – the Po-lu-sha-po-lu of the Chinese pilgrim Hsüan Tsang, the Sanskrit Purushapura, and the early Muslim Purshapur or Pushabur – is Peshawar.

[4] *Aristotle's Meteorologica*, trans. H. D. P. Lee (1952), I, iii, 339b.

[5] In *De Caelo* 298(a) Aristotle writes: 'One should not be too sure of the incredibility of the view of those who conceive that there is continuity between the parts about the Pillars of Hercules and the parts about India, and that in this way the ocean is one. As further evidence in favour of this they quote the case of elephants, a species occurring in each of these extreme regions, suggesting that the common characteristic of these extremes is explained by their continuity.' And in *Topica*, 116(a), 38, he implies that India (i.e. the land of the Indus) is the farthest inhabited region of the earth in the east.   [6] *Meteorologica*, II, i, 354a.

rivers, extraordinary both in number and in size, among them the Phasis (Rion). The Caucasus is the largest mountain range, both in extent and height, towards, the summer sunrise (north-east).[1]

Such was the sum of geographical knowledge when Alexander set out on his conquests: a small, restricted world in which, except for Greece, Europe was of no great account, and in which Egypt was subject to the Persians, whose empire extended over habitable Asia, beyond which lay the Ocean. Were the legend true that, after his return from India to Babylon, Alexander sighed for yet more lands to conquer, there would be nothing remarkable about it, for his knowledge of the actual world was that of the geographers of his age.

Although Alexander's world was only a fraction of what it is now known to be, his theatre of war was immense. It extended from south of the Danube to beyond the Indus, and from the Syr Daria to the Nile. Besides the Balkan peninsula, of present-day countries it included Asiatic Turkey, Syria, Palestine, half of Egypt, Iraq, Iran, Afghanistan, the Punjab, Sind, Baluchistan and southern Turkestan; in all about 2,000,000 square miles – that is, two-thirds the extent of the United States – which it has been estimated was inhabited by some 50,000,000 people.

It included every type of terrain: fertile plains, arid deserts, vast mountain ranges and great rivers; a complex and difficult theatre of war. Present-day Iran (Airiya of the *Avesta*, land of the Aryans or the 'Illustrious'), then the central and eastern sections of the Persian empire, covers most of the highlands which extend from west of the Indus to the Tigris; an arid plateau 5,000 feet above sea level at Kerman and Isfahan, 4,000 feet at Shiraz and Yezd, and 3,000 feet at Tehran and Meshed. In winter the temperature at times falls below zero, and in summer has been known to rise to as high as 129 degrees Fahrenheit.[2] Throughout history it has experienced changes of climate, and in Alexander's day probably it was considerably more fertile than now. This has been noted by Ellsworth Huntington, who points out that today an incredible number of ruins are to be found in the more arid regions, that 'mighty cities of the dead crowd such places as Seistan, the province of Kirman, the piedmont region of Afghanistan, and the northern border of the great desert of Dasht-i-Lut'; and that 'though the divisions of Alexander's army which marched through Afghanistan under Krateros appear to have had no special difficulty . . .

[1] *Meteorologica*, II, xiii, 350a.
[2] See *A History of Persia*, Sir Percy Sykes (1921), p. 8.

it would certainly puzzle a Krateros now-a-days to march his elephants and heavy baggage from the Helmund to Narmashir', because the greater part of this march of 180 miles is now 'absolutely desert'.[1]

Some of the rivers have dried up, others have changed their courses, and among them it would appear that the Oxus not only flowed into the Aral Sea, but also along the Uzboi Channel into the Caspian.[2] When Huntington explored this region in 1903 he discovered 'strands lying at various heights up to six hundred feet above the present water level' of the Caspian Sea; and he is of the opinion that, in all probability, 2,200 years ago 'the Caspian stood nearly a hundred and fifty feet higher than now, and almost coalesced with the Sea of Aral'.[3]

In the Punjab changes in the courses of its rivers have been on a stupendous scale, but nothing is known of them until after the Arab invasion of 712. Since then the Bias has forsaken its ancient independent bed and become a tributary of the Sutlej, while the Indus, Jhelum, Chenab and Ravi have repeatedly changed their courses and points of junction. Since Akbar's reign (1556–1605) it is known that the delta of the Indus has advanced more than fifty miles and that accretion and denudation have much changed the coast line of Makran. Because during the 1,000 years before the coming of the Arabs equally great changes are likely to have occurred, Vincent A. Smith considers it probable that in Alexander's day 'the "lost river of Sind", the Hakra or Wahindar, then existed, and that the Panjāb rivers, including the Indus, joined it, and formed one stream, afterwards known as the Mihrān of Sind'.[4] This is supported by Aristobulus, who records that when he was sent on some business into an unspecified region – possibly Bahawalpur – 'he saw a tract of land deserted, which contained more than a thousand cities with their dependent villages; the Indus, having left its proper channel, was diverted into another on the left hand much deeper, and precipitated itself into it like a cataract, so that it no longer watered the country by the (usual) inundation on the right hand from which it had receded, and this was elevated above the level not only of the new channel of the river, but above that of the new inundation'.[5]

[1] *The Pulse of Asia*, Ellsworth Huntington (1907), pp. 314–18.

[2] According to Aristobulus, cited by Strabo (XI, vii, 3), large quantities of Indian merchandise were conveyed by the Oxus 'to the Hyrcanian Sea, and ... thence into Albania (Azerbaijan) by the Cyrus (Kur or Kura) and through the adjoining countries to the Euxine'. See also *The Greeks in Bactria and India*, W. W. Tarn (1938), pp. 113 and 491–3, and 'The voyage of Anthony Jenkison in 1558', *Voyages*, Richard Hakluyt (Everyman's Library, 1939), vol. I, p. 448.

[3] *The Pulse of Asia*, p. 337.

[4] *The Early History of India* (4th edit., 1924), p. 103.   [5] Strabo, XV, i, 19.

Should 'left hand' mean 'east', the new channel he refers to must be the southern part of the now dry bed of the Hakra; if 'west', the existing bed of the Indus.

Organization of the Persian Empire

In 552 B.C., when Cyrus, prince of Anshan, revolted against Media, the Persians were almost an unknown people who inhabited the region north of the Persian Gulf; but under his leadership and that of his son Cambyses, within a generation of the revolt four great kingdoms – Media, Lydia, Babylonia and Egypt – were welded into the Persian empire, which for over 200 years became the centre of world-history. The rapidity of these conquests was due not only to force of arms, but also to the tolerance shown to the conquered peoples. But, when Cambyses died childless in 522 B.C., the empire, only partially consolidated, fell into turmoil and during it Darius (521–486 B.C.), son of Hystaspes, Satrap of Parthia and Hyrcania and a kinsman of Cyrus, gained control. Once he had enforced his authority he began to strengthen the imperial frontiers. First, in 518 B.C. he pushed the eastern frontier, which Cyrus had established along the western slopes of the Hindu-Kush, beyond the Indus, and six years later, in 512 B.C., he advanced the western frontier over the Sea of Marmara to the Danube and so opened the long struggle between Persia and Greece.

Darius' place in history is, however, not that of a conqueror, but of an empire organizer and administrator whose work, in Breasted's words, was 'one of the most remarkable achievements in the history of the ancient Orient, if not of the world'.[1] It proved, writes Robinson, 'to be the model of all latter empires', including the Roman,[2] and without it the conquests of Alexander would not have been possible.

The empire over which Darius ruled was, like the British empire, not only vast in extent, but inhabited by a medley of peoples and nations bound together neither by unity of race, nor by a common language or religion, and, as with the British empire, his problem was threefold: How to win and maintain the loyalty of his subjects; how to delegate power without loss of central control, and how to secure the whole against invasion and internal revolt.

To meet the first of these requirements, which was the foundation of the second and third, he wisely adopted a policy of tolerance. Though an absolute monarch, he assured the rights and privileges of

---

[1] *The Conquest of Civilization* (1926), p. 199.
[2] *A History of Israel* (1945), vol. I, p. 5.

each ethnic or national group and paid great regard to their traditions and customs. In Babylonia he reigned as king of Babylon, in Egypt, as pharaoh and the successor of the pharaohs, he was looked upon as the son of Ammon-Ra. In Cyprus and Phoenicia he maintained the local kings, and in the Greek cities of Ionia the local tyrants. Though by faith a Zoroastrian, he respected the gods of his subjects and repaired and built their temples at the expense of the imperial treasury, among which was the temple of Ammon at Siwah. The only marks of subjection he imposed on his subjects were the payment of tribute and, in the event of war, a levy for service in the field. As Dr G. B. Gray points out, his was the first attempt in history 'to bring a large number of different races and nationalities under a single-government which assured to the whole the rights and privileges as well as the burdens and responsibilities of the members of the state'.[1]

Once he had established his rule, he divided his empire into twenty satrapies or provinces, each under a satrap or viceroy. This was not a new innovation, it had existed in the Assyrian, Babylonian and Median empires, and Xenophon mentions six satraps under Cyrus;[2] but he improved on it, and never before had it been applied on so extensive a scale.[3]

The satraps were always men of high birth, sometimes members of the royal family. Their appointments were indefinite; they had their own courts and body-guards and were the highest judicial authorities in their respective provinces. Their functions, both civil and military, were wide, and their main duties were to collect the tribute, maintain law and order within their satrapies, secure their communications, and mobilize their provincial militias when they were needed to reinforce the king's army in war.

The weak link in this system was that there was an ever-present tendency for an ambitious satrap to become independent; a contingency which later facilitated the conquests of Alexander. Darius resorted to the following preventive measures.

Besides the provincial levies he maintained a standing army. In peace-time it acted as a check on the levies should a satrap attempt to

[1] *The Cambridge Ancient History*, vol. IV, p. 184.
[2] *Cyropaedia*, VIII, 6, 7–8.
[3] A list of the twenty satrapies and the tribute they paid is given by Herodotus (III, 89–97); the total tribute amounted to 14,600 talents. Darius introduced a bimetallic coinage of gold darics and silver siglos; almost exactly equivalent to English pounds and shillings. A talent of gold (3,000 darics) was worth £3,313, and a talent of silver (6,000 siglos) was worth £331 (see *A History of Persia*, Sir Percy Sykes, p. 163).

break away from the king's authority, and in war-time the levies rein-forced the standing army. They were organized in divisions of 10,000 men, divided into ten battalions each of 1,000, and then again into hundreds and tens, each unit under its own commander. But as the levies were only mobilized in time of war, their organization usually remained on paper.

The standing army consisted of the king's body-guard of 2,000 cavalry and 2,000 infantry, and a division of 10,000 infantry known as the 'Immortals'. In war-time large forces of Persian cavalry were added to it; all these troops were either Persians or Medes. In war and on the line of march the army was maintained by the provinces it passed through, which suggests that in peace-time supply depots must have been established in readiness.

As a further check on the satraps, the cities and strategic points throughout the empire were garrisoned by Persian soldiers,[1] and from time to time a high official, known as the 'King's Eye', was sent to inspect the satrapies and report on the conduct of their governors. To guarantee an adequate supply of loyal officers, a Royal Academy was established at Susa. Xenophon writes of it: 'For all the sons of the Persian nobles are educated at the gates of the King [i.e. at his palace] where they may learn a lesson of virtuous conduct, but can see or hear nothing disgraceful . . . so that in their very childhood they may learn to govern and to obey.' [2] This, it may be conjectured, was also a check on the satraps and nobles, because these youths could be held as host-ages for the good behaviour of their fathers.

Because in so vast an empire it was imperative that troop move-ments should be speedy, and also to stimulate trade, Darius developed many of the old caravan routes into military roads, and though there is no evidence that they were comparable with those of the Romans, they were passable highways. Bridges or fords were provided at the river crossings, and on an average of every four parasangs[3] there were posting houses and caravanserais at which relays of horses were kept for the imperial couriers. Herodotus describes these couriers as follows:

Nothing mortal travels so fast as these Persian messengers. The entire plan is a Persian invention; and this is the method of it. Along the whole line of road there are men (they say) stationed with

---

[1] 'In accordance with the rules . . . laid down by Cyrus, the citadel garrisons and the captains of the guard are to this day appointed directly by the king, and have their names on the Royal list' (Xenophon, *Cyropaedia*, VIII, 6, 8).

[2] *Anabasis*, I, ix, 3.   [3] A parasang was three and two-fifths of an English mile.

horses, in number equal to the number of days which the journey takes, allowing a man and horse to each day; and these men will not be hindered from accomplishing at their best speed the distance which they have to go, either by snow, or rain, or heat, or by the darkness of night. The first rider delivers his despatch to the second, and the second passes it to the third; and so it is borne from hand to hand along the whole line, like the light in the torch-race, which the Greeks celebrate to Vulcan [Hephaestus].[1]

These military highways may be divided into two groups, the western and eastern. In the former, the main artery was the great western road, known as the 'Royal Road', which is fully described by Herodotus;[2] and in the latter, the great eastern road, details of which were given by Ctesias in his lost history of Persia.

The Royal Road linked Sardes (Sart) with Susa (Shust); it ran for 1,500 miles and at the common rate of travel a journey from Susa to Sardes took ninety days; but thanks to the relay system the imperial couriers could cover it in seven. From Sardes, its western half – which approximately followed the present railway from Smyrna to the Gulf of Iskanderum – passed through Ipsus (northeast of Ak Shehr), Iconium (Konia), the Cilician Gates in Mt Taurus, and Tarsus to Issus (? Aisse north of Alexandretta). From Issus the eastern half crossed the Euphrates at Zeugma (Balkis) and then passed through Carrhae (Herran), Nisibis (Nisibin), and crossed the Tigris at Nineveh (near Mosul), after which it went on to Arbela (Erbil) and then proceeded in a south-easterly direction to terminate at Susa near the river Pasitigris (Karkheh). From Ipsus a loop road ran by way of Pessinus (a city in Phrygia) and Ancyra (Ankara) to the river Halys (Kizil-Irmak) at Pteria (? Boghaz Keui) in Cappadocia; then it again crossed the Halys to lead to Mazaka (Kayseri) and the Cilician Gates.[3]

From Nineveh, which was a road centre, a road went northward to Trapezus (Trebizond) on the Black Sea, and another westward to Thapsacus (Dibsi), from where it turned southward through Syria, and by way of Damascus, Tyre, and Gaza led to Pelusium and Memphis in Egypt.

From Babylon and Susa the great eastern road passed through Ecbatana (Hamadan), Rhagae (Rei) and the Caspian Gates to Meshed, from where its northern branch went on to Bactra (Balkh) and the

---

[1] VIII, 98. [2] V, 52–4.

[3] This varies from Herodotus' version, because he mixes up the loop road with the main Royal Road. See 'The Royal Road in Herodotus', W. M. Calder, *The Classical Review*, vol. XXXIX (1925), pp. 7–11.

Oxus (Amu Daria), and its southern to Herat. At Herat the road forked, one branch passed eastward up the Hari-Rud to Kabul and thence to Attock on the Indus, and the other southward through Seistan, Kandahar and the Mulla pass to the Indus. From Kandahar a road proceeded south-eastward to Gulashkird, then to Persepolis and Pasargadae, from where one branch led to Ecbatana and the other to Susa.

Still further to improve his communications, at some time during his reign Darius sent Scylax, a Carian Greek, to discover a sea route between India and Persia. According to Herodotus, Scylax set out from Caspatyrus (Peshawar) in the Pactyican country (Gandhara) and sailed down the Indus to the sea, from where he skirted the coasts of Persia and Arabia, sailed up the Red Sea and landed in the neighbourhood of Suez. After this remarkable voyage we are told, 'Darius conquered the Indians [the Punjab and Sind] and made use of the sea in those parts'.[1] He also had a canal cut from the Nile to the Red Sea,[2] by means of which water communication was established between India and the Mediterranean.

Persia in the Fourth Century

After the death of Darius the Persian empire entered its decline. With the defeat of his son Xerxes (485–465 B.C.) at Salamis and Plataea, the foothold in Europe was abandoned, and under his successors Artaxerxes I (464–424 B.C.) and Darius II (424–405 B.C.) the palace rule of women led to frequent revolts, and in 404 B.C. to the loss of Egypt. In 401 B.C. came the rebellion of Cyrus the Younger against his brother Artaxerxes II (404–358 B.C.) which, though crushed at Cunaxa, was followed by constant struggle between the central government and the outlying provinces, during which the conquests of Darius I east of the Hindu-Kush and south of the Black Sea were permanently lost. Under his successor, Artaxerxes III (358–338 B.C.), Egypt was reconquered and the Egyptian gods brutally insulted; an ass was stabled in the temple of Ptah and the sacred Apis bull was roasted for a banquet. In 338 B.C. Artaxerxes was assassinated by his vizier Bagaos, who raised to the throne a collateral of the Achaemenid house, who became Darius III (336–330 B.C.). He was a mild and virtuous prince and totally unfitted to cope with the rising power of Macedonia.

[1] IV, 44.
[2] 'I commanded to dig this canal from the Nile ... to the sea which goes from Persia ...' On one of Darius' inscriptions (see *The Cambridge Ancient History*, vol. IV, p. 200).

During the latter years of this decline, the degeneration of Persia since the days of Cyrus and Darius I is described by Xenophon:

Noble achievement in the old days was the avenue to fame, the man was honoured who risked his life for the king, or brought a city or a nation beneath his sway. But now, if some Mithridates has betrayed his father Ariobarzanes, if some Reomithres has left his wife and children and the sons of his friend as hostages at the court of Egypt, and then has broken the most solemn of all pledges – it is they and their like who are loaded with the highest honours, if only they are thought to have gained some advantage for the king. With such examples before them, all the Asiatics have turned to injustice and impiety. For what the leaders are, that, as a rule, will the men below them be. Thus has lawlessness increased and grown among them. And injustice has grown, and thieving. Not only criminals, but men who are absolutely innocent are arrested and forced to pay fines for no reason whatsoever: to be known to have wealth is more dangerous than guilt, so that the rich do not care to have any dealings with the powerful, and dare not even risk appearing at the muster of the royal troops. Therefore, when any man makes war on Persia, whoever he may be, he can roam up and down the country to his heart's content without striking a blow, because they have forgotten the gods and are unjust to their fellow-men. In every way their hearts and minds are lower than in days gone by.[1]

There may be much truth in this, but there is also much anti-Persian propaganda, and when Xenophon turns to the Persian army and says that its cavalry was no better than butlers, flunkeys and cooks, who possessed no fighting value, his strictures, judged in the context of Alexander's battles, are palpably absurd. His criticism that it was a great mistake to abandon the short spear with which Cyrus armed his horsemen for the javelin is just, as also is his castigation of reliance on quantity instead of on quality, on hordes of untrained levies and attempts to make good their lack of national spirit by the hire of foreign mercenaries. Plato says much the same thing: 'in theory', he writes, 'their forces are reckoned by countless thousands, but all these thousand are worthless for service. Hence they hire mercenaries and aliens, as though they had no troops of their own, and look to them for their salvation.' [2]

The army of Darius III was nothing like the size attributed to it

[1] *Cyropaedia*, VIII, 8, 4–7.   [2] *The Laws*, III, 697–8.

by Arrian and other historians, for there can be no doubt that the enormous numbers quoted by them are either propaganda figures, or what is as probable they represent paper establishments – that is, the number of men of fighting age who could be called up for war, and not the numbers mustered. The royal army, it would appear, consisted, as in the past, of the king's body-guards – possibly 4,000 strong – some 20,000 Greek mercenaries, and an indefinite number of cavalry, which Tarn calculates to have been at a maximum 50,000 horsemen, of which Darius never succeeded in marshalling anything like that figure.[1] The 10,000 Immortals would seem to have disappeared.

Therefore, in 336 B.C., circumstances favoured the would-be invader of Persia although there was a great distance to be traversed before the vitals of the empire could be reached; the command of the sea was in Persian hands, and by means of his hoarded wealth the Persian king could, as had become customary, rely on corrupting his enemy by bribery. The Persian king was a weakling, his satraps unreliable, his native levies of low fighting value, and though his empire was still highly organized and well-roaded, these assets favoured a bold and judicious enemy.

[1] *Hellenistic Military and Naval Developments*, pp. 153–5.

5

STRATEGICAL NARRATIVE

❦

Securing the Home Base

When Philip was assassinated Alexander was barely twenty years of age and as yet so inexperienced and untried that it seemed to all Greece that the Macedonian empire was about to dissolve. Nor was his succession unchallenged, for many Macedonian nobles favoured the claims of Amyntas, son of Philip's brother Perdiccas while others championed the princes of the Lyncestian line.[1] Fortunately for Alexander, his two leading generals, Antipater and Parmenion, remained loyal; Antipater was in Macedonia, and Parmenion with Attalus in Asia; he was Attalus' father-in-law and his defection might have done irretrievable harm.

In Athens the news of the assassination was received with an outburst of joy; a vote of thanks was passed to Philip's assassin, and a letter was addressed to Attalus urging him not to recognize Alexander. Demosthenes was the soul of the revolt; he appeared in the Assembly garlanded as if for a festival, assured the Athenians that Alexander was a braggart of no consequence, persuaded the people by decree to depose him from his position of Captain-General of the League and to prepare for war, and again entered into relations with the king of Persia. This set Greece ablaze: Aetolia recalled her exiles, whom Philip had banished; Ambracia expelled her Macedonian garrison; Thebes, Argos, Elis and Arcadia prepared to break away, and in Thessaly the anti-Macedonian party gained the upper hand. The situation at home and abroad was so threatening that Alexander's counsellors urged him to abandon all the Greek states south of the northern limits of Thessaly and to placate the Illyrian, Paeonian, and Thracian tribes, who were

[1] Soon after 393 B.C., Argaeus, chief of the Lyncestian clan, for a brief spell usurped the throne of Amyntas II, Alexander's grandfather.

preparing to throw off the yoke imposed upon them by Philip and invade Macedonia.

Genius is a baffling word. It is neither high talent,[1] nor outstanding intelligence, nor is it the product of learning, or of discipline or training. It is, so it would seem, a creative gift, intuitive and spontaneous in its manifestations, that endows its possessor with a god-like power to achieve ends which reason can seldom fathom. It is neither capable of analysis nor explicable, it is solely demonstrative, and from the very opening of Alexander's reign we are brought face to face with genius in its highest flights. Confronted with a situation which made the boldest tremble, he swept aside advice, fears and trepidations, and before any of the conspirators could act, not only did he have their leaders put to death,[2] but he was on his way, not to secure his frontiers, not to punish the rebels, but to proclaim to all Greece that he was her master.

Should there be an ingredient which affirms his genius, it is the startling rapidity with which he always acted: no situation caused him to pause; all difficulties were immediately stormed; though risks were immense, to him success seemed foreordained. Time was his constant ally; he capitalized every moment, never pondered on it, and thereby achieved his end before others had settled on their means.[3]

Without waiting to reorganize his kingdom or to assure himself of the allegiance of the tribes bordering it, Alexander swept like a whirlwind southward along the coast into Thessaly at the head of his army. At Tempe, the Thessalians bade him halt outside the pass while they deliberated whether to admit him. To avoid battle and yet circumvent the pass, he ordered his men to cut steps in the sea-face of Mount Ossa and appeared on the farther side of the pass before the Thessalians guessed what he was up to. This was sufficient to make up their minds, for when they found themselves at his mercy they elected him in his father's place as head of their federation and placed at his disposal a strong force of cavalry.

---

[1] 'Talent is that which is in a man's power; genius is that in whose power a man is' – James Russell Lowell, *Among my Books,* 1st Series, p. 356.

[2] Amyntas and Attalus and all the male relatives of Attalus, except Parmenion, were put to death; also two of the Lyncestian princes, but the life of their only surviving brother was spared for the time being. On her own initiative, it would seem, Olympias had Philip's second wife, Cleopatra, and her infant daughter murdered.

[3] Napoleon also possessed this quality—'In the art of war, as in mechanics, time is the grand element between weight and force.' So did Francis Drake – 'The advantage of time and place in all martial actions is half of victory, which being lost is irrecoverable.' So did Charles XII of Sweden, and so did Joan of Arc in an occult way.

From Tempe he swept on to Thermopylae, the gateway of central Greece, where the Amphictyonic Council, then in session, promptly recognized him hegemon of the League. He pushed on, entered Boeotia and encamped before Thebes. He was then forty miles from Athens. Promptly the Athenians, who were not prepared to stand a siege, reversed their attitude toward him and dispatched an embassy, including Demosthenes, to plead for mercy. Alexander, who needed the cooperation of the Athenians, was pleased to pardon them and did so in so generous a way that they overwhelmed him with honours even more numerous than those they had conferred upon his father. All semblance of resistance then collapsed, and at an assembly of representatives of the League he was acclaimed hegemon for life and entrusted with his father's office of Captain-General in the war of revenge against Persia. All this was accomplished without a sword being drawn. Speed had been his weapon and it paralysed his enemies.

On his way back to Macedonia he visited Delphi to consult Apollo concerning his expedition against Asia and, according to Plutarch, when the priestess refused to perform her office because the day was not one lawful to prophesy, he impetuously dragged her toward the tripod, 'whereupon, as if overcome by his ardour, she said: "Thou art invincible, my son!" On hearing this, Alexander said he desired no further prophecy, but had from her the oracle which he wanted.' [1]

Once he had mastered Greece, Alexander's next task was to secure his home base before he left for Persia. Thebes and Athens had surrendered under compulsion, and Sparta was hostile and not a member of the League. In order to maintain his authority and that of the League during his absence, he decided to leave Antipater in Greece with a force sufficient to contain Sparta and to quash a rebellion. That before his departure he did not subdue Sparta, which he could have done, was dictated by his commission, which was to wage war on Persia, and though strategically it would have been advantageous for him to have rid himself of Sparta before he left Greece, if he had done so he would have turned his hegemony into a despotism. Throughout his life Alexander consistently subordinated strategy to policy, which is the essence of grand strategy.

So that Antipater might be free to deal with Sparta as well as a rebellion, it was incumbent to relieve him of the task of garrisoning in strength the northern frontier, so before setting out against Persia Alexander decided to bring to heel the turbulent tribes between Macedonia

[1] 'Alexander', XIV. For the genuineness of this story, see Tarn's *Alexander the Great*, vol. II, appx. 21.

and the Danube and then make that natural line of defence his northern frontier. Also, had not the Danube been crossed by the Persians, and was not he as bold a general as Darius I? The campaign was to be not merely of subjugation, but also of prestige; a campaign that would make his name resound throughout Greece. It was to be the prologue of his grand drama, in which he was to play the part of a Macedonian Cyrus.

In the spring of 335 B.C. Alexander ordered a squadron of warships to sail from Byzantium up the Danube to some unspecified spot at which he would meet it with the army. Then he set out from Amphipolis, crossed the river Nestus (Mesta) and the Rhodope mountains, and arrived at Mount Haemus (the Balkans) where, probably at the Shipka pass, he was opposed by a tribe of Thracian mountaineers.[1] He cleared the pass by a skilful enveloping movement; crossed the Balkans; advanced into the land of the Triballians, and arrived at the river Lyginus, a tributary of the Danube. Syrmus, king of the Triballians, forewarned of his approach, ordered the bulk of his army to hold him back while he withdrew with the women and children to an island in the Danube called Peuce. When Alexander came up, by a skilful manœuvre he forced the Triballians to battle and killed some 3,000 of them, and then advanced to the Danube where he was joined by his ships. He intended to occupy Peuce and embarked a body of archers and hoplites, but when he reached the island he found the current of the river so swift and the banks of the island so precipitous that he was compelled to forgo a landing.

In the meantime the Getae, a Thracian tribe that inhabited the region north of the Danube, had collected in force to bar his way. This was a challenge Alexander could not resist, and as Darius had crossed the river so would he.[2] He collected such boats as he could find, made rafts of tent-covers stuffed with straw, and secretly, under cover of night, ferried over to the northern bank, at 'a spot where the corn stood high',[3] 1,500 cavalry and 4,000 infantry. Then, hidden by the crops, he surprised the Getae horde and scattered it. Though tactically, this operation was a small affair, morally its consequences were startling. That he should have been able to cross 'the largest of rivers' in a single night without first bridging it, as Darius had done, so amazed the tribesmen that from as far away as the Ionian Gulf (Adriatic), they, as

[1] For this operation, see Chapter 8.

[2] Compare Julius Caesar's operations on the Rhine and his reason for crossing it in 55 B.C. (*The Gallic War*, IV, 16).

[3] Arrian, I, iv, 1.

well as the Triballians, looked upon him as invincible and dispatched envoys to him to tend their submission.

No sooner was this campaign at an end than Alexander learnt that Cleitus and Glaucias, two Illyrian chiefs, had entered into alliance and that Cleitus had seized Pelion, an important western Macedonian border fortress on the river Apsus (Devol). He set out at top speed to retake it before Glaucias could support Cleitus.[1] Unable to carry the fortress by assault, he decided to lay siege to it; but no sooner had he opened his works than Glaucias, at the head of a large army, came up on his rear, occupied the hills to the east of Pelion, and blocked Alexander's line of retreat. It would seem that Alexander's over-eagerness to retake Pelion made him commit an error of judgment, for he found himself placed in a critical position between two hostile forces. He re-opened his communications by a brilliant ruse and manœuvre and three days later, when he learnt that Glaucias had linked up with Cleitus and that their two armies were encamped outside Pelion, he made a night advance on them and surprised them when many were still asleep. He regained Pelion, and his victory was so decisive that only one outbreak on the northern and western borders of Macedonia is recorded during the remainder of his reign.

When Alexander was engaged in Thrace and Illyria, Darius III, who was fully aware of the danger which threatened Persia from the west, seized the opportunity offered by Alexander's absence from Greece to send envoys to the Greek states with large sums of gold to bribe them to revolt. Only Sparta – not a member of the League – accepted a subsidy; but there can be little doubt that many of the leaders of the anti-Macedonian party in the cities had their palms well greased, for though Athens refused the Persian gold, Demosthenes personally accepted 300 talents and with them bought arms for the Thebans, many of whose exiles were then congregated in Athens. Next, a rumour was circulated that Alexander had fallen in battle in Illyria, and if it was not Demosthenes who invented this canard, in order to promote revolt he exploited it to the full and in evidence produced a soldier, said to have been wounded in the same battle, who declared that he had seen Alexander fall.[2]

Soon belief in the rumour became widespread and under cover of the excitement it aroused the Theban exiles were secretly smuggled into

[1] For this operation, see Chapter 8.
[2] Demades, a contemporary Athenian politician, says he 'all but showed the corpse of Alexander there on the bema before our eyes' (cited by Benjamin Ide Wheeler in his *Alexander the Great*, 1925 edit., p. 166).

Thebes where they successfully urged the inhabitants to revolt. After two of Alexander's officials had been killed the freedom of the city was proclaimed and siege was laid to the Macedonian garrison that held the Cadmea. The news spread, Aetolia, Arcadia, and Elis prepared to support the rebels, and the Athenians, spurred on by Demosthenes, made ready for war.

At this juncture it is as well to emphasize the need to bear in mind that the rising of the Thebans was not a revolt against Alexander, but against the League, of which Thebes was a member. Had Alexander been dead, it might have been justifiable, because the hegemony would have lapsed; but as he was alive it was treason, and it presented him, as hegemon, with the god-sent opportunity to quash the rebellion on the part of the League and at the same time to escape the onus of his actions. Thus it came about – though at the time he may not have realized it – that the impetuous acceptance and exploitation by Demosthenes of his rumoured death placed him in a position once and for all to impose his will on Greece, not as king of Macedonia, but as hegemon of the League.

When the news of the revolt reached Alexander, he had only just occupied Pelion; he was some 300 miles from Thebes and his troops badly needed rest. But as he feared that Athens, Aetolia, and Sparta would unite with Thebes against him, his problem again was time: would he be able to reach Thebes before this could happen? In order to make time the master, he brushed all difficulties aside and set out by forced marches through the roadless mountains of western Macedonia. On the thirteenth day after he had left Pelion he entered Boeotia, where he was joined by contingents of Phocians, Plataeans and Boeotians, all members of the League. His advance was so rapid that the Thebans did not know that he had passed Thermopylae until he reached Onchestus, a city seven miles north-west of Thebes. Even then they continued to delude themselves that he was dead and that the approaching army was that of Antipater from Macedonia. Next day their doubts were dispelled – Alexander was before Thebes.

He first called on the Thebans to submit and honour their oath to the League, because his desire was that all Greek cities should be his allies and not his enemies. When no response was made, on the following day he moved his camp to the Electra gate so that he might command the road to Athens and be nearer to the Cadmea. He still refrained from attack in the hope that the Thebans would negotiate. But instead they sent him an insulting reply and launched an attack on his advanced guard and drove it back.[1] Then Alexander brought forward the phalanx, drove the Theban forces which were outside the walls back on the Electra gate, and entered Thebes on the heels of the rout before the gate could be closed. The garrison of the Cadmea then joined the fray and a massacre followed in which 6,000 Thebans are said to have perished.

Once Thebes was in his hands, in his capacity of hegemon Alexander called an extraordinary meeting of the *Synhedrion*, because the punishment of Thebes was its task and not his. As only the neighbouring allies, the Plataeans, Phocians, and Boeotians, can have had time to send deputies, and as they all detested the Thebans, their decision was that Thebes should be razed to the ground and its inhabitants sold into slavery.[2] There is little doubt that Alexander could have modified the severity of this decision, which by some has been held to have been one of his major military crimes. Also it is recorded that at a later date he regretted the destruction of Thebes. But at the time, if he was to be assured of a stable home base from which to operate once he crossed into Asia, it was strategically imperative for him to teach the Greeks a lesson they would not readily forget. Further, the destruction of Thebes meant that the only refractory states of importance left in Greece would be Athens and Sparta, and as they were separated from each other by the isthmus of Corinth, not only was it difficult for them to combine, but a comparatively small Macedonian army stationed in the vicinity of the isthmus could make it impossible.

The fall of Thebes struck Greece like a thunderbolt and consternation swept far and wide. The Arcadians slaughtered their anti-Macedonian leaders; the Eleans received back from exile their pro-Macedonian exiles; the Aetolians craved pardon, and most contemptible of all the Athenians dispatched to Alexander an embassy to congratulate him on his safe return from Illyria. At first he demanded the surrender of Demosthenes and eight others, mostly orators,[3] which caused Demosthenes to bribe Demades, a pro-Macedonian, with five talents to entreat Alexander to be merciful. After some hesitation he granted the request because he did not want to drive the Athenians to despair and was eager to set out for Persia. Besides, Demosthenes was now discredited; Demades and Phocion were in power in Athens, and above

[1] This is Arrian's version; that of Diodorus is that, on receiving the reply, he then and there assaulted Thebes.
[2] The Thebans in 373 B.C. had punished Plataea in the same way. Thirty thousand Thebans were sold into slavery and their sale realized 440 talents. Thebes was refounded by Cassander in 316 B.C.
[3] According to Plutarch ('Demosthenes', XXIII) Callisthenes was among them.

all it was incumbent on Alexander to neutralize the Athenian fleet and so prevent it going over to Persia.

He marched to the isthmus of Corinth, presided over a meeting of the *Synhedrion*, arranged what contingents should be provided by its members, revisited Delphi, and before the winter of 335 B.C. had set in he was back in Macedonia.

Establishing the Overseas Base

While Alexander warred in Greece, Parmenion advanced southward down the Asiatic coast, and though part of his army suffered defeat at the hands of Memnon, who commanded the Greek mercenaries in the Persian service, he held fast to his all-important bridgehead at Abydus (Chanak). Alexander, on his return to Macedonia, recalled Parmenion to help him and Antipater to marshal the expeditionary force.

It was decided that Antipater should remain in Greece as regent of Macedonia and deputy hegemon of the League with 9,000 foot and a body of horse to garrison the home base, and that the army of invasion, with Parmenion as Alexander's second in command, should consist of 30,000 infantry and 5,000 cavalry[1] – these are round numbers. Of the infantry, 12,000 were Macedonians, made up of six battalions of the phalanx (9,000 men) under Craterus, Perdiccas, Coenus, Amyntas, Meleager, and Philip, son of Amyntas, and three battalions of hypaspists (3,000 men), under Nicanor, son of Parmenion; 7,000, under Antigonus, were allied Greek hoplites and peltasts raised by the League; 5,000, under Menander, were mercenaries, and 6,000 Agrianian javelin-men (Attalus), Thracian peltasts (Sitalces), and Cretan archers (Clearchus). Of the cavalry, 2,000 were Companions under Philotas, another son of Parmenion; 2,000 Thessalians under Calas, and 1,000 Thracian (Agathon), Paeonian (Aristo), Lancers (Amyntas the Lyncestian), and Greek allied horse (Philip, son of Menelaus). That the League's contingent was not larger was probably due to Alexander's distrust in his Greek allies; in any case he is unlikely to have wanted to encumber his army with second-rate troops. Why he did not raise a stronger force of mercenaries may have been because he lacked money to pay them; he tells us that when he set out 'he had not even sixty talents in the treasury', and was 1,300 talents in debt.[2] There must

[1] Arrian (I, xi, 3) says: 'over 30,000 infantry together with light-armed troops, and more than 5,000 cavalry'.
[2] Arrian, VII, ix, 6. Plutarch ('Alexander', XV) says 70 talents and only thirty days' supplies.

have been also a considerable number of artillerists, engineers, transport drivers, pack-horse leaders, servants, camp followers, and women; all told, the number under Alexander's command probably exceeded 40,000.[1]

It would appear that Parmenion's reverse in Asia made Darius assume that the likelihood of an invasion had been removed; or it may be he still believed that were invasion attempted, gold and Sparta would be sufficient to ruin it. Memnon, who was an experienced soldier, had under his command some 20,000 Greek mercenaries in Asia Minor, many of whom were serving in the Persian fleet of some 400 warships; it was vastly superior to the fleet of the League, which numbered 160.

That the Persian fleet was not mobilized to hold the Dardanelles may have been due to the narrowness of its waters, which in battle discounted its numerical superiority. But what would appear more probable is that from the first Memnon's plan was not to oppose a landing, but to let Alexander cross the Dardanelles and when he advanced inland, to waste the country and burn the villages and towns and thus deprive his army of provisions, fodder, and shelter. Then, while Alexander's army starved, he would use the fleet to transport a striking force to Greece and make Greece the seat of war.[2] It was this plan that he urged the Persian generals to adopt shortly before the battle of the Granicus, and there is no reason to suppose that it was a sudden inspiration. But Spithridates and Arsites, the satraps of Lydia and Hellespontine-Phrygia, would not listen to it; Arsites asserted that he would not allow a single house in his satrapy to be burnt, and the generals agreed with him.

Before Alexander's first campaign against Persia is considered, it is imperative to bear in mind the aim of the war. It was to avenge the wrongs done to all Hellas by Xerxes. The war was, then, to be ideological, a conflict between right and wrong and, as Vattel pointed out in the eighteenth century, when two nations are equally convinced that they are fighting for their rights, there can be no peace between them until one of them is completely crushed.[3] But it is highly improbable that when Alexander set out his idea was to subdue the entire Persian empire. At first his idea may have been what Isocrates envisaged, to

---

[1] According to Droysen (*Alexander le Grand*, pp. 132–3), under a ruling issued by Philip each cavalryman was allowed a mounted squire, and each ten phalangites a baggage carrier, which Droysen assumes also applied to the allied contingents and mercenaries. Whether this ruling was adhered to by Alexander is not known; but if it did, then the non-combatants must have numbered at least 10,000.

[2] See Arrian, I, xii, 9, and Diodorus, XVII, 30, 1.

[3] See his *The Law of Nations*, trans. Joseph Chitty (1834), pp. 381–3.

conquer Asia Minor up to the river Halys, but because from the start
his policy was psychological – not merely to avenge Greece on Persia,
but to attack Persia internally by winning the Persians to him by con-
siderate treatment – it drew him on from one situation to the next,
until eventually the farthest limits of his enemy's empire were reached.
At bottom it was to be a war between two cultures and civilizations,
and therefore a war of expansion for the more virile.

A battle of Alexander: detail from a floor mosaic, found in the House of the
Faun in Pompeii, now in the National Museum, Naples. *The Bettman Archive*

When preparations for the invasion were completed, early in the
spring of 334 B.C. Alexander entrusted the safekeeping of Macedonia
and Greece to Antipater and led his army by way of Amphipolis to
Sestus (Kilid Bahr) on the Dardanelles, where Xerxes had crossed 146
years earlier. He left Parmenion there to supervise the crossing to
Abydus while he steered his own ship down the Dardanelles to Ilium
to lay a garland on the tomb of his ancestor Achilles and borrow his
shield. Arrian says of this visit that Alexander is reported to have pronounced Achilles fortunate in having Homer 'as the herald of his fame
to posterity', and adds that this was the reason which induced him to
write his history of Alexander, since Alexander had not been as fortunate as Achilles in his historians.

When he had concluded his pious mission, Alexander proceeded to

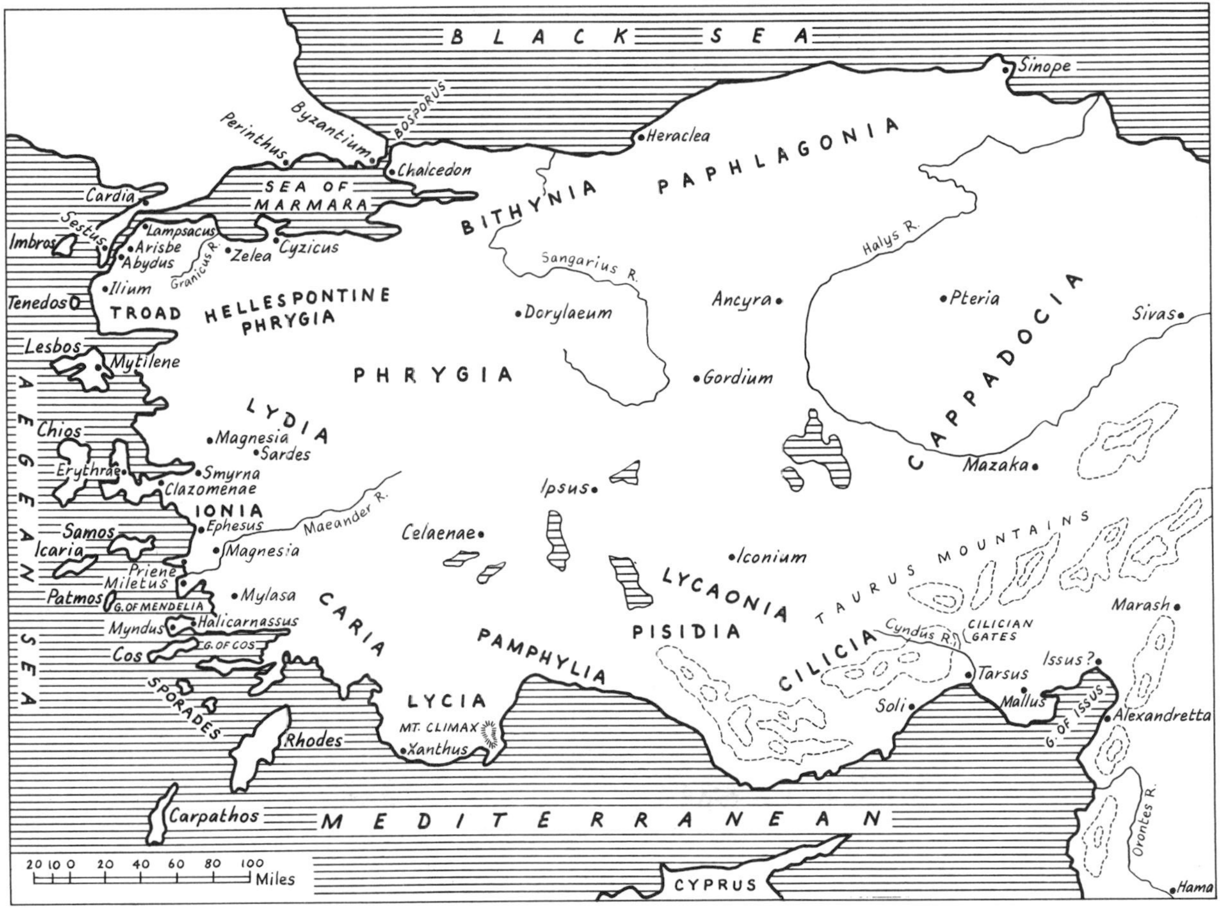

2 WESTERN ASIA MINOR

Arisbe, a town near Abydus, where he found Parmenion and the army encamped.

On the following day he set out northward along the coast to Lampsacus (Lamsaki) to meet the satraps who had hastily collected their forces to oppose him. From Lampsacus the army turned eastward, and at Hermotus a cavalry reconnaissance discovered the Persians in position on the right bank of the river Granicus (Bigha), a few miles upstream from its mouth in the Sea of Marmara. There Alexander won his first great victory;[1] it made him master of Asia Minor, which remained Greek until the Turkish invasions of the eleventh century.

Immediately after the battle he visited and cheered up his wounded; buried his own and the Persian dead; granted exemption of taxes to the relatives of the killed and, to propitiate his Macedonians, ordered Lysippus to make statues of the twenty-five Companions who had fallen and have them set up in the temple of Zeus in Dium. Then he did three things which are illuminating.

The first was that he sent to Athens 300 suits of Persian armour as a votive offering to be hung in the Acropolis with the following inscription fixed over them: 'Alexander, son of Philip, and all the Greeks, except the Lacedaemonians, present this offering from the spoils taken from the foreigners inhabiting Asia.'[2] It will be noticed that he does not describe himself as king, or mention his Macedonians, but implies that he is Captain-General of the League and therefore the League's servant.

The second action is equally remarkable. He sent back the captured Greek mercenaries in fetters to Macedonia to till the soil, 'because, though they were Greeks, they were fighting against Greece on behalf of the foreigners in opposition to the decrees the Greeks had made in their federal council'.[3] He did not treat them with ignominy because they had fought against him, but because they had fought against the League.

The third action is more remarkable still. It heralded his policy to win the war through conciliation. In the place of Arsites, who had fled the field, he selected Calas, a Macedonian general, to govern Hellespontine-Phrygia. He did not give him a Macedonian title, but the old Persian title of 'satrap', and he ordered him to collect the same tribute the inhabitants had paid to Darius. This gives the first inkling of Alexander's pro-Persian policy. Further, in order to pacify the conquered territory before he moved on, he ordered those who had fled to the mountains to return to their homes, and he acquitted the people of Zelea of blame, 'because he knew that they had been compelled to

---

[1] See Chapter 6.   [2] Arrian, I, xvi, 7.   [3] Ibid., I, xvi, 6.

assist the Persians in the war' [1] – a remarkable act of moderation for a conqueror of any age.

Although the battle of the Granicus had opened western Asia Minor to Alexander, it was no more than an advanced guard victory. The Persian main army had still to be reckoned with; Memnon, who had survived the battle, had withdrawn the remnants of his defeated mercenaries southward; and the Persian fleet remained intact. Alexander had to secure his overseas base and its sea communications, and to do so he had not only to occupy the western shore of Asia Minor but, as he advanced, he had to leave in his rear a peaceful and friendly country that would not require a large garrison; if he did not do so he would be unable to concentrate the maximum force against his enemy.

Alexander was an absolute monarch and in no way predisposed to favour democracy, but he was fully aware that the Persian king ruled the Greek cities in Asia Minor by means of friendly oligarchies and tyrants, and that they were abhorrent to the majority of their citizens, who were democrats. As these citizens were the enemies of Persia, he decided to make them his friends by offering to the Greek cities not only freedom from Persia, but also self-determination – that is, he would leave to their citizens the choice of government they preferred. In brief, he decided to enter into alliance with every anti-Persian faction he contacted, irrespective of their political outlook, and with their aid create an inner front which, as he advanced, would progressively destroy the Persian imperium and leave a friendly country in his rear. Besides this, by winning over city by city, particularly the coastal cities, he would deprive the Persian fleet of its bases and thereby restrict its operations against his sea communications. From this time, freedom and self-determination were to become the pillars of his policy and his strategy was developed in accordance.

From the Granicus he marched to Sardes, the capital of Lydia, and as Mithrines, the Persian garrison commander, surrendered the city without a fight, he treated him with honour and 'granted the Sardians and the other Lydians the privileges of enjoying the ancient laws of Lydia and permitted them to be free'.[2] At Sardes he reorganized the Persian satrapal system which he had adopted. Under this system the satraps combined all civil, military, and financial powers, which made them so powerful that they frequently rebelled. Alexander decided to deprive his satraps, who in Asia Minor were Macedonian generals, of their control over finance, as well as to keep the coining of money in his own hands. Once Sardes had been occupied, he appointed Asander

---

[1] Arrian, I, xvii, 2.   [2] Ibid., I, xvii, 4.

satrap of Lydia with Pausanias as garrison commander of Sardes; but he placed the collection of tribute and taxes under Nicias.

From Sardes he went to Ephesus. There he recalled from exile all men who had been banished from the city, broke up the oligarchy and established a democratic government. But to Alexander freedom did not include licence, and when the democrats began to slaughter their private enemies as well as the oligarchs and their adherents, he put a stop to mob rule. Through this, according to Arrian, he gained 'great popularity'. He then sent Parmenion with 2,500 infantry and 200 cavalry to liberate the Greek cities in Carian Magnesia, and Alcimachus with an equal force to the Aeolic cities, with orders 'to break up the oligarchies everywhere, to set up the democratic form of government, and to remit the tribute which they were accustomed to pay to the foreigners (Persians)'.[1] After this, he sacrificed to Artemis, and with the remainder of his army set out for Miletus.

There he was opposed by Hegesistratus, in command of the Persian garrison, who at first offered to surrender but took courage and changed his mind on the approach of the Persian fleet. Unfortunately for him, Alexander had anticipated this and had ordered the fleet, under Nicanor, to occupy the mouth of the harbour of Miletus. Nicanor did so three days before the Persian fleet could come up. Parmenion, who had now rejoined Alexander, advised him to fight a sea battle, but Alexander rejected the proposal, not only because of the vast superiority of the Persian fleet, but also because if the battle were lost, loss of prestige might detonate a revolution in Greece. He decided to take the city by storm; brought up his siege engines, battered down parts of the walls and captured the city. Yet in spite of the opposition he had met with he pardoned the citizens for their resistance and granted them their freedom. After this, he cut off the Persian fleet from its water supply in the mouth of the Maeander – some ten miles from Miletus – and compelled it to abandon its operations. The islands of Mytilene, Tenedos, and Chios became members of the League of Corinth, but, according to Tarn, none of the Greek cities on the mainland did so.[2]

Winning Command of the Sea

With the capture of Miletus, the last predominantly Greek city on the western shore of the Aegean, from which a subsidiary line of communications could be opened with Greece by way of the islands of Samos, Icaria, Myconos, Tenos, and Andros, Alexander completed the

---

[1] Ibid., I, xviii, 2.   [2] *Alexander the Great*, vol. i, p. 31.

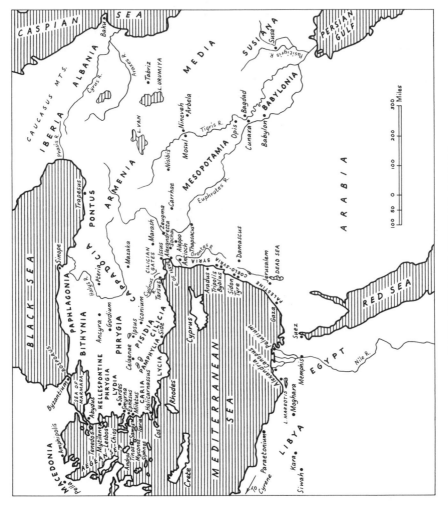

3 THE WESTERN PERSIAN EMPIRE

establishment of his overseas base. His next problem was how best to advance eastward from it.

On land he was in no immediate danger, for Darius was still far away; but at sea he was threatened by the Persian fleet. How should he deal with it? Since he could not hope to defeat it in battle, he decided to throttle it by advancing along the southern coast of Asia Minor and deprive it of its bases. As this strategy did not entail the direct use of his fleet, he decided to disband it except for a few vessels to carry his siege train, among which, Diodorus informs us, were the twenty triremes provided by the Athenians[1] – obviously retained as hostages for the good behaviour of their donors. Further reasons for adopting this course were that during the winter Persian naval operations would be restricted, and that for lack of money he could not afford to maintain his fleet in idleness until the spring; besides, its disbandment would release some 30,000 men.

In spite of these reasons, to abandon the sea to Memnon was to accept a considerable risk, although this was mitigated in part because the establishment of democracies in the Greek cities had already badly shaken the Greek contingents of the Persian fleet, for they were largely composed of exiles and poor democrats. Also, the brutal treatment meted out to the Cyprians and Phoenicians by Artaxerxes III had not been forgotten, with the result that, except for the Tyrian squadron, those provided by the Cyprians and Sidonians were disaffected.[2]

From Miletus Alexander advanced on Halicarnassus (Bodrum), the capital of Caria, a city more Carian than Greek and to which, since the battle of the Granicus, Memnon had withdrawn. There Alexander was so strongly opposed that he was forced to lay siege to the city, which soon after he carried by assault, except for its two citadels of Arconnesus and Salmacis.[3] He ordered that the Halicarnassians who remained in their homes were not to be molested and then he arranged for the government of Caria.

The step he took to effect this shows how far he was from following any rule of thumb in the administration of his satrapies. Thus far he had appointed Macedonians in the place of the ousted Persian satraps; but this time he appointed a Carian woman. When he entered Caria he had been met by Ada, sister of the former satrap Mausolus, whom she had succeeded[4] before she had been dispossessed of her authority by her

---

[1] Diodorus, xvii, 22, 5.   [2] See *The Cambridge Ancient History*, vol. VI, p. 22.
[3] For the siege of Halicarnassus, see Chapter 7.
[4] It would appear that matriarchy, which had been prevalent in the pre-Greek Mediterranean, still survived in Caria.

brother. Because she had welcomed Alexander, surrendered the fortress of Alinda to him and had adopted him as her son; and because Alexander's policy was always to present himself as the liberator of subjected peoples, he reinstated her and made her satrap. In the eyes of the Carians he became the son of their ruler. But he introduced a modification that was to become a guiding principle whenever he appointed an Oriental to a satrapy: though he conferred on Ada the civil functions of government, he separated from them the military command, which he gave to a Macedonian officer.

He then sent back on leave to Greece, under Ptolemy, son of Seleucus, those of his Macedonian soldiers who had married soon before the campaign opened, and ordered him to return with them by the end of the winter with fresh reinforcements of horse and foot. 'By this act more than any other,' writes Arrian, 'Alexander acquired popularity among the Macedonians.' [1] Alexander left Parmenion with 3,000 Greek infantry and 200 horse to reduce the two citadels of Arconnesus and Salmacis and marched into Lycia to gain command of the coastland, 'and by that means render the enemy's fleet useless'. [2]

At Side, in Pamphylia, he appointed Nearchus satrap of Lycia and Pamphylia; then struck northward, subdued Pisidia, and advanced into Phrygia. At Celaenae (Dinar), which capitulated to him, he appointed Antigonus satrap of Phrygia and allotted to him 1,500 mercenaries to garrison the city, and then directed his march on Gordium (Bela-Hissar), the capital of the old Phrygian kings. There Ptolemy rejoined him with the newly-married men and 3,000 Macedonian foot and 650 horse he had brought as reinforcements. While at Gordium an appeal was received from Athens praying Alexander to release the Athenian prisoners captured at the Granicus. He refused because, as Arrian writes, he 'did not think it safe, while the war against Persia was still going on, to relax in the slightest degree the terror with which he inspired the Greeks'. [3]

When Alexander was in Phrygia Memnon bestirred himself and, according to Arrian, decided to prosecute his original plan of campaign to carry war into Greece by means of his fleet; but what would appear more probable is that his plan was to strike at Abydus, cut Alexander's communications; force him to weaken his army in order to retake Abydus, and then slip away. The operations which followed bear this out. First, Memnon gained possession of Chios through treachery and then he occupied all Lesbos, except Mytilene, which he blockaded. But

---

[1] Arrian, I, xxiv, 1.   [2] Ibid., I, xxiv, 3.
[3] Ibid., I, xxix, 6. Later, on his return to Syria from Egypt, he released them.

he suddenly fell sick and died and the chief command devolved on his nephew Pharnabazus, to whom the Mytilenians capitulated on the understanding that they should become allies of Darius in accordance with the terms of the Peace of Antalcidas. Pharnabazus immediately violated these terms and set up a despotism. After this, he occupied Tenedos at the mouth of the Dardanelles – thirty miles from Abydus.

When the news of Memnon's counter-attack reached Alexander it appeared so threatening that he ordered Hegelochus to reform the fleet while Antipater collected all the ships he could and destroyed a small Persian squadron off Siphnos. The alarm was short-lived because after the death of Memnon Darius decided to recall his mercenaries and transfer the war from sea to land. He ordered Pharnabazus to send the mercenaries, less 1,500 men, by sea to Tripolis in Phoenicia and in order to meet Alexander, should he continue his advance eastward, he assembled an army at Babylon and there spent over a year in recruiting it. In the autumn of 333 B.C. he advanced with it to a place named Sochoi (site unidentified), which lay west of Aleppo and east of the Amanus mountains, to await Alexander's arrival.

From Gordium Alexander advanced on Ancyra (Ankara) and then through Cappadocia toward the Cilician Gates (Golek-Boghaz), the chief pass over the Taurus mountains into Cilicia. If properly held, it was impregnable; it was so narrow that pack animals had to be un-loaded before they could pass through it. It was held in strength by Arsames, satrap of Cilicia. Alexander left Parmenion, who had by now rejoined him, with the heavy troops in rear, and with the hypas-pists, Agrianians and archers set out at top speed to take the pass. In a day and a night he covered the sixty-two miles that separated the pass from his starting point, and though his march was not unobserved it would seem that its speed so completely upset Arsames' plans that he abandoned the Gates and hastily withdrew to Tarsus. But when Alexander pressed on, Arsames was forced to continue his retreat. At Tarsus, Alexander bathed in the cold water of the Cydnus river (Kara-sui) and was taken seriously ill. A halt had to be called.

The topography of the region Alexander was about to enter (see Map 7) is relevant to the understanding of subsequent events. The Amanus mountains (Giaour Dagh) stretched before his line of advance from Antioch, on the river Orontes, in a northerly direction to present-day Marash. About twenty miles north of Antioch and a little south of Alexandretta is a pass through the mountains, now traversed by the motor road to Aleppo, then known as the Syrian Gates (Beilan Pass); some fifteen miles north of it, where the mountains come down to the coast, is a narrow defile called the Pillar of Jonah, and twenty-seven miles to the north of it is another pass, the Amanid Gates (Bogtche Pass), through which the railway to Aleppo now runs. It would seem that the last of these three passes was either unknown to Alexander, or that he considered it of no importance, because, after he had recovered from his illness and while he was engaged in pacifying the country south of Tarsus, he sent Parmenion with a strong force of allied mercenary troops to occupy the Syrian Gates,[1] but left the Amanid Gates unguarded. Then, when his own operations were concluded,[2] and when he was at Mallus, on the western shore of the Gulf of Alexandretta, he learnt that Darius was encamped with his army at Sochoi, about a two-day march from the Syrian Gates. This news greatly excited the army, and Alexander, eager to meet Darius, set out for the Syrian Gates the following day. Two days later, after he had left his sick at Issus, at the head of the Gulf of Alexandretta, he encamped his army outside Myriandrus (near Alexandretta), the first town in Syria or Phoenicia.[3] His intention was to advance through the Syrian Gates on Sochoi, which must have lain some thirty miles east of the pass, and approximately half-way between it and Aleppo.

When Alexander was in Cilicia, Darius made ready to withstand him at Sochoi. He was supported by Amyntas, son of Antiochus, who some years before had fled from Pella and was now in command of his Greek mercenaries. He urged Darius not to move forward from the flat, open country around Sochoi because it was favourable for the deployment of a large army, whereas the mountainous region was not. But when Alexander, delayed by his illness and his operations in Cilicia, did not appear, Darius concluded that he did not intend to advance farther east: a reasonable assumption, because the Taurus range would make a nearly impregnable eastern frontier for the Macedonian empire. He set Amyntas' advice aside and decided to assume the offensive. First he sent his heavy baggage and field treasury to Damascus, over 200 miles to the south of Sochoi, an extraordinary spot to select as both Aleppo or Thapsacus lay on his communications and either would appear to have been more suitable. Then he set out for the Amanid Gates, where he learnt that far from being in Cilicia, Alexander was on his way southward from Issus. He turned in that direction to come up on his rear and at Issus found Alexander's field

---

[1] So Arrian says; but it would seem more probable that it was the Pillar of Jonah.

[2] During these operations Alexander learnt that at length the citadels of Halicarnassus had been captured.

[3] Again the march was rapid, because by road Mallus is at least sixty-seven miles from Alexandretta.

hospital and butchered its inmates; a stupid thing to do for they could do him no harm and their slaughter would antagonize his enemy. From Issus he moved on to the river Pinarus (Deli), and took up a defensive position on its right bank. This was an inexcusable blunder, for as he had caught his enemy in *flagrante delicto* he should have pressed on at top speed.

Alexander was so certain that Darius would remain at Sochoi that he made no attempt to keep him under observation, which he readily could have done, and when he learnt that he and his army were in his rear he would not believe the report. To verify it he embarked a party of Companions in a galley to reconnoitre the Gulf of Issus. They confirmed the report. Alexander assembled his generals, explained the situation and aroused their enthusiasm. On the following day, late in October or early in November, 333 B.C., he reversed his order of march and headed for the Pinarus. There can be little doubt that he had blundered badly – over-eagerness had led him into a trap.

Alexander fought his second great battle on the Pinarus – that of Issus.[1] The Persian army was disastrously defeated; Darius fled to Thapsacus and his camp with his mother, wife and children, and 3,000 talents was captured. Amyntas with some 8,000 of his mercenaries escaped through the mountains to Tripolis, from where, by way of Cyprus, they sailed to Egypt and soon after, in an attempt to conquer the country, Amyntas was killed.[2]

Second only in importance to Darius' defeat was the influence of Alexander's victory on Greece. There, although the Persian fleet controlled the Aegean, Hegelochus had recaptured Tenedos and had thrown the Athenians into an uproar by seizure of their grain ships coming from the Black Sea. Demosthenes was again broadcasting wishful reports, hints, and insinuations that Alexander and his army were doomed to destruction,[3] and when the battle of Issus was fought, while Agis, king of Sparta, conferred with Pharnabazus at Siphnos on a joint plan to liberate Greece, the news of Alexander's victory fell

---

[1] For the battle of Issus, see Chapter 6.

[2] After his death his mercenaries entered the service of Agis, king of Sparta, and fought at Megalopolis.

[3] 'But when Darius came on with all his forces, and Alexander, as you [Demosthenes] claimed, was locked up in Cilicia and in sore straits, and was going to be, as your phrase had it, "speedily trampled under foot by the Persian horse", then, with the city not big enough to hold your swagger, you pranced about with epistles dangling from your fingers, pointing people to my countenance as that of a miserable, despairing wretch, and called me a bull ready for the sacrifice, with gilded horns and garlands on the head, the moment anything happened to Alexander' (Aeschines, *Against Ctesiphon*, 164).

like a thunderbolt on them and all Greece. Pharnabazus sailed back to Chios to forestall a revolt, the Athenians abandoned their intrigues, and with their homelands directly threatened the Cyprian and Phoenician squadrons of the Persian fleet broke away and sailed homeward to defend them. Step by step, as he fought his way along the Asiatic coast, Alexander steadily won command of the Aegean.

After the battle, Alexander appointed Balacrus and Menon satraps respectively of Cilicia and Coelo-Syria and sent Parmenion on to Damascus to seize the Persian field treasury, which relieved him of further financial anxiety. At Damascus Parmenion found Spartan, Theban, and Athenian ambassadors awaiting the arrival of Darius to seek his aid. But with Issus to his credit, Alexander could afford to be lenient.   He kept the Spartan in custody, released the Theban, and the Athenian, Iphicrates, son of the noted Iphicrates, he kept in attendance on himself as long as he lived, 'both from friendship to the city of Athens and from recollections of his father's glory'.[1]

Though no general knew better than Alexander how to exploit a victory, after the battle of Issus he adhered to his aim – to win command of the sea – which could only be achieved finally by the occupation of the Phoenician coastal cities. He did not pursue Darius, but advanced southward along the Syrian coast. When on the march he was met by Straton, prince of the Aradians, who surrendered to him his island stronghold of Aradus (Arwad, Biblical Arvad) and the city of Marathus, which lay opposite to it on the mainland.

While at Marathus Alexander received an embassy with a letter from Darius in which he begged him to release his mother, wife and children, and in return offered him friendship and alliance. In his reply Alexander first set forth the wrongs done to Macedonia and the rest of Greece by Darius' ancestors, and wrote that to avenge them he had been appointed Captain-General of the Hellenes. Further, he accused Darius of instigating the murder of Philip; of unjustly seizing the Persian throne contrary to the laws of the Persians, and of urging the Greeks to wage war on Macedonia. 'I took the field against you', he wrote, 'and since I have vanquished your generals . . . I am, by gift of the gods, in possession of your land . . . Come to me then, and ask for your mother, wife and children, and anything else you wish. For whatever you ask for you will receive; and nothing shall be denied you. But for the future, whenever you send to me, send to me as the king of Asia, and do not address to me your wishes as to an equal . . . and if you dispute my right to the kingdom, stay and fight another battle for it;

[1] Arrian, II, xv, 4.

but do not run away. For wherever you may be, I intend to march against you.' [1]

This letter discloses what was then in Alexander's mind – a radical change of policy. After the battle of the Granicus he had emphasized his hegemony of the Hellenic League, after Issus he appears as claimant to the lordship over the entire Persian empire. Even before the battle of Issus, he had said in his harangue to his Companions: 'After the conflict nothing would be left for them to do, except to take possession of all Asia . . .' [2] After the battle he was in a better position to do so, although he must have known that as long as Darius was in the field his words were no more than a terrifying boast. His sole alternative was to follow the advice of Isocrates and limit the Macedonian conquests to Asia Minor; but this would have meant a defensive war and Alexander was not a defensively-minded general.

From Marathus he continued his march southward. Byblus (Gebal) and Sidon (Saida) capitulated to him and on his way he was met by an embassy from Tyre, sent to ascertain his demands.   He ordered it to return to Tyre and tell the Tyrians that he wished to enter their city and offer sacrifice in the temple of Heracles. [3] But they were afraid to admit him, and because they believed their island fortress to be impregnable – it had vainly been besieged by Nebuchadrezzar for thirteen years – they rejected his request. Yet its occupation meant the end of Persian naval power; Alexander had to take it and he decided to besiege it. [4]

His strategical outlook at this time is described in a remarkable speech he delivered to his generals. It is of such outstanding importance that it is quoted here in full:

Friends and allies [he said], I see that an expedition to Egypt will not be safe for us, so long as the Persians retain the sovereignty of the sea; nor is it a safe course, both for other reasons, and especially looking at the state of matters in Greece, for us to pursue Darius, leaving in our rear the city of Tyre itself in doubtful allegiance, and Egypt and Cyprus in the occupation of the Persians. I am apprehensive lest while we advance with our forces towards Babylon and in pursuit of Darius, the Persians should again forsooth conquer the maritime districts, and transfer the war into Greece with a larger army, considering that the Lacedaemonians are now waging

---

[1] Ibid., II, xiv, 4–9.   [2] Ibid., II, vii, 6.
[3] The Tyrian god Melkart (Syrian Baal) was identified by the Greeks with Heracles.   [4] For the siege of Tyre, see Chapter 7.

war against us without disguise, and the city of Athens is restrained for the present rather by fear than by any good-will towards us. But if Tyre were captured, the whole of Phoenicia would be in our possession, and the fleet of the Phoenicians, which is the most numerous and the best in the Persian navy, would in all probability come over to us. For the Phoenician sailors and marines will not dare to put to sea in order to incur danger on behalf of others, when their own cities are occupied by us. After this, Cyprus will either yield to us without delay, or will be captured with ease at the mere arrival of a naval force; and then navigating the sea with the ships from Macedonia in conjunction with those of the Phoenicians, Cyprus also having come over to us, we shall acquire the absolute sovereignty of the sea, and at the same time an expedition into Egypt will become an easy matter for us. After we have brought Egypt into subjection, no anxiety about Greece and our own land will any longer remain, and we shall be able to undertake the expedition to Babylon with safety in regard to affairs at home, and at the same time with greater reputation, in consequence of having appropriated to ourselves all the maritime provinces of the Persians and all the land on this side of the Euphrates.[1]

When this speech was made, unknown to Alexander the news of Darius' defeat at Issus had already disintegrated the Persian fleet. Soon after the siege opened, on their return from the Aegean all the Phoenician squadrons, except the Tyrian, accepted service under Alexander; the Cyprian squadron followed suit soon after. This placed at his disposal a fleet of 220 warships, a force considerably more powerful than that of king Azemilk of Tyre.

Yet another Persian embassy arrived during the siege to inform Alexander that Darius was willing to pay 10,000 talents (£2,440,000)[2] in ransom for his mother, wife and children, to give him one of his daughters in marriage, and to surrender to him all the land west of the Euphrates to the Aegean Sea.

When Alexander announced these proposals at a conference of his generals, Parmenion is said to have told Alexander that 'if he were Alexander he would be glad to put an end to the war on these terms'. Alexander replied: 'So would he also do, if he were Parmenion.' Then he replied to Darius 'that he was neither in want of money . . . nor

---

[1] Arrian, II, xvii. Tarn (*Alexander*, vol. II, pp. 286–7) accepts this speech as genuine, and is of opinion that, though it may have been a speech, it more probably 'reflects a manifesto issued by Alexander to the army on the eve of the siege'.

[2] At 1913 value.

would he receive a part of his territory instead of the whole; for that all his money and territory were his; and that if he wished to marry the daughter of Darius, he would marry her . . . He commanded Darius to come to him if he wished to experience any generous treatment from him.' [1]

Both Sir William Tarn and Ulrich Wilcken, in their respective histories of Alexander, point out that in all probability this story of the divergent views held by Alexander and Parmenion on Darius' offer indicates the first rift between Alexander and the old Macedonians who had served Philip. Wilcken's opinion is that had Philip advanced as far as Alexander had, he would certainly have accepted the offer of the Euphrates frontier; but that Alexander had transcended the comparatively limited outlook of a Macedonian king and already felt himself 'King of Asia'—a supranational monarch. [2] As this appeared to mean the submergence of Macedonia in an Asiatic empire, the idea was abhorrent to the older Macedonians, who looked upon Parmenion as their leader.

Either at the end of July or the beginning of August, 332 B.C., Tyre was stormed after a siege of seven months and 8,000 Tyrians were slaughtered in its sack. According to Arrian, the reasons for this massacre were the fury of the Macedonians at the length of the siege, and also because to mock the besiegers the Tyrians had slaughtered a shipload of captured Greeks on the tops of their walls and had cast their bodies into the sea. Only those who had taken refuge in the temple of Heracles were, on Alexander's express orders, given amnesty; the remainder of the inhabitants and mercenary soldiers were sold into slavery. [3]

The capture of Tyre gave Alexander Syria and Egypt, which were to be held by Greeks and Romans for nearly 1,000 years. More immediately important, with its occupation he achieved his aim—supremacy over the eastern Mediterranean. The Persian fleet had ceased to exist and all its naval bases were in his hands. He had little to fear for the security of his home base, and his strategy could be devoted solely to land operations.

---

[1] Arrian, II, xxv, 3.

[2] *Alexander the Great*, pp. 111–12.

[3] Professor Freeman (*Historical Essays, Second Series*, p. 198) points out that 'the mere slaughter of the prisoners, was no breach of the Greek laws of war . . . But the mockery and the denial of burial were direct sins against all Greek religious notions. We therefore cannot be surprised that the successful assault of the city was followed by a merciless slaughter.' Concerning the respect of the Macedonians for their dead, see Curtius, V, iii, 2.

Securing the South-Western Frontier

Because Alexander's uncompromising reply to Darius' second appeal meant that the war would continue, to have advanced against Darius immediately after the fall of Tyre would have led Alexander on a wild goose chase. There was nothing very definite to strike at. It may be conjectured that what he then had in mind was a decisive battle, which once and for all would make good his lordship over Asia, and as it could not be fought until Darius had mustered another army it logically followed that while he did so Egypt was Alexander's next most profitable objective. Egypt was the south-western province of the Persian empire, but also, as the Egyptians were bitterly opposed to Persian rule, if he occupied Egypt Alexander could once again play the part cf liberator and appear as the champion of oppressed peoples. Further, to leave a secure and contented Egypt in his rear was a strategical necessity, as it would round off his hold on the eastern Mediterranean, and because Egypt was one of the great grain-producing countries its occupation would go far to solve the perennial food shortage in Greece, which in Athens particularly was an outstanding cause of social and political unrest.

Because the occupation of Egypt had to be accomplished before Darius took the field, once again time became the decisive factor; after the fall of Tyre Alexander did not pause to organize the administration of Syria but left Parmenion to supervise that country and advanced southward. At Gaza, the frontier fortress that guarded southern Syria, he was vigorously opposed by Batis, its Persian governor, and was compelled to lay siege to it;[1] this delayed him for two months. According to Arrian, all its male inhabitants died fighting and, after Gaza was taken, Alexander sold their wives and children into slavery and repeopled the city from neighbouring settlements. Curtius relates[2] that in imitation of the treatment of Hector's dead body by Achilles, Alexander had the valiant Batis lashed living to a chariot and dragged him to death around the walls of Gaza, but this is manifestly an invention, for in the *Iliad*, which Alexander venerated, Homer expressly condemns the action of Achilles as a 'shameful outrage'.[3]

From Gaza Alexander followed the coast to Pelusium, the frontier fortress of Egypt on the eastern mouth of the Nile, where the fleet waited for him. Egypt fell to him without a fight; everywhere he was hailed as liberator. Mazaces, the Persian satrap, surrendered 800

---

[1] See Chapter 7.   [2] IV, vi, 29.
[3] For this incident, see Tarn's *Alexander the Great*, vol. II, appx. 11.

talents and Memphis, where Alexander was formally crowned king of Egypt and became pharaoh in the eyes of the people. Though the sole authority for his coronation is *The Romance* of pseudo-Callisthenes, Wilcken points out that 'hieroglyphic texts . . . testify that Alexander bore the traditional royal titles, like his Persian and Egyptian predecessors . . . As "Horus" he was called "the strong prince" . . . or "the protection of Egypt". As "King of Upper Egypt and King of Lower Egypt" he was called "beloved of Ammon and selected of Ra"; and finally as "Son of Ra" he was called "Alexandros" . . . These titles prove two things of Alexander, his special sovereignty over Egypt and his consequent deification.' [1]

At Memphis Alexander sacrificed to Apis and other gods; a political act of high importance that made a profound impression on the Egyptians, for nothing had outraged them more than the desecration of their temples and the slaying of the sacred Apis bull by Cambyses and Artaxerxes III. These sacrifices were followed by gymnastic and musical contests, after which Alexander embarked the hypaspists, Agrianians, archers, and the Royal Squadron of the Companions and sailed down the western branch of the Nile past the Greek settlement of Naucratis[2] (Nibireh) to Canopus (Abukir).

A few miles to the west of Canopus, between lake Mareotis (Maryut) and the island of Pharos, at the village of Rhacotis, he founded the first of his seventeen known Alexandrias.[3] There Hegelochus came to him from the Aegean to report that all Persian resistance was ended; that Lesbos, Chios, Tenedos, and Cos had been liberated, but that Pharnabazus had escaped.

Because the oracle of Ammon in the oasis of Siwah[4] was as famous among the Greeks as those of Delphi and Dodona, and because legend affirmed that it had once been visited by Alexander's ancestors Perseus and Heracles, naturally Alexander – the 'Invincible' of Delphi – was eager to emulate them and consult its god.[5] He set out with a small party along the coast to Paraetonium (Matruh), some 200 miles west of Alexandria, and there he received and accepted the offer of alliance tended to him by the Greek colony of Cyrene. From Paraetonium he struck south across the desert, and as he approached the oasis he was

[1] *Alexander the Great*, p. 114.
[2] Founded by Amasis, king of Egypt, in the sixth century B.C.
[3] For these, see Tarn's *Alexander the Great*, vol. II, appx. 8, 1.
[4] A description of the oasis is to be found in Arrian, III, iv, and in Diodorus, XVII, 50.
[5] Another reason may have been that Cambyses' attempt to reach it, in order to destroy the temple, ended in complete disaster (Herodotus, III, 26).

met by a priest who saluted him as 'Son of Ammon'. Much has been woven around this salutation, but it was no more than the traditional greeting made to every pharaoh, and since his coronation, in the eyes of the Egyptians Alexander was the son of Ammon-Ra. Alexander and the priest entered the inner shrine, but what was divulged to him is unknown, for all we are told is that in a letter to his mother he 'received certain secret responses, which he would tell to her, and to her alone, on his return',[1] but he did not live to do so. From Siwah he took the desert road, by way of Kara and Moghara, back to Memphis.

At Memphis Alexander found embassies from Greece, also 400 Greek mercenaries and 500 Thracian horse sent by Antipater. It would seem probable that it was then that he met the Egyptian philosopher Psammon and listened to his teachings. According to Plutarch, Alexander was much pleased by his statement that 'God was king of all mankind', but that when he had meditated on it, he arrived at a deeper philosophical conclusion, that 'although God was indeed a common father of all mankind, still, He made peculiarly his own the noblest and the best of them'.[2] 'This, on the face of it,' writes Tarn, 'is a plain statement that all men are brothers, and, if true, is the earliest known, at any rate in the Western world.' [3]

At Memphis Alexander reorganized the administration of Egypt on very different lines from those he had hitherto adopted. Because Egypt was naturally a strong and rich country, he decided that it would be unsafe to entrust it to the care of one man and he divided its government between several. He appointed two Egyptians, Doloaspis and Petisis, as governors – not as satraps – of Upper and Lower Egypt, and when Petisis resigned he handed over to Doloaspis the whole country. The provinces which bordered on Libya in the west, and on Arabia beyond Heroopolis (a city near Suez) in the east, he gave to two Greeks, Apollonius and Cleomenes of Naucratis. Cleomenes was also appointed minister of finance, with powers to collect, but not to levy the taxes, which was to remain in the hands of the native tax-gatherers: this gave great satisfaction to the Egyptians. He appointed Pantaleon and Megacles, two of his Companions, to command the garrisons of Memphis and Pelusium; Lycidas, an Aetolian, to command the Greek mercenaries; Peucetas and Balacrus generals of the

---

[1] Plutarch, 'Alexander', XXVII. According to Tarn (*Alexander the Great*, vol. II, appx. 22), Alexander never called himself son of Zeus or son of Ammon, though he acquiesced when people called him the former.

[2] 'Alexander', XXVII.

[3] *Alexander the Great*, vol. II, appx. 25, p. 435.

army left in Egypt, and Polemon admiral of the fleet. In this division of responsibilities it will be seen that he separated the military commands and financial control from the civil government, and thereby rendered it difficult for any one official to gain control of the whole administration and set up an independent kingdom.

In the spring of 331 B.C. Alexander bridged the Nile near Memphis and set out on his return to Tyre, where his fleet awaited him. There he received yet another appeal from Athens to release the Athenians he had captured on the Granicus; this time he consented. He dispatched 100 Phoenician and Cyprian warships from Tyre to reinforce those he had already sent to Antipater. He appointed Asclepiodorus satrap over Syria, with Coeranus to levy tribute in Phoenicia, and Philoxenes to collect it in Asia as far as the Taurus; but, except for Tyre and Gaza, which were garrisoned, the autonomous Phoenician cities were allowed to keep their laws and kings and were not subject to Asclepiodorus' control.

Winning Political Supremacy

Alexander's rear was secure and he was in a position to challenge Darius for his throne, so he sent Parmenion ahead to Thapsacus to bridge the Euphrates, along the eastern bank of which Mazaeus, late satrap of Syria, in command of the Persian advanced guard, had deployed his 3,000 cavalry and 2,000 Greek mercenaries. Soon afterward Alexander set out to join him, but when Mazaeus learnt of his approach, he feared that he would be overwhelmed by so great an army and withdrew eastward from the Euphrates. The bridges, already three-quarters built, were then finished and the river was crossed; but instead of following the main road, Alexander marched in a north-easterly direction through Mesopotamia, because fodder and provisions were more plentiful along that route. Soon contact was gained with Darius' scouts, and those who were captured reported that the king and his army were near the Tigris. Alexander pushed on at top speed, but when he reached the Tigris he found the report to be false and the river unguarded. The stream was swift-flowing and the army crossed it with considerable difficulty. While encamped on its eastern bank the moon was eclipsed (September 20, 331 B.C.) and Alexander sacrificed to the moon, sun, and earth before, after a short rest, the advance was resumed. On the fourth day after crossing the Tigris scouts reported that Darius' advanced cavalry were visible on the plain about Gaugamela, a village now identified with the mound of

Tel Gomel on the Khazir river,[1] a tributary of the Great Zab and east of the plain of Keramlais (see Map 9). It was a spot which called for retribution; for it was near Gaugamela that after the battle of Cunaxa, in 401 B.C., the treacherous Tissaphernes had seized and murdered Clearchus and the leading generals of the Ten Thousand.[2]

There, on October 1, Alexander fought and won the battle of Arbela (also called Gaugamela).[3] 'The greatest battle in the record of the ancient world had been fought', writes Professor Wheeler, and adds, 'The issues of centuries had struck their balance in a day. The channel of history for a thousand years had been opened with a flying wedge.'[4]

When in the middle of the battle Alexander made his decisive cavalry charge, broke through the Persian front and rode toward Darius, Darius was one of the first to flee. But on the following day, when the pursuit reached Arbela (Erbil), it was found that Darius, accompanied by Persian and Bactrian cavalry and 2,000 Greek mercenaries, had abandoned the main road and was hurrying up the Lesser Zab to gain the mountainous country of Media. His reason for this was that he expected Alexander to follow the main road because the one he had chosen for his flight was difficult for a large army with baggage. He was right, but for the wrong reason. Alexander chose the main road because the occupation of Babylon and Susa were politically more important to him than to chase a shattered army through mountainous country in which Darius could easily effect his escape. Alexander advanced on Babylon and approached it in full order of battle; led by their priests and rulers the inhabitants came out to greet him and offered the surrender of their city and its treasury.[5]

As in Egypt, Alexander's first act was religious – to base his lordship over Babylon on the sanction of its gods. He commanded the Babylonians to rebuild all the temples Xerxes had destroyed, and in particular the temple of Marduk, the chief Babylonian god, and then, in accordance with the ritual laid down by the priests, he sacrificed to Marduk and through this acknowledgment of his divinity became in the eyes of the Babylonians their sanctified ruler.

[1] See *The Geographical Journal*, vol. C.1942, pp. 155–64, 'Notes on Alexander's Crossing of the Tigris and the Battle of Arbela', Sir Aurel Stein.

[2] Xenophon's *Anabasis*, II, v.   [3] For this battle, see Chapter 6.

[4] *Alexander the Great* (1925), p. 368. Arrian (III, xiv) says that before charging Alexander drew up his Companion cavalry in a wedge formation.

[5] According to Diodorus (XVII, 64, 3) Alexander found 3,000 talents of silver in Arbela. Of the money surrendered in Babylon 'he gave to every horsemen six minas (£24); to every auxiliary, five (£20); to each of the Macedonian phalanx, two (£8), and to every foreign mercenary, two months' pay'.

His next task was to organize the government of Babylonia, and in this he was faced with a new problem. Although Darius had escaped, he had been so decisively defeated at Arbela that the battle had made Alexander *de facto*, if not *de jure*, King of Kings. Still a king in the eyes of his Macedonians, Fortune had crowned him emperor over many nations, and in the near future was to put more nations under his sway. His problem was not only how to reorganize his conquests, but how, with Macedonia and Greece, to weld them into one world power. This his genius told him he could never do by force alone; but only through the willing co-operation of the conquered peoples. For the first time he selected a Persian as satrap,[1] and appointed Mazaeus, the general who had ably commanded Darius' right wing at Arbela and who after the battle had sought refuge in Babylon, satrap of Babylonia. Politically it was an astute decision; firstly, it was more likely to please the people to be ruled by a Persian rather than by a Macedonian or Greek; secondly, as long as Darius was at liberty, it was an inducement to those satraps who were still loyal to him to desert his cause. In accordance with his now settled policy, to limit Mazaeus' powers he appointed a Macedonian general to command the troops left in Babylon, and another Macedonian as collector of the Babylonian revenue.

Once affairs in Babylon were settled, Alexander set out on a twenty-day march to Susa, which was surrendered to him on his arrival by Abulites, the Persian satrap. He found no less than 50,000 talents in its treasury and among the royal property he recovered the bronze statues of Harmodius and Aristogeiton,[2] which Xerxes had brought with him from Greece; these he returned to Athens as a token of friendship and he also sent 3,000 talents to Antipater. Another acquisition, which was to become a factor of outstanding importance at a later date, was that at Susa the Royal Academy, at which the sons of the Persian nobles were educated to serve the king,[3] fell into Alexander's hands. This gave him a hold over their fathers and toward the close of his reign enabled him to create the cadres of a native Persian army to supplement his own, or to act as a counterpoise to it. For the time being, it deprived his enemy of his main source of potential officers.

At Susa he was reinforced by several thousand fresh troops from

[1] Later he appointed Persians as satraps of Susiana, Media, Persis, Parthia and Hyrcania, Tapuria, Paraetacene, Aria, Drangiana, the Paropamisadae, Bactria and Carmania.
[2] The tyrannicides who in 514 B.C. murdered Hipparchus, brother of the tyrant Hippias, and lost their lives.   [3] See Xenophon's *Anabasis*, I, lx, 3.

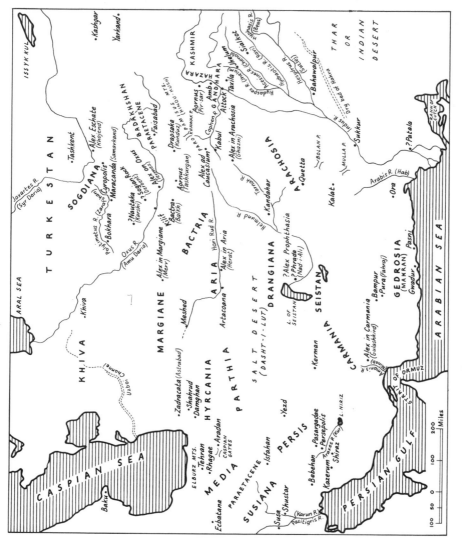

4 THE EASTERN PERSIAN EMPIRE

Macedonia; the mounted men he incorporated into his Companion cavalry, and at the same time he made it more mobile by dividing each of its regiments (*ilae*) into two squadrons (*lochoi*) of 100 men or more, each under its own squadron leader (*lochagos*). He retained Abulites as satrap, appointed a separate garrison commander and then set out for Persepolis and Pasargadae, which lay close together.

He invaded the country of the Uxians on his way and brought its wild tribesmen to heel[1] and compelled them to pay a tribute in horses, cattle, and sheep, which they had refused to do to the Persian kings.

After this he sent Parmenion with the baggage train, Thessalian cavalry, and the more heavily armed soldiers ahead by way of the Shiraz road, while he and the Companion cavalry and the lighter-armed troops made a forced march through the mountains to seize a defile, known as the Persian Gates,[2] held by Ariobarzanes, satrap of Persis, with an alleged 40,000 infantry and 700 cavalry. His first attempt failed, but his second, a skilful turning movement combined with a frontal holding attack, was successful; after which he advanced with such speed that he arrived at Persepolis before its garrison could remove its treasury. There he found the enormous sum of 120,000 talents, and 6,000 more at Pasargadae – the old capital founded by Cyrus.

At Persepolis occurred the memorable burning of the palace of Xerxes. The story as given by Diodorus and Curtius, based on Cleitarchus, that the palace was fired during a drunken revel by Alexander and the courtezan Thais, is fiction. It is certain that it was a deliberate act on the part of Alexander, which Parmenion with some justification opposed. Its purpose was to proclaim to all Greece that the campaign of vengeance had been won. Its wisdom is to be doubted, because it must have encouraged the older Macedonians to press for the conclusion of the war – the last thing Alexander contemplated.

The ruins of Persepolis are still an impressive sight, and in Omar Khayyám's day – as now – they were known as Takht-i-Jamshid ('Jamshid's Throne'), and he believed that they contained the last resting-place of Cyrus. They are referred to as follows in the xviiith quatrain of the Rubáiyát:

> They say the Lion and the Lizard keep
> The Courts where Jamshýd gloried and drank deep:
> And Bahrám, that great Hunter – the Wild Ass
> Stamps o'er his Head, but cannot break his Sleep.

[1] For this operation, see Chapter 8.   [2] For this operation, see Chapter 8.

Cyrus' tomb was, and still is, at Pasargadae.[1]

While Alexander wintered at Persepolis he learnt that soon after the battle of Arbela had been fought, in a stiff fight Antipater had defeated and killed Agis of Sparta near Megalopolis, a city in Arcadia founded by Epaminondas, and still bearing the same name. Thus the last potential threat to Alexander's rear was removed; Sparta was at last compelled to enter the League of Corinth.

Since his defeat at Arbela, Darius, accompanied by Bessus, satrap of Bactria, other satraps, and his remaining Greek mercenaries, had established his headquarters at Ecbatana (Hamadan), from where he sent on his baggage column to the Caspian Gates, now known as the passes of Sialek and Sadar. When, about midsummer 330 B.C., Alexander learnt where Darius was, he at once set out for Media. When he was three marches from Ecbatana he was met by Bistanes, a son of Artaxerxes III, who informed him that Darius, with 3,000 cavalry, 6,000 infantry, and 7,000 talents, had left Ecbatana five days before. Darius' intention was to withdraw through Parthia and Hyrcania to Bactria, wasting the land on his way to impede any attempt by Alexander to follow him.

With the League war at an end, Alexander paid off at Ecbatana the Thessalians and all his Greek allies, and sent them back to Greece with a donation of 2,000 talents. From this time he made increasing use of mercenaries, not to augment his striking force, but to garrison and colonize the Persian provinces as they were captured. This was a wise policy, because so many of the mercenaries were either homeless men or exiles. He also ordered that all the gold and silver he had seized at Susa, Persepolis, and Pasargadae, which amounted to 180,000 talents (£43,920,000 at the 1913 value of the pound), was to be brought to Ecbatana and stored in its citadel. This vast sum he entrusted to Harpalus, his imperial treasurer, with instructions to establish a royal mint and coin the bullion into gold staters and silver tetradrachms. He entrusted the safe-keeping of the imperial treasury to Parmenion, who was also appointed commander of the communications of the army eastward of Ecbatana. For these tasks Alexander allotted to him a strong body of Thracian mercenaries.

Alexander then set out after Darius,[2] and on the eleventh day arrived at Rhagae (Rei, five miles south-east of Tehran), 'distant from

---

[1] For a description of the tomb, see Strabo, XV, iii, 7.

[2] For this pursuit, see 'Notes on the march of Alexander the Great from Ecbatana to Hyrcania', A. F. von Stahl, *The Geographical Journal*, vol. LXIV, 1924, pp. 312–29.

the Caspian Gates', writes Arrian, 'one day's journey to one marching as Alexander did' [1] – actually they were forty-four miles east of Rhagae.

At Rhagae, he learnt from deserters that Darius had already passed through the defile; as this meant that he could not catch up with him for several days, he decided to call a five-day halt to rest his exhausted men and horses before he renewed the pursuit. When he did, he advanced to the Gates, camped near them, and on the following day passed through to encamp again, probably at Aradan, where he sent out foragers to collect supplies because the local inhabitants told him that the country ahead was waterless desert. While there, a Baby-lonian noble who had deserted Darius, Bagistanes, surrendered and told him that Bessus had deposed Darius, and held him captive. Alexander did not even wait for his foragers to come in, but set out at top speed at the head of a picked force, carrying two days' rations. He marched all night until noon on the following day, rested his army until nightfall, then went on again until he reached the village from which Bagistanes had set out. There he learnt that Bessus was in supreme command.

In spite of his exhausted horses and men, he pushed on. Again he set out by night, and at noon the following day came to a village which Bessus had occupied the day before. There he was told of a short-cut through the desert by which he might be able to head off Bessus; but as his infantry could no longer keep up, he dismounted 500 of his cavalry and mounted infantry upon their horses. In the afternoon he set out again, and, as Arrian says, 'led the way with great rapidity'. After he had advanced forty-seven miles during the night he came unexpectedly upon his quarry, a little before daybreak, 'going along without any order and unarmed'.[2] Bessus had Darius stabbed before he effected his escape with 600 horsemen, and when Alexander came up, he found that his rival was dead. He sent his body back to Persepolis to be given a royal burial and 'his children received from Alexander, a princely rearing and education just as if their father were still reigning'.[3]

Darius is thought to have been murdered either at Damghan or Shahrud; Damghan is 208 miles from the Caspian Gates and Shahrud 253. One or other of these distances was traversed in seven days; if the former, at an average daily march of slightly over twenty-nine miles, and if the latter, thirty-six miles – a tremendous feat of endurance

[1] III, 20, 2.
[2] Their arms were presumably in their wagons, a common custom.
[3] Arrian, III, xxii, 5.

when it is remembered that it was midsummer[1] and much of the country waterless desert.

For Alexander, the death of Darius was not only most opportune, but decisive. Had he lived a prisoner, he would have become the centre of intrigue, and to have put him out of the way was contrary to Alexander's code of royalty. It was decisive because by right of conquest it raised Alexander to the position of Great King, and as such his genius told him that for his empire to endure he had to overcome the centuries-old antagonism between Greeks and Persians. With victory his, there was no longer any place in his empire either for victor or vanquished. He also realized that its existence depended not on his mortal life and endeavours, but on the goodwill and contentedness of its peoples; to expunge his victories from their minds and show them he was one of themselves, he introduced Persian etiquette into his court and donned Persian attire. He demanded that they should pay him the same homage (*proskynesis*) they had paid to Darius, which they were ready to do; indeed, they would have had little respect for him had he not demanded it. As regards attire, Plutarch informs us that he adopted a composite dress 'midway between the Persian and the Median, more modest than the one and more stately than the other',[2] and that he did so, not from personal predilection, but because 'as a sovereign of both nations . . . he strove to acquire the goodwill of the conquered by showing respect for their apparel, so that they might continue constant in loving the Macedonians as rulers, and might not feel hate toward them as enemies'.[3]

Unlike Hephaestion and Craterus, who supported this policy of conciliation, the bulk of the Macedonians failed to understand its political motive. They were wholly military-minded men and that Alexander should demand homage and don oriental attire in order to obliterate the memory of his victories in the minds of his new subjects was quite beyond their mental grasp; now that victory had been won, all they yearned for was to enjoy its fruits. With Darius' death they felt that the war should be ended, so that they might return to their homes with their booty. That this feeling was pronounced is corroborated by the fact that Alexander considered it advisable to summon an assembly of the army and make clear to it the necessity of a further advance.[4] Though by sheer force of personality he convinced his soldiers of the

[1] Arrian (III, xxii, 2) says that Darius died in the month of Hecatombaeon. According to Chinnock, in the year 330 B.C. the first of Hecatombaeon fell on July 1.
[2] 'Alexander', XLV.   [3] *On the Fortune of Alexander*, 330, 8.
[4] See Curtius, VI, 6–10.

rightness of his motives, their longing for peace and home was to endure, and their abhorrence of his policy of conciliation to continue.

Securing the North-Eastern Frontier

Alexander did not follow Bessus in his flight towards Bactria, but advanced into the Elburz mountains to subdue the tribes of the Tapurians and Mardians – the Mardians had never acknowledged Persian supremacy – and to force the surrender of those of Darius' followers who, with the remnant of his Greek mercenaries, had sought refuge in their fastnesses. This was an imperative task; his rear had to be clear before he could take up the chase.

With two columns, one under Craterus, who increasingly replaced Parmenion as his second-in-command, and the other led by himself, Alexander rapidly swept through the mountains and subdued the tribesmen; after which Nabarzanes, Darius' chiliarch (vizier), Phrataphernes and Autophradates, his satraps of Parthia and Tapuria, Artabazus, father of Pharnabazus, and 1,500 Greek mercenaries accompanied by the Greek envoys accredited to the Persian court, surrendered. Nabarzanes was pardoned, the two satraps reinstated, and Artabazus was received with honour and admitted to the Macedonian court because he had been a friend of Alexander's father and had remained faithful to Darius. Those of the mercenaries who had entered the Persian service before the creation of the League of Corinth were set free; but those who had not, though pardoned, were incorporated with their leader Andronicus in the army. The envoys from Athens and Sparta were imprisoned, but those from Sinope and Chalcedon, not members of the League, were granted their liberty.

Alexander then marched to Zadracata (Astrabad), where he halted for fifteen days before he set out to follow Bessus. At Meshed he received the submission of Satibarzanes, satrap of Aria, retained him in his satrapy and allotted to him a small police force for road protection. There he learnt that Bessus had assumed the upright tiara and the title of Artaxerxes, and that he expected the Scythians (Sacas) to enter into alliance with him.

On his way from Meshed along the main road toward Bactra (also called Zariaspa, the modern Balkh), Alexander received the news that Satibarzanes had massacred his police force and was collecting an army at Artacoana to support Bessus. Alexander could not leave Aria in revolt in his rear, so he set out with his Companion cavalry and his light-armed troops on a two-day forced march of seventy miles. He surprised Satibarzanes, but though his soldiers deserted him he effected his escape; soon after he was caught and killed.

A little to the east of Artacoana Alexander founded Alexandria of the Arians (Herat) and appointed a Persian, Arsames, satrap in the place of Satibarzanes. He advanced into Drangiana, then part of the satrapy of Arachosia, and because its satrap, Barsaëntes, had joined in the rebellion, he had him put to death. At Phrada (? Nad-i-Ali in Seistan) the conspiracy of Philotas came to light, which so shocked Alexander that he decided no longer to entrust his Companion cavalry to a single leader. He divided the Companions into two divisions, each of four squadrons, and placed one under his bosom friend Hephaestion, and the other under Cleitus the Black. At Phrada he founded Alexandria Propthasia ('Anticipation').

Then, eager to catch Bessus, he advanced up the Helmund and came across a people, formerly called the Ariaspians, but later named Euergetae ('Benefactors') because they had rendered loyal service to Cyrus. When he learnt that they 'not only enjoyed a form of government unlike that of the other barbarians in that part of the world, but laid claim to justice equally with the best of the Greeks, he set them free, and gave them besides as much of the adjacent country as they asked for themselves'.[1] At the same time he received the submission of the satraps of Gedrosia and Carmania; appointed Menon satrap of Arachosia with orders to reduce that country, and in October, or November, 329 B.C., advanced up the Tarnak river and, according to Sir William Tarn, founded Alexandria in Arachosia at Ghazni, and not at Kandahar as generally held.[2]

Since crossing the Hellespont in the spring of 334 B.C., Alexander had advanced nearly 2,500 miles and had subdued the whole of the Persian empire except for the satrapies of Bactria and Sogdiana, which together constituted a great bastion that guarded its north-eastern approaches. Though he could have little realized it, the reduction of these two satrapies was to test his generalship to the full and engage his energies for two years. The reasons were that the Bactrians and Sogdians were a warlike people of pure Aryan stock, who were determined to fight for their freedom. Added to this, they inhabited one of the most difficult regions in the world for any type of army to operate in. Bactria (Badakshan and Afghan Turkestan), which lay between the Paropamisus (Hindu-Kush)[3] and the Oxus (Amu Daria),

---

[1] Arrian, III, xxvii, 5.   [2] *Alexander the Great*, vol. II, appx. 8.1, p. 234.
[3] Arrian calls them 'the Caucasus', because in his day it was still held that the Hindu-Kush were an extension of the Caucasus. See also Strabo, XI, viii, 1.

was largely a tangled mass of mountains, and most of Sogdiana (Bokhara and Turkestan) was either open steppe land or desert. Except for Bactra, the last great city of the Persian empire, there were no towns to strike at; the people were either village-dwellers or nomads.

In this theatre the whole mode of fighting was to differ from what it had been. No great battles awaited Alexander; he was to be faced by a people's war, a war of mounted guerrillas who, when he advanced would suddenly appear in his rear, who entrenched themselves on inaccessible crags, and when pursued vanished into the Turkoman steppes. To overrun such a theatre of war and subdue such an enemy demanded generalship of the highest order, much higher than needed against an organized enemy on the plains. It is in his campaigns in Bactria and Sogdiana that Alexander's generalship reaches its zenith, and that he was able to subdue these two satrapies in a little over two years is a feat of arms seldom rivalled.

Unfortunately Arrian and the other historians tell us little about the tactical changes Alexander introduced although we may assume that there was a considerable expansion of light troops, both foot and horse; yet all we hear of is the introduction of mounted javelin-men and that Alexander lightened the equipment of part of the phalanx.[1] Whatever the changes, one thing is certain, they were based on mobility and flexibility, coupled with the use of a large number of military posts and military colonies that restricted his enemy's mobility while they added to his own.

Alexander rested his army at Ghazni before he crossed the mountains into Paropamisadae in the spring of 329 B.C.; founded Alexandria of the Caucasus near Kabul; appointed Proexes, a Persian, satrap of this region, with one of the Companions as his military commander, and then prepared to cross the Hindu-Kush into Bactria. Bessus, with 7,000 Bactrians and Dahae, accompanied by Spitamenes and Oxyartes, two great barons of Sogdiana, held Aornus (Tashkurgan) near the upper Oxus; yet, although the Hindu-Kush was deep in snow, Alexander crossed that range by the Khawak pass (11,600 feet high), descended into fertile country and then advanced northward to Drapsaka (Kunduz) to turn Tashkurgan from the east. Bessus withdrew beyond the Oxus; both Tashkurgan and Bactra submitted without resistance, and Artabazus was made satrap of Bactria.

From Bactra Alexander next marched to the Oxus opposite Kilif, where the river was about three-quarters of a mile wide. It was crossed by means of skins stuffed with chaff, like those used to cross

[1] Arrian, III, xxix, 7, and IV, vi, 3.

the Danube in 335 B.C.; it took in all five days.[1] Then, during a forced march to Bessus' reported position, a message was received from Spitamenes that Bessus had been arrested and was in chains, and that Spitamenes was willing to surrender him. Alexander dispatched Ptolemy with a powerful force to accept the surrender, and after completing 'ten days' march in four days' he arrived at the camp where Spitamenes had bivouacked the day before. But Spitamenes had changed his mind. As speed was now more than ever essential, Ptolemy ordered his infantry to follow up, and pressed on with his cavalry to a village in which he found Bessus abandoned; he seized him and set out on his return.

While Ptolemy was on his mission, Alexander remounted those of his troopers who had lost their horses in the Hindu-Kush, and when Ptolemy returned, he marched to Maracanda (Samarkand, the future capital of Tamerlane), one of the two royal residences in Sogdiana; the other was Bokhara. There he left a garrison before he advanced to Cyropolis, a fortress founded by Cyrus near the Jaxartes (Syr Daria), and the strongest of eight fortified posts the Persians had built to protect their north-eastern frontier against the nomadic Massagetae who inhabited the steppes beyond the Jaxartes. He garrisoned these posts with mercenaries, and as he now believed that Sogdiana had submitted, he summoned all the Sogdian barons to meet him in durbar at Bactra.

Sogdiana was far from subdued, and the capture of Bessus would appear to have misled him; for it was not he but Spitamenes who was the true leader of the Sogdians, and when this able man received the summons, he felt it foreboded nothing good for either himself or his people, and decided to put himself at the head of a national and not merely a local revolt. It was skilfully planned and it took Alexander by surprise.

The revolt broke out suddenly in Alexander's immediate rear; Cyropolis and the other fortified posts were caught napping, stormed, and their garrisons massacred. Alexander marched against the nearest fortress, Gaza, and sent Craterus against Cyropolis with orders to besiege it. Gaza he stormed and put its defenders to the sword, and in the two following days reduced four other forts. Then he marched to Cyropolis, which after a determined resistance was carried by assault.[2]

---

[1] At this time Curtius (VII, 5, 28–35) records Alexander's massacre of the Branchidae, a family group of the Milesians whom Xerxes had settled in Bactria. According to Tarn (*Alexander the Great*, vol. II, appx. 13) the story is without foundation and an invention of Callisthenes. Mr A. K. Narain disagrees; he believes the massacre to be true, because it is attested by at least three classical sources. See his *The Indo-Greeks* (1957), pp. 2–3.   [2] See Chapter 8.

The remaining two forts were then recaptured, and in each case the severity meeted out was abnormal; for, according to Aristobulus, all their garrisons were slain.

It would appear that the reason for this butchery hinged on the strategic importance of Sogdiana – a march satrapy and bulwark protecting the north-eastern approaches into Persia – coupled with Alexander's eagerness to conclude a campaign prolonged beyond his expectations. He could not proceed farther east with an unconquered Sogdiana on his northern flank; it seemed that he hoped to extinguish resistance by terror, as he had done in the case of Thebes. Should this be correct, events proved his policy to be mistaken; far from subduing the Sogdians, the terrible punishment meted out to them provoked in them a resistance born of the fury of despair. Other reasons may have been that the 'Asiatic Scythians' (Massagetae, part of the Saca confederacy) had assembled large numbers of horse-archers on the right bank of the Jaxartes ready to fall upon the Macedonians should they fail to quell the revolt; simultaneously news reached Alexander that Spitamenes had laid siege to Maracanda to the west.

It would appear that Alexander did not realize how serious the rebellion was, for when he learnt that Maracanda was besieged, he dispatched to its relief no more than sixty Companion cavalry, 800 mercenary cavalry and 1,500 mercenary infantry, under Pharnuches, a diplomatist and not a soldier, because he expected to win the favour of the barbarians by negotiation and not by battle.

He founded Alexandria Eschate (Alexandria the Farthest, now Khojend) on the left bank of the Jaxartes as a bulwark against the nomads, and when, after twenty days, its citadel had been built, he settled in this new Alexandria a body of Greek mercenaries, some of the local inhabitants, and those of his Macedonians who were no longer fit for service. He then sacrificed to the gods and held a gymnastic contest.

In the meantime the Scythians remained on the right bank of the Jaxartes, and as the river was narrow at this point, they shouted insults at Alexander and dared him to cross over to them. He took them at their word and ordered skins to be prepared for its passage. Then followed a remarkable operation;[1] for though Alexander had no experience in 'Parthian' tactics, which at times could be annihilating, as they were at Carrhae in 53 B.C., he devised a tactics of his own and was completely successful. One thousand of the Scythians were slain and 150 captured; in all probability many more would have been taken in the pursuit had not Alexander fallen seriously ill after drinking foul

[1] See Chapter 8.

water. Their defeat was sufficiently decisive to induce them to send an embassy to Alexander to apologize for what had happened and to assure him that their king was willing to obey any command he might give him.

While Alexander was thus engaged, a very different battle was fought near Maracanda. When Spitamenes learnt of the approach of the relieving column under Pharnuches, he raised the siege, was joined by 600 Scythian horsemen, and on the level plain south of the Polytimetus river (Zarafshan) he ambushed Pharnuches and annihilated his column.[1]

This was the first disaster suffered by Alexander's army since it crossed the Hellespont. Retribution was immediate; Alexander set out with half the Companions, the hypaspists, archers, and 'the lightest men of the phalanx'; covered the 1,500 stades (170 miles)[2] between Khojend and Maracanda in three days and a few hours, and at dawn on the fourth day came near the city. Spitamenes and his followers fled with Alexander at their heels, but when he reached the field of battle he halted to bury Pharnuches' dead. He then laid waste the rich lands that bordered the Polytimetus[3] and marched back to Bactra where he went into winter quarters.

It was a busy time. Bessus was brought to Bactra for trial, and because he had assumed the tiara was punished according to Persian law. After his nose and ears had been cut off he was sent to Ecbatana to be put to death. Arrian condemns this brutal treatment, but it was a common Persian custom and the same that had been meted out to the pretender Fravarish by Darius I.[4] At Bactra Alexander received large reinforcements from Greece, and the western satraps brought to him fresh drafts of mercenaries, a type of soldier he increasingly needed to garrison his fortified posts, on the lines of Constantine's *limitanei*, and to provide men for military colonies. Pharasmanes, king of the Chorasmians, a people who inhabited the country between the Caspian and Aral Seas (province of Khiva), visited Alexander at Bactra to offer alliance. He also offered to guide Alexander by way of

[1] See Chapter 8.

[2] If the short stade is meant, Tarn makes the distance 135 miles (*Alexander the Great*, vol. I, p. 69). The length of railway now connecting Khojend and Samarkand is about 150 miles.

[3] At the end of the nineteenth century Lord Curzon described the basin of the Zarafshan as 'a veritable garden of Eden, and incomparably the most fertile part of Central Asia' (*Russia in Central Asia*, 1889, p. 205).

[4] *The Cambridge Ancient History*, vol. IV, p. 179. Tarn says of this mutilation: 'It is the only occasion on which Alexander is recorded on any reputable authority to have used torture' (*Alexander the Great*, vol. I, p. 70).

the northern trade route to the Black Sea, but Alexander replied that for the time being he was engrossed on plans to conquer India, and that when he had done so, on his return to Greece he would explore the land east of the Euxine.

But before any move towards India could be made, the Sogdians had first to be subdued; the terror had not forced their submission but had broken them into bands, which held the strongholds and mountain fastnesses. In the spring of 328 B.C., Alexander returned to the Oxus, and while encamped there a spring of petroleum was discovered near his tent.[1]

Before he set out to subdue Sogdiana, Alexander left Craterus with a strong force in Bactra with orders to patrol the country and prevent a rising; then he divided the rest of his army into five columns under Hephaestion, Ptolemy, Perdiccas, Coenus and Artabazus, and himself. He led his own column to Maracanda, while the others swept the countryside, reduced the Sogdian strongholds, and then joined up with him at Maracanda: it was probably then that Cleitus was murdered. Next, he sent out Hephaestion to build fortified posts and plant colonies, and he instructed Coenus and Artabazus to advance their column into Scythia (Turkestan), where Spitamenes had sought refuge.

When Alexander set out to reduce all the places still held by the Sogdians, Spitamenes suddenly appeared in his rear with a body of Massagetae, overwhelmed one of the Bactrian border forts, and then moved on Bactra, which was garrisoned with oddments and sick soldiers. Those who were fit enough to fight were led out by Peithon, son of Sosicles. They engaged the invaders and killed a number of them; but on their return fell into an ambush and were nearly annihilated, Peithon was wounded and captured. When Craterus learnt of this disaster, he set out by forced marches, came up with the Massagetae and killed 150 of them; but Spitamenes again escaped.

After Alexander had established his network of fortified posts, he allotted to Coenus two battalions of the phalanx, two squadrons of Companions, all the mounted javelin-men and the newly raised Bactrian and Sogdian light horse, and instructed him to continue the operations against Spitamenes while he rested the army at Nautaka.[2]

---

[1] Arrian, IV, xv, 7-8; also Strabo, XI, xi, 5. Herodotus knew of oil pits at Ardericca near Babylon. Marco Polo in his *Travels* came across oil in Zorzania (Baku, Georgia). 'There is a fountain of oil', he writes, 'which discharges so great a quantity as to furnish loading for many camels' (Edit. Everyman's Library, 1939, bk. I, chap. V).

[2] Sir Percy Sykes suggests that to-day it is represented by Karshi, between Samarkand and the Oxus (*A History of Persia*, p. 269).

There, because of his age, Artabazus was relieved of his satrapy and Amyntas, son of Nicolaus, appointed in his stead; also Alexander removed Autophradates from Tapuria, added it to the satrapy of Phrataphernes and restored Atropates, Darius' former satrap, to Media.

'But', writes Arrian, 'when Spitamenes saw every place was occupied by the Macedonians with garrisons, and that there was no way of flight left open to him', he decided to attack Coenus, and by offers of plunder he persuaded 3,000 Massagetae to join him. When Coenus heard this he set out against him; a sharp encounter followed in which 800 Massagetae were killed, and Spitamenes' Sogdian and Bactrian followers deserted to Coenus. Soon after, when the Massagetae learnt that Alexander was on his way, they seized Spitamenes, cut off his head and sent it to Alexander. Thus perished the most formidable opponent who ever faced Alexander. Except for his tragic end, Spitamenes' career is closely paralleled by that of Christian De Wet in the Anglo-Boer War of 1899–1902.

After Spitamenes' death, Coenus and Craterus rejoined the army at Nautaka: it was now mid-winter 329–328 B.C. But they were not to remain there for long, because four great Sogdian barons – Oxyartes, Chorienes, Catanes, and Austanes – were still under arms and, in spite of the lateness of the season, Alexander was determined to settle his account with them. Late in the winter of 328 B.C. he attacked Oxyartes' stronghold, known as the 'Sogdian Rock' (? near Derbent). Oxyartes was away, but his family was there, and though the snow was deep on the mountains, and the approaches of the rock citadel were precipitous, by an extraordinary feat of rock-climbing the stronghold was captured.[1]

Among the captives was Oxyartes' daughter Roxane, reputed to be the most beautiful woman in Asia, and because Alexander wished to reconcile the Sogdian barons and bring the national war to an end, as an act of policy he decided to marry her. The wedding was celebrated according to the Persian ritual, which suggests that Alexander's idea of equality between Persians and Macedonians, at first imposed on him as a military necessity, had now become his fixed policy.[2] It was an astute arrangement and the very opposite of the terror he had relied on, for when Oxyartes learnt of the marriage he surrendered

---

[1] See Chapter 8.

[2] According to Curtius (VIII, iv, 25), Alexander said of this marriage, 'that it was important for establishing his empire that Persians and Macedonians be joined in wedlock; that only in that way could shame be taken from the conquered and haughtiness from the victors'.

to Alexander and accompanied him to the siege of the rock fortress of
Chorienes (near Faisabad).[1] After its surrender, Alexander appointed
Chorienes governor of that region, left Craterus to reduce Catanes and
Austanes in Paraetacene (in Sogdiana), and returned to Bactra. In a
sharp battle in which Catanes was killed and Austanes captured,
Craterus brought the war of Sogdian independence to an end. He re-
joined Alexander at Bactra, which was refounded as an Alexandria,
as well as two others, one at Merv and the other at Termez on the
Oxus. Besides these, many military defensive colonies were established
in Bactra and Sogdiana.

It may have been at Bactra that Alexander arranged for 30,000
native youths to be educated and trained in Macedonian fashion – presumably at the Royal Academy at Susa – in order to provide reinforcements for the army, and if so, this, as well as his marriage with
Roxane, would appear to have outraged some of the Macedonians. It
was at this time that the Callisthenes incident over *proskynesis* occurred;
it came to a head in the spring of 327 B.C. and was soon followed by
the conspiracy of the Pages and the execution of Callisthenes.

With the pacification of Sogdiana Alexander finally secured his
north-eastern frontier on the Jaxartes,[2] and though he knew that
beyond that river lay the land of the Scythians (Sacas), he believed that
on its far side streamed the Ocean, and therefore that this frontier
would be faced by no great danger from the east. Nevertheless, he was
aware that trouble might come from the lands about the Caspian Sea,
and his reply to the king of the Chorasmians was no idle one; for, as
we know, shortly after his return to Babylon from India its exploration
was the first project which engaged his mind.

Search for the Eastern Frontier

Alexander made ready at Bactra for the invasion of India, which he
was aware had at one time been the most easterly of the Persian satrapies. He believed India to be a peninsula of no great depth, which
jutted eastward to the sea, and that on its northern flank it was bordered by the chain of the Paropamisus mountains, north of which, at
no great distance beyond the Jaxartes, flowed the Ocean, which
washed their foothills and swept round the eastern end of the peninsula.

[1] See Chapter 8.
[2] The consolidation of Bactria and southern Sogdiana was so complete that the
Greek kingdom, eventually established there, endured until 130 B.C., when it was
extinguished by the Yueh-chi.

To Alexander, India meant the land of the Indus, and whether that river was the source of the Nile, or whether it flowed into the ocean was beyond his ken. It seems that he knew nothing of the voyage of Scylax, although Aristotle mentions the *Periplus* of that intrepid navigator in his *Politics*.[1] He had two objectives: to complete the conquest of the Persian empire (that is, of Asia), and to solve the problem of Ocean, which for so long had intrigued the geographers. To help him in this, in the autumn of 328 B.C. he had sent instructions to Egypt and Phoenicia to send him shipwrights and sailors.

While preparations were under way, he received large reinforcements; according to Curtius, 19,400 foot and 2,600 horse.[2] Many of these men were mercenary troops needed for colonization, and those who were not were drafted into the army as replacements. Of the total forces assembled, 10,000 foot and 3,500 horse were allotted to Amyntas, satrap of Bactria, as garrison troops, and the strength of the phalanx was raised from six to seven battalions. In all, from 27,000 to 30,000 troops were allotted to the army of invasion.[3] To these must be added an unknown yet considerable number of non-combatants, because the army was now a mobile state and the administrative centre of the empire; it included the civil and military services, the commissariat, engineers, scientists, merchants, soldiers' wives, and schools for training and educating their children.

When engaged on his preparations, Alexander was joined by Sasigupta, an Indian rajah from Gandhara, which lay between the Kunar and Indus rivers. Alexander learnt from him that the rajah or king of Taxila,[4] whose domains lay between the Indus and Jhelum, was eager to appeal to him as Great King for aid against Porus, king of the Pauravas east of the Jhelum, with whom he was at loggerheads.

In the early summer of 327 B.C. Alexander set out for India, recrossed the Hindu-Kush, and after a ten-day march arrived at Alexandria of the Caucasus at their foot. He found things amiss there, appointed Nicanor governor, and Oxyartes satrap of Paropamisadae, and sent a summons to Taxiles and other rajahs west of the Indus to come and meet him. They did this, not because they looked upon him

---

[1] VII, xiv, 1332b.

[2] VII, x, 11–12. Pierre Jouguet estimates that between the battle of Arbela and the invasion of India, in all Alexander received 41,000 foot and 6,530 horse (*Macedonian Imperialism and the Hellenization of the East*, English edit., 1928, p. 78).

[3] Tarn's *Alexander the Great*, vol. I, p. 84.

[4] Taxila is not far from Rawalpindi. This rajah's personal name was Omphis (Ambhi), but usually he is referred to as Taxiles.

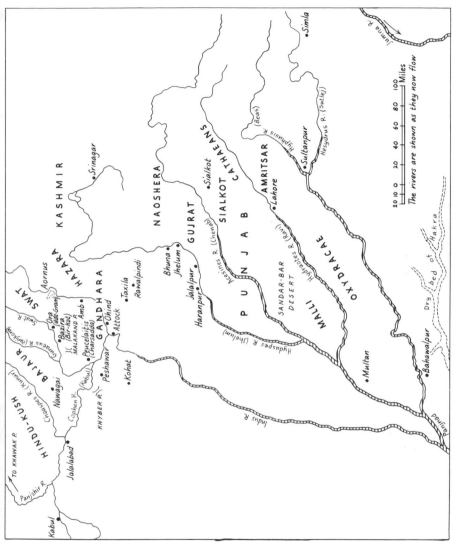

5 THE NORTH-WEST FRONTIER OF INDIA AND THE PUNJAB

as a conqueror, but because they regarded him as their rightful protector. Alexander must have learnt from them, as well as from Sasigupta, how erroneous were many of his views on India; but of this nothing has been written.

His plan was to advance half the army and the impedimenta, under Hephaestion and Perdiccas, accompanied by Taxiles, down the Cophen (Kabul) river to the Indus, with orders to bridge that river; while, to protect their left flank and line of communications, he moved with the remaining half up the Choaspes (Kunar) river and through the mountains of Bajaur and Swat, to rejoin Hephaestion and Perdiccas on the Indus.

He was vigorously opposed on the Choaspes by the Bajaur tribesmen, called by the Greeks Aspasians, who collected in their strongholds to block his advance: some of these hill forts had to be besieged, others were stormed, while others capitulated or were abandoned. At Arigaion (possibly Nawagai, the present capital of Bajaur), a pitched battle was fought in which, with obvious exaggeration, Ptolemy states that 40,000 of the hillmen and 230,000 head of cattle were captured. The finest of the cattle Alexander sent to Macedonia to improve the native stock – a journey of well over 3,000 miles.

Next, he crossed the Guraeus (Panjkora) river and entered Swat, the land of the Assacenians, who had concentrated their forces at the chief stronghold Massaga (unidentified), and who were supported by 7,000 Indian mercenaries from beyond the Indus. Unexpectedly they did not await their enemy's attack, but advanced on the Macedonians as they pitched camp. By a rapid feint withdrawal Alexander frustrated their intentions: first he drew them away from their stronghold, then turned about, drove them into it, and laid siege to it.[1] The Assacenians eventually surrendered on terms, but as these were broken, the Indian mercenaries, who had pledged themselves to enter Alexander's service, were surrounded and massacred.[2]

Alexander next took and garrisoned the towns of Ora (Ude-gram) and Bazira (Bir-kot), and crossed either the Malakand or a near-by pass into the district of Peucelaitis (part of the Peshawar valley) which Hephaestion had failed to subdue. There, after he had received the surrender of Peucelaitis (Charsadda), which he garrisoned, he marched

[1] See Chapter 8.
[2] See Arrian, IV, xxvii, and Tarn's *Alexander the Great*, vol. I, p. 89, where he considers whether this massacre was a justifiable act of war. It would seem that either they had to serve in the Macedonian army or perish, because Alexander could not afford to run the risk of allowing them to withdraw over the Indus and sell their services to his future enemies.

to Embolina (unidentified), which lay two days' march from Aornus,[1] a mountain stronghold north of Attock and near the Indus in which large numbers of tribesmen had sought refuge.

In 1926 Aornus was identified by Sir Aurel Stein as Pir-sar, a flat-topped ridge with precipitous cliffs that commands the Indus 5,000 feet below it. Legend affirmed that it had been unsuccessfully besieged by Heracles, and that this was sufficient reason for Alexander to try to outdo his ancestor. Should this story be true, then it can have been put about only for purposes of prestige and propaganda, because it must have been obvious to Alexander that, as Aornus was a rallying point for the tribesmen, and because it flanked his line of communications up the Kabul valley as well as any crossing he might make over the Indus, he could not afford to leave it in enemy hands. Strategically, it was imperative for him to occupy it, also it was morally imperative; for it was considered impregnable and its capture would demoralize the tribesmen far and wide. He decided to take it. He left Craterus with the bulk of the army at Embolina to gather supplies and, probably in March, 326 B.C., he set out at the head of a picked force to reduce it, which he accomplished after one of the most remarkable of mountain warfare exploits.[2] He left Sasigupta with a garrison to hold Aornus, and then for a few days pursued the fugitives.

Next, he ordered timber to be felled for the building of ships and floated down the Indus to Ohind, sixteen miles above Attock, where Hephaestion and Perdiccas had bridged the river. Then he set out to join them. He crossed the Indus and marched to Taxila, the largest city between the Indus and Hydaspes (Jhelum) rivers,[3] where he established his advanced base for the conquest of the Punjab.[4] He was received with every sign of friendship by Taxiles and was met by envoys from Abisares and other hill state rajahs of Kashmir; but Abisares was actually in league with Porus.

At Taxila Alexander reorganized his cavalry. He separated the *agema* (Royal Squadron) from the Companions, and took personal command of it; the remainder, less the horse-archers and a few mercenaries, he divided into five hipparchies, each of 1,000 men. Four of them were composed of one squadron (300 men) of Companions,

---

[1] Possibly a corruption of the Sanskrit '*avarana*', a fort, enclosure, or refuge.
[2] See Chapter 8.
[3] Taxila is now represented by more than 12 square miles of ruins.
[4] Land of the five rivers: in English, Greek, and Sanskrit the names of the rivers are: Jhelum, Hydaspes, Vitasta; Chenab, Acesines, Asikni; Ravi, Hydraotes, Parushni; Beas, Hyphasis, Vipas; and Sutlej, Hesydrus, Sutudri. In Sanskrit the Indus is Sindhu, it gave its name to India.

with whom 700 eastern Iranian horsemen were brigaded; the remaining hipparchy was almost entirely Iranian.[1]

While engaged on preparations for the next move, news was received by Alexander that Porus was marshalling his army along the eastern bank of the Jhelum to oppose his advance, and was expecting Abisares' assistance. He sent back instructions to the Indus to have all ships already built cut into sections and transported by wagons to the Jhelum. He then garrisoned Taxila, made Philip, brother of Harpalus, satrap of Gandhara, and accompanied by Taxiles set out at the head of his army for the Hydaspes, which he reached early in June; exactly where, is unknown (Sir Aurel Stein suggests probably at Haranpar, seventeen and a half miles below Jalalpur).[2] There he found Porus, who held its eastern bank.

His problem was how to cross the river and bring Porus to battle, and its solution was urgent because the rainy season had already set in. By a series of feints he misled Porus about the selected place of crossing, and then he moved upstream one night with part of the army, crossed with difficulty to the eastern bank, brought Porus to battle and decisively defeated him.[3] As related in Chapter 3, he did not impose his will on him, but went into alliance with him, respected his kingdom and soon after enlarged it.

It is improbable that he adopted this course solely out of admiration for a valiant antagonist, because Alexander was a statesman as well as a knight errant. It may be assumed that he realized that the only way he could hold the Punjab with any certainty was to establish a balance of power between its leading potentates, and as he had already enlarged the domains of Taxiles, it was necessary to enlarge those of Porus as a counterpoise. His policy closely resembled that of the British in India in the eighteenth century – to divide and rule. It was no longer a question of satrapies but of local kingdoms, whose mutual rivalries and antagonisms would enable him to play off one against the other and remain master of both. Further, in order to strengthen his hold over the conquered country, immediately after the battle he founded two Alexandrias; 'one where the battle took place', named Nicaea, and the other at 'the spot whence he started to cross the river', Bucephala, named after his famous war-horse Bucephalus, who fell dead during the battle.[4]

---

[1] See Tarn, *Alexander the Great*, vol. I, pp. 92–3.
[2] See Sir Aurel Stein, *Geographical Journal*, vol. LXXX, 1932.
[3] See Chapter 6.
[4] Arrian V, xix, 4; also Strabo, XV, i, 29.

Though it was as much his alliance with Porus as his victory over him that had gained for Alexander the western Punjab, it was imperative that he should continue his advance eastward, not only that he might add to Porus' kingdom, but also to reach the eastern ocean which, apparently, he still believed to be close at hand; that alone could give him the secure eastern frontier he sought.

By this time, some of his hazy views on India must have become more consonant with geographical realities. At least it seems that he had learnt that the Indus was in no way related to the Nile; that it was an independent river which flowed into the southern ocean and that the Jhelum was one of its tributaries. This is supported by the fact that before he resumed his advance he left Craterus on the Jhelum, not only to superintend the building of Nicaea and Bucephala and supply his forward communications, but to build a fleet. Though no statement of his purpose has survived, it must have been so that after he had reached the eastern ocean, he could return to the Jhelum and sail down it to the southern sea. Nicaea and Bucephala were, then, also to be his base for this southern voyage of exploration.

The rested army set out for the river Acesines (Chenab) in pouring rain, for the summer monsoon was at its full. After considerable difficulty it crossed it; marched on to the Hydraotes (Ravi), and as it went dropped defended posts on its communications to facilitate Craterus' task of forwarding supplies. When it neared the Ravi, a column under Hephaestion was detached to subdue Porus' nephew, also named Porus, who had revolted. Hephaestion did this and the nephew's domains were added to his uncle's. In the meantime the army crossed the Ravi and entered the land of the Cathaeans, a warlike and kingless people who inhabited the region between the Ravi and Beas. To the south, between the Chenab and the Ravi, dwelt the Malli, and between Ravi and Sutlej the Oxydracae, kindred folk.[1] The chief city of the Cathaeans was Sangala (unidentified), where the army met with stubborn resistance and suffered heavy losses in its assault.[2] Its fall and destruction terrified the Malli and Oxydracae into submission, which was fortunate for Alexander, for his losses were so serious that he was short of troops[3] and was compelled to allow Porus to garrison the conquered territories. Alexander then set out for the Hyphasis (Beas) to subdue the peoples beyond it.

[1] At this date the Beas and Sutlej were probably independent rivers.
[2] See Chapter 8.
[3] Anyone who has spent a summer in the eastern Punjab will realize that his casualties due to climate must have been crippling.

On the Beas the army mutinied. It was now eight years since it had set out from Amphipolis; it had marched nearly 17,000 miles,[1] and since it had left the Jhelum the heat had been suffocating and the rain incessant.[2] Also it had picked up rumours – as soldiers always do – that the country beyond the Beas was thickly populated; that its men were 'of very great stature' who 'excelled in valour', and that its kings possessed innumerable elephants.[3] Rumours, magnified by terror of the unknown, hardships, exhaustion, rain, and heat broke down Macedonian morale – it is astonishing it had endured so long. 'Conferences', writes Arrian, 'were held throughout the camp, in which those who were the most moderate bewailed their lot, while others resolutely declared that they would not follow Alexander any farther, even if he should lead the way.'[4]

What was Alexander's reaction to the mutiny? His speech to his generals, attributed to him by Arrian,[5] has been discounted by Tarn as an after-day compilation; and words need not be wasted on whether Alexander had or had not heard of the existence of the Ganges. Wilcken affirms that he had, and therefore at length he was brought to realize that the eastern ocean must be far away;[6] Tarn affirms that he had not.[7] But Tarn's assertion that when on the Beas Alexander still thought 'that the eastern ocean was quite close',[8] is to be doubted, because Alexander was a highly inquisitive man, as is shown by the story of how when a boy he questioned the Persian ambassadors at his father's court on the roads and nature of their country.[9] Since he had crossed the Indus, the ocean, which he believed to be so near, and which Aristotle assumed could be seen from the Hindu-Kush, had, like a will-o'-the-wisp, eluded him. He must have questioned Indians about it many times through his interpreters, and though a few may have told him that it was far off, undoubtedly most of them did not even know what the word 'ocean' meant; it was 1,200 miles away from the Beas. His mind must, therefore, have been filled with doubts: was the ocean near, was it far away – did it in fact exist? And when Coenus, the spokesman for the army, replied to his speech and said: 'Do not lead us now against our will; for then thou wilt no longer find

---

[1] This is Colonel Dodge's estimate, see his *Alexander*, vol. II, appx. C.

[2] Strabo (XV, i, 27), following Aristobulus, writes: 'He was prevented from proceeding further, partly from regard to some oracles, and partly compelled by his army, which was exhausted by toil and fatigue, but whose principal distress arose from their constant exposure to rain.'

[3] Curtius (IX, ii, 2–3) mentions one king who possessed 3,000.

[4] Arrian, V, xxv, 6.   [5] Ibid., V, xxv–xxvi.   [6] *Alexander the Great*, p. 185.

[7] *Alexander the Great*, vol. II, appx. xiv, p. 280.

[8] Ibid., p. 284.   [9] Plutarch's *Life of Alexander*, V.

us the same men in regard to dangers, since free-will will be wanting to us in the contests'[1] – which rings true – Alexander retired to his tent to think things over for three days. Had he still firmly believed that the eastern ocean was to be found but a few marches ahead, it may be accepted with assurance that he would have refused to give way to his men, as he refused to do in the next great mutiny. With equal assurance then, it may be assumed that he decided, wherever the eastern ocean might be, the state of the army prohibited further successful advance. So he ordered sacrifices to be offered for the passage of the Beas, and when they proved to be unfavourable, he 'made known to the army that he had resolved to march back again'.[2]

His soldiers rejoiced wildly and said that, 'because of them alone he suffered himself to be conquered'.[3] This also rings true; for it was better to forego the problematical ocean than lose the army. His eastern frontier was never established – it was the one great failure in his career.

Then he ordered twelve towering altars to be built on the western bank of the Beas to mark the limits of his conquests; he sacrificed, held gymnastic contests, and after he had added the country as far as the Beas to the domains of Porus, led his army back to the Jhelum to prepare for its journey of 800 miles to the southern sea.

Linking the Empire by Sea

The reasons which induced Alexander to embark on his southern venture are not in doubt. One was that, as the lower Indus valley had at one time been ruled by the Great King and he was his successor, it was his right and duty to reconquer it. The other was, not only his determination to reach the ocean, cost what it might, but also to discover whether it was feasible to establish a sea route between the mouths of the Indus and Euphrates and so avoid the long and tedious land route he had followed. When he determined on this venture is not known, but since he first crossed the Indus and thought that he had discovered the source of the Nile because he found crocodiles on its banks, 'which he had seen in no other rivers except the Nile', he had learnt from the natives 'That the Hydaspes unites its water with the Acesines, as the latter does with the Indus, and that the last-named river has two mouths, through which it discharges itself into the Great Sea.'[4] In this there is nothing remarkable, for since time

---

[1] Arrian, V, xxvii. This speech, or at least the bulk of it, also is obviously a late interpolation.   [2] Ibid., V, xxviii, 4.   [3] Ibid., V, xxix, 1.   [4] Ibid., VI, i, 5.

immemorial the Indus and its tributaries had been main thorough-fares, and seagoing trade from the mouth of the Indus westward along the coast of Makran was carried on centuries before Alexander's day.[1]

On the Jhelum he found, according to Curtius, that during his absence Harpalus had sent out to him 5,000 horse and 7,000 foot as reinforcements, as well as sets of armour for 25,000 men;[2] that eighty 30-oar warships had been built or were under construction with horse-transports and supply ships, and that a vast number of native river craft had been collected. In all, it would appear that, when ready, the fleet numbered about 1,000 vessels.[3] The warships were manned, at least in part, by Phoenicians, Cyprians, Carians, and Egyptians and one can only suppose that a host of Indians were engaged or pressed into service to sail the native craft.

The order of march was as follows: while Alexander with the hypaspists, Agrianians, Cretan archers, and the *agema* of the Com-panions sailed down the Jhelum, the rest of the army was to march in three columns; one under Craterus on the right bank, a second under Hephaestion on the left bank, and a third under Philip, satrap of Gandhara, three days' march in the rear. Nearchus was given command of the fleet.

In November, 326 B.C., all was ready, and after sacrifices had been made to the gods and Alexander had poured a libation into the river from the prow of his ship, the great armada set out.[4] But the voyage was not to be peaceful. Before the advance had reached the confluence of the Chenab and Jhelum news was received that the Malli and Oxydracae were preparing to oppose it.

The army encamped below the confluence and a remarkable cam-paign followed in which surprise and celerity were again combined in a masterful way.[5] But this campaign, the last of importance fought by Alexander, ended in a near disaster. When several strongholds had been taken and the army stormed the chief Mallian town, Alexander saw his men falter, impetuously seized a ladder and planted it against the wall and mounted it crouched under his shield. He was followed immediately by Peucestas, his shield-bearer, who carried the sacred shield of Ilium, and by his body-guard Leonnatus, while a soldier

---

[1] Arabian voyages to north-west India, and Phoenician trading in the Persian Gulf, were known before 650 B.C. Also, 'there was an age-old coasting commerce between North-West India and the eastern coasts of Africa' (*The Ancient Explorers*, M. Cary and E. H. Warmington, 1926, pp. 59, 60).   [2] Curtius, IX, iii, 20.
[3] Curtius (IX, 13) says 1,000; Nearchus (*Indica*, XIX), 1,800, and Arrian (VI, ii, 4) 'short of 2,000'.
[4] Arrian (VI, iii) gives a vivid description of the start.   [5] See Chapter 8.

named Abreas mounted a second ladder. Then others rushed forward to emulate them, but under their weight the ladders collapsed, and Alexander was left on the wall to face the Malli. He leapt down into the citadel to avoid their missiles, and with his back to the wall kept his opponents at bay with his sword. Abreas fell, shot through the forehead with an arrow, while another arrow pierced Alexander's corselet and penetrated deep into his breast. Choked by a rush of blood he fell upon his shield, while Peucestas and Leonnatus, both of whom were wounded, protected him as best they could. When all seemed lost, the storming party scaled the wall and a desperate conflict over Alexander's body followed until some of the soldiers opened a gate, when the Macedonians rushed into the town. Infuriated by the fall of their king, they fell upon the inhabitants and spared neither woman nor child.

For several days Alexander lay near to death, but when rumours spread through the camp that he was dead he had himself carried on a litter to a ship and rowed along the river bank so that all his men might see that he was still alive.

After he had recovered from his wound, the fleet and army advanced down the Chenab to its confluence with the Indus. There Alexander ordered an Alexandria to be built; he extended Philip's satrapy to include all the country east of the Kunar river to the confluence of the Chenab and Indus, and allotted to him a body of Thracians. At the same time he appointed Peithon satrap of Lower India – that is, of the region extending southward of Philip's satrapy to the sea. Then the advance continued. At an unspecified place on the Indus Alexander learnt of disturbances in Arachosia and Drangiana and decided to send Craterus with three battalions of the phalanx, some archers, men unfit for further service, and the heavy baggage and elephants, probably by way of the Mulla Pass,[1] through those provinces to Carmania, where he was to await his own arrival. It may be assumed from this that he had also decided, when the fleet set out from the mouth of the Indus on its westward voyage, to march homeward by way of Gedrosia (Makran). In July, 325 B.C., after some minor forays, the great expedition reached Patala, at the apex of the Indus delta as it then was.

Alexander began to build a harbour and dockyard at Patala, as he intended to make it the eastern base of his sea communications between India and Persis; this shows, as Sir Thomas Holdich points out, that he was well aware of the way by sea to the coast of Persia.[2] He then sailed down each of the two main arms of the Indus to discover

[1] According to Holdich (*The Gates of India* (1910), p. 147) the Bolan-Quetta route did not come into use until recent times.   [2] Ibid., p. 155.

which of them was the easier to navigate, and decided on the eastern one; in 325 B.C. it probably flowed into the Rann of Cutch. Then he consulted with Nearchus about the command of the coastal expedition, and after several of his officers had been approached and had excused themselves from accepting the command, Nearchus proposed himself. At first Alexander demurred because of the hazards of the voyage, for Nearchus was one of his oldest and dearest friends, but in the end he gave way. This greatly encouraged the crews, because they felt that Alexander would never have appointed Nearchus unless he counted on success. The instructions given to Nearchus were to explore the coast, to discover what harbours, islands, and gulfs existed, whether there were any coastal towns, and whether the country was fertile or barren.[1]

How many ships took part in the expedition is unknown: Tarn suggests 100 or 150, with crews of from 3,000 to 5,000 men, as well as some archers, mercenaries, and catapults.[2] It would seem that not more than ten days' rations and five days' water could be carried in the ships[3] and frequent landings would have to be made; but this would be necessary in any case, because in classical times ships usually put into land for the night. In late September, 325 B.C., the fleet dropped down the eastern arm of the Indus to await the north-east monsoon, which was due to start at the end of October.[4]

Shortly before Nearchus left Patala, Alexander set out on his march through Gedrosia.[5] His object was not to outdo the exploits of Semiramis and Cyrus the Great, though their legends may have intrigued him, but to dig wells and establish food depots for the fleet along the coast and, in order to facilitate landings, to subdue the independent inhabitants of southern Gedrosia. He must have been well aware of the dangers ahead; but he had to face them if he wanted to help the fleet. He took with him four battalions of the phalanx, the hypaspists, the Agrianians, the archers, and all the Macedonians of the Companions as well as the horse-archers; the rest of the native troops he sent back to their homes.

From Patala he marched to the river Arabis (Hab), and from there turned southward to the coast to dig wells and subdue the independent Orietae. At their chief city, Ora (near Bela), he founded an Alexandria; appointed Apollophanes satrap, and left with him a strong force under Leonnatus. His instructions to Apollophanes were that he

[1] *Indica*, XXXII, 11.
[2] *Alexander the Great*, vol. I, p. 105, and *Indica*, XXIV, 8.
[3] *Indica*, XXIII, 8, and XL, 11.   [4] Ibid., XXI, 1.
[5] In 1893 Sir Percy Sykes travelled through Makran, and in his *A History of Persia* (p. 277) states how truthful is Arrian's description of Gedrosia.

should supply Nearchus and collect supplies of food to forward to the army. As there was no shore route, he was then compelled to strike inland along the track subsequently travelled in the days of Arab ascendancy, which connects Makran and Sind;[1] from this route, from time to time, he sent parties with supplies to the coast. The country through which he marched was devoid of water for long stretches, and the heat was so intense that he had to march by night. After nearly all the baggage had been lost – the transport animals either died or were eaten – the army again reached the coast at Pasni, and at Gwadur struck the road which led to the Persian royal residence at Pura (Fahraj). There the army rested after its terrible sixty-day march from Ora. According to Tarn, except for the non-combatants, most of whom perished, Alexander 'extricated the army without much loss'.[2]

While he was at Pura Alexander deposed Apollophanes because he had failed to carry out his instructions to forward supplies, and it was there that he learnt that Philip, satrap of Upper India, had been murdered in a mutiny. He did not replace him, but sent instructions to Taxiles to take over the administration of the satrapy. Then he marched to Gulashkird in Carmania, founded yet another Alexandria, and was joined by Craterus.

While Alexander toiled through Gedrosia, Nearchus coasted along the northern shore of the Arabian Sea. In his *Indica* he gives a detailed and truthful account of his voyage, which includes a considerable amount of geographical information; it must have pleased Alexander. Eighty days after it had begun its voyage his fleet entered the Strait of Ormuz and cast anchor in the mouth of the river Amanis (Minab). It had been a most successful voyage, and by no means costly, for Nearchus lost only four ships. It had been as remarkable a voyage as that of Columbus, not because of physical danger, but because of the enormous fears born of imagination with which Nearchus had had to contend in order to hold panic in leash.

Soon after the crews had landed, Nearchus learnt from a Greek wanderer that Alexander's camp was no more than a five-day journey from the sea. He left with Archais and five others and their meeting with the king is touchingly described in the *Indica*.[3] At first Alexander found it difficult to recognize Nearchus and his companions because of their long hair, tattered clothing and shrivelled bodies. He thought that the men who stood before him were the sole survivors of the expedition, and he asked Nearchus in what manner the ships and army had perished? But when Nearchus told him that both ships and army were safe, Alexander wept with joy and said that the grief he would have felt if they had perished would have obliterated the memory of all his other successes.

A great festival was held, at which thanksgiving sacrifices were offered to Zeus, Heracles, Apollo, Poseidon and other sea gods, and in the procession that followed Nearchus was pelted with flowers by the soldiers. He returned soon afterward to his fleet and sailed along the coasts of Carmania and Persis and up the Karun river to a boat-bridge near Susa, where he moored his ships. He had proved to the western world that the Indus could be linked with the Euphrates, and Patala with Susa.

Imperial Unification

Early in 324 B.C. Alexander set out for Pasargadae, and the farther west he went the more numerous were the reports on gross irregularities within the empire. He had been absent from its centre for five years, during which the belief that he would never return, reinforced by repeated rumours of his death in India, had loosened the cement of his authority. With lightning speed he proceeded against the miscreants: Baryaxes, a Mede, who had assumed the upright tiara, and his followers were put to death; Orxines, who had usurped the satrapy of Persis, was hanged; so was Ordanes for raising an insurrection in Carmania, and Abulites for misgoverning Susiana. Cleander and Sitalces, the two generals who had assassinated Parmenion, were put to death for their tyrannous and rapacious behaviour towards the people; the tomb of Cyrus, which had been rifled, was restored to its former state, and all private armies raised during Alexander's absence were disbanded. Alone among the malefactors, Harpalus, the imperial treasurer, escaped; he had spent vast sums on riotous living, had erected temples to his courtezan mistress, and on Alexander's approach had fled westward with 6,000 mercenaries and 5,000 talents to urge the Athenians to revolt. He was subsequently assassinated in Crete by one of his followers.

But more than punishment was demanded to reinstate Alexander's good name among the Persians, and the first step he took was to appoint Peucestas satrap of Persis and Susiana; the province of Persis was the cradle of the Persian nation. It was a popular choice, because Peucestas spoke Persian and had adopted Persian manners and dress.

Soon after, when Alexander reached Susa, the second step was taken. A great feast was held to celebrate his victorious return, during which symbolic of his policy of partnership between the races of his empire, a mass-marriage was celebrated. He and Hephaestion wedded Barsine and Drypetis, daughters of Darius; over eighty of his generals and companions were given as wives daughters of the noblest of the Persians and Medes, and 10,000 of his soldiers were married to their Asiatic concubines and received generous dowries.

Alexander also undertook to pay all debts incurred by his soldiers, and to find out how many debtors there were, he invited all who were in debt to enter their names and the amounts they owed in a register. Few did so, because the soldiers suspected that his hidden intention was to discover those who had lived extravagantly. But a deeper motive for their distrust and lightly disguised hostility would appear to have been that the governors of the newly-built cities were bringing to army headquarters the 30,000 native youths known as *Epigoni* ('Descendants' or 'Successors') who at some time previously Alexander had ordered to be recruited, disciplined, and armed in Macedonian fashion. Their arrival, writes Arrian, 'is said to have vexed the Macedonians, who thought that Alexander was contriving every means in his power to free himself from future need of their services', and 'was becoming altogether Asiatic in his ideas, and was holding the Macedonians themselves as well as their customs in contempt'.[1] Another cause of complaint was that the mass marriages had been celebrated in Persian fashion.

When Alexander was informed of his soldiers' reluctance to register their names he was deeply wounded and said that a king should not deal otherwise but sincerely with his subjects; nor should any of those ruled by him think that he would deal otherwise than sincerely with them. He cancelled registration and ordered that all debts of those who could show a bond were to be paid without the recipients giving their names in writing. Once again he bowed to the will of his men, but it was to be the last time.

Alexander turned to affairs in Greece where, during his absence, the high-handed policy of Antipater toward the democratic city-states had swamped the country with an ever-increasing number of homeless anti-Macedonian exiles. To stamp out factional discord was no easy task, because Alexander's relationship with the members of the League of Corinth was very different from his relationship with the Persians. Though, as the successor of the Great King, the whole of Asia was now within his jurisdiction, as hegemon of the League he

[1] Arrian, VII, vi, 2.

had no legal power to interfere in the internal affairs of its constituent members. But if his empire were to be united, it was as imperative for him to establish peace within and between the Greek cities as it was between Greeks and Persians. He saw that there could be no peace as long as *stasis* (factional discord) endured and hordes of exiles continued to roam from town to town or gather at the great market for mercenaries at Taenarum (Cape Matapan) to sell their services to the highest bidder. In spite of his legal disabilities he issued a decree, under which all states were ordered to receive back their exiles and their families, and in September, 324 B.C., it was read out at Olympia by Nicanor, adopted son of Aristotle, to the Greek delegates and some 20,000 exiles who had gathered there to attend the Olympic Games.[1] Though this decree violated the Covenant of the League, it was a statesmanlike act, generous because so many of the exiles belonged to the anti-Macedonian factions. Alexander restored his former enemies to their cities.

To overcome the legal difficulty, some scholars, among whom Tarn is numbered, hold that this decree was accompanied or preceded by a request for deification, because though the Covenant bound Alexander the king, it 'did not, and would not', as Tarn writes, 'bind Alexander the god, and he could therefore set it aside without losing his self-respect'.[2] Other scholars reject this hypothesis, mainly because they consider its sources to be too flimsy to justify it.[3] Should the hypothesis be accepted, it is as well to bear in mind that the request had nothing to do with Macedonia or Alexander's Asiatic empire, in both of which Alexander was already an autocrat; only in Egypt was he accepted as a god. Further, it is unlikely that it shocked the Greek conscience because, as Professor W. S. Ferguson points out, when the question of deification during the Hellenistic age is considered, it was an axiom of Greek political theory for men of genius to be held above the law.[4] What then was their position to be?

The answer [replies Ferguson] was suggested repeatedly by Aristotle. 'If', he argued in a famous passage of the *Politics*,[5] 'there exists in a state an individual so pre-eminent in virtue that neither the virtue nor political capacity of all the other citizens is comparable with his . . . , he should not be regarded as a member of the

---

[1] Diodorus, XVII, 109, 1.   [2] *Alexander the Great*, vol. II, appx. 22, iii, p. 370.
[3] See D. G. Hogarth, *English Historical Review*, II (1887), 322 sqq., and J. P. V. D. Balsdon, in *Historia*, I (1950), pp. 383–8.   [4] Plato, *Politics*, 294A, 296 sqq.
[5] III, 13, 1284a. Aristotle's outlook on the exceptional man is very similar to that of Confucius in his *Analytics* on the 'superior man'.

state at all. For he will be wronged if treated as an equal when he is thus unequal in virtue and political capacity. Such a man should be rated as a god among men.' [1]

Before Alexander crossed over into Asia, living men had been deified in Greece; for instance, 'Lysander by the Samian aristocrats, Dionysius and Dion by the Syracusan partisans, Philip by some of his subjects, and Plato by his scholars'.[2] Also:

> As it was in Greece (Egypt apart) that the deification of rulers originated, so it was there that it was perpetuated . . . What lay behind these repeated acts of deification [writes Ferguson] was doubtlessly the same motive which led the Samians and Alexander to the idea in the first instance – political convenience and political thought. The same political problem presented itself again and again: the need of finding a legal basis in a constitutional state for an extra-constitutional authority . . . . Since it was the fact that kings had to be obeyed, deification was a way, consonant with Hellenic feeling, of legalizing absolutism.[3]

Although these considerations do not prove that Alexander issued a request for deification, they show that if he did, there is no reason to suppose that the Greek cities looked upon it as other than reasonable.

Soon after the decree ordering the return of the exiles was published, and when the army was at Opis (the future Seluceia, near Ctesiphon), Alexander decided to send Craterus back to Macedonia with all veterans past further service. When this became known, and was coupled with his policy to unify the races of his empire, which demanded the effacement of all differences between victor and vanquished within the ranks of the army, Curtius states that the soldiers, who assumed that Alexander's intention was to establish the permanent seat of his government in Asia, 'filled the camp with mutinous talk'.[4] When Alexander assembled the army to hear his decision, this pent-up hostility flamed into open mutiny, in which all units, except the *agema* of the hypaspists, were involved. At first it seems that the men listened to him in sullen silence, but when he had spoken they lost control over themselves and shouted in reply that they would all go home together,

---

[1] *The Cambridge Ancient History*, vol. VII, p. 13.   [2] Ibid., p. 13.
[3] Ibid., pp. 15–16.
[4] Curtius, X, ii, 12. This fear was well founded, because for political and strategical reasons no Greek city could possibly have been chosen by Alexander as the capital of his empire. The same fear was unleashed before the battle of Actium (31 B.C.), when the people of Rome believed that were Antony victorious, he would transfer the seat of government from Rome to Alexandria. (See *Dio's Roman History*, L.4.)

and for all they cared he might take the field in company with his father Ammon.

The mention of Ammon, which touched upon the most sacred spiritual experience in Alexander's life, so roused his fury that he leapt down from the platform from which he spoke; pointed out the thirteen ringleaders to the hypaspists, had them arrested and led off to execution.[1] Then he returned to the platform to pour words of burning reproach upon his ungrateful men.[2] He reminded them of what his father had done for them, how he had found them poor herdsmen dressed in skins, and had made them the rulers of Greece; how he himself had raised them to the lordship of Asia. He spoke of their many labours, their victories, and their wounds, and that no one under his leadership had ever been killed in flight. At length, overmastered by his passionate words and beside himself with fury, he cried: 'And now, as you all want to go, go, every one of you, and tell them at home that you deserted your king who had led you from victory to victory across the world, and left him to the care of the strangers he had conquered; and no doubt your words will win you the praises of men and the blessing of heaven. Go!'[3]

If any single incident in Alexander's life is worthy to acclaim him a demi-god, surely it is this mutiny, in which by the overpowering forcefulness of his personality and demonic rage, he imposed his will on his turbulent men without making a single concession.

When he had spoken, Alexander leapt down from the platform, withdrew to his palace, and refused to see anyone for two days. On the third day he summoned to him the leading Persians and began to organize out of the 30,000 *Epigoni*[4] a Persian army on Macedonian lines. This broke the mutineers' resistance; they crowded together in front of the palace gates, cast down their weapons in token of supplication, and beseeched that they be allowed to enter and surrender their ringleaders. When Alexander was informed of this, with tears in his

[1] Oliver Cromwell acted in a similar manner. When faced by Lilburne's mutinous regiment, he suddenly wheeled round his horse, and with drawn sword charged headlong into its ranks, scattered the mutineers, and forced them to shoot their ringleader.

[2] This speech has been minutely analysed by Tarn (*Alexander the Great*, vol. II, appx. 15). The parts written by Ptolemy, or compiled from his notes, he holds to be genuine, and much of the rest the additions of subsequent editors.

[3] This is Tarn's translation of the final section of the speech, after interpolations have been deleted (ibid., p. 295).

[4] These now highly trained but as yet unregimented men were at that moment Alexander's ace of trumps; for without them he would have been at the mercy of the mutineers.

eyes, he left the palace and went to the main gate, and there an old soldier, Callines, a captain of the Companions, said: 'O King, what grieves the Macedonians is, that thou hast already made some of the Persians kinsmen to thyself, and that Persians are called Alexander's kinsmen, and have the honour of saluting thee with a kiss; whereas none of the Macedonians have as yet enjoyed this honour.' Alexander interrupted him: 'But all of you without exception I consider my kinsmen, and so from this time shall call you.'[1] Callines and others saluted him with a kiss and the men took up their weapons to return to the camp shouting and singing songs of thanksgiving.

After this reconciliation Alexander sacrificed to the gods, and ordered a vast feast to be prepared, to which, according to tradition, 9,000 guests were invited. The Macedonians sat around their king, and next to them the Persians, after whom came representatives of the other nations of the empire. When the feast ended, all drew wine for the libation from 'a huge silver crater which had once belonged to Darius',[2] and the whole 9,000 made libation[3] led by the Greek seers and Persian magi. It was followed by a prayer for peace by Alexander, a brief summary of which is given by Arrian, who writes: 'He prayed for other [the usual] blessings, and especially that harmony and community of rule might exist between the Macedonians and Persians.'[4] Or, as Sir William Tarn translates it: 'prayed for the other good things and for Homonoia between, and partnership in rule between, Macedonians and Persians'. 'Or', he writes, 'we can read it: Alexander "prayed for the other good things, and for Homonoia, and the partnership in the realm between Macedonians and Persians".' This he holds is the correct reading, because 'He *could* not have prayed for a joint rule of Macedonians and Persians; it had no meaning. His two realms, Macedonia and "Asia", were not two Empires but one, united in his own person as equally ruler by both. . . . .'[5]

This supreme moment in Alexander's life was followed by the cheerful departure of the 10,000 discharged veterans under Craterus who, on his return to Macedonia, was to replace Antipater as deputy hegemon and instruct him to join Alexander with Macedonian reinforcements.

As these old soldiers set out homeward toward what Fate was to

---

[1] Arrian, VII, xi, 7.

[2] Tarn, *Alexander the Great*, vol. I, p. 116. All at the king's table drew wine from this crater, and those at the other tables from craters notionally part of it (ibid., vol. II, appx. 25, vi, p. 442).

[3] The libation was not drunk, but poured out as an act of worship.

[4] Arrian, VII, xi, 9.   [5] *Alexander the Great*, vol. II, appx. 25, vi, pp. 443–4.

decide to be no happy future, the twilight of Alexander's reign set in with the sudden death of Hephaestion from a malignant fever. It was a cruel blow; Alexander and Haphaestion were of the same age, and since childhood had been the closest of companions and the dearest of friends. Although it was mid-winter, Alexander set out to distract his sorrow on a successful campaign against the Cossaeans, who inhabited the mountainous region between Susa and Ecbatana, and in the spring of 323 B.C. he was back in Babylon, where envoys from Libya, Bruttium, Lucania, and Etruria came to congratulate him on his conquests.

He turned to two projects that had for long intrigued him;[1] the exploration of the Caspian, and the Persian Gulf and Arabian Sea. He sent Heracleides and a company of shipwrights into Hyrcania to cut timber for ships with which to ascertain whether in fact the Caspian Sea was a lake or a gulf of the ocean. For the second expedition, which he intended to lead in person, he ordered a great harbour to be excavated near Babylon, large enough to afford anchorage for 1,000 warships, and adjoining it dockyards to be built. Also he sent 500 talents to Phoenicia for the hire of seamen and colonists. He intended to settle the colonists on the shores of the Persian Gulf. Further, he intended to circumnavigate Arabia, and reconnaissances were sent out to report on the Arabian coast. While the ships were built, Alexander sailed down the Euphrates to the Pallacopas canal, which carried off the flood waters of the river; he rectified the irrigation system and founded a fortified city for Greek mercenaries.

When he returned to Babylon he found awaiting him 20,000 trained Persian soldiers under Peucestas, satrap of Persis and Susiana, as well as reinforcements of Cossaeans, Tapurians, Carians, and Lydians, and a body of Macedonian cavalry. With contingents of these men he decided to remodel the Macedonian phalanx. Each decade, or file, which hitherto had consisted of sixteen Macedonian spearmen, was to be replaced by one of four Macedonians and twelve Persians in order from front to rear – a Macedonian file-leader followed by two Macedonians, then twelve Persians, and a Macedonian file-closer. As before, the Macedonians were to be armed with the sarissa, but the Persians were to carry either a bow or javelins.[2]

---

[1] The plans attributed to Alexander by Diodorus (XVIII, 4, 2–5), which include the conquest of Carthage and the Mediterranean basin, as well as the construction of a coastal road from Alexandria to the Pillars of Hercules, are discounted by Tarn as late forgeries (see *Alexander the Great*, vol. II, appx. 24).

[2] Asclepiodotus, a first century B.C. writer, makes mention of this type of phalanx in his *Outline of Tactics*, II, 1 (Loeb edit. 1933). If this reform has been correctly

Though this mixed phalanx was never formed, its projection is interesting because it points to the realization by Alexander that with his conquests at an end, his problem had become how to maintain law and order in his empire. The army of occupation he would require must be more flexible than his old army, hence the mixture of light and heavy troops. Another characteristic was that it combined missile power and shock.

On June 2, 323 B.C., a few days before he intended to set out on his Arabian expedition, Alexander fell sick with fever – probably malaria – and by June 7 was so critically ill that he could no longer give orders to his generals. On the 10th he was speechless. As rumours of his death were being bruited about, on the 12th his soldiers were admitted to his chamber and filed past his bed. With difficulty he moved his head or hand slightly toward those he recognized. At sunset on June 13 he closed his eyes for ever; he was not quite thirty-three years of age, and he had reigned for twelve years and eight months. He left no testament and no appointed successor, and even had he done so, no one of his companions with success could have taken his place; for by universal consent it was recognized that the genius of the king surpassed human measure.[1]

reported, it would seem probable that Alexander's intention was not to combine shock and missile troops in one formation, but rather to brigade them, so that he could base his offensive or defensive tactics on whichever type circumstances demanded.

[1] See Polybius, XII, 23 and Arrian, VII, xxx, 2.

Part II

✿✿✿✿

THE ANALYSIS

6

ALEXANDER'S GREAT BATTLES

The Battle of the Granicus

Before Alexander crossed the Dardanelles, when the Persian satraps set aside Memnon's plan and decided to protect their provinces by opposing Alexander should he attempt to invade them, they assembled their forces at Zelea. According to Arrian, they numbered 20,000 Persian cavalry and nearly as many Greek mercenaries;[1] of local levies he makes no allusion, but there must have been a considerable force of them. These figures are certainly exaggerated. Though there may have been 20,000 Greek mercenaries in Asia Minor, many were sailors, and we are told by Diodorus that soon after Alexander's accession Darius ordered Memnon with 5,000 mercenaries to occupy Cyzicus on the Sea of Marmara.[2] It may be conjectured from this that 5,000 is much nearer the actual strength of the mercenaries at the battle of the Granicus than Arrian's 20,000. It would seem equally improbable that the Persian cavalry numbered anything like 20,000; 10,000 would appear more reasonable.

Whatever the numerical effective strength of the Persian army may have been, it is clear that it was inferior to Alexander's. A strong defensive position, which Alexander would be compelled to attack and from which he could be repelled, had to be sought to make good numerical inferiority. Such a position was to be found on the lower Granicus, which when occupied would draw Alexander away from Sardes; for if he advanced on Sardes before he had defeated the Persian army he would risk the loss of his communications with the Hellespont. The strategical initiative, then, was with the Persians.

The Granicus is a mountain stream that descends from Mount Ida

---

[1] Arrian, I, xiv, 4. Diodorus says 10,000 horse and 100,000 foot.
[2] Diodorus, XVII, 7, 3.

and flows into the Sea of Marmara; the southern flank of its lower reach was safeguarded against a turning movement from its western side by a lake, now called the Edje Göl, and north of this lake the eastern bank of the river rose steeply above the western bank. Elsewhere the country was flat, and as it was the month of May the river was swollen, although still fordable in many places.

The choice of this position was admirable; but the way the Persian satraps set about holding it was as defective as could be. They did not deploy the Greek mercenaries along the eastern bank, with the Persian cavalry on their flanks, and also in their rear to counter-attack any force that might break through the infantry, but as Wilcken says: 'By a glaring error of tactics, they placed their excellent cavalry in front on the steep bank, where they were unable to charge', with the mercenaries in rear.[1] Tarn disagrees. He writes:

> The Persian leaders had in fact a very gallant plan; they meant if possible to strangle the war at birth by killing Alexander. They massed their cavalry on the steep bank of the lower Granicus, put the Greeks behind them, and waited. It has often been explained since that this was not the way to hold a river-bank; but that was not their intention.[2]

There can be no doubt whatever that they hoped to kill Alexander, because to kill the opposing general-in-chief was a set aim in nearly every classical battle, and not a few modern ones.[3] But as the Persian cavalrymen were armed with javelins and not with lance or spear, they were not true shock troops and incapable of meeting shock troops on equal terms. Arrian does not tell us how many javelins the Persian horseman carried; but to be effective his javelin must have been of moderate weight, not merely a light dart, so it is probable that like the Roman *hastati*, he carried two.[4] For cavalry other than mounted infantry, the javelin must have been an indifferent weapon as was the pistol in a later age, and to hurl it with accuracy from a moving horse must frequently have been impossible. Further, if only two javelins were

---

[1] *Alexander the Great*, p. 84.   [2] *Alexander the Great*, vol. I, p. 16.
[3] As late as the Second World War a British Commando was sent out to kill General Rommel.
[4] Polybius, VI, 22. Polybius says that there were two types of Roman javelins (*pila*), a thick and a fine, and that the latter was like a moderate sized hunting spear, about three cubits long (4 ft. 6 in.). The effective range of the *pilum*, without thong, has been estimated at 30 to 40 paces. Xenophon in his *The Cavalry Leader* (XII, 12) says that he prefers two short spears to one long one. In his *Cyropaedia* (VIII, 8, 20) he champions the short spear adopted by Cyrus.

carried, the missile power of the Persian cavalry must have been rapidly exhausted; for there is no record that the Persian cavalry were accompanied by pack animals carrying loads of missiles as were Surena's horse-archers at Carrhae (53 B.C.).

If the sole aim of the Persians was to kill Alexander, then the best way to do so was to meet his cavalry charge with a hedge of spears; let him shatter himself against it, and then, should he break through, overwhelm him with javelins. Some other reason for this peculiar distribution must be looked for, and one is not far to seek. Throughout history the cavalry soldier has despised the infantryman, and to have placed the Greek mercenaries in the forefront of the battle would have been to surrender to them the place of honour. Military etiquette forbade it; pride of rank is sufficient to explain this particular tactical folly, as it also explains the conduct of the Gothic horsemen at Taganae (A.D. 552), of the French chivalry at Crécy, and the arrogance of the mounted warrior in scores of battles up to the First World War.

From Lampsacus Alexander advanced eastward preceded by an advanced guard of lancers and light-armed troops, and when near the Persian army, because Parmenion did not think it feasible to cross the swollen Granicus in face of Persian opposition, he suggested to Alexander that the camp should be pitched on the western side of the river to give the enemy, whom he believed to be thoroughly scared, the opportunity to decamp during the night. This shows how little he understood his young master; for it must have been the one thing Alexander wanted to prevent. Not only was he eager to open his war against Persia with a resounding victory, but what above all things he must have wished to avoid was a stern chase over most of Asia Minor. His reply to Parmenion was: that the Hellespont, which he had crossed so easily, would blush for shame should he be afraid of so paltry a stream as the Granicus, and that to refrain from attacking his enemy would only rouse his courage; because so far the Persians had suffered no defeat there was no warrant for the fear of him Parmenion attributed to them.

Then he drew up his army in order of battle, and though Arrian's detail of it is somewhat confused, the order generally accepted, sometimes with slight variations, was as follows:

The phalanx was marshalled in the centre, with its six battalions in order from right to left: Perdiccas; Coenus; Amyntas, son of Andromenes; Philip, son of Amyntas; Meleager; Craterus.

On the right of the phalanx stood the hypaspists, under Nicanor, son of Parmenion; next to them a combined force made up of the lancers,

the Paeonian light horse and the squadron of Socrates,[1] the last under
Ptolemy, son of Philip, and all three under the command of Amyntas,
son of Arrhabaeus; next to this force came the Companion cavalry,
under Philotas, son of Parmenion; and lastly, on their right, the Cretan
archers under Clearchus and the Agrianian javelin-men under Attalus.

Alexander the Great: detail from a bronze statute in the National Museum, Naples. *The Bettmann Archive*

On the left of the phalanx stood the Thracian cavalry, under
Agathon; then the allied Greek cavalry, under Philip, son of Menelaus;
and lastly the Thessalian cavalry, under Calas.

The right wing of the army, which consisted of the three right
battalions of the phalanx and all on their right, was commanded by
Alexander, and the three left battalions and all on their left constituted
the left wing, under Parmenion.

The Persian order of battle, as given by Grote,[2] was as follows: the
Median and Bactrian cavalry on the right, under Rheomithres; the

---

[1] This was the Apolloniate squadron of the Companion cavalry, whose turn it
was on this day to take the lead.   [2] *History of Greece*, vol. X, p. 31.

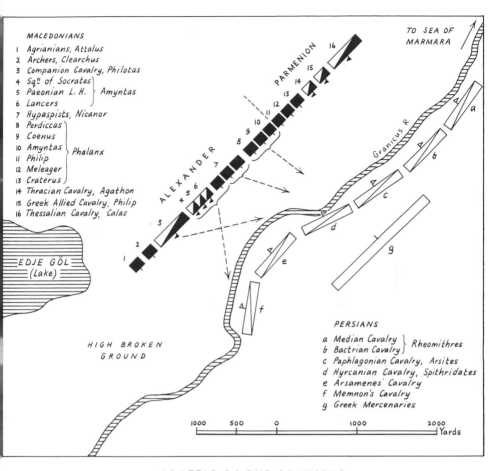

MACEDONIANS

1 Agrianians, Attalus
2 Archers, Clearchus
3 Companion Cavalry, Philotas
4 Sqⁿ of Socrates ⎫
5 Paeonian L.H.   ⎬ Amyntas
6 Lancers   ⎭
7 Hypaspists, Nicanor
8 Perdiccas ⎫
9 Coenus   ⎪
10 Amyntas   ⎬ Phalanx
11 Philip   ⎪
12 Meleager   ⎪
13 Craterus   ⎭
14 Thracian Cavalry, Agathon
15 Greek Allied Cavalry, Philip
16 Thessalian Cavalry, Calas

PARMENION

ALEXANDER

Granicus R.

TO SEA OF
MARMARA

EDJE GÖL
(Lake)

HIGH BROKEN
GROUND

PERSIANS

a Median Cavalry ⎫
b Bactrian Cavalry ⎬ Rheomithres
c Paphlagonian Cavalry, Arsites
d Hyrcanian Cavalry, Spithridates
e Arsamenes' Cavalry
f Memnon's Cavalry
g Greek Mercenaries

1000   500   0   1000   2000
                                 Yards

6 BATTLE OF THE GRANICUS

Paphlagonian and Hyrcanian cavalry, under Arsites and Spithridates, in the centre; and on the left the cavalry divisions of Memnon and Arsamenes. There is no definite list, but from the casualties among the Persian leaders, it will be seen that there were several other commanders. The Greek mercenaries were deployed in rear of the cavalry.

For a time silence prevailed; but when from the brightness of his armour and his personal following the Persian leaders recognized Alexander and watched him marshalling his Companion cavalry on his right wing, they concluded that his intention was to attack their left wing, which they reinforced. Though they could see every movement Alexander made, they could not penetrate his plan. It was to launch his main attack not against their left, as they suspected, but against the left centre of their front.

To effect this, Alexander instructed Amyntas, son of Arrhabaeus, to strengthen his combined force with a battalion of hypaspists; then to open the battle by advancing diagonally to the right across the front of the Companion cavalry to attack the extreme left of the Persian line. The object of this attack is clear; it was to induce the Persians to draw off cavalry from their centre to their left, and thereby weaken their centre, against the left of which Alexander intended to lead the Companion cavalry, supported on their left by two battalions of hypaspists and the three right battalions of the phalanx. Although there is no record, it is probable that Parmenion was instructed to carry out a somewhat similar operation with his left wing.

Amyntas moved forward at the appointed time, to be met when he reached the river by showers of javelins. A cavalry engagement followed which is thus described by Arrian:

> Then ensued a violent struggle on the part of the cavalry, on the one side to emerge from the river, and on the other to prevent the landing. From the Persians there was a terrible discharge of javelins; but the Macedonians fought with spears. The Macedonians, being far inferior in number, suffered severely at the first onset, because they were obliged to defend themselves from the river, where their footing was unsteady, and where they were below the level of their assailants; whereas the Persians were fighting from the top of the bank, which gave them an advantage, especially as the best of the Persian horse had been posted there. Memnon himself, as well as his sons, were running every risk with these; and the Macedonians who first came into conflict with the Persians, though they showed great

valour, were cut down by them, except those who retreated to Alexander, who was now approaching.[1]

Once Amyntas had engaged his enemy and had drawn the attention of the Persians toward their left flank, Alexander, heralded by a blare of trumpets, followed by shouts of '*Enyalius*',[2] led the Companion cavalry forward, wheeled them half-left, and in column of squadrons advanced obliquely toward the Persian left-centre. He rushed the river at the head of the Royal Squadron, scrambled through it and fought his way up its eastern bank. When the Persian leaders recognized him by the white plumes on his helmet, they rode to engage him in hand-to-hand fight. The impetuous assault of the Royal Squadron eased the way for the troops on its flanks; for we are told that while the struggle raged round Alexander, 'one rank of the Macedonians after another easily kept on crossing the river'. At this juncture Arrian describes the fighting as follows:

> It was a cavalry struggle, though on infantry lines; horse pressed against horse, man against man, wrestling one with another, Macedonians trying to push, once for all, the Persians from the bank and force them on to the level ground, the Persians trying to bar their landing and hurl them back into the river. Already, however, Alexander and his guards were getting the best of it, not only through their forcefulness and their discipline, but because they were fighting with stout cornel-wood lances against short javelins.[3]

To appreciate correctly the tactics both of the battle and of the period, it should be borne in mind that war was still in its heroic phase; much of the decisive fighting took the form of duels between heroes.[4] Leadership was personal and not delegated: a general-in-chief led his army into battle and did not direct it from the rear; not only was he the moral dynamo of his army, but also its brain – its general staff. That was why it was all-important to kill him, for once he was slain, panic more often than not seized upon his men and his army disintegrated. To engage him and slay him in single combat not only glorified the victor but was in itself a decisive victory; that is why the somewhat common assumption that when a classical historian depicts a duel between opposing protagonists, he does so to gain dramatic effect, or to

---

[1] Arrian, I, xv, 2–4.   [2] The Homeric name of the Greek war-god.

[3] Arrian, I, xv, 4–5.

[4] As late as the Thirty Years War, hand-to-hand encounters between generals-in-chief were still frequent, such as the battle duel between Archduke Leopold and Piccolomini at the second battle of Breitenfeld, in November, 1642.

champion a favourite general, should generally be discounted, for he is usually depicting *the* decisive incident in the battle.

Though it is to be regretted that Arrian does not say much about the details of this battle, his brief description of the Homeric struggle around Alexander was its central incident. He writes that when Alexander was in personal conflict, his spear was shivered and he turned to one of his body-guard for another. But as this man's spear was also broken, Demaratus the Corinthian – the man who had settled the quarrel between Alexander and his father – spurred up to him and gave him his own. No sooner had Alexander seized it than Mithridates, son-in-law of Darius, who was riding ahead of his squadron, rode up. When Alexander saw him he charged him, thrust him in the face with his spear, and rolled him to the ground. As he did so, Rhoesaces, another Persian leader, smote him on the head with his battle-axe and sheared off part of the helmet and with it one of its two white plumes. Alexander wheeled round, hurled him to the ground and with his spear pierced through the cuirass into his breast. Spithridates, who was in rear of Alexander, raised his axe to cut him down, but Cleitus the Black severed his sword-arm and saved Alexander's life. The sudden loss of these three Persian leaders, and possibly others not mentioned by Arrian, decapitated their respective divisions and was the decisive moment in the battle.

While this Homeric contest was waged, squadron after squadron of the Companions succeeded in crossing the Granicus, as also did the hypaspists and the three right battalions of the phalanx,[1] against whose sarissas the confused masses of leaderless Persian horsemen could put up but slight resistance. Then the whole Persian centre caved in. It can only be conjectured that the three left battalions of Parmenion's wing crossed or were crossing at about the same time; we are told by Diodorus that the Thessalian cavalry on Parmenion's left showed undaunted courage, and 'next to the king, they were most highly applauded and gained exceeding honour and reputation'.[2]

When the centre of the Persian army gave way, its wings took to flight; but the fleeing horsemen were spared pursuit because the Greek mercenaries still stood in Alexander's path. Although flight could not have saved them, that they resisted the general panic shows discipline of a high order. According to Plutarch, they asked for quarter, which meant that they were willing to enter Alexander's service. But he is said to have ignored their request, and should this be true, then his most likely reason was that he decided to make an example of them in order

---

[1] See Plutarch's 'Alexander', XVI.   [2] Diodorus, XVII, 21, 4.

to deter other Greeks from offering their services to Persia: in his eyes they were traitors. He ordered up the hypaspists and the phalanx to assault them in front, while the cavalry attacked them in flank and rear, and after many had been cut down, 2,000 surrendered unconditionally.

According to Arrian, the Macedonian losses were twenty-five Companions, sixty other cavalry, and thirty infantry killed, which is probably an underestimate. But when the unknown number of Greek mercenary casualties is omitted, the 1,000 Persian cavalrymen he records as killed is also a low figure, because in Alexander's battles practically all enemy losses are grossly exaggerated for propaganda purposes. The main Persian losses were not in men, but in leaders, who fought with extreme bravery. Among those known to have fallen were: Rhoesaces, Niphates and Petines, presumably cavalry commanders; Spithridates, satrap of Lydia; Mithrobazarnes, satrap of Cappadocia; Mithridates, son-in-law of Darius; Arbupales, grandson of Artaxerxes; Pharnaces, brother-in-law of Darius; Omares, commander of the mercenaries; and although Arsites, satrap of Hellespontine-Phrygia, did not die on the field, he committed suicide soon after the battle because he was deemed to have been the cause of the Persian defeat. This loss of Persian leaders was not the least of the events that opened western Asia Minor to Alexander's subsequent advance.

The Battle of Issus

Late in October, or early in November, 333 B.C., Darius entered Issus on the evening of the day on which Alexander had set out from it in the early morning on his forced march to Myriandrus. If Darius had arrived at Issus twenty-four hours earlier he would have interposed his army between those of Alexander and Parmenion, and his position would then closely have resembled that of Napoleon immediately before the battles of Ligny and Quatre-Bras in 1815.

When he learnt that Alexander had passed through Issus earlier in the day, on the following morning he marched southward to catch up with him; but after he had advanced no more than eight miles he halted his army on the river Pinarus (Deli), a small mountain stream which descended from the Amanus mountains and flowed in a south-westerly direction into the Gulf of Alexandretta. According to Callisthenes, who was present as an onlooker at the battle: 'The width of the ground from the foot of the mountain to the sea was not more than fourteen stades (a little over one and a half miles) through which the

A statue of Alexander the Great by Pierre Puget (1622–1694), in the Louvre, Paris.
The Bettmann Archive

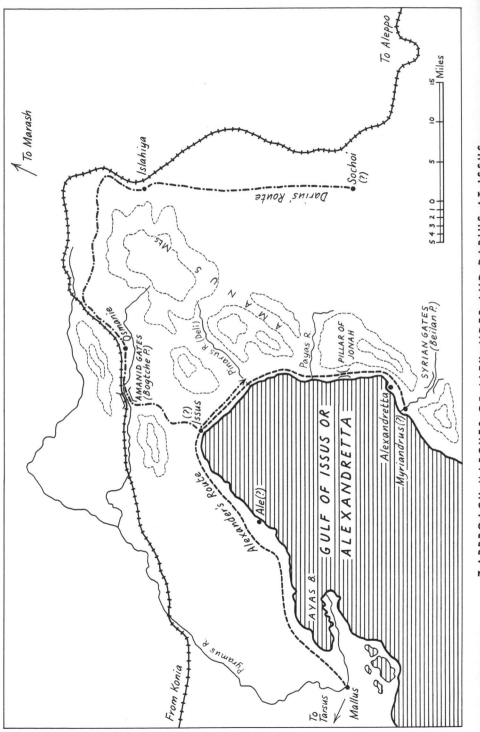

7 APPROACH MARCHES OF ALEXANDER AND DARIUS AT ISSUS

Labels on map:

To Aleppo

To Marash

Islahiya

Sochoi (?)

Darius' Route

AMANUS Mts

Osmanie

AMANID GATES (Bogtche P.)

Pinarus R. (Deli)

AMANUS

Payas R.

PILLAR OF JONAH

Issus (?)

Alexander's Route

SYRIAN GATES (Belan P.)

Alexandretta

Ale (?)

GULF OF ISSUS OR ALEXANDRETTA

Myriandrus (?)

AYAS B.

From Konia

Pyramus R.

To Tarsus

Mallus

Miles

5 4 3 2 1 0   5   10   15

river ran diagonally.' [1] In places its banks were steep and broken, but near its mouth, so it would appear from the battle, they offered no obstruction, and throughout its course it was easily fordable either on horseback or on foot.

The strength of the Persian army encamped along the northern bank of this small river can only be conjectured, because of the fantastic figures quoted by the classical historians. Arrian states that the gross strength was 600,000 men, of whom 30,000 were Greek

A mosaic of Alexander and Craterus fighting a lion, discovered during excavations at the site of Pella, the ancient capital of Macedonia and Alexander's birthplace. *Keystone*

mercenaries and 60,000 Cardaces, who he classes as hoplites.[2] Diodorus and Justin quote totals of 400,000 foot and 100,000 horse; Callisthenes, cited by Polybius, mentions 30,000 cavalry and 30,000 Greek mercenaries, and Curtius also says that there were 30,000 Greeks. Whatever the total strength may have been, the Greek mercenaries probably numbered over 10,000 men, because it is stated that after the battle 8,000 under Amyntas got away, and 2,000 rejoined Darius. The Persian cavalry was still armed with the javelin and,

[1] Cited by Polybius, XII, 17.

[2] According to Strabo (XV, iii, 18–19) the Cardaces were young Persians trained to use bows and javelins, who were also employed on planting trees, making armour, and on other useful work; they would appear to have been a kind of Hitler Youth. From the age of twenty they served in subordinate positions in the army, and could fight either on foot or mounted. All but certainly they were not hoplites, but, as Callisthenes says, 'peltasts' (Polybius, XII, 17). Had they been hoplites, it is highly improbable that Alexander would have charged them with his cavalry.

according to Curtius, both horse and horsemen were protected by linked armour which, like the byrnie (mail shirt) of the Carolingian army, covered the rider to the knees.

Before the events which followed the arrival of the Persians on the Pinarus are described, it is useful to bear in mind certain road distances; but as the sites of Issus and Myriandrus are still unidentified, they can be no more than approximate. Granted that Issus was three miles to the east of the northern extremity of the Gulf of Alexandretta, and Myriandrus at the mouth of the torrent which flows out of the Syrian Gates and enters the gulf three miles south of Alexandretta, then they are as follows: Mallus to Issus – thirty-eight to forty miles; Issus to the Pinarus – eight to nine miles; the Pinarus to the Jonah Pass – twelve to thirteen miles; and the Jonah Pass to Myriandrus – nine to ten miles. Therefore, when Alexander reached Myriandrus, his army had marched from between sixty-seven and seventy-two miles in forty-eight hours,[1] and it must have been exceedingly tired. Added to this, because of heavy rain, Alexander – fortunately for himself – decided to camp near the city and rest his weary men.

While the Macedonians rested Alexander received the startlingly unexpected news that the Persian army, which he thought to be at Sochoi, was in his rear. What effect this had on him is not recorded, but it may be assumed with some certainty that it caused widespread consternation among his exhausted and rain-sodden men; there is nothing soldiers dread more than to feel that their line of retreat has been blocked.

When Alexander had verified that the Persian army was encamped on the Pinarus, which cannot have been until some time in the afternoon, he made up his mind to precipitate his army on his enemy with such speed that Darius would be surprised in his turn. He sent out a small force to reconnoitre the road in his rear and then, after he had ordered his men to eat their dinners, he marched them to the Jonah Pass, which they occupied at midnight, and ordered his men to bivouac under cover of outposts.

In an interesting article, entitled *La Bataille d'Issus*,[2] based on an immense unpublished study of 679 folio pages by Commandant Bourgeois, M. Marcel Dieulafoy sets out to prove that the battle of

---

[1] In Napoleon's 1797 campaign in Italy, Masséna's corps set out from Verona at 7 p.m. on January 13; marched twenty-eight miles in ten hours; arrived on the battlefield of Rivoli on the morning of the 14th; fought until the evening; then set out on a forty-four mile march to Mantua, and arrived under its walls on the evening of the 15th: a total of seventy-two miles in forty-eight hours, including a battle.

[2] In *Mémoires de l'Institut National de France*, vol. xxxix (1914), pp. 41–76.

Issus was not fought on the Pinarus, but on the river Payas, which flows into the Gulf of Alexandretta some eight miles to the south of it. His theory is based on carefully worked out space and time calculations by which he proves that it would have been impossible for Alexander to have reached the Pinarus from the Jonah Pass in time to fight the battle in daylight; therefore the Pinarus must have been the Payas and not the Deli. His arguments are vitiated by the assumptions that three hours must be allotted for the battle and one for the pursuit. These are unwarranted, because, as will be seen, it is highly unlikely that the battle lasted for more than one hour, and because of nightfall the pursuit was of the briefest.

Arrian writes that 'at the approach of dawn', which would be at about 5.30 in early November,[1] Alexander set out from the Jonah Pass in column of route, the infantry ahead with the cavalry in rear. The distance he had to march to the Pinarus was twelve miles; this would take four and a half hours. But as a series of deployments had to be made *en route* to enable the rear units to come up on the flanks of the leading troops, it is advisable to double the time and make it nine hours; also an additional hour – better, an hour and a half – should be added for a rest before battle, a minor preliminary engagement, and the final arrangements. So if Alexander set out, as assumed, at 5.30 a.m., the probability is that the battle opened at 4 p.m. or a little later, approximately an hour before sunset. Let us now see what happened.

When, three miles north of the pass, the track led into the coastal plain between the mountains and the sea, Alexander began to deploy his infantry from column of route into line of battle. First he moved forward the hypaspists under Nicanor – probably his leading troops – toward the mountains on his right, and next, on their left, the battalions of Coenus and Perdiccas; these formed the infantry of the right wing, under his personal command. On the left of this wing and toward the sea he posted the battalions of Craterus, Meleager, Ptolemy, and Amyntas, all under Craterus, and appointed Parmenion in command of the left wing. He instructed him to keep its left close to the sea, so that his outer flank should not be turned.

According to Tarn,[2] Alexander's army was smaller than at the Granicus because many of the Allied troops had been left with Calas, as well as 4,700 mercenaries in Caria and Phrygia. When reinforcements are allowed for, Tarn calculates that it may have been composed

---

[1] Dieulafoy supplies the following timings in the region of Issus for November 1: Beginning of morning twilight – 5.13 a.m.; sunrise – 6.42 a.m.; sunset – 5.18 p.m.; and end of evening twilight – 6.47 p.m.   [2] *Alexander the Great*, vol. I, p. 26.

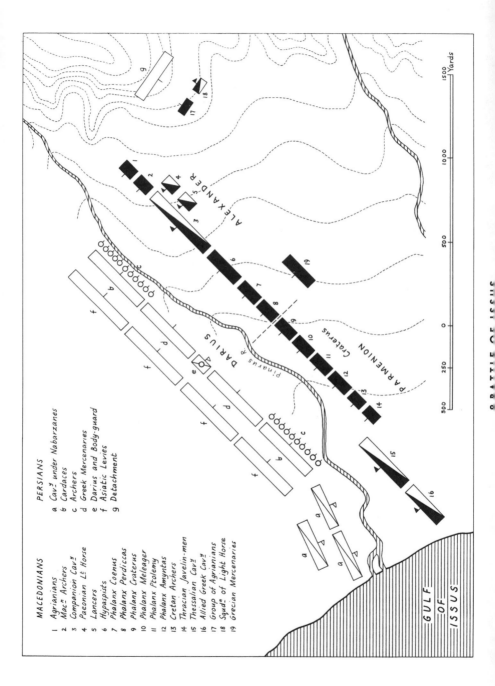

MACEDONIANS

1 Agrianians
2 Maced Archers
3 Companion Cavy
4 Paeonian Lt Horse
5 Lancers
6 Hypaspists
7 Phalanx Coenus
8 Phalanx Perdiccas
9 Phalanx Craterus
10 Phalanx Meleager
11 Phalanx Ptolemy
12 Phalanx Amyntas
13 Cretan Archers
14 Thracian Javelin-men
15 Thessalian Cavy
16 Allied Greek Cavy
17 Group of Agrianians
18 Squadn of Light Horse
19 Grecian Mercenaries

PERSIANS

a Cavy under Nabarzanes
b Cardaces
c Archers
d Greek Mercenaries
e Darius and Body-guard
f Asiatic Levies
g Detachment

BATTLE OF ISSUS

of from 20,000 to 24,000 effective infantry, and probably 5,000 horse. But as is not uncommon between classical scholars, Wilcken disagrees, and states there is no doubt that 'through accessions it was somewhat larger than his command at the Granicus'.[1]

It seems that soon after Alexander began to deploy his troops their presence was reported to Darius who, to safeguard his own deployment, sent forward south of the Pinarus the whole of his cavalry supported by light-armed troops. Under their cover he formed up his Greek mercenaries, under Thymondas and Amyntas, in the centre, with strong bodies of Cardaces, covered by archers, on their flanks. To secure his left from being turned, he posted a force, probably of light troops, on the foothills and in advance of his line of battle. The remainder of his infantry, presumably Asiatic national levies, he drew up in rear of his battle front, and when his order of battle had been formed he withdrew the covering force and posted all but a fraction of his cavalry, under Nabarzanes, on the right wing, because the ground near the seashore was suitable for cavalry action. He ordered stockades to be built on those parts of the Pinarus which were easy to cross; but there can hardly have been sufficient time to do more than erect some abattis. Lastly, he took up his position in the centre, as was customary among the Persians.

Since Curtius writes that 'Darius chose to make it a contest of cavalry, in the belief that the phalanx was the main strength of the Macedonian army',[2] it seems that his plan was to break through his enemy's left flank, then to take the Macedonian phalanx in flank and reverse, and lastly, when it was disorganized, to drive it towards the mountains.

In the meantime Alexander continued his advance, and as the coastal plain widened out he brought forward his cavalry; posted the Companions, Thessalians, lancers, and Paeonian light horse on his right wing, and sent the Allied Greek cavalry to Parmenion on his left. Later, when he was sufficiently near to observe his enemy's order of battle, which must have been clearly visible from the foothills, Alexander completed his own. Because he saw that Darius had drawn up the whole of his cavalry close to the sea, he ordered the Thessalian cavalry with speed to reinforce Parmenion, and so that their change of front might go unobserved he instructed them to ride round to the left flank in rear of the phalanx. Next he ordered the lancers, under Protomachus, and the Paeonian light horse, under Ariston, to take up position near the Companions, with the archers, under Antiochus, and

---

[1] *Alexander the Great*, p. 103.   [2] III, xi, 1.

the Agrianians, under Attalus, probably on their right.[1] Some of the Agrianians with a small body of horse he threw out *en crochet* on the foothills on his right rear to observe and contain the detachment Darius had posted on them. On the left of Amyntas' division of the phalanx he instructed Parmenion to post the Cretan archers and Thracian javelin-men, under Sitalces, with the cavalry of the left wing in advance of them. The Greek mercenaries he drew up in reserve behind his front.[2]

Lastly, he decided to clear his right flank before he engaged battle, and to do so he reinforced the detachment on his right with two squadrons of mercenary horse, some archers, and some Agrianians, who drove the Persian detachment back into the foothills. He then left 300 horse to observe it and withdrew the remainder to his right wing.

Alexander's plan of battle was much the same as that of his adversary; it was, while Parmenion held back the Persian right, to hurl his Companion cavalry at the Cardaces on the left of Darius' Greek mercenaries, break through them and then take the mercenaries in flank and rear.

After his men were marshalled, he ordered them to rest awhile; then he led them forward at a slow pace in order to maintain their dressing. When near the enemy, he rode down the ranks to see that all was in order and to encourage his soldiers, he called aloud the names, not only of their generals, squadron-leaders and captains, but also those of the men who had performed conspicuous deeds of valour. As he did so, from all sides there came shouts to lead them to the attack. But he continued the advance at a slow pace until within bow-shot.

At the battle of the Granicus, after a fierce struggle Alexander broke through the Persian cavalry; this time he was faced with infantry – the Cardaces. That they were hoplites, as Arrian asserts, is contradicted by the fact that Darius posted archers in front of them; for to do so with hoplites who, unless in disorder, could not be successfully charged by cavalry, would be to impede them. Darius obviously placed no great reliance in the Cardaces. Peltasts could be ridden over, as they had been by the Persian cavalry at Cunaxa (401 B.C.), and if the Cardaces were peltasts then it was a reasonable precaution to cover them with bowmen. But it was dangerous unless previous arrangements had been made for the Cardaces to open their ranks to allow the archers to retire through them once they had shot a few volleys of arrows. This,

---

[1] Curtius (III, ix, 9) writes that before his battle line Alexander 'stationed a band of slingers mingled with bowmen', but he does not say exactly where.

[2] Although Arrian calls them a 'reserve', they do not appear to have been used as such, and are not mentioned during the battle.

it may be assumed, was done, but was rendered ineffective by the rapidity of Alexander's assault.

At the head of the Royal Squadron, followed by the other squadrons of the Companions, with, so we may assume, the hypaspists on their left and the light horse and Agrianians on their right, Alexander trusted more to speed than to force of arms to strike terror into his enemy and took the river at a gallop. What followed can be pictured: As his horsemen splashed through the Pinarus with a yell, the Persian archers fled; but such was the speed of the assault that, before the Cardaces could open their ranks, or as they did so, the Companions were upon them and the whole of the Persian left wing took to its heels.

Much the same was to happen at the battle of Breitenfeld in 1631, when Fürstenberg and Isolani, the cavalry leaders of Tilly's right wing, charged the Saxon infantry on the Swedish left; for at the first shock they also fled the field. But Darius was no Gustavus Adolphus; his reserves, the Asiatic levies, were useless, and when he saw his left wing in flight, instead of attempting to draw the left of his Greek mercenaries back while he faced Alexander with his body-guard, he turned his chariot about and fled in panic. A little later, when the ground became cut up by ravines, he cast aside his mantle, bow and shield, mounted a horse and continued his headlong flight – as the Elector of Saxony did at Breitenfeld.

The second phase of the battle opened, and for a spell the Macedonian phalanx was in jeopardy. It would seem that Alexander's impetuous assault carried forward with it the two right battalions of the phalanx, which were part of Alexander's wing, while the four left battalions of Parmenion's wing continued to move at a slow pace. The result was that the phalanx broke in two, or as Arrian writes:

> For the Macedonian phalanx had been broken and had disjointed towards the right wing; because Alexander had dashed into the river with eagerness . . . but the Macedonians in the centre (i.e. the four left battalions) had not prosecuted their task with equal eagerness; and finding many parts of the bank steep and precipitous, they were unable to preserve the front of the phalanx in the same line (i.e. in line with the two right battalions).[1]

The opportunity offered by this break in the Macedonian phalanx was immediately exploited by the Greek mercenaries. They moved forward and pushed their disordered enemy back into the river, where

[1] Arrian, II, x, 4–5.

a desperate struggle followed in which Ptolemy, son of Seleucus, and 120 Macedonians fell. For a moment the battle in the centre was in doubt; but once the rout of the fleeing Cardaces had cleared the field and Alexander was able to grasp the position, he wheeled his hypaspists and the two battalions of the phalanx half-left and attacked the Greek mercenaries in flank.

While this engagement was fought, another was in progress on the left of the Macedonian front. There, in accordance with Darius' plan, the heavily armoured Persian cavalry crossed the Pinarus, charged Parmenion's Thessalians and continued to press them back until it was learnt that Darius had fled and that the Greek mercenaries were being cut down. Then the Persian horse broke off their attack and fell back. What happened to the Cardaces on their left is unrecorded; but as we are told that in the retreat of the Persian cavalry many men were trampled to death, not a few of them are likely to have been Cardaces. As the Persian horse withdrew, the Thessalians set out in pursuit and cut down many of the fugitives who, we are told, were impeded in their flight by the weight of their armour.

The sun must have set when the battle ended, and Arrian writes that Alexander did not start to pursue until the Greek mercenaries and Persian cavalry had been driven from the river. By then it must have been nearly dark, for, according to Arrian, night came on soon after Darius fled. It saved the Persians from annihilation. Most of the Persian cavalry withdrew into Cappadocia, where with the local inhabitants they caused Alexander serious trouble by attacks on his communications; it cost Antigonus three battles to keep them open. As mentioned earlier, 8,000 of the Greek mercenaries, under Amyntas, escaped over the mountains to Tripolis, and 2,000 rejoined Darius later.

Though the Persian losses were probably heavy, the figures given by all the classical historians are as fantastic as the numbers they attribute to the Persian army: they are 100,000 infantry and 10,000 cavalry killed. But they are no more fantastic than many publicized for purposes of propaganda during the Second World War.[1] According to Curtius, Alexander's losses were 450 infantry and cavalry killed and 4,500 wounded.[2] If correct, they are high figures for a victorious army.

---

[1] On one occasion, in the Second World War, 'according to a reliable report' – so it was stated at the time – in a single short battle 200,000 Germans were *killed* on a comparatively short sector of the Russian front. If so, following normal battle statistics, the German army engaged must have numbered 15,000,000 men.

[2] III, xi, 27.

Head of Alexander by the Greek sculptor, Lysippus, in the Constantinople Museum.
The Bettmann Archive

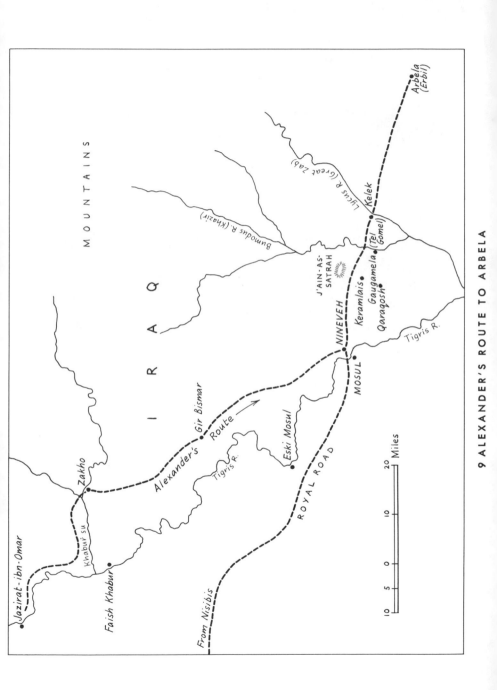

9 ALEXANDER'S ROUTE TO ARBELA

The Battle of Arbela

On the fourth day after it had crossed the Tigris (? at Jazirat-ibn-Omar) the Macedonian army reached the vicinity of Nineveh,[1] and when its scouts reported that more than 1,000 Persian horsemen were to be seen in the distance, Alexander rode forward with a body of

Obverses of three gold staters of Lysimachus, King of Thrace 323–281 B.C. The head is that of the deified Alexander which several of his successors used as a type on their own coinage after the death of the Macedonian conqueror.
American Numismatic Society

cavalry. After a chase of about eleven miles he captured some prisoners from whom he learnt that Darius and his army were encamped on the plain near Gaugamela, a village on the Bumodus river (Khazir), about 150 stades (some seventeen miles) to the east of Nineveh. Further, they told him that Darius had levelled the ground where it was uneven in order to facilitate the movements of his cavalry and chariots. On the strength of this information Alexander halted where he was for four days to rest his men and to build an entrenched camp for his baggage train and unfit soldiers.[2] Then he set out on a night march so timed

[1] See *The Geographical Journal*, vol. C (1942), 'Notes on Alexander's Crossing of the Tigris and the Battle of Arbela', Sir Aurel Stein, p. 157.

[2] According to Arrian (III, ix, 2) Darius learnt, apparently from the scouts who escaped capture, that Alexander was advancing, and that his army was about sixty stades away. Therefore Alexander's entrenched camp must have been situated about seven miles west of the eventual battlefield, or if the reckoning is by the short Macedonian stade, which was three-quarters of the Attic (see Tarn, *Alexander the Great*, vol. II, appx. 2, p. 170), then a little over five miles.

that he would come into contact with his enemy at break of day. But when he had advanced about thirty stades and the Persian camp fires were within sight, he halted and deliberated with his leading generals whether or not to attack.

Most were in favour of an immediate attack, but Parmenion suggested that the army should bivouac and the ground in front carefully reconnoitred to ascertain whether it was free from artificial obstacles. Alexander agreed, and, while the army rested, he rode forward with the Companion cavalry, followed by some light troops, to examine the whole countryside. Then he assembled another conference at which he told his generals that the forthcoming battle would decide the fate of Asia, that strict discipline was to be observed and complete silence maintained during the approach so that orders might be heard and transmitted with promptness; only when the battle was joined was the battle cry to be raised. After the conference Parmenion came to his tent to urge him to make a night attack on the enemy. Alexander refused to consider this, and though in his reply he said, 'I will not steal my victory',[1] he was far too good a general not to realize the impossibility of directing a great battle in the dark; that to strike in the dark was to strike not so much at Darius as at his own genius, and that at night time, even among the staunchest troops, the danger of sudden panic is ever-present.

When Darius was informed of his enemy's approach he began to draw up his motley host of national contingents into line of battle; Arrian mentions no less than twenty-four nationalities and supplies the names of fifteen of their leading generals. As at Issus, the strength of the Persian army, recorded by the classical historians, is both fabulous and fantastic. Arrian quotes 40,000 cavalry, 1,000,000 infantry, 200 scythed chariots, and fifteen elephants; Diodorus gives 200,000 cavalry, 800,000 infantry and 200 chariots; Curtius, the most modest of the three, 45,000 cavalry, 200,000 infantry and 200 chariots. Whatever its actual strength may have been, numerically it must have considerably exceeded that of Alexander, because its line of battle extended far beyond his flanks. In cavalry – well trained and valiant horsemen – it must have surpassed that of Alexander; but in effective infantry it was at a discount, because its only hoplites were 2,000 Greek mercenaries and the royal body-guard, presumably 2,000 strong.[2] This

---

[1] Plutarch, 'Alexander', XXXI, and Arrian, III, x, 2.

[2] In Arrian's order of battle of the Persian army no mention is made of the 10,000 Infantry, which in the days of Darius I were called 'the Immortals' (see Herodotus, VII, 83).

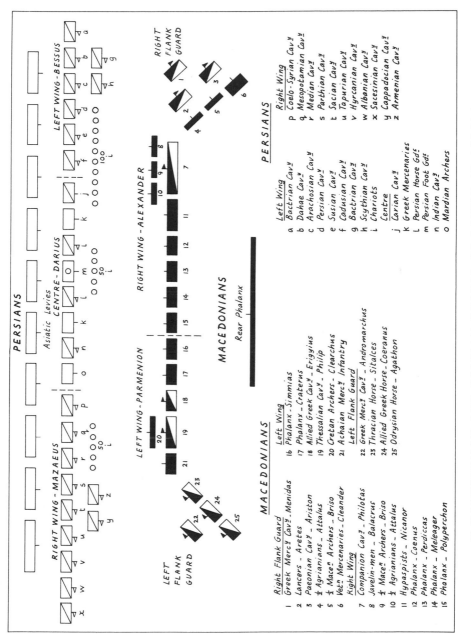

10 MACEDONIAN AND PERSIAN ORDERS OF BATTLE AT ARBELA

PERSIANS

LEFT WING - BESSUS

RIGHT WING - MAZAEUS

Asiatic Levies
CENTRE - DARIUS

RIGHT
FLANK
GUARD

RIGHT WING - ALEXANDER

LEFT WING - PARMENION

MACEDONIANS

Rear Phalanx

LEFT
FLANK
GUARD

MACEDONIANS

Right Flank Guard
1 Greek Merc^y Cav^y - Menidas
2 Lancers - Aretes
3 Paeonian Cav^y - Ariston
4 ½ Agrianians - Attalus
5 ½ Macⁿ Archers - Briso
6 Vetⁿ Mercenaries - Cleander

Right Wing
7 Companion Cav^y - Philotas
8 Javelin-men - Balacrus
9 ½ Macⁿ Archers - Briso
10 ½ Agrianians - Attalus
11 Hypaspists - Nicanor
12 Phalanx - Coenus
13 Phalanx - Perdiccas
14 Phalanx - Meleager
15 Phalanx - Polyperchon

Left Wing
16 Phalanx - Simmias
17 Phalanx - Craterus
18 Allied Greek Cav^y - Erigyius
19 Thessalian Cav^y - Philip
20 Cretan Archers - Clearchus
21 Achaian Merc^y Infantry

Left Flank Guard
22 Greek Merc^y Cav^y - Andromarchus
23 Thracian Horse - Sitalces
24 Allied Greek Horse - Coeranus
25 Odrysian Horse - Agathon

PERSIANS

Left Wing
a Bactrian Cav^y
b Dahae Cav^y
c Arachosian Cav^y
d Persian Cav^y
e Susian Cav^y
f Cadusian Cav^y
g Bactrian Cav^y
h Scythian Cav^y
i Chariots

Centre
j Carian Cav^y
k Greek Mercenaries
l Persian Horse Gd^s
m Persian Foot Gd^s
n Indian Cav^y
o Mardian Archers

Right Wing
p Coelo-Syrian Cav^y
q Mesopotamian Cav^y
r Median Cav^y
s Parthian Cav^y
t Sacian Cav^y
u Tapurian Cav^y
v Hyrcanian Cav^y
w Albanian Cav^y
x Sacesinian Cav^y
y Cappadocian Cav^y
z Armenian Cav^y

meant that the infantry base from which the Persian cavalry would be called upon to manœuvre was extremely weak. There was plenty of mobility, but little stability in Darius' army.

The plan of attack adopted by Darius was dictated by his cavalry superiority and his chariots; it was to envelop both flanks of his enemy, an operation facilitated by the greater length of his battle front. He based his hopes on two powerful cavalry wings.

The army was marshalled in two lines; the forward line, except for its centre, consisted exclusively of cavalry, and the rear line mainly, if not entirely, in infantry, mostly hillmen, unsuited for a pitched battle in the plains either against hoplites or charging horsemen. Its centre was commanded by Darius, who was also in supreme command; its left wing by Bessus, satrap of Bactria and of royal blood; and its right wing by Mazaeus, former satrap of Syria. From the order of battle found in the royal camp after Darius' defeat, the distribution of the Persian troops was as follows:

On the left wing, from left to right, first came the Bactrian cavalry, then the Dahae (Saca), Arachosian, Persian (intermingled with foot) and Susian horsemen, and lastly the Cadusian. In front of these regiments were posted 1,000 mailed Scythian (Saca) cataphracts brigaded with 1,000 Bactrian cavalry, and 100 chariots.

In the centre stood the Royal Foot-Guard, the so-called 'Apple-bearers'; the Persian Horse Guard; the Greek mercenaries in two divisions, each presumably 1,000 strong; the Indian and Carian[1] cavalry, and the Mardian archers. In front of the centre were posted fifty chariots and fifteen elephants,[2] and it appears that in rear were contingents of Uxians, Babylonians, Arabs and Sitacenians.

On the right wing, from right to left, first came the Coelo-Syrian cavalry, then the Mesopotamian, Median, Parthian, Sacian, Tapurian and Hyrcanian horsemen; and lastly the Albanian and Sacesinian cavalry. In front of this wing the Cappadocian and Armenian cavalry and fifty chariots were drawn up.

Since the battle of Issus, Darius had provided his soldiers with more effective arms; instead of the javelin his horsemen were armed with a longer sword and a short thrusting-spear, such as the Macedonian cavalry carried, in part at least they were provided with link-armour, and the infantry were given a larger shield. He placed great faith in his four-horsed chariots, which were equipped with a long, heavy spear-

---

[1] They had been removed forcibly from Caria to central Asia.

[2] No mention of the elephants is made during the battle, nor are any reported to have been captured.

headed pole that projected in front, and had scythes fitted to the hubs of their wheels.[1] His confidence in them is hard to understand, because at Cunaxa they had proved completely ineffective.[2]

The day before the battle, when Darius had finished marshalling his army, because his front was not entrenched and he feared a night attack, he decided to keep his troops under arms in battle order during the night – this must seriously have fatigued them.

In contrast with the Persian army, the strength of the Macedonian is known. Arrian states that it consisted of 7,000 cavalry and about 40,000 infantry,[3] and there is no reason to doubt his figures. But unfortunately, like other classical historians, he seldom if ever defines the tactical aims of the opposing commanders-in-chief and leaves it to his readers to disentangle them from the battles he describes. What was Alexander's tactical aim at Arbela? This is an important question, because no clear picture of his generalship is obtainable until it is answered. What were the facts, and what were the steps he decided to take to turn them to his advantage?

As regards the facts, two were outstanding:

(1) In contrast with its length at Issus, the Persian line of battle at Arbela was considerably longer than the Macedonian – possibly twice its length – because Arrian tells us that when Alexander advanced the Macedonian right wing was opposite the Persian centre;[4] therefore it must have been overlapped, and, presumably, on the Macedonian left flank it was much the same. Further, unlike the battle of Issus, there was no possibility for Alexander to rest his flanks on an unturnable obstacle – no sea and no mountains.

(2) The Persian front, composed mainly of cavalry, was an offensive (mobile) and not a defensive (stable) front. This meant that when the battle opened the Persian cavalry would move forward, and because the Persian infantry in rear of the cavalry were incapable of establishing a defensive front even were they to occupy the places vacated by the cavalry, a number of undefended gaps would occur in the Persian front on both sides of its small hoplite centre.

There were three steps that Alexander decided to take:

(1) His first step was to assume a defensive order of approach, more especially on the flanks, because his centre – the phalanx – was

---

[1] See Curtius, IV, viii, 3, and Diodorus, XVII, 59, 5.

[2] Xenophon's *Anabasis*, I, 8, 19–20.

[3] III, 12, 5. Tarn (*Alexander the Great*, vol. II, pp. 159–60) estimates the strength of Alexander's cavalry at: Companions 2,000; Thessalians 2,000; mercenary horse in two bodies each 500; Greek allied cavalry about 700; and Balkan horse-lancers, Paeonian, Thracian, and Odrysian about 1,300.   [4] III, 13, 1.

defensively strong in front and weak on the flanks, and to maintain this defensive order until an opportunity arose in which to assume the offensive – that is, when gaps appeared in the Persian front.

(2) His second step was to advance in oblique order with his right leading. This would throw the Persian line out of gear; it would draw its right wing forward toward his own refused left wing and place the rear of the Persian right wing in jeopardy should the Persian left wing be penetrated, as had happened at Issus. Therefore both Alexander's wings would have to be mobile and capable of withstanding envelopment; the left, if necessary, by sacrificing ground, but not so the right, because its task was to press forward. Therefore the right would have to be stronger than the left.

(3) Lastly, when the two wings had drawn the Persian cavalry toward themselves and were engaged in defensive action, Alexander with his *corps de rupture*, his Companion cavalry, would charge through one or other of the gaps in the enemy's front caused by the forward movement of the Persian cavalry. This would demand the most exact timing.

Dictated by his numerical inferiority, the nature of the battlefield, the dispositions of his enemy, and his obvious intentions, Alexander's aim was to defeat an attack of double-envelopment by an attack of penetration, and to achieve it his tactical order was based on the idea embodied in Napoleon's maxim: 'The whole art of war consists in a well-reasoned and extremely circumspect defensive followed by rapid and audacious attack.' [1]

Alexander's order of battle was as follows:

Centre: The phalanx was drawn up in the centre in order from right to left: first Coenus' battalion, then those of Perdiccas, Meleager, Polyperchon, Amyntas (commanded by Simmias), and lastly Craterus. The four right battalions were to co-operate with the right cavalry wing, under Alexander, and the two left battalions (both under Craterus) with the left cavalry wing, commanded by Parmenion.

Right Cavalry Wing: This wing consisted of the Companion cavalry, commanded by Philotas, with the Royal Squadron, under Cleitus, in front, and in its rear the squadrons of Glaucias, Ariston, Sopolis, Heraclides, Demetrius, Meleager, and Hegelochus. On the left of the Companions came the hypaspists, under Nicanor, and on the front of the whole wing were deployed half Attalus' Agrianians, half the Macedonian archers, under Briso, and Balacrus' javelin-men.

Left Cavalry Wing: On the left of Craterus, first came the Allied

---

[1] *Correspondance*, No. 10558, vol. XIII, p. 10.

A

B

South →

THE VILLAGE OF KERAMLAIS

This photograph faces east toward the Bumodus (khazir) river. When taken on September 21, 1928, by the 6th Squadron (R.A.F.) of the Iraq Levies a slight dust haze covered the plain.

← North

←North

South→

A

B

THE TEL OR MOUND OF KERAMLAIS

This photograph immediately adjoins the first one on its right along A–B. From the mound a full
view is obtained of the battlefield of Arbela.

Greek cavalry, under Erigyius, and next on their left the Thessalian cavalry, under Philip, son of Menelaus. Next to the Thessalians, or more probably in front of them, Clearchus' Cretan archers and the Achaean mercenary infantry were deployed.[1] The Pharsalian horse, the *élite* and strongest squadron of the Thessalians, was detailed to act as Parmenion's body-guard.

Right Flank Guard: Toward the right front of the Royal Squadron was posted the Greek mercenary cavalry, under Menidas; and in their rear, thrown back *en crochet*, Aretes' lancers, Ariston's Paeonian cavalry, the remaining halves of the Agrianians and archers, and close to the latter Cleander's veteran mercenary cavalry.

Left Flank Guard: The left flank guard was also thrown back *en crochet*; it consisted of the Thracian light horse, under Sitalces; then the Allied Greek cavalry, under Coeranus, the Odrysian cavalry, under Agathon, and lastly the Greek mercenary cavalry, under Andromarchus.

Rear Phalanx or Second Line: To be prepared to meet envelopment, and in consequence an attack in rear, a second phalanx, or rear line, was deployed at an unspecified distance behind the front line, which with the front line and the two flank guards, when wheeled backward, would together form a hollow square, as in another context described by Xenophon.[2] Of this arrangement Curtius writes: 'Therefore the front was not better protected than the flanks, nor the flanks than the rear.'[3]

The Camp and its Guard: A small body of Thracian infantry was detailed to protect the camp; but where was it located, because it was to play a part of no small importance in the battle? If it was still the camp Alexander built during his four-day halt, then it was seven or five miles in rear of the battle front, and as there is no evidence that it was shifted closer to the front, it is assumed that it was there when the battle was fought.

The site of the battlefield has been determined by Sir Aurel Stein;[4] it lay on the plain north and south of Keramlais, a village six miles to the west of the mound of Tel Gomel (Gaugamela), on the Khazir (Bumodus) river. This mound lies six miles to the north of the junction of the Khazir and Great Zab (Lycus), and about a mile south of the Royal Road from Nineveh. The present-day road still crosses the Great Zab at Kelek, where Darius bridged the river, and then follows

---

[1] Arrian does not mention these two units, Diodorus does. Their normal place was on the left wing.   [2] *Anabasis,* III, ii, 36.   [3] IV, xiii, 32.
[4] *The Geographical Journal,* vol. C (1942), 'Notes on Alexander's Crossing of the Tigris and the Battle of Arbela', pp. 155–64.

on to Erbil (Arbela), which by the present highway is less than thirty miles from the Lycus, and therefore about thirty-six miles from Tel Gomel, and not 600 stades (about sixty-nine miles) as Arrian states.[1] The plain of Keramlais, which is remarkably level, extends for fully eight miles from south-east to north-west, with a maximum width of about seven miles. To its south the plain is flanked by low, flat-topped hills inclined toward the Tigris, and on its northern side is overlooked by the steep Jabal 'Ain-as-Satrah, which culminates in a rugged crest. Sir Aurel Stein is of opinion that when Alexander in his approach march turned obliquely to his right to avoid the levelled plain, he was making toward the low hills near Qaroqosh; also that the hill, which Curtius mentions[2] was occupied by Mazaeus in a reconnaissance before the battle, was probably the Jabal 'Ain-as-Satrah.

The sun was already high in the heavens when, on the morning of October 1, 331 B.C., Alexander broke bivouac and led his army toward the Persians. But when he saw how greatly they outflanked him, and that his right wing faced the Persian centre, he inclined his advance more and more to the right, so as to bring that wing opposite the Persian left flank. This oblique movement drew Parmenion's wing nearer to the Persian centre; also it induced Darius to side-step his line of battle towards his left, and to head off his opponent he sent out a body of Scythian horse, but apparently, it was brushed aside, because we are told that Alexander 'continued to march towards his right, and almost entirely got beyond the ground which had been cleared and levelled by the Persians'.[3]

When Darius saw that if Alexander reached the unlevelled ground – the low hills mentioned by Sir Aurel Stein – his chariots would become useless, he ordered Bessus with the troops in advance of his wing – the brigaded Scythian and Bactrian horse – to wheel round Alexander's right and bring it to a halt. But immediately Alexander became aware of their intention he ordered Menidas to charge them with his mercenary cavalry; Menidas charged, but through weight of numbers was driven back. Next, Alexander ordered Ariston with his Paeonians and Cleander with his Greek mercenary horse to charge the Scythians, upon which they began to waver and give way. But before they could be driven from the field Bessus brought forward the Bactrians of his left wing – those who were posted in rear of the advanced Scytho-Bactrian brigade – and when they had reinforced the Scythians, for a spell the battle swung in favour of the Persians. In this way, we are told, a general cavalry engagement was brought about in

[1] III, 15, 5.   [2] IV, xii, 15 and 18.   [3] Arrian, III, xiii, 1–2.

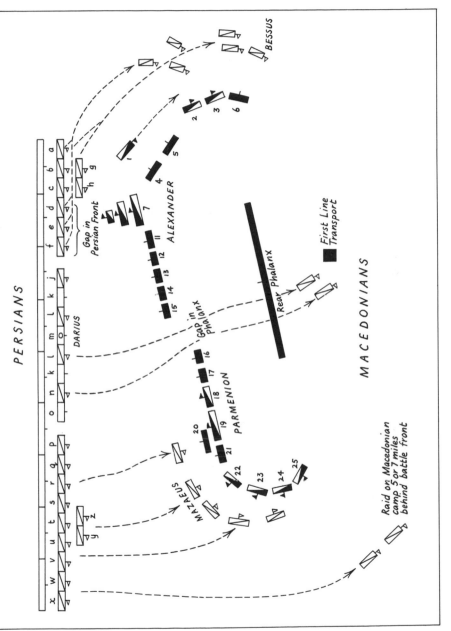

11 BATTLE OF ARBELA

which many of Alexander's men fell, overwhelmed by the multitude of their adversaries; also 'because the Scythians themselves and their horses were much more completely protected by armour'. But 'the Macedonians stood up against their onsets, and falling on them stoutly, squadron by squadron, broke their formation'.[1]

Who were these 'Macedonians'? Tarn argues that as the only Macedonians on Alexander's right flank were his Companion cavalry, the Scythians broke through the flanking column and 'got into the ranks of the Companions'.[2] Mr G. T. Griffith and Mr A. R. Burn disagree;[3] their argument is that, in the present context, Arrian uses 'Macedonians' not in an ethnical but in a general sense, as he does on other occasions, and that it was the flank guard and not the Companions who threw the Scythians back. Burn pertinently points out that because Alexander still had Aretes' lancers in hand, and that probably they were between the Scythians and the Companions, why should he use the Companions, 'whom he was reserving for the decisive charge against the Persian King, without using Aretes' lancers to check them'? More interesting than this controversy is Burn's summing up of the engagement.

> This part of the narrative [he writes] lets us see in how masterly and economical a fashion Alexander 'fed the battle' – incidentally, using the units of his flank-guard in just the order that one would expect from their position in the original formation; first, the outermost units of his flank-guard, from front to rear: Menidas', Ariston's, Kleandros' regiment . . . while still keeping the Companions, on the flank of the main line, covered by Aretes' lancers and the Agriânes and archers.

At this juncture, Darius sought to take advantage of the temporary success the Scythians and Bactrians had gained and launched his left wing chariots against the right of the Macedonian phalanx with the aim of throwing it into confusion. But his expectations were short-lived; no sooner did they race forward than they were met with volleys of javelins, hurled by the Agrianians and men of Balacus, posted in front. A wild confusion followed in which not a few of the charioteers were dragged out of their chariots, and those who got through caused little harm; as they neared the phalanx, the Macedonians opened their

---

[1] Arrian, III, xiii, 4.   [2] *Alexander the Great*, vol. II, pp. 185–6.
[3] See *The Journal of Hellenic Studies*, vol. LXXII (1952), 'Notes on Alexander's Campaigns, 332–330', A. R. Burn, p. 87, and ibid., vol. LXVII (1947), 'Alexander's Generalship at Gaugamela,' G. T. Griffith, pp. 80–81.

ranks and let them through,[1] and left it to the grooms in rear to over-power them.

Either immediately after the chariot charge, or what would seem more probable, at the time it was launched, two things happened. The first was that because Bessus was wheeling round Alexander's right flank guard to attack it in rear, Alexander sent in Aretes and his lancers, presumably to fall upon Bessus' rear. The second was that when Darius saw from his command post that Alexander had engaged his last mobile reserve, he believed that Bessus was succeeding in his mission and decided that the moment had come to launch his two decisive enveloping attacks. Our authority for this is, that he then 'set his whole phalanx in motion'[2] – that is, his whole line of battle – and this can only mean that he released all or most of his remaining cavalry on both his wings with the aim of crushing Alexander on the left and Parmenion on the right. What happened is uncertain, but the crucial mistake would appear to have been that instead of most of the cavalry of the Persian left wing being directed against Alexander's Companions, and the others sent to the support of Bessus, the whole galloped towards Bessus. This may have been due to a misunderstanding of verbal orders, or to the instinctive urge of masses of horsemen to follow those in the lead,[3] or again – assuming that part was ordered to charge the Companions – it may have been because it was met by such a hail of missiles from the javelin-men and archers who were posted in front of the Companions that the horsemen instinctively swerved to their left to avoid it[4] and then joined those galloping toward Bessus.

Whichever of these assumptions is accepted, the moment Alexander had awaited had arrived, and here Arrian's description is crystal clear. He writes:

> But when the Persians had made a break in the front line of their army, in consequence of the cavalry sallying forth to assist those who were surrounding the right wing, Alexander wheeled round towards

[1] One would like to know what the drill was which enabled broad lanes to be rapidly formed; it must have been very simple, and discipline must have been of the highest.

[2] Arrian, III, xiv, 1.

[3] In Cavalry engagements the excitement of man and horse is often so overmastering that, when a body is ordered to charge, neighbouring bodies either join in or are unable to hold back their horses. A classical example of this is the twice repeated unauthorized charges of Lefebvre-Desnouettes' and Guyot's cavalry divisions at the battle of Waterloo.

[4] This happened at the battles of Taganae and Crécy. Neither the Gothic horse nor the French chivalry would face the arrows of the Romans and English; instinctively, both man and horse turned away from them.

the gap, and forming a wedge as it were of the Companion cavalry and of the part of the phalanx which was posted here [that is the hypaspists and the four right battalions of the phalanx], he led them with a quick charge and a loud battle-cry straight towards Darius himself. For a short time there ensued a hand-to-hand fight; but when the Macedonian cavalry, commanded by Alexander himself, pressed on vigorously, thrusting themselves against the Persians and striking their faces with their spears, and when the Macedonian phalanx in dense array and bristling with long pikes had also made an attack upon them, all things together appeared full of terror to Darius, who had already long been in a state of fear, so that he was the first to turn and flee.[1]

Meanwhile, what was happening on Parmenion's flank? From the initial dispositions of the Persian army it is clear that the tasks set to Bessus and Mazaeus were identical; each was called upon to envelop one of Alexander's wings. Unfortunately, Arrian tells us nothing of the earlier engagements on Parmenion's flank and only takes up the story at the time Alexander launched his decisive assault. The situation is in no way clarified by Tarn, who holds, on the authority of the pre-battle speech attributed to Darius by Curtius, that Mazaeus' task was to rescue the royal family captive in Alexander's entrenched camp, seven or five miles in rear of the battlefield.[2] The speech is a rodomontade of over 1,000 words, and among other things Darius is made to say: 'Rescue my flesh and blood from bonds; restore to me my dear ones, mother and children for whom you yourselves do not refuse to die . . .'[3] It is not directly addressed either to Mazaeus or to Bessus, but to 'the troops who stood about him'. On the strength of this appeal – it is nothing more than an appeal – Tarn writes that: 'The army had Darius' express orders to rescue his family who were in Alexander's camp . . .'[4] Certainly Bessus did not interpret it as such, why then should Mazaeus?

Here Diodorus comes to our rescue and, in part at least, fills the gap in Arrian's narrative. He tells us that, when Bessus engaged Alexander's flank guard, 'Mazaeus, likewise, in the right wing, with a brave body of cavalry, charged with that briskness that he laid many at his feet in the first onset. Then he ordered two thousand Cadusian

---

[1] III, xv, 1-3.
[2] Curtius (IV, xiii, 35) says that Alexander's camp was placed not far from the field of battle on a high hill; and from Arrian (III, ix, 3) we learn that when Alexander halted and ordered a camp to be entrenched, it was on or near high ground.   [3] Curtius, IV, xiv, 22.   [4] *Alexander the Great*, vol. II, p. 110.

horse, and a thousand more of the Scythians, to take a compass round the enemy's wing, and to break in upon the trenches that defended their carriages . . .' [1]

Nothing is expressly said about rescue of the royal family, and beyond all doubt, as apparently Mazaeus had horsemen to spare, it was a sound tactical and not a sentimental manœuvre, aimed to distract Alexander and compel him, or Parmenion, to detach troops to rescue the camp. Further, it was undoubtedly facilitated by Alexander's oblique approach, which is likely to have largely uncovered the camp.

The raid was a complete success; Parmenion, when he learnt of it, hurriedly sent Polydamus to Alexander, 'both to notify him of the danger and to ask what he ordered to be done'. Alexander replied: 'Go report to Parmenion, that if we win the battle, we shall not only recover our own property, but shall seize what belongs to the enemy . . . let him scorn the loss of our packs and fight valiantly.' [2] Though the raiders found the royal family in the camp, Sisygambis, Darius' mother, refused to be rescued,[3] so, after they had rifled the carriages they returned to Mazaeus, presumably by the way they had come.

It is time to return to the Macedonian centre. On its right the four right battalions of the phalanx pressed on vigorously; but its two left battalions were held back by Mazaeus with the result that a gap developed in its front beween the left of Polyperchon's and the right of Simmias' battalions.

It is at this moment that Arrian abruptly records that some of the Indian and the Persian cavalry[4] 'burst through the gap towards the baggage of the Macedonians' and 'fell upon their adversaries, being mostly unarmed men', who 'never dreamt that anyone would make a charge through the phalanx, doubled as it was', which means that they broke through the rear, as well as the forward phalanx. The Persian prisoners found with the baggage were released[5] and joined in the fray. But when the commanders of the troops 'which formed the reserve to the first phalanx' – that is, of the rear phalanx – learnt what had

---

[1] Diodorus, XVII, 59, 5. Curtius (IV, xv, 5) also refers to this raid, but times it with the chariot charge. He writes: 'Mazaeus also struck them with fear in their panic by ordering his 1,000 cavalry to wheel about in order to plunder the enemy's baggage'. Plutarch ('Alexander', XXXII) also says that Mazaeus sent 'horsemen round outside the line of battle'.

[2] Curtius, IV, xv, 6–8.

[3] That the old lady was in the camp is also a pointer that Alexander did not move it into the battle area, which would certainly have upset her.

[4] This must have been the Persian Horse Guards in the centre of the Persian line, and the Indians not far from their right.

[5] Released from what today would be the advanced prisoners' cage.

happened, they turned about, and 'appeared in the rear of the Persians and slew large numbers of them, crowded together as they were round the baggage animals'.[1] In the meantime Mazaeus continued his attack on Parmenion's left flank.

Tarn's comment on this action is: 'Arrian does not say why the [Persian] Guard, after cutting the phalanx in half, did not take it in rear . . . but just rode on to the camp.' He gives as the reason that, according to Curtius, 'Darius had ordered the Guard to rescue his family, and they threw away the best chance of the day from a mistaken sense of loyalty to their worthless king.'[2] Surely the best chance was when the battle opened and the best way to reach the camp the one described by Diodorus, and not by hewing a path through the double phalanx.

But did the Persian Guard hew their way to Alexander's camp which was some seven or five miles to the rear of the second phalanx? Arrian makes no mention of either camp or royal family; he speaks of 'baggage animals'. Further, he hints at a considerable number of Persian prisoners, and it is unlikely that there were many of them in the camp. Also, if the raiders 'round the baggage animals' were eventually slaughtered by the rear phalanx, then, should 'camp' be correct, the men of the rear phalanx must have marched at least five miles to catch up with them; this would take about two hours, a timing which will be referred to subsequently.

Really, this will not do, and in clarification it is suggested that the Persian Guard never reached Alexander's camp, because the 'baggage animals' mentioned were the Macedonian first-line transport and not the Macedonian wagon train, which *was* in the camp; that the prisoners released were those captured during and not before the battle, for of the latter there cannot have been sufficient to put up a fight worth recording. Although there is no mention of first-line transport except as 'baggage animals', it must have existed, because no organized army, ancient or modern, could have operated successfully without it. Why it had not been placed within Alexander's elastic square is the sole puzzling item.

From the point of view of generalship, the most interesting problem in the battle will now be discussed. What with the break-through of the Persian Guard and Indians and the incessant attacks on the Macedonian left wing, Parmenion was in a desperate plight; so he sent a messenger to Alexander to tell him of his critical position and to seek his aid. According to Arrian, the message was delivered to him when

---

[1] Arrian, III, xiv, 5–6.   [2] *Alexander the Great*, vol. II, appx. 5, pp. 187–8.

he was in pursuit of Darius; whereupon he abandoned the chase,[1] wheeled round his Companions, and led them against the Persian right wing.

Was he pursuing Darius? Mr Griffith asks this question,[2] and it is a pertinent one. How could Alexander dare to pursue, when as yet he knew little or nothing of the progress of the battle on his left wing, and was fully aware that his right wing was still hard pressed? He was no Rupert,[3] a man to be carried away by the excitement of a gallop, and to risk the loss of the battle by a premature pursuit would class him as a third-rate general. Griffith's assumption is – and if it does not fit Arrian's narrative, it fits Alexander's known generalship at Issus – that once Alexander had penetrated the gap in the Persian front and had caused Darius to flee and his whole centre to crumble, he turned right in order to extricate his right flank guard which was fighting against heavy odds. 'By this interpretation', Griffith writes, 'Alexander, after his sucessful charge and the flight of Darius, wheeled *to the right* with his "Companions" in order to deal with that sector of the battle which he *knew* to be in danger and in order to relieve the only group of his forces which he *knew*, at the moment, to be in some need of relief.'

His first opponents would be squadrons of the Persians left wing, which, as mentioned, had moved forward, and his next opponents the brigaded Scytho-Bactrians who had opened the battle. He dispersed the Persian left wing, and the Scytho-Bactrians, when they witnessed its rout, got away before he could engage them.

This assumption tallies with Curtius' confused description of the fighting on Alexander's wing immediately before the fictitious meeting of Alexander and Darius on the battlefield. While the Scythians, he writes, plundered the Macedonian baggage,[4] Aretes[5] rode up and killed their leader. Next, the Bactrians overwhelmed Aretes, whose men fled back to Alexander. He rebuked them, led them forward and attacked the thinned ranks of the Bactrians – many had already fled.

[1] Curtius (IV, xvi, 10) says that Alexander had reached the Lycus river, twelve miles from the battlefield, before he turned back to assist Parmenion, which is absurd.   [2] Op. cit., pp. 83–4.

[3] Whose reckless pursuits ruined the battles of Marston Moor and Naseby in 1644 and 1645 respectively.

[4] IV, xv, 18. Should this be correct, then the 'baggage' cannot have been in the camp. Therefore it must have been the first-line transport of the right flank guard. A little later on (IV, xv, 22) Curtius says that the Bactrians also plundered 'the enemies' baggage'.

[5] All Arrian (III, xiv, 1) says of Aretes is that Alexander, immediately before his assault, ordered Aretes to charge the Persian cavalry who were wheeling round the right wing. This he did, and put them to flight. Since he was outnumbered by probably four to one, it would appear that something is missing here.

But the Persians tried to surround Alexander, who was saved by the Agrianians who 'put spurs to their horses [sic] and attacked the barbarians', and 'by slashing at their backs compelled them to turn and face them'.[1]

Should this garbled account be timed to have taken place shortly after, instead of shortly before Darius fled, as Curtius times it, it not only reinforces Griffith's assumption, but also fills in the gap in Arrian's narrative. When the later timing is accepted, then it was *after* Alexander had routed the Persians and Bactrians on his right flank that he received Parmenion's message. In any case, had he already been on his way to Arbela, and he was not wont to pursue at a trot, no messenger could have caught him up, not only because he would have been too far away, but because the messenger would have had to have ridden through the routed Persian army. Also, the cloud of dust must have been so dense that it would have been little short of a miracle had the messenger found him.[2]

When Alexander received the message – as we know he did – he turned back through the now extensive gap between his right flank guard and the advancing phalanx to aid Parmenion; and soon after he came in head-on collision with large forces of retiring horsemen, whom Arrian describes as 'Parthians, some Indians, and the main host (and the strongest) of the Persians'.[3] These can only have been the Indians and the Persian Guard who had broken through the double phalanx, and the Parthians, who at the opening of the battle were in the right flank of the Persian line, and who probably had been engaged against Parmenion's left flank guard, must have ridden round it and joined up with the Indians and the Guard as they looted the Macedonian baggage.

The time required by Alexander to assault the Persian left centre and carry out his alleged pursuit of Darius, or if he had instead carried out the assumed rescue of his right flank guard, is unlikely to have been more than an hour, or at the very most an hour and a half, so the probability is that within an hour, or a little more, after he broke the Persian centre, he was on his way to rescue Parmenion.

Because it is known that the Indians and Persian Guard broke

---

[1] Curtius, IV, xv, 19–22.

[2] Curtius (IV, xv, 32–3) writes: 'the cloud of dust which rose to the sky made it impossible to see'; and Diodorus (XVII, 60, 4): 'the horses in their flight raised so great a cloud of dust, that Alexander and his men, who pursued close after the enemy, could not see which way Darius fled'. Anyone who has witnessed a cavalry charge in the dry weather over an Indian *maidan* will be able to picture what the dust at Arbela was like. On one such occasion the writer remembers that visibility was reduced to four or five yards.   [3] III, xiv, 1.

through the gap in the Macedonian phalanx immediately after Alexander led his Companions to the assault, the question arises: Could they, within an hour and a half, have ridden to Alexander's camp, looted it, and on their return have met him on his way to help Parmenion? Of course not, because to reach the camp and return from it entailed a ride of either ten miles or fourteen, and as they must have been engaged for two hours or more in looting before the rear phalanx came up and ejected them, in all their raid must have taken three hours at the very least. It follows that unless it is assumed that Alexander spent three hours, instead of one, or one and a half hours, in his assault and his rout of Bessus, or, if preferred, in his assault and his abortive pursuit of Darius, the raiders of his camp could not possibly have met him on his return as Arrian alleges.

It is clear from these timings that the Persian Guard and the Indians never got near Alexander's camp. Instead, and although it is an assumption, it fits the timings, once they broke through the rear phalanx they could not resist the temptation to loot the Macedonian first-line transport;[1] then, after the rear phalanx had pulled itself together and ejected them, they set out on their return. In what direction is not known, but as they must have seen a wide gap between the dense dust cloud that smothered the left and centre of the battle, and another dust cloud toward its right, where Bessus was in flight, what more natural than for them to ride for the gap, either to exploit it or escape? Then, out of the second cloud galloped Alexander at the head of his Companions. Their surprise was complete, and before they could turn tail Alexander was upon them.

> Here raged the fiercest cavalry engagement of the whole action [writes Arrian]. For being drawn up by squadrons, and so in column, the Persians wheeled round and clashed with Alexander's troops front to front: There was no javelin-throwing and no manœuvring of horses, such as are usual in a cavalry engagement, but each tried to break his way through whatever opposed him, pressing on as if this were their one hope of safety. So they continued beating and battered, with no quarter given as men now no longer fighting for someone else's victory, but for their very own lives. There about sixty of the Companions of Alexander fell . . .[2]

---

[1] Ever since the battle of Megiddo in 1479 B.C., the first clearly recorded battle in history, countless examples can be cited of battles lost or rendered abortive because victorious troops abandoned their task to loot their enemy's camp or baggage.

[2] III, xv, 2. The whole description shows clearly that the Persians were fighting to open their line of retreat.

Many of the Persians broke through the Companions and took to headlong flight.

Alexander did not pursue them but pressed on towards the Persian right wing – as usual he stuck to his objective. But the general rot had set in, the men of the Persian right wing were already taking to their heels, vigorously pressed by the Thessalians. Alexander wheeled the Companions about and set out on his pursuit of Darius. The chase was kept up as long as there was daylight; at the same time Parmenion pushed forward. Alexander found the bridge over the river Lycus (Great Zab), about twelve miles from the battlefield, intact and he rested his men there while Parmenion occupied the Persian royal camp at Gaugamela. At midnight Alexander pressed on again, hoping against hope to capture Darius; but early on the morning after the battle when he reached Arbela he found that the bird had flown northward toward the Kurdish mountains.[1] The battle of Arbela, which changed the political axis of the ancient world, had ended.

Though the losses suffered by the Persians, more especially during the pursuit, must have been exceedingly heavy, the figures given by Arrian, Diodorus, and Curtius are as fabulous as those given for Issus. Arrian gives 300,000 Persians killed and more than 300,000 captured; Diodorus, 90,000 killed; and Curtius, 40,000. The figures for the Macedonians are more interesting: Arrian gives 100 killed and 1,000 horses killed or dead of exhaustion, and 'among these nearly half of the Companions' horses'; Curtius increases the Macedonian dead to 'less than 300'; and Diodorus to 500. Both the last two writers include Hephaestion, Perdiccas, Coenus, and Menidas among the wounded, of whom Diodorus says there were 'great multitudes'.

The Battle of the Hydaspes

Among the many battles fought by invaders who entered the plains of India from the north-west, the first recorded in history is the battle of the Hydaspes, and in Hogarth's opinion, when coupled with the crossing of the river, together they 'rank among the most brilliant operations of ancient warfare'.[2]

The starting point of this most famous of Alexander's campaigns was Taxila, and there is justification for assuming that while he rested his army there he learnt from Taxiles all that was to be known of the nature of the country he would have to traverse, and of the best

---

[1] Bessus accompanied Darius, and Mazaeus escaped to Babylon.
[2] *Philip and Alexander of Macedon*, p. 239.

road to follow. But nothing of this is recorded except that, according to Pliny, the distance between Taxila and the Hydaspes, as measured by Alexander's surveyors Diognetus and Baeton, was 120 Roman miles – that is, 110½ English miles;[1] and that, according to Strabo, 'the direction of march, as far as the Hydaspes, was for the most part towards the south'.[2]

Before he set out from Taxila Alexander had learnt that Porus, king of the Pauravas, whose realm lay between the Hydaspes and Acesines, had occupied the eastern bank of the Hydaspes in order to oppose his passage. He instructed Coenus, son of Polemocrates, who was still on the Indus, to cut the smaller vessels into two parts, and the thirty-oared galleys into three, and have the sections conveyed to the Hydaspes by wagon. Then, accompanied by Taxiles and 5,000 of his Indians, he advanced to the Hydaspes. The river was broad, and along its eastern bank Porus had posted his elephants to command the fords. Before describing how Alexander overcame this difficulty, it is important to consider where his crossing was probably made.

Information on this is scanty. It is known from Frontinus that Alexander 'led his army across at a higher point of the stream'[3] – that is, upstream from his camp; and the description of the point of crossing as given by Arrian, is as follows:

> From the bank of the Hydaspes projected a headland, where the river made a considerable bend; it was thick with every sort of tree, and opposite it was an island in the river, wooded and desolate. . . . Observing this island opposite the headland, both being well wooded, and suited to hide the attempt at crossing, Alexander determined to take his army over at this point. The headland and island were about a hundred and fifty stades [seventeen miles] distant from the great camp.[4]

In addition to this Curtius writes that 'there was an island in the river larger than the rest, wooded also and suitable for concealing an ambuscade, moreover in a very deep ditch [nullah] not far from the bank which he himself [i.e. Alexander] held he could conceal not only foot-soldiers but even men and their hosrses'.[5]

On this slight information four theories have been built. The first, by Sir Alexander Burnes and Monsieur Court, one of Ranjit Singh's French generals, is that Alexander pitched his camp at Jhelum.[6] This

---

[1] *Natural History*, VI, xxi, 62.   [2] XV, i, 32.
[3] *Stratagems*, trans. E. Bennett (1925), I, iv, 9.   [4] V, xi, 1–2.   [5] VIII, xiii, 17.
[6] *Journal of the Asiatic Society of Bengal*, 1836, pp. 387 sqq. and 1839, pp. 304 sqq.

theory was adopted by General Sir James Abbott who, in 1848, suggested that from Taxila Alexander marched down what is now the Grand Trunk Road to Jhelum, where the river makes a considerable bend, but where there is no headland or deep nullah; that from there

Right-hand portion of a mosaic from the floor of the House of the Faun in Pompeii depicting a battle of Alexander. *National Museum, Naples*

he marched ten miles upstream to Bhuna, crossed the river and fought his battle between its eastern bank and the Pabbi Hills.[1]

The second theory was put forward by General Alexander Cunningham in 1863,[2] according to which Alexander advanced south of the Grand Trunk Road over the Salt Range, and came down to the river at Jalalpur, some thirty miles south of Jhelum; from there he marched eight miles upstream to Dilawar, where there is an island, and the river makes a slight bend, but again there is no headland or deep nullah; he then crossed at Dilawar, and fought his battle on the

[1] *Journal of the Asiatic Society of Bengal,* 1848, pp. 619 sqq.
[2] *Archaeological Survey Report of 1863–1864,* II, pp. 175 sqq.

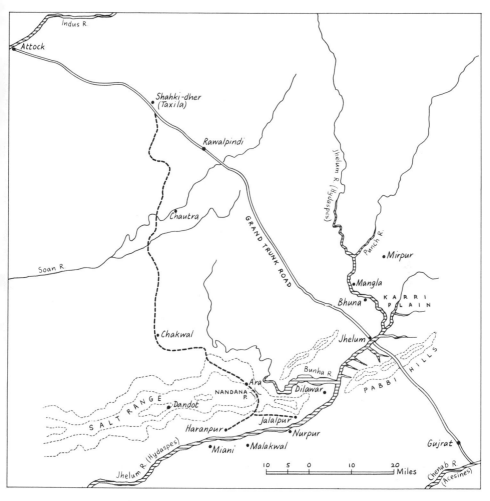

12 ALEXANDER'S ROUTE TO THE HYDASPES

Sarcophagus reputed to be that of Alexander the Great. Musees d'Archeologie, Istanbul

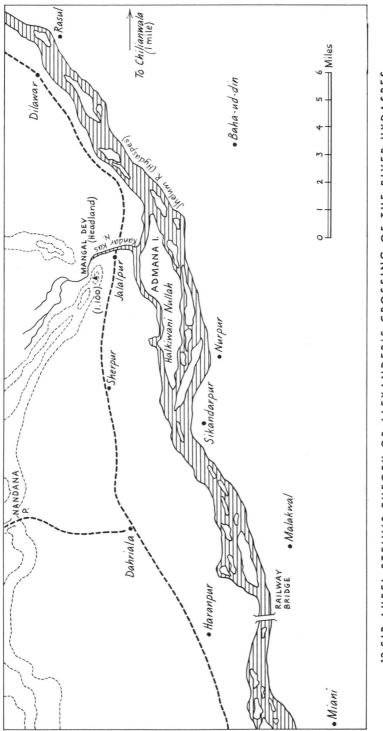

13 SIR AUREL STEIN'S THEORY OF ALEXANDER'S CROSSING OF THE RIVER HYDASPES

eastern side of the river at some spot not far from his camp on the western side.

In 1931, Sir Aurel Stein, after a close examination of the ground, rejected both these theories;[1] the first because the valley between the river and the Pabbi Hills (rising to 1,300 feet) – which because these hills and the Salt Range cannot have changed much since the battle was fought – is too restricted for the deployment of large forces; it is cut up by numerous gullies, nullahs and quicksands and is virtually impassable even after the rains of the hot weather. Although the second theory overcame these difficulties, Sir Aurel Stein considers it more likely that, as in Alexander's day the most practical, and historically the oldest, of the several tracks leading from Taxila over the Salt Range is the one by way of Chakwal, Ara, and the Nandana Pass to Haranpur, where the railway bridge now spans the Jhelum, it was this track which Alexander followed.[2] It also agrees with Strabo's statement that Alexander advanced 'towards the south', and with Pliny's statement that the distance from Taxila to the Hydaspes was 110½ miles, which approximately it is by way of this track, whereas by way of the Grand Trunk Road to Jhelum it is about eighty miles. At Haranpur, now a large village near the Jhelum, the river flows in a single channel with a well-defined bed of about half a mile in width, and it was here, Sir Aurel Stein suggests, that Alexander pitched his camp. Further, he suggests that he marched seventeen and a half miles upstream to Jalalpur, at which place, though the river makes no more than a slight bend, there is a well-defined headland, the Mangal Dev, which rises to a little over 1,100 feet above the river bed. Immediately to the east of the town lies the wide winding mouth of the Kandar Kas nullah, which Stein identifies with Curtius' 'deep ditch', and he adds, 'Nowhere else along its course after debouching from the mountains does the Jhelum touch ground which could possibly be described as a headland or promontory.'[3] The Kanda Kas flows into the Halkiwani nullah, the northern branch of the Jhelum, which from April to August is unfordable. The latter skirts the island of Admana, the largest in the whole course of the Jhelum under consideration here. In 1931 the island was over six miles in length, with a maximum width of one and a half miles, and was thickly wooded. Because, except for

---

[1] *The Geographical Journal*, vol. LXXX (1932), pp. 31–46, and *Archaeological Reconnaissances in North-Western India and South-Eastern Iran* (1937), pp. 1–36.

[2] It was followed by Sultan Mahmud of Ghazni in 1014, and by the Emperor Babur in 1519, in their invasions of India.

[3] *Arch. Rec.*, p. 27. The headland, not the island or the bend, is the important clue, because it is unlikely to have changed since Alexander's day.

'the considerable bend',[1] all the points mentioned by Arrian, Curtius, Pliny and Strabo fit into Stein's theory, Jalalpur is accepted here as Alexander's most probable crossing place.[2] But as Sir William Tarn points out, this question will only be settled when the city of Bucephala, which Alexander built at the crossing point after the battle, is located and identified by excavation.

It is assumed that Alexander encamped at Haranpur; opposite him on the eastern bank of the Hydaspes was Porus, who was seen to have with him a large number of elephants. The strength of his army is variously given: Arrian's estimate is 4,000 cavalry, 30,000 infantry, 300 chariots, and 200 elephants;[3] Diodorus gives 3,000 cavalry, over 50,000 infantry, over 1,000 chariots and 130 elephants;[4] and Curtius – who omits all mention of cavalry – gives 30,000 infantry, 300 chariots and 85 elephants.[5]

Because all fords were held by pickets and elephants, Alexander realized that his horses could neither be swum nor rafted across the river, because they would not face the trumpeting of the elephants and would become frantic when in the water or on their rafts. He resorted to a series of feints. While small parties were dispatched to reconnoitre all possible crossing places, he divided his army into columns, which he marched up and down the river as if he sought a place of crossing. Then, when shortly before the summer solstice the rains set in and the river became swollen, he had corn conveyed from all quarters to his camp so that Porus might believe that he had resolved to remain where he was until the dry weather. In the meantime he reconnoitred the river with his ships and ordered tent skins to be stuffed with hay and converted into rafts. Yet, as Arrian writes, 'all the time he was waiting in ambush to see whether by rapidity of movement he could not steal a passage anywhere without being observed'.[6]

At length, and we may be certain after a close personal reconnaissance, Alexander resolved to make the attempt at the headland and island described by Arrian, and in preparation he decided on a manœuvre almost identical with that adopted by General Wolfe in his

---

[1] It is possible that Ptolemy mistook the slight bend round the pronounced headland as a considerable one, because he never went round the corner to have a look at it. Every motorist will appreciate this.

[2] The fourth theory is put forward by Professor B. Breloer in his *Alexander Kampf gegen Poros* (1933). It is that Alexander advanced by the Grand Trunk Road, pitched his camp at Jhelum, and crossed at a point two and a half miles below the fort of Mangla – thirteen miles above Jhelum – and then advanced fifteen miles down the left bank of the river and engaged Porus in battle. It is demolished by Stein in his *Arch. Rec.*

[3] V, xv, 4.   [4] XVII, 87, 2.   [5] VIII, xiii, 6.   [6] V, x, 1.

1759 Quebec campaign.[1] Under cover of night he sent out his cavalry to various points along the western bank of the river with orders to make a clamour, and from time to time to raise the battle-cry; for several nights Porus marched his elephants up and down the eastern bank to block an attempted crossing until he got tired of it, kept his elephants in camp, and posted scouts along the eastern bank. Then 'when Alexander had brought it about that the mind of Porus no longer entertained any fear of his nocturnal attempts, he devised the following stratagem':[2] Upstream and along the western bank he posted a chain of sentries, each post in sight and hearing of the next one, with orders to raise a din and keep their picket fires burning, while visible preparations were made at the camp to effect a crossing.

Before Alexander's plan is outlined it is as well to set down the names of Alexander's leading generals, because many changes in command had been made since the battle of Arbela. The regiments of the Companion cavalry, recently organized on a five hipparchy basis, were now commanded by Hephaestion, Perdiccas, Craterus, Coenus and Demetrius. The number of battalions of the phalanx had been raised from six to seven; they were commanded by Antigenes (who replaced Coenus), Meleager, Polyperchon (Perdiccas' brother), Alcetas (Amyntas' brother), Attalus, Gorgias, and Cleitus the White. Seleucus commanded the hypaspists and Tauron the archers; possibly during the battle all the light-armed troops were under the latter's command.

Alexander's plan is one of the most interesting ever devised for the crossing of a strongly defended river. Porus had to be kept unaware of the turning movement, and in order to surprise him the turning force had to be kept sufficiently small to permit it to cross the river under cover of one night; also it had to be sufficiently powerful to bring Porus to battle without undue risk of being overwhelmed. To solve these seemingly incompatible requirements, Alexander decided to leave Craterus at Haranpur with a force of sufficient strength to deceive Porus and to organize the turning force in two groups; the leading group, under his own command, was to cross the river at Jalalpur and the rear group was to take up covered positions at selected fords between Haranpur and Jalalpur. Then, when he had crossed with the leading group and by a move downstream had compelled the Indians who blocked the fords to withdraw from them, the rear group

[1] Hannibal's crossing' of the Rhône bears so close a resemblance to Alexander's crossing of the Hydaspes, that it would seem probable that he based his plans on the latter's (see Livy, XXI, 26–7). Polybius (III, 46) provides an interesting description of the rafts Hannibal had made for the ferrying of his elephants. Possibly Alexander's horse-rafts were of similar construction.   [2] Arrian, V, x, 4.

was to cross and join him. This is Tarn's interpretation of an obscure passage in Arrian's *Anabasis*,[1] and should he be right, it follows that the fords in question must have been not far west of Jalalpur. The detail of his plan was as follows:

The Holding Force. Craterus was instructed to remain in the camp with his hipparchy, the Arachosian and Parapamisadae horsemen, the battalions of Alcetas and Polyperchon, and Taxiles' 5,000 Indians; in all about 3,000 cavalry and 8,000 infantry. His orders were, not to attempt to cross the river before Porus either moved northward to face the turning force, or took to flight.

> But [said Alexander], should Porus take a part of his army and lead it against me, and another part be left behind at his camp, and any elephants, do you still stay where you are; if, however, Porus leads all his elephants against me, but some portion of the army is left behind at the camp, then do you cross with all dispatch; for it is only the elephants which are dangerous to disembarking horses; the rest of the force will not trouble them.[2]

The Turning Force. The leading group consisted of the Royal Squadron (300 men); the hipparchies of Hephaestion, Perdiccas, Coenus and Demetrius (4,000); the Dahae horse-archers (1,000); the hypaspists (3,000); the battalions of Antigenes and Cleitus (3,000); the Agrianians (1,000); the archers (2,000), and the javelin-men (1,000).[3] Besides these troops, Arrian mentions 'the cavalry from Bactria and Sogdiana and the Scythian horsemen'.[4] When these horsemen are omitted – they are not mentioned in the battle – in all the assumed strength of the leading group was approximately 5,000 cavalry and 10,000 infantry.

To the rear group Alexander allotted the battalions of Meleager, Attalus and Gorgias, and with them the Greek mercenaries, both horse and foot. Where they were posted is not known, nor is the strength of this group, but possibly is was 500 cavalry and 5,000 infantry.[5]

When Porus had been lulled into a sense of false security and all preparations were completed at the camp and the crossing place, Alexander set out secretly and kept at some distance from the western bank of the river so that his march would not be observed. At Jalalpur

---

[1] *Alexander the Great*, vol. II, appx. 6, pp. 190–1.
[2] Arrian, V, xi, 4.   [3] The strengths are Tarn's.   [4] V, xi, 2.
[5] Although Arrian (V, xii, 1) states that the three phalanx battalions were ordered to cross independently, he makes no further mention of them.

he found all in readiness; but it would seem more likely that the thirty-oared galleys and boats which had been brought there in sections, as well as the rafts, were concealed in the Kandar Kas nullah rather than in the woods, as Arrian states.

Embarkation began immediately under cover of night in a violent storm of rain, the thunder of which drowned the noise of the troops. Near dawn, when the cavalry were on their rafts and the infantry in their boats, the fleet, hidden as it was by the island from the eastern bank of the Hydaspes, set out down the Halkiwani channel to its junction with another branch of the river at the western end of the island. Soon after, as the leading galleys passed the island, they were observed by Porus' scouts, who galloped to Porus with the news. Meanwhile Alexander disembarked with his body-guard and the cavalry on what he believed to be the eastern bank, but after a short advance it was found to be another island, separated from the eastern bank by a wide channel which, though fordable during the dry weather, was now so swollen by the rains that a considerable time was spent before a ford was discovered. 'At its shallowest', it 'was over the breasts of the foot-soldiers', and 'so deep that the horses only kept their heads above the river'.[1]

Certain points in this remarkable river crossing need to be considered.

The basic fact is, that a force of approximately 5,000 cavalry and 10,000 infantry was embarked by a little before dawn on the day the battle of the Hydaspes was fought. Then, should it be assumed that the embarkation was completed by 3 a.m. and that the battle opened at 6 p.m., the following operations were carried out in fifteen hours: A voyage of several miles down the Halkiwani channel; a disembarkation on the second island; the search for a ford; the wade over to the eastern bank and the marshalling of the forces there, and finally, a minor engagement and an advance of probably five or six miles before battle was joined. How was it possible to carry out all these operations in the assumed fifteen hours? All we can answer is, that the staff work of the Macedonian army must have been superb.

There is another question, which also has no answer. How was it possible within a few weeks of his arrival on the Hydaspes for Alexander to collect and construct sufficient river craft to transport 15,000 men and 5,000 horses? Though the number of the vessels is unknown, it must have been enormous. One of the few operations over water to parallel Alexander's is that of William the Conqueror in 1066, and it has been calculated that he must have built or acquired some 350

[1] Arrian, V, xiii, 4.

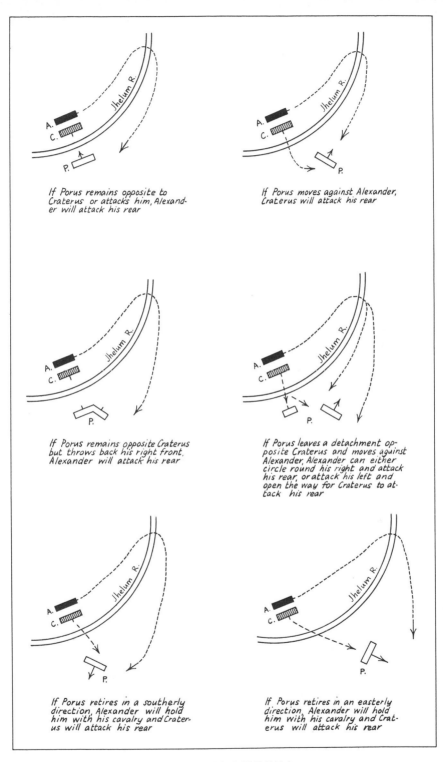

If Porus remains opposite to Craterus or attacks him, Alexander will attack his rear

If Porus moves against Alexander, Craterus will attack his rear

If Porus remains opposite Craterus but throws back his right front, Alexander will attack his rear

If Porus leaves a detachment opposite Craterus and moves against Alexander, Alexander can either circle round his right and attack his rear, or attack his left and open the way for Craterus to attack his rear

If Porus retires in a southerly direction, Alexander will hold him with his cavalry and Craterus will attack his rear

If Porus retires in an easterly direction, Alexander will hold him with his cavalry and Craterus will attack his rear

14 PORUS' DILEMMA

open boats to transport his 2,000 knights and their horses, and his 3,000 foot over the English Channel.[1] These administrative questions continually crop up in Alexander's campaigns, and though the classical historians barely if ever mention them, they are proof positive of the amazing efficiency of the services of the Macedonian army, without which Alexander's conquests would have been impossible.

When his cavalry began to land, Alexander threw forward the horse-archers as an advanced guard and under their cover drew up his order of battle. On the right he marshalled the hipparchies of Hephaestion, Perdiccas, Coenus, and Demetrius, and ordered the hypaspists, under Seleucus, and the two battalions of the phalanx, commanded by Antigenes and Cleitus, with bodies of archers, Agrianians, and javelin-men on their flanks, to form up on their left.

Because he believed himself to be superior to the enemy in cavalry, he decided to lead his Companions forward, supported in rear by Tauron's archers, while the infantry completed their crossing of the river and then followed at a slow pace. From Arrian we learn that his plan embraced three alternatives: to overwhelm Porus with his cavalry while he was changing front; or should this be found impossible, to operate defensively until his infantry came up; or, should Porus retire, to pursue him *à outrance*.

What of Porus? The disembarkation and marshalling of Alexander's forces must have taken several hours, and as Porus had learnt of his approach soon after, or even before, his landing on the second island, he had time to consider his problem, which was – to discover whether the turning movement was or was not a feint. If the former, were he to move the bulk of his army against the turning force he would risk the loss of the Haranpur ford; but if it were not a feint, if he did not concentrate against it he would be placed in a most critical position. His dilemma was profound, and is illustrated in Diagram 14.

He did the right thing, but he did it too late. According to Ptolemy, he sent out one of his sons with 2,000 cavalry and 120 chariots, and although the orders he gave him are unknown, because the forces allotted to him were overpowerful for a mere reconnaissance, it can be assumed that their aim was to drive back the invaders into the river.[2] Were this done, his dilemma would dissolve.

---

[1] *The Decisive Battles of the Western World*, J. F. C. Fuller (1954) vol. 1, p. 372. Incidentally, it took William twelve hours to disembark at Pevensey, and in 1415 Henry V spent three August days in disembarking 8,000–10,000 men at Harfleur.

[2] According to Polyaenus (*Stratagems*, IV, iii, 21) 'Pikatos, a grandson of Porus [Arrian calls him Spitaces] endeavoured to arrest Alexander's march in a narrow valley terminating in a straight defile [? a nullah]'.

When the younger Porus appeared on the scene, Alexander at first believed that his force was the advanced guard of the Indian army and that it could be held by his horse-archers, and he led on his cavalry to clinch with the main body before it could deploy. But when he learnt from his scouts of its strength, he decided to annihilate it. A cavalry action followed in which Porus' son was killed as well as 400 of his horsemen, and all his chariots were driven into the clayey land that bordered the Hydaspes and captured. It was probably then – although it is not recorded – that Meleager, Attalus, and Gorgias crossed the river and joined up with Antigenes and Cleitus.

Next came the battle, and although the site of the battlefield has not been determined, should Stein be correct in placing Alexander's crossing at Jalalpur, it probably lay five or six miles south-west of the village of Nurpur, which is situated on the open plain that stretches south-westward on the left bank of the Jhelum river toward the villages of Malakwal and Miani. Not far from Nurpur is the village of Sikandarpur, but, as Stein points out, because the name Sikandar ('Alexander') is so common in the Punjab, it carries no significance.

When the refugees from the disaster told Porus that his son was dead and Alexander over the river with a powerful army, at first Porus hesitated on the course he should adopt, because Craterus was then trying to cross from Haranpur. At last he decided to leave a fraction of his army with a few elephants to face Craterus, and to march against Alexander with the rest. When he found a place both free from clay and hard and level, he drew up his army in order of battle. When his son's losses are deducted, he had with him 3,600 cavalry, 30,000 infantry, 180 chariots and 200 elephants. He deployed them as follows:

> First the elephants on the front, distant each from each about a hundred feet, so that they should form a line in front of the whole infantry line, and at all points terrify the cavalry of Alexander. For in any case he did not expect that any of the enemy would dare to force a way through the gaps between the elephants, certainly not on horseback, since the horses would take fright, and still less foot-soldiers, who would be kept back by the heavy armed troops advancing in line and then would be trampled down by the elephants turning upon them. Behind these elephants were stationed the foot soldiers, not in the same front as the elephants, but holding the second line after them, so that the columns were fitted more or less,

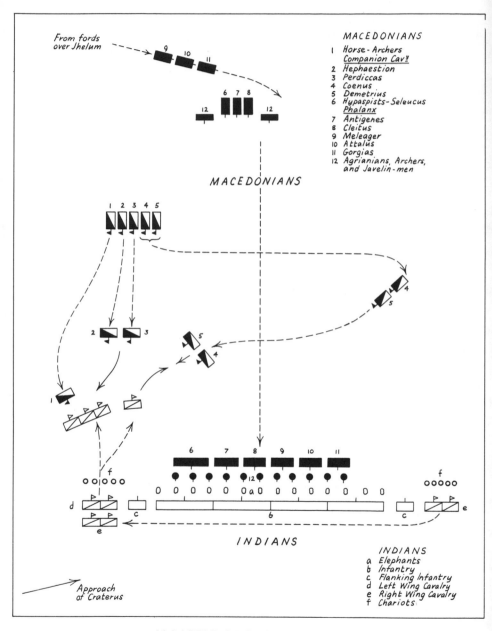

MACEDONIANS

1 Horse - Archers
  Companion Cav.ˣ
2 Hephaestion
3 Perdiccas
4 Coenus
5 Demetrius
6 Hypaspists – Seleucus
  Phalanx
7 Antigenes
8 Cleitus
9 Meleager
10 Attalus
11 Gorgias
12 Agrianians, Archers,
   and Javelin-men

From fords
over Jhelum

MACEDONIANS

MACEDONIANS

INDIANS

INDIANS

a Elephants
b Infantry
c Flanking Infantry
d Left Wing Cavalry
e Right Wing Cavalry
f Chariots

Approach
of Craterus

15 BATTLE OF THE HYDASPES

into the intervals left by the animals.[1] Porus had besides stationed on the wings foot soldiers, stretching even beyond the line of elephants. Then on each flank of the infantry the cavalry was posted, and in front of the cavalry the chariots, on both sides.[2]

According to Plutarch, when Alexander engaged Porus' son he was '20 furlongs'[3] in advance of his own infantry, and, according to Arrian, when at some time after this engagement he observed Porus forming his line of battle, he halted his cavalry so that the infantry might catch up with him. Actually he must have halted them long before this, and in all probability under cover from view, because it must have taken at least two to three hours for Porus to have received the news of his son's defeat, made up his mind, and changed front. When the infantry came up Alexander halted them, and while they rested he decided on his plan of action. It was to lead to one of the most remarkable cavalry engagements in history.

So much muddled tactical comment has been made on this battle that, first of all, Arrian will be quoted fully and then by means of a few common-sense assumptions, the reader may get a clear picture of what in all probability happened.

Arrian begins by stating that when Alexander examined his enemy's array he saw that the whole of his front was covered by his elephants, and accordingly he set aside all thought of a frontal attack and decided to advance with his numerically superior cavalry obliquely against Porus' left wing. Then Arrian seemingly contradicts himself. He continues:

Coenus he sent to the right,[4] with the regiments of Demetrius and his own; he commanded him so soon as the Indians should perceive the solid body of cavalry and advance their cavalry to meet it, he should keep behind them. Seleucus, Antigenes and Tauron Alexander commanded to lead the infantry phalanx; but they were not to take part in the action till they observed the enemy's main body of infantry and their cavalry thrown into confusion by his own cavalry force.[5]

---

[1] Because a line composed of spearmen in small columns would be inherently weak, the columns were probably of double depth – that is, each contained sufficient men to fill in the gaps immediately in rear of the elephants when a continuous front was needed. If the normal depth of the phalanx was ten ranks, then the columns would be in twenty or more ranks, according to the width of the deployment required.   [2] Arrian, V, xv, 5–7.   [3] 'Alexander', LX.

[4] It is almost generally accepted that this means toward the Indian right flank.

[5] V, xvi, 3.

When still out of bow-shot, Alexander launched his horse-archers against the Indian left wing in order to throw it into confusion and then rode rapidly toward the enemy left wing to charge it with the Companion cavalry when it was in confusion and before it could close its ranks.

> Meanwhile [writes Arrian] the Indians had collected their cavalry from all parts, and were riding along, advancing out of their position to meet Alexander's charge. Coenus also appeared with his men, according to his instructions. The Indians, observing this, were compelled to make the line of their cavalry face both ways; the largest and best part against Alexander, while the rest wheeled round against Coenus and his forces.

The appearance of Coenus 'at once upset the formations and intentions of the Indians, and Alexander perceiving the opportunity . . . attacked'. The Indians did not wait to receive the charge, 'but fell hurriedly back upon their elephants, as if to some friendly sheltering wall'.[1] So much for Arrian's description of the cavalry action.

Tarn's interpretation radically differs from this, and is more clearly given by him in *The Cambridge Ancient History*[2] than in the first volume of his *Alexander the Great*. It reads:

> Out of bowshot he [Alexander] halted . . . and Porus seeing the massed cavalry, brought all his own cavalry round to his left. Alexander began by sending his horse-archers to attack the infantry of Porus' left wing[3] outside the elephants and keep them occupied; his own infantry had orders not to attack till he had defeated Porus' cavalry. He desired to draw that cavalry away from the elephants; he therefore ordered Coenus to take two hipparchies and move off towards Porus' right (Alexander's left); then, when the Indian cavalry, seeing the force opposed to them, should charge his orders were to take them in rear. If Alexander knew that the Indian cavalry, a weaker force than his own, would charge him, this could only be because he inteded to make them do so; the inducement was the division of his force; they would imagine Coenus was going to support the horse-archers, and would only see two hipparchies with Alexander. The plan worked; the Indians attacked Alexander's two hipparchies, and while Alexander met

---

[1] V, xvii, 1-2.   [2] Vol. VI, p. 408.

[3] Surely the left-wing cavalry, not the infantry, or the horse-archers would have been ridden over by the former. The effective range of the horse-archer's bow was considerably less than that of the infantry bow.

them Coenus swung round and took them in rear; after a sharp fight they were driven to take refuge behind the elephants.[1]

Should Tarn's interpretation be correct,[2] then two things follow: the first is that tactically Porus must have been blind; and the second, that Alexander was a most indifferent cavalry general, which so far he certainly had not shown himself to be.

As regards Porus, Arrian does not say that when Alexander halted out of bow-shot he sent Coenus toward the Indian right; but that he did so before this halt. Had he done so just before he sent out his horse-archers, as Tarn assumes he did, Porus must have seen Coenus' move towards the Indian right, and he could not possibly have thought that Coenus' intention was to support the horse-archers, because they were engaged on the Indian left – that is, in the opposite direction – and probably were no more than a few hundred paces in advance of Alexander's two hipparchies. Instead, Porus would have at once fathomed what was in Alexanders' mind, and would either have wheeled round part of his cavalry to face Coenus much earlier than he did, or else have withdrawn the whole of his cavalry behind his elephants – the last thing Alexander wanted.

As regards Alexander's generalship, no cavalry general worth his salt would await a cavalry charge when he was in position to deliver one, because the *raison d'être* of heavy cavalry *is* to charge, and when halted, their defensive power is negligible.[3] When stationary, even if

---

[1] Again in *Alexander the Great* (vol. II, appx. 6, pp. 193–7), after a minute examination of the meaning of Arrian's Greek, Tarn writes that, when Porus had concentrated all his cavalry on his left flank, 'the whole body charges Alexander's advancing cavalry'. Also, 'his orders to Coenus show that he was not going to charge, but was going to make the Indian cavalry charge *him*, to get them away from the elephants and give Coenus the opportunity of taking them in rear'.

[2] Some other interpretations are: Wilcken (*Alexander the Great*, p. 182) makes Alexander charge the Indian left-wing cavalry before the right-wing cavalry reinforced it, and no sooner was it reinforced, than Coenus fell on the rear of the combined Indian cavalry; Bury (*History of Greece*, p. 804) makes Coenus ride toward the Hydaspes – that is, toward the Indian left; Wheeler (*Alexander the Great*, p. 442) does the same; while Dodge (*Alexander the Great*, vol. II, p. 558) makes Coenus ride round the Indian right and rear and emerge on the Indian left. Vincent A. Smith (*The Early History of India*, pp. 69–73) also makes Coenus gallop round Porus' right wing. Further, he locates the battlefield on the Karri Plain east of Bhuna, and because there is not sufficient room there to deploy 200 elephants in line, he considers it probable that they were marshalled in eight ranks. There is no warrant for this assumption, and tactically it would be absurd.

[3] Though Tarn asserts (see reference 1, *above*) that Alexander's cavalry were 'advancing' and not halted, the difference is immaterial because, unless they were advancing *with the intention to charge*, which Tarn says they were not, they were at as great a disadvantage as if halted.

charged by an inferior force, they are liable to be thrown into wild confusion.[1] If Alexander wanted to draw the enemy cavalry away from the elephants he would not have waited to be charged; he would have fallen back, in order to persuade his enemy to follow him. Whatever the correct reading of Arrian's Greek may be, it is beyond belief that Alexander – of all men – should plan to be charged.

Since, from Arrian's account, it is clear that Coenus' attack came as a surprise to the Indian cavalry, then it logically follows that from the time Alexander dispatched him toward the Indian right until the moment when, according to Arrian, he 'appeared'[2] in rear of the Indian cavalry, his whereabouts were unknown to Porus. Granted this logical assumption, everything becomes clear, and without violation of Arrian's account of what happened before Coenus launched his rear attack, events may be reconstructed as follows:

When, after his engagement with Porus' son, Alexander halted his cavalry, as we have suggested he kept it out of view, and we may assume that either he or his scouts kept the enemy in view; Porus then, was unable to estimate Alexander's cavalry strength, whereas Alexander could estimate that of Porus. Because Alexander was aware that his cavalry would not face the elephants, he was also aware that his phalanx would have to advance against them without cavalry support and so, to secure the phalanx against cavalry attack on its flanks or rear, he had to destroy the Indian cavalry before the phalanx assaulted. How could he do this? Only by inducing Porus to concentrate the *whole* of his cavalry on *one* of his flanks, and then to overwhelm it.

Let us step into Alexander's shoes. His forces are out of sight; he has taken a rapid survey of the battlefield and of the enemy's line of battle, and has decided to attack Porus' left flank. He turns to his generals and says:

'When we have drawn nearer, I am going to send forward the horse-archers as a covering force with orders to annoy the enemy's left-wing cavalry. Next, I shall manœuvre against the enemy's left-wing cavalry with my two leading hipparchies, a force I judge to be sufficiently inferior to the total cavalry forces of the enemy that it will

---

[1] At the battle of Balaclava (October 25, 1854) General Scarlet's three leading squadrons (300 horse) of the Heavy Cavalry Brigade charged a mass of Russian cavalry which outnumbered them by over ten to one. The latter were thrown into wild confusion, because, as Kinglake writes, they had been kept 'at a halt, and condemned (in violation of the principles which govern the use of cavalry) to be passively awaiting the attack' (*The Invasion of the Crimea*, Student's edit., 1899, p. 283).

[2] 'Appeared' suggests that previously he had not been seen.

persuade Porus to reinforce his left-wing cavalry with his right-wing cavalry in order to be superior to me.'

Then he turns to Coenus and says:

'I want you to take your hipparchy and Demetrius' and move in the direction of the enemy's right flank under cover from view along that dip in the ground there (points it out). And when you see me move forward toward the enemy cavalry, which by then I hope will be massed on his left flank, you will at once gallop for all you are worth and charge the mass in flank and rear, while I charge it in front.'

In this interpretation the sole assumptions are, that Alexander halted his cavalry out of sight of Porus, a precaution every cavalry leader would take, and that, when he resumed his advance, although his two hipparchies were visible to Porus, because of the formation of the ground Coenus' two hipparchies were not. The rest follows as Arrian describes it.

When the Indian cavalry was driven back on the elephants, the mahouts on the left of the Indian line urged forward their animals against Alexander's cavalry; thereupon the Macedonian phalanx boldly advanced and the battle became general. Because we are told by Arrian that as the elephants pressed forward their mahouts were met with showers of javelins, and that at times they and their elephants were ringed by javelin-men who volleyed them from all sides, Tauron's light-armed troops must have preceded the phalanx into battle.

The action [writes Arrian] was unlike any of the previous contests; for wherever the beasts could wheel round, they rushed forth against the ranks of infantry and demolished the phalanx of the Macedonians, dense as it was. The Indian cavalry also, seeing that the infantry were engaged in the action, rallied again and advanced against the Macedonian cavalry. But when Alexander's men, who far excelled both in strength and military discipline, got the mastery over them the second time, they were again repulsed towards the elephants and cooped up among them. By this time the whole of Alexander's cavalry had collected into one squadron, not by any command of his, but having settled into this arrangement by the mere effect of the struggle itself; and wherever it fell upon the ranks of the Indians, they were broken up with great slaughter. The beasts being now cooped up into a narrow space, their friends were no less injured by them than their foes, being trampled down in the wheeling and pushing about. Accordingly there ensued a great slaughter of the cavalry, cooped up as it was in a narrow space around the elephants. Most of the keepers of the elephants had been killed by the javelins, and some of the elephants themselves had been wounded, while others no longer kept apart in the battle on account of their sufferings or from being destitute of keepers. But, as if frantic from pain, rushing forward at friends and foes alike, they pushed about, trampling down and killing them in every kind of way. However, the Macedonians inasmuch as they were attacking the beasts in an open space and in accordance with their own plan, got out of their way whenever they rushed at them; and when they wheeled round to return, followed them closely and hurled javelins at them; whereas the Indians retreating among them were now receiving greater injury from them. But when the beasts were tired out, and were no longer able to charge with any vigour, they began to retire slowly, facing the foe like ships backing water, merely uttering a shrill piping sound. Alexander himself surrounded the whole line with his cavalry, and gave the signal that the infantry should link their shields together so as to form a very densely closed body, and thus advance in phalanx. By this means the Indian cavalry, with the exception of a few men, was quite cut up in the action; as was also the infantry, since the Macedonians were now pressing upon them from all sides. Upon this, all who could do so turned to flight through the spaces which intervened between the parts of Alexander's cavalry.[1]

While the battle raged, Craterus forced his way over the Haranpur ford. When he saw that Alexander was winning a brilliant victory he pressed on and, as his men were fresh, took over the pursuit. Yet, in spite of the carnage and the rout, unlike Darius, Porus refused to abandon the field as long as any part of his troops held their ground. Though wounded, he battled on bravely until, tortured by thirst and weak from loss of blood, he surrendered himself to an Indian, Meroes, an old friend of his, who had been sent by Alexander, overcome with admiration for the valour Porus displayed, to appeal to him not to sacrifice his life in vain. The battle then ended.

The casualties recorded by Arrian are: of the Indians 20,000 infantry and 3,000 cavalry killed, all the chariots destroyed, and all the surviving elephants captured. Among the Indian dead were two sons of Porus and his grandson Spitaces, the governor of the province in which the battle was fought, the commanders of the elephants and chariots as well as other commanding officers. Arrian states that the Macedonians

[1] V, xvii, 3–7.

lost eighty infantry, ten horse-archers and 220 cavalry killed, including twenty of the Companions. Diodorus' figures appear more realistic. They are: Indians, more than 12,000 killed and 9,000 captured, as well as eighty elephants; Macedonians, 280 cavalry and 700 infantry killed.

7

ALEXANDER'S SIEGES

✕✕✕

The Siege of Halicarnassus

The three major sieges undertaken by Alexander were those of Halicarnassus, Tyre, and Gaza. Halicarnassus, the present-day Bodrum, was the capital city of Caria and the Persian main naval base commanding the southern approach to the Aegean. It was situated on the southern shore of a small peninsula that jutted westward between the gulfs of Mendelia to the north and of Cos to the south, and was strategically well placed because it was linked with Attica by the islands of the Cyclades, and with Crete by the Sporades (Dodecanese), of which Rhodes was the most important. As a step toward command of the Aegean, and thereby to secure his sea communications with Macedonia, it was imperative for Alexander to wrest Halicarnassus from the Persians.

Two complementary accounts have survived, one by Arrian, based on Ptolemy and Aristobulus, written from the point of view of the besiegers; the other, by Diodorus, which follows a lost mercenary source,[1] tells the story from the point of view of the besieged. Though they differ in detail, in general they agree.

By nature and art Halicarnassus was a strongly defended city; on its landward side it had a towered wall surrounded by a moat forty-five feet broad and twenty-two feet deep. It possessed three citadels; the original acropolis at its north-western corner, the Fortress of Salmacis on the sea close to the south-western corner, and the King's Castle on the small island of Arconnesus at the entrance of the harbour and near the shore. It was strongly garrisoned by 2,000 or more Greek mercenaries under Ephialtes, an Athenian exile, and a large force of Asiatics, commanded by Orontobates, satrap of Caria. Memnon, who had recently

---

[1] See Tarn's *Alexander the Great*, vol. II, p. 73.

been appointed governor of lower Asia, was in supreme command of
both the army and the fleet, and he had supplied the city to withstand
a long siege; its magazines were full, and it possessed many defensive
engines. Further, he had moored a squadron in the harbour, and its
crews could be called upon to reinforce the garrison. Lastly, because
Alexander had disbanded his fleet, the Persians held absolute command
of the sea and could reinforce and supply the city at will.

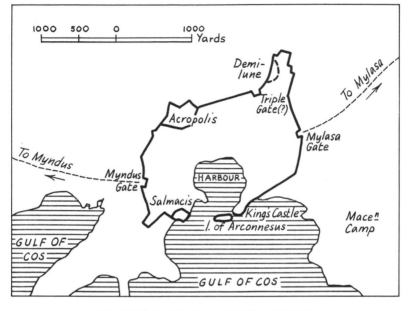

16 SIEGE OF HALICARNASSUS

After the capitulation of Miletus in the autumn of 334 B.C., Alexander advanced on Halicarnassus. Its siege was to prove the most formidable enterprise he had as yet undertaken; unlike at Miletus, his
approach was restricted to its landward side. He encamped his army
near the south-eastern corner of the city, and not far from the Mylasa
gate, from which a road ran to Mylasa (Milas) twenty-five miles to the
north-east.

His first operation was a reconnaissance of the walls in the vicinity
of the Mylasa gate, but he was surprised by a sudden and violent sortie
of the garrison which, though repulsed, must have caused considerable
confusion, because the attackers were in no way hindered in regaining
the city. This slight setback persuaded Alexander to seek another spot.

A few days later he moved from the eastern to the western side of Halicarnassus to reconnoitre the walls in the neighbourhood of the Myndus gate, from which a road ran to Myndus, some twelve miles west of Halicarnassus and at the western extremity of the peninsula upon which Halicarnassus stood. He also intended to occupy Myndus, because a faction of its citizens had offered to betray their city to him.

He took with him the hypaspists, Companion cavalry, the battalions of Perdiccas, Amyntas, and Meleager, the Agrianians, and the archers, and passed round to the western side. From there he made a night advance on Myndus, but as he approached its walls, the signal agreed upon with the traitors was not made. As Alexander had not brought his siege train with him, he made an abortive attempt to undermine its walls before the approach by sea of enemy reinforcements made him abandon all idea of storming the city and withdraw to Halicarnassus.

The siege then opened in earnest and an attempt to breach the city wall was made at the northern extremity of the city. Alexander had a section of the moat filled in to enable his siege towers and rams to be moved close to the wall, and had pent-houses and mantlets built in order to protect the miners detailed to undermine its foundations. Before the work had progressed far, the garrison made a night sally to set fire to the towers before they could be brought into position. They were repulsed, but in the engagement Neoptolemus, brother of the deserter Amyntas, and 170 of the garrison fell; sixteen Macedonians were killed and 300 were wounded. According to Arrian, the disproportion between the Macedonian dead and injured was because the sally had been made under cover of night, which made it difficult for the besiegers to protect themselves with their shields against the volleys of missiles hurled at them.

A few days later, when two towers and the intervening curtain wall had been battered down and a third tower badly shaken, and while the besieged were hastily building a *demi-lune* of brick to cover the breach, an unexpected incident precipitated an engagement. Two drunken soldiers of Perdiccas' battalion who had been boasting of their respective prowess, decided to prove who was the braver, armed themselves and set out to attack the *demi-lune*. When their approach was seen from the walls flanking the breach the defenders leapt down and slew them, and then attacked the Macedonian outposts. Perdiccas rushed reinforcements forward and more of the garrison joined in the fray. A stiff fight followed, but again, as Arrian relates, the Macedonians drove back their attackers and nearly captured the city because its walls were denuded of troops.

Diodorus has a different story to tell, according to which, the Macedonians, hurried forward by Perdiccas, were severely repulsed, and not until Alexander appeared on the scene with reinforcements did Memnon withdraw his troops. That the garrison had the best of this encounter is supported by an incident which Ptolemy does not mention, presumably because it would be derogatory to Alexander. It was that, once the action was over, '. . . the king sent a trumpeter to make a truce, in order to carry off those Macedonians that were slain before the walls'.[1] This shows that the Macedonians got the worst of it. The request was opposed by Ephialtes, but it was granted by Memnon.

The next day Alexander moved forward his towers and rams to breach the *demi-lune*, but again a sally was made and this time part of the pent-house erected against the wall and one of the wooden towers were burnt. The rest were saved by Philotas and Hellanicus, and when Alexander came forward, the sally party threw down their torches and fled back to the city.

> Yet at first [writes Arrian] from the position, which was commanding, the besieged had the best of it, and did not only volley straight ahead along their line at the advance guard of the engines, but also from the towers left standing on either side of the breach, which enabled them to volley on the flanks, and almost at the rear, of those who approached the new-built wall.[2]

After this engagement, Ephialtes pointed out at a council of war assembled in Halicarnassus, that, were the city to be saved, an offensive must be assumed. Memnon agreed. Though the plan, as given by Diodorus, is somewhat obscure, it would appear to have been as follows: 2,000 Greek mercenaries, in two groups of 1,000 each, were to sally out; one column carrying lighted fire-brands was to advance from the *demi-lune* and set fire to the enemy's engines, and the other, under Ephialtes, was to issue out from the 'triple gate', which presumably was situated on the flank of the breach, but at no great distance from it. Then, when the first column's attack on the engines had drawn the enemy to their rescue, the second column was to fall on the enemy's flank. Lastly, should this surprise attack succeed, Memnon with the bulk of the Persian troops was to come to the support of Ephialtes and deliver the *coup de grâce*. Should this be the correct reading of Diodorus, it shows that Alexander was faced by no mean foe.

Next, Arrian writes that when, a few days after the last engagement,

[1]Diodorus, XVII, 27, 6.   [2] Arrian, I, xxi, 6.

Alexander brought forward his engines to attack the *demi-lune*, suddenly he was 'attacked near the breach', and immediately after by a second group of the enemy, who 'issued out of the triple gate, the last place the Macedonians looked for a sally'.[1] Then, after a description of the fight around the engines, he writes:

> As for those who sallied by the triple gate, Ptolemaeus, captain of the body-guard of Alexander, met them, bringing up the battalions of Addaeus and Timander,[2] and some of the light troops; these too fairly easily drove back the sallying party. This also suffered in the retreat over a narrow bridge thrown over the moat; the bridge gave way under their numbers, many fell into the moat, some were trampled by their comrades, some the Macedonians shot down from above. The greatest slaughter was round about the gates themselves; for the gates were shut prematurely in panic, the defenders fearing lest the Macedonians, pressing hard upon the fugitives, might enter also; thus many friends were shut out, to be destroyed by their foes close to the walls. The city indeed came near to capture, had not Alexander sounded the retreat, desirous even now of saving Halicarnassus if the citizens would surrender without further hostility.[3]

Diodorus' account differs. He writes that, when all was in readiness, at dawn on the day of the counter-attack the gates were suddenly flung open and the first column rushed out and cast its fire-brands among the engines. Immediately afterward, Ephialtes issued forth, formed his men into a deep phalanx and 'charged upon the Macedonians, who were hastening to preserve and defend the engines. . . . Noise and clamour filled the camp, and the trumpet giving the alarm to battle, they fell to it', and though the Macedonians easily quenched the fire, in the conflict 'Ephialtes got the better'. Then Memnon came on the scene, and with so powerful a force that Alexander 'knew not well what to do'. Then he writes:

> On a sudden the tables were turned: for the Macedonians (who by reason of their age were to this time dispensed with, and not called to fight, though formerly victorious in many battles under King Philip) now, at this very instant, were stirred up to their ancient courage and resolution; and, being both valiant and expert soldiers (far beyond all the rest), they upbraided the cowardice of the freshwater soldiers, who turned their backs, with most bitter taunts and reproaches. These presently getting into a body and clapping their

---

[1] Arrian, I, xxii, 1.   [2] These were not phalanx battalions.   [3] Ibid., I, xxii, 4–7.

bucklers one into another, fell in upon the enemy (now confident of an assured victory), and, having killed Ephialtes, and many others, forced the rest into the city; and the Macedonians, being mixed with the others in the night-time, entered pell-mell with them within the walls; but the king ordered a retreat to be sounded, and so they returned into the camp.[1]

In explanation of this, it would appear that the troops Ephialtes first engaged – the battalions of Addaeus and Timander – were composed of young and inexperienced soldiers,[2] and that not until the veteran Macedonians – Philip's old soldiers – came up was Ephialtes repulsed. This is alluded to by Curtius who, in his account of the fatal quarrel between Alexander and Cleitus, makes the latter say: 'You scorn the soldiers of Philip, forgetting that if old Atarrhias . . . had not called back the younger men when they shrank from battle, we should still be lingering around Halicarnassus.'[3]

The conclusion of Arrian's description of the Persian counter-attack and its repulse – the sounding of the retreat – seems to lack something which would have made it more intelligible. If, as he writes, the city was nearly captured, unless Alexander had full assurance that at least some of its citizens were prepared to join him, he was too good a general not to have pressed on. It may be that he was unable to do so because of the confusion Diodorus says his troops were in, and because it was night-time; but what would seem as likely is, that all along he had been in contact with an anti-Persian faction within Halicarnassus, the adherents of which were prepared to welcome him as their liberator.[4] This is suggested by the decision taken by Memnon and Orontobates immediately after their repulse, to set fire to the city and withdraw their troops to the King's Castle and Salmacis. The reasons given for the decision are that because part of the city wall had been lost and casualties had been heavy,[5] the city was no longer tenable. Although this may have been so, it would seem more probable that as Alexander had gained a footing within the walls they feared a rising of the people

---

[1] XVII, 27, 1–4.

[2] Though our authorities do not mention it, presumably because it was so obvious to them, the miners and workers of the siege engines would be escorted by light-armed soldiers – javelin-men and archers – and not by phalangites, who were shock troops, and therefore were unsuited to cover the siege operations.

[3] VIII, i, 36.

[4] It will be remembered that there was an anti-Persian faction in Myndus.

[5] We are told that they numbered 1,000 men killed, which is probably an exaggeration as Alexander's casualties are given at no more than forty. (Arrian, I, xxii, 7).

and, if so, the conclusion is that it was Alexander's liberal policy as much as force of arms that delivered the city into his hands.

The firing of the city took place about midnight. When Alexander saw the flames spread, he sent troops into the city to put to the sword all incendiaries caught in the act; but all citizens who remained in their houses were to be spared. When, as dawn broke, he learnt that Memnon had withdrawn his men to the King's Castle and Salmacis, he decided not to lay regular siege to these fortresses, but only to invest them. This course was dictated because of their strength, because they were unlikely to be taken through treason, and because they were open to the sea, which meant that they could not be starved out. According to both Arrian and Diodorus, he next ordered the city to be razed to the ground, but this is most unlikely because he had no intention to reduce the inhabitants to slavery and only a few hours earlier had ordered all incendiaries to be put to death. It is more probable that he had the houses in their neighbourhood demolished in order to throw up defensive works in the vicinity of the two fortresses. Then he left Ptolemy, son of Lagus, with 3,000 Greek infantry and 200 cavalry to blockade the fortresses while he marched into Phrygia. That he was wise not to attempt a regular siege of the fortresses is supported by the fact that it was not until shortly before the battle of Issus, in the autumn of 333 B.C., that Orontobates was defeated by Ptolemy and Asander in pitched battle and the King's Castle and Salmacis surrendered to them.[1] The two citadels had held out for just twelve months.

The Siege of Tyre

After the battle of Issus, Alexander's problem was the conquest of Phoenicia; like Greece it was a land of city-states, each a trading community. Intense rivalry existed between them, especially between Tyre and Sidon, and at times they subjected their neighbours, as Aradus did Marathus, and although they acknowledged the suzerainty of Persia, they were virtually independent, monarchial principalities. There were twenty-five of them in all, many quite small, and the most important were Tyre (Es Sur), Sidon (Saida), Aradus (Arvad), Byblus (Gebal), and Tripolis.[2]

When Alexander set out southward with his customary speed these cities were placed between the horns of a dilemma. If they opposed him, uncombined as they were, they risked falling one by one; if they sub-

[1] Arrian, II, v, 6-7.
[2] For further information, see *History of Phoenicia*, George Rawlinson (1889), chap. IV.

mitted to him with their fleets still in the Aegean with many of their chief men and several of their kings,[1] then their ships might be seized by Darius and their crews held in hostage for their fidelity. The first city in Alexander's path was Aradus; though small it was immensely strong, for it was situated on an island of rock, 800 yards in length and 500 in breadth, two and a half miles from the shore. Its walls were of immense thickness, and in places were built of hewn stones of fifteen to eighteen feet in length, strongly cemented together; parts of the walls still rise to a height of over thirty feet.[2] As it could not long withstand a siege without a fleet to supply it, Straton, son of Gerostratus, who had been left in command, decided to surrender his fortress to Alexander. He also yielded the cities of Marathus, Sigon, and Mariamme, which were under his sway. Byblus, whose king was also absent, was the next to open its gates to him, and Sidon, whose inhabitants loathed the Persians, welcomed him. These submissions isolated Tyre, the most powerful of the cities. King Azemilk was still in the Aegean, so to avert a siege the Tyrians sent envoys to tell Alexander that they had decided to accept whatever terms he might propose. He expressed his desire to sacrifice in the temple of the Tyrian Heracles (Melkart), but was unaware that according to the Tyrian custom only the king was allowed to do so;[3] were the envoys to grant his request, it would carry with it acknowledgment of him as their king.[4] The envoys did not explain this to him but replied that they would grant him anything except sacrifice and, as they trusted in the strength of their walls, they added that they would have neither Persian nor Macedonian within their city. This so angered Alexander that he dismissed them, assembled his commanders, and addressed them in terms of the speech quoted in full in Chapter 5.

[1] Enylus of Byblus, Gerostratus of Aradus, and Azemilk of Tyre.

[2] It had an ample water supply: Strabo (XVI, ii, 13) writes, 'The inhabitants are supplied with water partly from cisterns containing rain water, and partly from the opposite coast. In war time they obtain water a little in front of the city, from the channel (between the island and the mainland) in which there is an abundant spring. The water is obtained by letting down from a boat . . . and inverting over the spring (at the bottom of the sea), a wide-mouthed funnel of lead, the end of which is contracted to a moderate-sized opening; round this is fastened a (long) leather pipe . . . which receives the water forced up from the spring through the funnel. The water first forced up is sea water, but the boatmen wait for the flow of pure and potable water, which is received into the vessels ready for the purpose, in as large a quantity as may be required, and carry it to the city.' The fountain is now known by the name of Ain Ibrahim, Abraham's fountain.

[3] See Wilcken's *Alexander the Great*, p. 109.

[4] Although Tyre was not a Greek city Alexander might have suspected this, because Aristotle, in his *Politics* (III, 1285b), discusses the ancient Greek kingdoms, and says that only their kings had the right of presiding over the sacrifices.

Old Tyre (Palaetyros) was situated on the mainland twenty miles to the south of Sidon, and a little over two miles to the north-west of it and half a mile from the shore lay a group of rocky islets parallel with the coast. The two largest in the centre of the group had been linked together by filling in the intervening channel, and on them New Tyre was built; according to Pliny,[1] its circumference was two and three-quarter miles.

The city was surrounded by a lofty wall, which rose to the height of 150 feet on its eastern side, and on its southern side its foundations, which may still be traced, were laid in the sea. Like Sidon, it possessed two harbours, both on its eastern side; the northern was called the Sidonian harbour and the southern the Egyptian harbour. The houses were built in many stories to save space and were crowded together;[2] the city was full of dye works and its inhabitants would seem to have numbered about 40,000. A long account of their trading activities is to be found in the Book of Ezekiel, Chapter XXVII.

Because Alexander had determined to occupy Egypt before seeking a final decision with Darius, he could not leave an unsubdued Tyre on his line of communications. In Grote's opinion,[3] since the main value of the Phoenician cities lay in their ships, had Alexander insisted on their withdrawal from Persian service and surrender to him, the cities would in all probability have complied and the siege of Tyre would have been unnecessary. But he overlooks the fact that as Aradus, Byblus, Sidon and all the lesser cities had already surrendered to Alexander, on their return from the Aegean their fleets would have had to follow suit. Further, in all probability he was aware that immediately after the Tyrian envoys returned to Tyre, the Tyrians began to send their wives and children to their old colony of Carthage, and he may also have learnt that they had received a promise from the Carthaginians to come to their aid with a powerful fleet.[4] Even though he did not have a fleet, not a moment was to be lost in laying siege to Tyre.

In January, 332 B.C., the siege was opened. The first step taken by Alexander was to order the construction of a mole across the half mile of water that separated the mainland from the island city, and though the sea was mainly shallow, on the island side it reached the depth of three fathoms. According to Diodorus, the breadth of the mole was 200 feet, and though this may be an exaggerated figure, when finally built it was sufficiently solid to resist erosion by the sea and, widened by

---

[1] *Natural History*, V, xvii, 77.   [2] Strabo, XVI, ii, 23.
[3] Vol. X, p. 82.   [4] Curtius, IV, ii, 10–12.

silt, it remains to this day in the form of the isthmus that links the original island to the mainland.

Besides the soldiers, thousands of the local inhabitants were pressed into labour gangs, stone was obtained by demolishing Old Tyre, and wood gathered in abundance from the forests of the Lebanon. The work, like all others throughout the siege, was supervised by

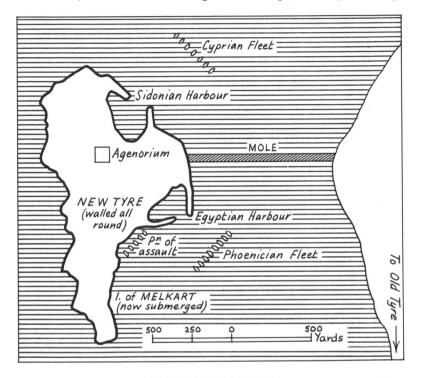

17 SIEGE OF TYRE

Alexander's chief engineer, Diades of Thessaly, helped by Charias, Poseidonius, and Philippus. The work was pushed forward with the greatest energy. It is recorded that Alexander explained each step that had to be taken and encouraged the workers by rewards for those who worked hardest and most efficiently. Only when the deeper water near the city was reached was work seriously impeded by missiles showered down on the workers from the summit of the wall, and because of the depth of water the Tyrian galleys were able to row up to the mole and attack the working parties.

To frustrate these attacks and to gain command of the wall,

o

Alexander had two wooden towers, protected against fire-arrows by raw hides, built and moved up to the far end of the mole. As they had to be man-handled, this must have been a remarkable feat of engineering. They were the same height as the wall – 150 feet – and are supposed to have been the highest ever built.[1] From their summits missiles were projected by catapults against the defenders of the wall, and from their lower stories they were hurled against those Tyrian galleys which came within range.

Like their kinsmen, the Carthaginians, the Tyrians were expert engineers and were in no way disconcerted by their enemy's towers; they soon took counter-measures to destroy them. They converted a horse transport into a fire-ship by loading her with dry branches and other combustible wood, fenced round her deck to gain additional room, and filled this space with shavings, pitch, and sulphur. Then they lashed two yardarms to each of her masts, and suspended cauldrons from them – probably filled with naphtha – which when the yardarms burnt through would fall on the combustibles. Lastly, they heavily ballasted the stern of the ship to raise her prow out of the water, so that it would project over the mole.[2]

The Tyrians waited for a favourable wind and then the fire-ship was towed into position by galleys. We read:

> When they came near the mole and the towers, they lighted the material and as violently as possible hauled with the triremes and dashed the ship on the edge of the mole. The crew of the ship, already burning fiercely, easily swam off. Soon enough a great fire fell on the towers, and as the yards broke, they poured into the fire anything that had been made ready to feed the flame. The men in the triremes lay to near the mole, and shot at the towers, so that it was not safe for anyone bringing materials to quench the fire to get near. At this stage, the towers being well alight, the citizens sallied in large numbers, and jumped into small boats put in at different parts of the mole and easily tore down the palisade set up to protect it; besides, they burned all the engines which had not been caught by fire from the ship.[3]

This successful counter-attack must have made it apparent to Alexander that the Tyrians were to prove tough opponents. He ordered the mole to be widened so that more towers could be erected on it, and

---

[1] Tarn, *Hellenistic Military and Naval Developments*, p. 110.
[2] Most of the remarkable devices attributed to them by Diodorus are fictitious.
[3] Arrian, II, xix, 3–5.

while this was done the Phoenician naval contingents began to return from the Aegean. Alexander set out with the hypaspists and Agrianians for Sidon to collect the galleys that had returned there. He was convinced that it would be nearly impossible to take Tyre as long as he lacked command of the sea.

In the meantime Gerostratus and Enylus had returned with their fleets to Aradus and Byblus.[1] When they found that their cities were in Alexander's hands, they had no choice but to place their ships at his disposal, and when added to the Sidonian vessels in all they numbered eighty galleys. Then ten galleys arrived from Rhodes, three from Soli and Mallus, ten from Lycia, and soon afterward 120 galleys arrived from the kings of Cyprus who, when they heard of Darius' defeat at Issus, decided to back the winning side. These surrenders gave Alexander command of the eastern Mediterranean.

While the engines were constructed and the ships fitted for battle, Alexander, always restless, set out on a ten-day expedition to subdue the hillmen of the Antilibanus mountains. He returned to Sidon to find that during his absence 4,000 Greek mercenary reinforcements had arrived from the Peloponnese. The siege entered its second phase.

Alexander stood out with the fleet from Sidon for Tyre in battle order. Accompanied by all the Cyprian kings except for Pyntagoras of Cyprian Salamis, and the Phoenician kings, he took command of the right wing, while Craterus and Pyntagoras commanded the left wing. At first the Tyrians decided to accept battle, but when they sighted his fleet they were astonished by the number of his ships, for they were unaware that all the Cyprian and Phoenician ships had joined him. Instead they wore about and blocked the entrance of their two harbours so that their enemy would be denied an anchorage. Because of this, an attempt was made by some Phoenician ships to force the narrow entrance of the Sidonian harbour, and three of the Tyrian galleys were sunk. After this small success Alexander withdrew the fleet and ordered it to moor along the shore not far from the mole, where it would be sheltered from the winds. On the following day he ordered the Cyprian contingent to blockade the Sidonian harbour on the north side of the mole, while the Phoenician contingent blockaded the Egyptian harbour on its southern side.

In the meantime many technicians skilled in the construction of siege engines were collected from Cyprus and Phoenicia; new towers were erected on the mole, and a large number of catapults and rams were built. Alexander had some of the rams mounted in the transports

[1] Presumably, at the same time, Azemilk and his contingent returned to Tyre.

he had brought with him from Sidon, as well as in some of the slower galleys; the only case known of battering rams used on ships.[1] Although there are no details of this device, it proved to be Alexander's ace of trumps and the following conjectural description of it may make the subsequent siege operation easier to understand.

Alexander's problem was to breach the city wall, and to do so from the mole meant that he was restricted to an assault frontage of some 200 feet, if Diodorus' figure is correct. Because this meant that the Tyrians could assemble a large number of their defensive weapons on this narrow front, it was imperative for Alexander to extend it. This he could only do from the sea; hence the idea to mount rams in ships. But this was only part of the problem; the rams would prove ineffective unless the ships in which they were mounted were firmly anchored and as the ships would have to be brought to anchor close to the foot of the wall, they and the men working the rams would have to be protected against all types of projectiles hurled at them from its summit. It follows almost certainly that the ram-ships must have been roofed in like a conventional Noah's Ark; that these roofs were made as fire-proof as possible, and the ships themselves firmly anchored from their bows and sterns, as well as from their port and starboard sides, in order to obtain the firmest possible platforms for the rams to be worked from. Another question intrudes: was it possible to work a ram of sufficient power to break down the immensely strong Tyrian wall from a single ship? The largest rams that appear to have been made in classical times were those used by Demetrius in his siege of Rhodes (305 B.C.); they were either 180 or 130 feet in length and each required 1,000 men to work it.[2] Though nothing like so enormous a weapon can have been employed by Alexander, it would not seem improbable that, in order to obtain the necessary space for the men who swung the ram, another ship was lashed to the stern of the ram-ship, and by this means the platform extended.[3]

While Alexander made ready for his second assault, the Tyrians had not been idle. On the battlement facing the mole they built wooden towers to gain command of the new towers erected on the mole; also they assembled a large number of catapults on the battlement facing the mole, and it is recorded that they held at bay their enemy's ships – presumably the ram-ships[4] – by volleys of fire-arrows. But there was a

---

[1] Tarn, *Hellenistic Military and Naval Developments*, p. 109.   [2] Ibid., p. 110.
[3] Curtius (IV, iii, 14–15) mentions the lashing together of 'four-bankers' with their bows close together and their sterns apart, on which was built a triangular platform 'as a standing-place for soldiers'. He says that they were rowed up to near the wall, and from them 'missiles were showered upon the defenders'.
[4] They cannot have been catapult ships because the height of the wall (not the

more formidable difficulty to be overcome; it was discovered that near the end of the mole it was impossible to bring the ram-ships close to the wall because blocks of stone had been sunk in the sea at its foot. Before the ram-ships could be used, these under-water obstacles had first to be removed. Although from shipboard this was a most difficult task it was successfully contrived by fastening slip-knots to the stones and dragging them up by means of cranes. Though we are not told so, the ram-ships must then have anchored close to the wall.

This conjecture is borne out by the next move by the Tyrians. They armoured a number of ships – presumably against arrows and catapult projectiles by fencing in their decks – and bore down on the enemy ships and cut their anchor cables. In reply, Alexander had a number of thirty-oar galleys similarly armoured and brought into position alongside the cables. In no way nonplussed by this, the Tyrians made use of divers to cut the cables; Alexander replied by replacing them with chains. At last the ram-ships were able to approach close to the wall wherever a channel had been cleared of block-stones.

To relieve the pressure on the wall in the vicinity of the mole, the Tyrians resorted to a stratagem. They noticed that daily at about noon many of the crews of the Cyprian ships that blockaded the Sidonian harbour were withdrawn to the mainland for their mid-day meal, and that Alexander, who usually was with the Phoenician fleet, ate at the same time before he took his customary short siesta. They decided to turn this situation to their advantage by a surprise sortie while the crews were away. To keep their plan secret, they camouflaged the entrance of the Sidonian harbour with a screen of sails and behind it assembled ten of their most powerful ships, manned by picked crews and their best armed marines.

At about midday on the day of the sortie the sails were removed; the squadron rowed out, fell upon the Cyprian ships, and at the first onset sank four quinqueremes. But unfortunately for the Tyrians, though Alexander had withdrawn to the mainland, on this day he had forgone his siesta and had returned to the Phoenician blockading fleet earlier than usual, to find many of its crews ashore. When the news of the sortie reached him – probably signalled to him from the mole – he ordered all crews to be recalled and the entrance of the Egyptian harbour to be closely blockaded to prevent a break-out of the Tyrian ships. Next, with such quinqueremes as were fully manned and five

depth of the sea, as Curtius asserts) prevented artillery being brought into action from ships unless they were at a considerable distance from the wall (see Curtius, IV, ii, 9).

triremes, he sailed round the southern end of the island to the support of the Cyprian fleet north of the mole. Since this manœuvre was made in full view of the city, directly the Tyrians fathomed Alexander's intention they shouted and signalled frantically to their ships engaged with the Cyprian fleet to put about. But apparently the Tyrian ships were so closely involved that they were unable to disengage before the arrival of Alexander who, so it would seem, came up in rear of their left flank and fell upon them.[1] Several of their ships were put out of action and a quinquereme and a quadrireme were captured at the entrance of the harbour, but most of their crews saved themselves by swimming ashore.

There can be little doubt that in this action Alexander had been caught napping. The problem of the mid-day meal was not new; a similar ruse had been adopted by the Syracusans in 413 B.C.[2] Besides, one would have thought that, as the crews of a blockading fleet usually went ashore to eat, more vigilance would have been displayed when they did so; also that the erecting of the sail screen would have warned Alexander that something unusual was afoot. Had the Tyrians been bolder, had they made a sortie in full strength from both their harbours simultaneously instead of a limited sally from the Sidonian harbour alone, Alexander might have been placed in an extremely awkward position and the siege considerably prolonged.

After the sortie, the assault from the mole was pressed with the utmost vigour, but because of the strength of the wall, with no appreciable gain. Alexander shifted his ram-ships to the battlements near the Sidonian harbour; but as no weak spot could be found there, he brought them round to the wall immediately south of the Egyptian harbour and tested it at various points. At last at one place the wall was badly shaken and partly broken down. By means of a drawbridge lowered on to the breach he made a tentative attack, and although his assault was repulsed by the Tyrians without much difficulty, as he had found a weak spot, he decided on a general assault.

His plan was first to enlarge the breach he had already made which, he calculated, would compel the Tyrians to mass against him, and when they had done so and he was about to storm the enlarged breach, the Cyprian and Phoenician fleets were to force their way into the Sidonian and Egyptian harbours, while a squadron of galleys, carrying catapults and archers, was to circle round the island and put in wherever

---

[1] At best a galley could row at five knots; therefore, as the approximate distance to be rowed was 3,500 yards, it probably took Alexander a little under half an hour to reach the Sidonian Harbour.   [2] Thucydides, VII, 40-1.

it was possible, or lay within range, 'so that the Tyrians, being shot at from all quarters, might be distracted, and know not whither to turn in their distress'.[1]

Three days after the tentative attack, the ram-ships were brought up to the wall in a calm sea, and a considerable section was battered down. Then these vessels were withdrawn and replaced by two ships equipped with boarding bridges or 'crows'.[2] Each vessel carried a storming party, in one a body of hypaspists under Admetus, and in the other part of Coenus' battalion of the phalanx. Alexander accompanied the former.

When these ships grounded, the bridges were lowered and the stormers rushed over them and fought their way up the rubble. The hypaspists were in the lead, and cheered on by Admetus they captured part of the wall which flanked the breach; but as he led his men forward Admetus was killed by a spear thrust. Behind them came Alexander with the second wave; he drove the Tyrians before him and then pressed on through the battlements toward the Royal Palace. In the meantime the Phoenician ships broke through the boom at the entrance of the Egyptian harbour and the Cyprian ships forced their way into the Sidonian harbour; their storming parties occupied the city on that side.

When the Tyrians found themselves attacked from three quarters and driven from the walls, they fell back on the Agenorium (Shrine of Agenor) where they made a stand until the hypaspists under Alexander broke through their ranks and put them to flight. The final scene is described by Arrian:

> Great was the slaughter also made both by those who were now occupying the city from the harbour and by the regiment of Coenus, which had also entered it. For the Macedonians were now for the most part advancing full of rage, being angry both at the length of the siege and also because the Tyrians, having captured some of their men sailing from Sidon, had conveyed them to the top of the wall, so that the deed might be visible from the camp, and after slaughtering them, had cast their bodies into the sea. About 8,000 of the Tyrians were killed; and of the Macedonians, besides Admetus, who had proved a valiant man, being the first to scale the wall, twenty of the shield-bearing guard were killed in the assault on that occasion. In the whole siege about 400 Macedonians were slain.[3]

Alexander granted amnesty to those who had sought refuge in the temple of Heracles; among them were King Azemilk, many Tyrian

[1] Arrian, II, xxiii, 3.   [2] For details of, see Polybius, I, 22.   [3] II, xxiv, 3-4.

notables, and some envoys from Carthage. The rest of the surviving inhabitants, as well as the Tyrian mercenary troops, to the number of 30,000, were sold into slavery.[1]

When the butchery was at an end and order had been restored, Alexander offered sacrifice to Heracles and held a gymnastic contest and a torch race in celebration of his victory.

Tyre fell to him in the month of Hecatombaeon (July, 332 B.C.) after a siege of seven months. Nothing comparable had been seen since the siege of Motya by Dionysius in 398 B.C., which in several respects resembled it, and nothing like it was to be seen again throughout classical times; though the siege of Rhodes by Demetrius Poliorcetes, in 305 B.C., was on a more extensive scale, it was a failure, and even had it succeeded its political consequences would have been negligible.

The Siege of Gaza

After the fall of Tyre Alexander set out along the coastal road for Egypt. A march of some 150 miles brought him to Gaza, the most southerly of the old Philistine cities, situated at the edge of the Egyptian desert and about one mile from the sea.[2] For centuries it had been a considerable fortress perched on a high mound encircled by a lofty wall and surrounded by desert sand.[3] Its governor was Batis, probably an Iranian, and not a eunuch as Arrian describes[4] him. He was a resolute man who, in preparation to resist Alexander should he advance south from Tyre, had enlisted a force of Arabian mercenaries and had provisioned his stronghold to withstand a long siege.

When Alexander reached Gaza, he demanded its surrender, but as Batis, who believed it to be impregnable, refused the summons, he encamped near what seemed to him to be the easiest part of the city wall to attack. But his engineers pointed out to him that because of the height of the mound it would be impossible to bring the siege engines up to the wall. This encouraged Alexander all the more to make the attempt, because 'the miracle of the achievement would strike terror into his enemies', while not to take Gaza 'would be a blow to his

[1] The statement made by Diodorus (XVII, 46, 4) that after the siege Alexander hanged 2,000 young Tyrians (Curtius, IV, iv, 17, says crucified them) is discredited by Tarn (*Alexander the Great*, vol. II, p. 82). Curtius (IV, iv, 16) also says that the Sidonians, out of pity for the Tyrians, saved 15,000 of them by secreting them in their ships. This act is not mentioned elsewhere; the figure is obviously exaggerated.

[2] Strabo, XVI, ii, 30.

[3] Gaza means 'the strong'. Today it consists of four quarters, one of which stands on a flat-topped hill, the ruins of successive cities, which is the site of the city Alexander besieged.   [4] See Tarn, *Alexander the Great*, vol. II, appx. 11.

prestige when noised abroad to the Greeks and Darius'.[1] Though this fits Alexander's character, there was another and obvious reason why he had to occupy Gaza; he could no more risk leaving it in Persian hands on his line of communications than he could have left Tyre, also on his communications, in Tyrian hands. Gaza had to be taken before he could march safely to Egypt; it was an imperative and not a vainglorious operation.

The problem was very different from those he had solved at Halicarnassus and Tyre; it was, as his engineers had pointed out, impossible to bring his siege engines up to the city walls, and as they were built on a mound, there was only one way he could do it – to build a countermound, or ramp, against the mound, and on its summit plant his rams. He ordered this to be done and the work was put into hand opposite a section of the wall on the southern side of the city; undoubtedly the local inhabitants were impressed to assist in this task.

Before the ramp could be fully raised, Batis made a sally and drove the workers down it. Alexander brought up the hypaspists, but as he directed the counter-attack he was hit by a catapult bolt, that pierced his shield and corselet and severely wounded him in the shoulder.

The siege engines used at Tyre arrived by sea, and Arrian writes that on their arrival Alexander ordered the counter-mound to be extended round the whole of the city to a breadth of two stades and to a height of 250 feet. These figures are totally impossible; nothing approaching so gigantic a work could have been built in the time available, because, according to Diodorus, the length of the siege was no more than two months. The best that can be made of this extension of the counter-mound is that Alexander ordered works of contravallation to be dug around the fortress to prevent a sortie, and that he raised the height of the ramp and broadened it until it was level with the foot of the wall and extensive enough for the rams to work from it: this in itself must have been a tremendous task.

When the ramp was of sufficient height and breadth, the rams were hauled up on to it, and part of the wall was brought down. But it would seem that this was insufficient to create an operative breach because, under cover of showers of missiles, Alexander had to resort to mining of the wall.

In spite of the demolitions, the Gazans beat back three assaults, and it was not until another section of the wall had been battered down and scaling ladders planted on the débris that access to the city was gained by the men of the phalanx. Once inside, the assaulting parties broke

[1] Arrian, II, xxvi, 3.

down several of the city gates and admitted the rest of the army. The Gazans fought on until all their fighting men were slain, which can only mean that no quarter was given.[1] Thus the road to Egypt was opened and Alexander's line of communications rendered secure.

From the military point of view it is to be regretted that Arrian provides so bald an account of this remarkable siege. Although there was nothing new in throwing up a mound instead of erecting a tower in order to gain command of a city wall, when it is remembered that the bulk of the material at hand was loose desert sand and grit, it is not only difficult to picture how a ramp of sufficient solidity of anything like the height necessary was built, but also how so heavy and cumbersome an instrument as a battering-ram with its pent-house were hauled up the ramp to within a few yards of the wall. Compared with this counter-mound, the building of the mole at Tyre was a comparatively simple task. It is these lacunas, in what may be called the background of tactics, which throughout military history make it so perplexing to appreciate the difficulties and values of operations. But they should always be borne in mind, and particularly so in the following chapter, which abounds with them.

[1] Polybius (XVI, 22a) praises the courage of the people of Gaza.

8

ALEXANDER'S SMALL WARS

❦

The Balkan and Illyrian Campaigns

Alexander is distinguished from all the great generals in that he was uniformly successful in every type of war. Others have equalled him as the winners of pitched battles and great sieges, but few have also been called upon to undertake what throughout the history of war have, time and again, proved to be the most intricate and difficult operations: the quelling of national risings and revolts, the suppression of partisans and guerrillas, the conquest of warlike hill tribes and fleet desert nomads, and the policing and pacification of conquered territories of every description, all of which may be listed under the title of 'Small Wars'. Yet, in all these fluid, loosely organized and involved operations, Alexander was as successful as in his great battles and sieges; it is because his generalship was put to so universal a test that he takes his place at the head of the great captains.

The first of Alexander's small wars was his campaign in the Balkans, which he undertook immediately he had established his authority over Greece after his accession. From Arrian's account, its aim was to subject the Triballian and Illyrian tribesmen, who threatened Macedonia from the north and west, before he turned against Persia; actually, as the campaign shows, it was more than this. He saw that the subjection of these tribes was not enough; his northern frontier could only be rendered secure by pushing it forward to the Danube, and it was this strategic objective that impelled him northward. It was to be no mere punitive expedition, but a conquest in which he intended to show that he was master; this is partly corroborated by the fact that, before he set out, he ordered a squadron of warships from Byzantium to sail up the Danube and meet him and his army at a certain point.

The Triballians inhabited the region between the Danube and the

Balkans in the present province of Pleven (see Map 1). Southward of them were the lands of the Agrianians and Paeonians, and west of these tribes lay Illyria, a savage country whose tribesmen had constantly raided into Macedonia. From Macedonia two tracks led to the Triballians, one up the Axius (Vardar) valley and through the Paeonian and Agrianian country, and the other from Amphipolis northward through the territory of the free Thracians and across the Haemus mountains (Balkans). That Alexander chose the latter was probably because, as the Agrianians were faithful allies, and the free Thracians were not, by an advance along the eastern track he would be able to enforce his authority on the free Thracians on his way.

In the spring of 335 B.C. he set out from Amphipolis with Philippi on his left;[1] crossed the Nestus river (Mesta), and after a ten-day march reached the Balkans, probably at the Shipka Pass, which he found held by the free Thracians. They had drawn up their carts in the form of a stockade, and if hard pressed they planned to let them loose upon their enemy should he attempt to ascend the pass, so as to disrupt his ranks, and then, it may be presumed, to charge down on him when in disorder.

Because there was no way round the pass, Alexander decided to storm it frontally with the phalanx, but what is remarkable is that no sooner did the line of carts come into view than he penetrated his enemy's intention[2] and suspected that they might be launched against his men as they climbed. The slope, though steep, must have been level or Alexander would not have employed the phalanx; also the carts could hardly have been used as projectiles had the slope been encumbered with rocks or covered with trees and bushes. He warned his men of this possibility and instructed them that should the carts be launched against them, where the slope was level they were to open their ranks and form lanes through which the carts would pass, and where this could not be done they were to stoop or lie down and link their shields closely together, 'so that the carts coming at them and (as was to be hoped) bounding over them by their gathered impetus should pass through without doing harm'.[3] Next, he brought forward the archers on the right front of the phalanx and instructed them to bring their arrows to bear on the left flank of the Thracians should they rush down on the phalanx after the carts had been launched. Lastly, he led

[1] What his strength was is unknown. Probably moderate, because of the difficulties of supply.

[2] It is unknown whether this ruse was novel or not. If it was, few generals would have seen through it, instead they would naturally have assumed that the Thracians intended to fight behind their cart stockade.   [3] Arrian, I, i, 9.

the hypaspists and Agrianians to the left of the phalanx, presumably so that they could fall upon the Thracian right flank. According to Arrian, these movements were ordered after the carts were launched; but this is unlikely because then there would have been insufficient time to carry them out, and also, once Alexander had seen through the ruse, it must have been obvious to him that the real danger was not the carts, but the wild Killiecrankie charge (1689) which they would herald.

All we are told of the Thracian cart attack is, 'that it turned out just as Alexander conjectured'; the carts either bounded through the lanes or over the shields without killing a single man, though it would seem probable that an unrecorded number of legs must have been broken. The men of the phalanx then rose from the ground, advanced up the slope, and before Alexander could bring his own column into action, the Thracians, panic-stricken by the failure of their ruse, cast away their arms and fled helter-skelter down the mountain-side: 1,500 were killed, and a few were captured, as well as the women, children, and impedimenta found in the laager.

Alexander then crossed the Balkans, entered the land of the Triballians, and directed his march on the river Lyginus.[1] But before he set out, Syrmus, the Triballian king, in anticipation of his arrival had sent back his women and children for refuge to the island of Peuce[2] in the Danube, to which the Thracians had also fled and Syrmus himself had retired. As Alexander approached the main body of the Triballians withdrew and then counter-marched to occupy the passes in his rear. When Alexander learnt of this he followed suit and came up with them as they encamped in a woody glen, which the dense forest made difficult to attack. To persuade them to come out into the open he resorted to a stratagem. First, he ordered his archers and slingers to advance on the entrance of the glen and discharge their missiles on the enemy. At the same time, at some distance in their rear and hidden from view, he deployed the phalanx with cavalry on its front, and a column of cavalry on both of its wings. He reckoned that, when the Triballians found themselves faced with archers and slingers alone, they would rush out from the glen and pursue them into the open. Then he would advance the hidden phalanx and cavalry and attack them in front and on both flanks. The archers and slingers were to be a bait as well as an annoyance.[3]

[1] Probably either the Osma, Vid, or Isker.
[2] Strabo (VII, iii, 15) mentions a Peuce near the mouth of the Danube, but Arrian's Peuce must be another.
[3] Compare William's stratagem at the battle of Hastings in 1066 to draw Harold's men out of their defensive position.

As he anticipated, so it happened. Annoyed by the arrows and sling-stones, the Triballians fell into the trap; they rushed out of the glen, drove the archers and slingers back, and suddenly came face to face with the phalanx and the cavalry. The former, led by Alexander, crashed through their centre, while the two flanking cavalry columns swept round their flanks. Their defeat was complete, 3,000 were slain, but because of the dense forest and nightfall few prisoners were taken; the survivors crossed the Lyginus and effected their escape. Of the Macedonians, eleven horsemen and forty infantry were killed.

Again it was Alexander's insight that governed his tactics, and in this engagement, as at the Balkan pass, he penetrated what his enemy intended or was likely to do. He knew that the tribesmen, though adept at ambushes and ruses, because of their lack of discipline were prone to succumb to them; he offered them what appeared to be an easy victory in order to lure them to defeat. Throughout his small wars, whenever it was possible he based action on surprise, either by hidden manœuvre or hidden intention.

Three days after the battle Alexander reached the Danube, and was met by the warships he had sent north from Byzantium. These he filled with archers and heavy-armed troops, and sailed to Peuce to dislodge Syrmus, who held it with a considerable number of his tribesmen and Thracian refugees. An attempt to effect a landing made it clear that the force was inadequate, and as the current of the river was swift and the banks of the island precipitous, Alexander decided to abandon the operation and try another plan.

It was to achieve what to the tribesmen would appear to be the impossible: to cross the Danube in a single night and cut off Syrmus from the Getae,[1] a kindred Thracian people who inhabited what today are parts of Moldavia and Bessarabia. They had assembled a force, estimated to number 4,000 cavalry and over 10,000 infantry, on the left bank of the Danube to frustrate a crossing, and probably also to support the Triballians should an opportunity arise. It is here that, for the first time, Arrian makes use of the oft-recurring expression that Alexander 'was seized with a longing (*pothos*) to cross the river' – the desire to penetrate into the unknown and investigate the mysterious which, as Wilcken points out, 'in his later years took him irresistibly to the ends of the earth'.[2]

There is no detailed account of how the crossing of the greatest of European rivers in Alexander's day was organized and carried out in

[1] Strabo (VII, iii) has much to say on the Getae; like the Scythians they relied mainly on horse-archers.   [2] *Alexander the Great*, p. 68.

so brief a time. All that is recorded is that numerous fishing-boats fashioned out of single tree trunks, and rafts made by stuffing tent coverings with hay, were collected. That with such primitive means 1,500 cavalry and 4,000 infantry were ferried across the Danube in a single night would be a startling enough accomplishment today; it can well be imagined that to the Triballians and other tribes it must have appeared to border on the miraculous, and in their eyes exalt Alexander to a position little short of a god.

Early on the following morning, when it was still dark, Alexander marshalled his men on the left bank of the Danube under cover of a field of standing corn. Nicanor led the phalanx forward in square while Alexander advanced on the right with the cavalry. When the untilled ground on the far side of the corn was reached, the camp of the Getae came into view, and the cavalry charged the sleeping enemy who, in wild confusion, fled back to their settlement, some three and a half miles away. The phalanx then advanced, the settlement was stormed and the Getae scattered far and wide to disappear in the northern steppes. A halt was then called, the settlement razed to the ground, and after sacrifices had been made to Zeus, Heracles and the river gods, without the loss of a single man, the army recrossed the river in daylight and returned to its camp on the river's southern side.

The audacity of this almost incredible exploit achieved its purpose: Syrmus and his Triballians, awe-struck and terrified by its boldness, at once submitted, as also did other tribes, and it is recorded that even the Celts on the eastern coast of the Adriatic sent an embassy to seek Alexander's friendship.[1]

When the envoys had departed, Alexander set out southward for the lands of the Agrianians and Paeonians, presumably by the western track, and on his way he received the news that Cleitus, an Illyrian chieftain and son of Bardylis,[2] was in revolt; that Glaucias, king of the Taulantians, an Illyrian people in the neighbourhood of Durazzo, was about to join him, and that the Autariatians, also an Illyrian people bordering on Paeonia, were going to attack him on his line of march. This meant that most of Illyria would soon be ablaze, and the western frontier of Macedonia invaded.

To stamp out this outbreak before its flames spread demanded the utmost speed, and fortunately for Alexander, Langarus, king of the

[1] 'The terror Alexander inspired', writes Wilcken, 'had a long after-effect. It was almost fifty years before the Celts ventured to invade Macedonia and Greece' (ibid., p. 69).
[2] Defeated and slain by Philip in 359 B.C. Ten years later Philip subdued Cleitus.

Agrianians, with his body-guard was with him, and as a faithful ally he agreed to march against the Autariatians and keep them occupied at home, while Alexander advanced against Cleitus and Glaucias. By forced marches Alexander advanced to the Axius (Vardar), and thence up the Erigon river (Tzerna) to recover the Macedonian border fortress of Pelion which Cleitus had occupied, and where he awaited the arrival of Glaucias.

Pelion commanded the valley of the Apsus river (Devol), and the main route leading into western Macedonia. The fortress lay in a wide plain bordered by mountains, and for the most part the track was narrow and precipitous. Not only could it easily be defended, but unless Cleitus could be crushed before Glaucias joined him, a delay before Pelion, or the failure of Langarus to keep back the Autaria-tians, might lead to a loss of communications with Macedonia, when Alexander would be placed in a critical situation.

His trust in Langarus was not misplaced, for he carried out his task with complete success, and was highly rewarded by Alexander. When Pelion was reached Alexander encamped in its vicinity, and decided to carry it by assault; but before he could safely do so, in order that his rear might be secure, it was necessary to drive Cleitus from the neigh-bouring foothills. This Alexander set out to do, and when Cleitus withdrew his forces into Pelion Alexander decided to hem him in with a contravallation. But on the following day, Glaucias appeared with a large army and seized the heights which Cleitus had vacated, and thus once again Alexander's rear was placed in jeopardy. Hourly his position became more critical. Faced by Cleitus in Pelion, and threatened in rear by Glaucias, not only was he outnumbered, but so short of sup-plies that he sent out Philotas with all the baggage animals and an escort of 200 horsemen to gather in what he could. But when Glaucias got wind of this, he swooped down on the foragers in the plain, who were only saved from destruction by the timely arrival of Alexander with a strong force of cavalry, Agrianians and archers.

Because Alexander was not strong enough to hold Cleitus in Pelion and simultaneously to drive Glaucias from the foothills, his problem was how to draw Glaucias into the plain, where superior discipline would tell, and unless he could do this quickly his supplies would be exhausted. Aware that there was nothing like a military spectacle to attract a crowd, he decided to draw the Taulantians out of their positions, and induce them to assemble in an area which favoured attack by means of a parade battle drill, and then, when they had gathered to watch it, suddenly to fall upon them and scatter them to the winds.

As the terrain is not described by Arrian, it is difficult to picture what actually happened. All we know is, that Alexander crossed the Apsus at a ford, and on the plain, apparently close to the foothills, formed the phalanx up in an oblong 120 files deep with 200 horsemen on either flank. He bade the soldiers keep silent and obey his words of command smartly. Then he ordered them 'first to raise their spears upright, and then, on the word, to lower them for a charge, inclining first to the right their serried points, then to the left, and then wheeled it here and there on either wing'.[1]

We can only conjecture that this display – seemingly arranged for the edification of the Taulantians – caused such interest that they came running down the mountain-side, and to get a better view of it congregated in groups on the lower slopes of the foothills; and that when they were enthralled by it, or, as we are told, 'bewildered both at the smartness and the discipline of these manœuvres',[2] Alexander suddenly ordered the attack, on which, with a tremendous cheer[3] and a clanging of their spears on their shields, the men of the phalanx advanced at the double on the Taulantians, who fled in wild confusion and sought refuge in Pelion. Colonel Dodge writes of this manœuvre: 'Never was so curious, so magnificent a ruse employed in war before; never since.'[4]

In spite of this success, Alexander's line of retreat was still obstructed by a group of the enemy on a hill that commanded the ford. It was driven off it by a dismounted cavalry action, and the hypaspists, followed by the heavy infantry, were ordered to cross the ford while Alexander remained on the hill with the rear guard to cover their withdrawal. When tne Taulantians noticed that their enemy was in retreat, they advanced against the rear guard, but at once fell back when the heavy infantry turned about and made as if they intended to re-cross the river. The withdrawal was then continued, and last the Agrianians and archers began to cross.

> But when he [Alexander] saw the enemy pressing upon the men in the rear, he stationed his engines of war upon the bank, and ordered the engineers to shoot from them as far forward as possible all sorts

---

[1] Arrian, I, v, 2.   [2] Ibid., I, vi, 3.

[3] An unexpected and tremendous shout can at times be as effective as a volley of musketry, as happened at the storming of the Alamo during the Texan Rising of 1836.

[4] *Alexander*, vol. I, p. 204. A ruse of a somewhat similar kind was resorted to by Gylippus during the siege of Syracuse in 413 B.C. To seize the Athenian naval base of Plemmyrium, he drew its defenders out of their works by a feint naval action in the Great Harbour, and while they watched it he occupied Plemmyrium with a force he had hidden near it during the previous night (Thucydides, VII, 22–3).

of projectiles . . . He directed the archers, also, to enter the water, and shoot their arrows from the middle of the river. But Glaucias durst not advance within range of the missiles; so that the Macedonians passed over in such safety, that not one of them lost his life in the retreat.[1]

Three days later Alexander learnt that Cleitus and Glaucias were carelessly encamped outside Pelion; no defensive works had been thrown up, nor were the sentinels on guard. The reason for this negligence was they believed that Alexander had withdrawn through fear. Under cover of night Alexander re-crossed the river with the hypaspists, Agrianians and the archers; the rest of the army followed in rear. As he neared his quarry, he found the opportunity of attack so favourable that he decided to strike with the Agrianians and archers alone. They rushed the sleeping camp, slew many when still in bed, others when in flight, and the surprise was so complete that Alexander was able to pursue the panic-stricken fugitives as far as the Taulantian mountains. Meanwhile Cleitus, who had sought refuge in Pelion, when he found himself deserted, fired the fortress and escaped to Glaucias in his mountain fastness.

Thus ended Alexander's first small war, and although the paucity of detail supplied by Arrian makes it difficult to judge his generalship, as mentioned in Chapter 5, it would seem that he was fortunate to surmount the risks he ran by his impetuous advance through one of the most difficult regions to fight in to be found in eastern Europe. But he imposed his will on the Illyrians, and so far as is known they gave him no further trouble during his reign. One thing is outstanding, never once throughout this mountain campaign did he lose his nerve. However desperate a situation, he refused to be mastered by it; he always sought a way out and never failed to find one. 'Military genius', said Napoleon, 'is a gift from heaven; but the most essential qualities of a general-in-chief are firmness of character and resolution to conquer at whatever price'[2] – qualities, as this his first campaign shows, Alexander in no way lacked.

The Persepolis Campaign

After the siege of Halicarnassus, Alexander carried out a number of small war operations in Asia Minor, but few details have been recorded

[1] Arrian, I, vi, 8. This is the first recorded use of catapults as field artillery.
[2] *Récits de la captivité de l'empereur Napoléon à Ste Hélène*, Montholon (1847), vol. II, p. 240.

of them, and it was not until late in 331 or early in 330 B.C., when he advanced from Susa on Persepolis, that an operation is sufficiently described by Arrian and Curtius to warrant examination. Its aim was to occupy Persepolis, the residence of the Achaemenid kings; thereby to wipe out the insult offered to Athens by Xerxes in 480 B.C., and seize the vast treasure stored there. Persepolis was then the seat of government of Ariobarzanes, satrap of Persis, who with a large army held the formidable defile known as the Persian Gates, on the western line of approach to Persepolis and north of the Behbehan-Shiraz road.

Persepolis lay some forty-five miles north-east of Shiraz, near the present town of Kinareh, a few miles east of the Palvar river, an affluent of the Kur, and some 370 miles to the south-east of Susa. To reach it Alexander decided to pass through the land of the Uxians, a pre-Aryan people who inhabited both the plains and the mountains. The plainsmen were ruled by a Persian governor, but the hill tribesmen had never been subdued; they lived by brigandage, and hitherto, rather than subject them, the Persians had found it more convenient to pay them a toll for free passage through their mountains, much as centuries later the British at times paid the tribesmen of the North-West Frontier of India.

When Alexander set out from Susa, he first crossed the river Pasitigris (Karun) and then entered the land of the Uxians. Those who lived on the plains at once submitted to him; those in the mountains, who expected that he would follow the Persian custom, demanded the customary toll. In reply he sent a messenger to them to meet him at a certain pass to receive it; then with the royal body-guards, the hypaspists and 8,000 other troops he made a night march by an unfrequented track, fell upon the Uxian villages, and slew many while still in their beds. He then advanced swiftly to the pass at which the Uxians had gathered in force to exact the toll.

While still at the villages, he must have questioned the captured headmen on the nature of the pass and its vicinity, because on his way to it he sent Craterus ahead to seize certain heights that commanded the probable line of retreat the Uxians would take when he had dislodged them. He pressed on with utmost speed and occupied the pass before the Uxians could man it, drew his men up in battle order, and led them from a commanding position against the Uxians, who were 'astonished at Alexander's swiftness' [1] and fled in panic to seek refuge on the heights which, unknown to them, Craterus had occupied. Some were killed by Alexander in his pursuit, many, we are told, lost their

[1] Arrian, III, xvii, 3.

lives by falling over the precipices, and many more were destroyed by Craterus.[1]

In twenty-four hours Alexander settled a problem which for two centuries the Persians had feared to tackle. The Uxians were permitted to inhabit their territories in peace on payment of a yearly tribute of 100 horses, 500 oxen and 30,000 sheep. These, we read, 'were the "gifts" they received from Alexander'.[2]

After the subjection of the Uxians, Alexander's problem was not only how to get to Persepolis, a comparatively easy task, but how to prevent Ariobarzanes, who occupied the Persian Gates with 40,000 foot and 700 horse,[3] from withdrawing to Persepolis on his approach, and removing the vast treasure hoarded there. To prevent this was of the highest strategic importance, because bullion was the mainstay of Persian military power. Were Alexander to advance on Persepolis by way of the Behbehan-Kazerum-Shiraz main road, which skirted the foothills of the mountains south of the Persian Gates, when Ariobarzanes learnt of his approach, because he was nearer to Persepolis than Alexander would be, he would have ample time to fall back on it. But were Alexander to march by a shorter but more difficult way, which led through the mountains to the north of the main road, it might be possible to surprise Ariobarzanes before he could withdraw. As the essence of surprise is speed, Alexander decided that, while Parmenion with the baggage train, Thessalian cavalry, mercenaries and other more heavily-armed troops, advanced by the main road, he with the Companion cavalry, light cavalry, Macedonian foot, Agrianians and archers, would march by a mountain track, which Sir Aurel Stein has identified with the present caravan road which, after emerging from the cultivated plain around Fahlium (or Fehlian) passes eastward from 'the ruined "Bridge of the Myrtles" (*Pul-i-murd*) through the defiles of the Tang-i-Gerrau, a lower continuation of the Tang-i-Khas, up the very rocky slopes above the left bank of the stream in the latter', and then diverges south-east to enter the long and narrow defile of the Persian Gates north-west of Aliabad.[4]

When Parmenion set out along the Shiraz road with the impedi-

---

[1] Curtius' account (V, iii, 7–12) is obviously garbled, because he describes Alexander cutting timber for hurdles and mantlets, as well as bringing up siege-towers to storm the Uxian city and citadel; and Diodorus' account is only a little less garbled.

[2] Arrian, III, xvii, 6.

[3] These are Arrian's figures (III, xviii, 2); Curtius' (V, iii, 17) are '25,000 foot soldiers', and Diodorus' (XVII, 68, 1) '25,000 foot and 300 horse'.

[4] *The Geographical Journal,* vol. XCII (1938), 'An Archaelogical Journey in Western Iran', p. 314.

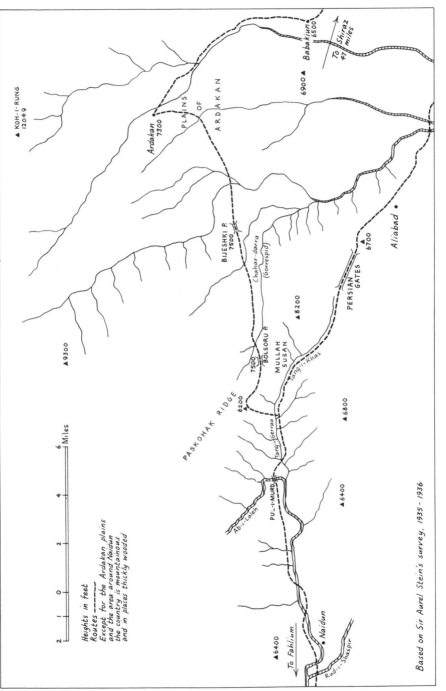

18 THE PERSIAN GATES

Based on Sir Aurel Stein's survey, 1935 - 1936

Heights in feet
Routes ----
Except for the Ardakan plains
and the area around Naidun
the country is mountainous
and in places thickly wooded

Miles
2 1 0   2   4   6

▲ KOH-I-RUNG
12049

▲9300

Ardakan
7300
PLAINS OF ARDAKAN

▲6900

Babakiun
6500

To Shiraz
47 miles

BIJESHKI P.
7500

Chahar-darra
(Gorrespid)

Aliabad ●

6700
PERSIAN GATES

7500
BOLSORU P.
MULLAH
SUSAN
▲8200

6200

PASKOHAK RIDGE

Tang-i-Khas

▲6800

Tang-i-Gerrau

Ab-i-Lalen

PU-I-MURD

▲6400

▲6400

To Fahlium

● Naidun

Rud-i-Shaspir

menta, Alexander 'marched at full speed through the hills',[1] and, according to Curtius, 'on the fifth day' he encamped on a spot 'open on all sides',[2] a little to the west of the Persian Gates, and on the following day he set out to assault them. But this time the rapidity of his march, which so often had paralysed his opponents, was of no avail; it was he and not his enemy who was surprised, for he found himself in a deep gorge blocked by a wall, which Ariobarzanes had built across it between two lofty cliffs. It was impossible to outflank it, so a frontal assault on the wall was made; but because of 'the rugged nature of the ground', and the catapults on the wall, when Alexander saw that 'his troops were suffering much damage',[3] he abandoned the enterprise and withdrew them to the camp. It was a definite repulse; that is why Arrian, following Ptolemy, says little about it.

Although Curtius' journalistic description is over-dramatized, it is not altogether unreal. After the depiction of a frantic scene in which huge rocks were rolled down from the heights upon the Macedonians, he describes how they were penned up 'like wild beasts caught in a pit', and then writes:

> Therefore their wrath turned to frenzy, and grasping the jutting rocks, they tried to clamber up and reach the enemy, lifting one another; but those very rocks, torn away by the hands of many who seized at the same time, fell back upon those who had loosened them. Therefore they could neither stand nor make any effort, nor be protected even by a tortoise-formation, since the barbarians were rolling down masses of such great size. The king was tormented, not alone by resentment, but also by shame for having inconsiderately thrown his army into those narrow quarters. Invincible before that day, he had risked nothing without success; he had safely entered the pass of Cilicia, he had opened a new route by sea into Pamphylia;[4] but now his good fortune was caught and had come to a standstill, and there was no other remedy than to return the way he had come. Therefore, having given the signal for retreat, he ordered his men to leave in close order, joining their shields above their heads. There were thirty stadia which were retreated.[5]

Sir Aurel Stein locates Alexander's camp on an open space known as Mullah Susan.

> It is here [he writes] that we can safely assume Alexander's camp to have stood after the attack along the caravan route to the pass had

---

[1] Arrian, III, xviii, 2. [2] Curtius, V, iii,17, and V, vi, 1. [3] Arrian, III, xviii, 3.
[4] The passing by Mt Climax, Arrian, I, xxvi, 2, and Strabo, XIV, iii, 9.
[5] V, iii, 20-3.

been beaten back. The track leading to it was clearly seen by us winding up under precipitous rocky slopes. These would make it easy for a force holding the heights to stop any advance towards the pass by the method of defence described in the texts. The distance between the open ground at Mullah Susan and the point where the caravan track enters a narrow defile before attaining the pass corresponds as closely as may be to the 30 stadia or 3½ miles which Curtius records as the distance over which Alexander withdrew when the assault was abandoned.[1]

Alexander was now in a serious predicament, and though, as Curtius writes, he may have been 'ashamed to desert the soldiers who were unburied, because it was an inherited usage that hardly any military duty was so sacred as that of burying their dead',[2] Parmenion must have been uppermost in his mind. He was by then well on his way toward Persepolis, and if Ariobarzanes were not defeated, he might turn on Parmenion before Alexander could retrace his steps and reinforce him. Even were Alexander to remain in face of Ariobarzanes, he could not be certain that he would be pinned down, because the Gates could be held by a fraction of the Persian army, while its bulk fell on Parmenion. The sole solution was to find a way over the mountains which would outflank the pass.

Fortunately for Alexander some prisoners had been captured, and these he now questioned. Among them was one who informed him that it was hopeless to seek a way round the defile over the mountain ridge; but that 'there were paths through the woods barely to be traversed in single file, that everything was covered with foliage, and that the interlaced branches of the trees made the forest continuous'. Alexander then asked him 'whether he had learned this by hearsay or by observation'? The man replied 'that he had been a shepherd and had roamed over all those paths'.[3]

Alexander made up his mind. He offered the man an enormous reward should his information prove true, and he ordered him to guide the army. He summoned Craterus and told him that while he himself with a flying column would attempt to turn the Persian Gates by way of the shepherd's track, Craterus was to remain in the camp with his own and Meleager's battalions of the phalanx, as well as 500 cavalry and some archers. He was to keep the full number of camp fires burning and Ariobarzanes under constant alarm. Further, when the flying

---

[1] *The Geographical Journal,* vol. XCII, p. 315.   [2] V, iii, 2.
[3] Ibid., V, iv, 4 and 10.

column approached the rear of the enemy's position, a trumpet signal would be sounded, and Craterus was then to assault the wall with all possible violence. Alexander ordered the men of the flying column to take three days' rations with them, and with the shepherd leading he set out by night through the dense forest.

All Arrian records of this desperate venture is that the 'road was rough and narrow'; that Alexander traversed some 100 stades (eleven and a half miles) 'at full speed',[1] and that on his way he detached Amyntas with Philotas and Coenus to bridge the Araxes (Palvar) river a little to the south-west of Persepolis. In contrast, Curtius, after a lurid description of the difficulties and the terrors of the march, realistically adds:

> Night also and the unknown country as well as the guide – since it was uncertain whether he was wholly to be trusted – increased their fear; for if he had deceived his guards, they themselves could be caught like wild game. The safety of their king and of themselves depended either on the trustworthiness or the life of a single prisoner. At last they reached the summit.[2]

From Sir Aurel Stein we learn that the 100 stades mentioned by Arrian 'closely agrees with the distance to be traversed from Mullah Susan to the Bolsoru pass and thence across the much broken ground to the rear of the pass held by the Persians above Aliabad'.[3] Also, when in 1935 he travelled through this region, the descent from the Bolsoru pass led down the slopes of the Paskohak massif, and throughout it was covered with dense oak forest. 'For close on 3 miles', he writes, 'it was so steep as to be barely practicable for laden mules', and a further two miles of descent brought him to Mullah Susan.[4] This compares so closely with the description of the path given by the shepherd in Curtius that, should Mullah Susan have been the location of Alexander's camp, then Sir Aurel Stein must approximately have traversed the path followed by Alexander.

Therefore the 'summit', mentioned by Curtius, was probably the Bolsoru pass, 7,500 feet above sea level, from which the track runs eastward to the fertile plains of Ardakan, and thence to the Araxes, close by the Shiraz road. If so, it must have been at this pass or a few miles beyond it that Alexander detached Amyntas and his companions. He had already detached Parmenion and Craterus, why then did he now further weaken himself by making this third detachment? We can

[1] III, xviii, 4–5.   [2] V, iv, 19.
[3] *The Geographical Journal*, vol. XCII, p. 316.   [4] Ibid., p. 315.

only conjecture that he considered the seizure of the treasure in Persepolis of even greater importance than the dislodging of Ariobarzanes,
and that should his surprise attack fail, he could turn about, catch up
with Amyntas, occupy Persepolis, and then advance against Ariobarzanes from the north, while Parmenion came up from the south. Thus,
even should he not succeed in destroying Ariobarzanes at the Gates,
he would be able to place him between two attacking forces should
he attempt to withdraw on Persepolis. It was an audacious decision;
but Alexander was an audacious general, who instinctively followed
Napoleon's maxim: '*Qui ne risque rien n'attrape rien.*'

Soon after he had detached Amyntas, Alexander took a track that
led to the right, and at mid-day he halted and rested his men. Then he
set out on another night march, of which Curtius gives a vivid description, and a little before dawn his advanced guard ran into three enemy
pickets; two were captured and the third dispersed. At dawn he was so
close to the Persian camp, which must have straggled along the gorge
eastward of the wall, that he sounded the trumpet signal and ordered
an assault. Then writes Arrian:

> So the enemy, caught on all sides, never so much as came to
> blows, but fled; even so they were hemmed in on all sides; Alexander
> was pressing hard upon them here, Craterus' troops were hastening
> up there, so that the greater number of the Persians were forced to
> turn back to the walls and seek escape there. But by this time the
> walls themselves were in Macedonian hands. For Alexander had
> expected to happen just that which did happen; and so had left
> Ptolemy there with some three thousand infantry, so that the
> greatest part of the Persians were cut down by the Macedonians at
> close quarters. Even those who were attempting flight, and the flight
> had become a panic, threw themselves over the cliffs and perished;
> but Ariobarzanes himself with a handful of horsemen escaped to the
> hills.[1]

Once the slaughter was over, Alexander retraced his steps 'at full
speed', gained the track Amyntas had followed, or the Shiraz road,
found the bridge over the Araxes built, crossed it, and 'once more at
full speed' [2] hurried on to Persepolis, to arrive there before its garrison
could plunder the treasury, which was found to contain 120,000

---

[1] III, xviii, 8–9. Curtius (V, iv, 33–4) says that Ariobarzanes with forty horse and
5,000 foot 'burst through the centre of the Macedonian line' and fled to Persepolis; but on reaching it was shut out by the garrison and killed by the pursuing
Macedonians.   [2] Arrian, III, xviii, 10.

talents (over £29,000,000 at 1913 value). 'There is no merit of the king that I could praise with more justice', writes Curtius, 'than his rapidity of action. Leaving his infantry forces, and riding all night with his cavalry, wearied though they were by a march of so great extent, he reached the Araxes at daybreak.' [1]

Thus ended one of the most hazardous, audacious, and certainly most profitable of mountain campaigns in the annals of history.

The Reduction of Bactria and Sogdiana [2]

When the death of Darius at the hands of Bessus raised Alexander by right of conquest to the Persian throne, it became his duty to hunt down the assassin, not only to reinstate the prestige of what had become his monarchy, but to eliminate a rival; this task carried with it the conquest of Bactria, the satrapy of the miscreant. But it was not until the spring of 329 B.C., when at Ghazni, that he was in a position to open his campaign against Bessus. Its progress has been outlined in Chapter 5, and it will be remembered that it included the crossings of the Hindu-Kush and Oxus; the chase and capture of Bessus by Ptolemy; the advance of Alexander to the Jaxartes, and his occupation of Cyropolis and seven fortified posts built by the Persians to guard their north-eastern frontier. Alexander was then so firmly under the impression that his task was almost accomplished, that he summoned the Bactrian and Sogdian barons to meet him at Bactra, presumably to discuss a general settlement. But the whole country suddenly flamed up behind him under the leadership of Spitamenes, the betrayer of Bessus.

The first thing Alexander heard was that the rebels – really patriots – had occupied Cyropolis and the seven forts and had massacred their garrisons. This meant the loss of his north-eastern defence line along the Jaxartes, and the high probability was that the Scythians (Sacas), who inhabited the steppes eastward of that river, would seize the opportunity offered to them to cross it and raid Sogdiana. This was a danger that could not be temporarily discounted; they were exceedingly mobile horse-archers, and were they to penetrate deeply into Sogdiana and link up with Spitamenes, it might lead to a long and exhausting campaign before they were driven out. The frontier had therefore to be restored, and that quickly.

Alexander's aim was not only to reoccupy Cyropolis and the fortified

---

[1] V, v, 3. The distance must have been between eighty and 100 miles.
[2] See Map 4.

posts, but to capture or exterminate their garrisons, because he was afraid that on his approach they might abandon them, seek refuge in the steppes, and then return when he moved against Spitamenes. To effect this, he ordered Craterus to lay siege to Cyropolis; to encamp near it, dig a ditch and plant a stockade round it, and fix together the siege engines. Next, he sent out his cavalry to two of the more distant posts with orders to surround them and prevent their garrisons from escaping, while he took by storm the three nearer ones; the sixth and seventh are not mentioned.

The first to be stormed, named Gaza, was surrounded by a low mud wall, and was carried by escalade under cover of a missile barrage. At the moment of assault the slingers, archers and javelin-men 'showered volleys upon the first line of defence on the walls, and missiles were hurled from the catapults, so that the wall was soon cleared of defenders by the great shower of missiles, and thus the setting up of the ladders and the ascent of the Macedonians to the wall were rapidly accomplished',[1] and the garrison put to the sword. Alexander then advanced against the next two forts, captured one on the same day, and the other on the day following. Meanwhile at the two more distant forts we read:

It fell out just as he [Alexander] anticipated, and the dispatch of the cavalry came none too soon. For those tribesmen who held the two yet untaken cities, seeing the smoke rising from the city next in front of them, when it was fired, and when a few who escaped its catastrophe gave first-hand information of the capture, attempted as fast as they could to escape from these cities in a mass, but ran straight into the close cordon of cavalry, and the greater number of them were cut down.[2]

Thus within forty-eight hours of the opening of the campaign five of the forts were captured.

Alexander next advanced on Cyropolis, which was surrounded by a high wall and garrisoned by a picked body of tribesmen. He ordered the battering rams to be brought up to the wall, and while this was done, on a reconnaissance he noticed that the river, a winter-torrent or nullah, which flowed through the city, was almost dry, and that the water in its channels which penetrated the wall was sufficiently shallow to allow of the passage of troops. He decided, directly the rams were got to work and the defenders' attention diverted by

[1] Arrian, IV, ii, 3.   [2] Ibid., IV, ii, 6.

them, secretly to gain access to the city by way of the channels or tunnels.[1]

Probably under cover of night or morning twilight, although this is not stated, at the head of the hypaspists, Agrianians and archers, 'he slipped through the channels, at first with only a few men, and penetrated into the city; then breaking open from within the gates which were on that side, he easily admitted the rest of the troops. Then the tribesmen, seeing that their city was already in the enemy's hands, none the less turned upon Alexander and his force, and they made a vigorous onslaught, and Alexander himself was struck violently with a stone upon his head and his neck; and Craterus was wounded by an arrow and many others of the officers also. Yet none the less they cleared the market-place of tribesmen. Meanwhile those who had assaulted the wall seized it, now denuded of defenders.' [2]

Eight thousand of the tribesmen are said to have been killed, and 15,000, who took refuge in the citadel, were on the following day forced to surrender through lack of water. The last two remaining forts were taken with little trouble.

While Cyropolis and the fortified posts were reduced, the Scythians continued to assemble on the right bank of the Jaxartes, and immediately after their reduction, news was received that Spitamenes had laid siege to Maracanda. To its relief Alexander dispatched a force of sixty Companion cavalry, 800 mercenary cavalry, and 1,500 mercenary infantry, under Pharnuches, 'an interpreter', or diplomatic officer, 'who knew well the speech of the natives . . . and in all other ways appeared skilful in dealing with them'.[3] He was accompanied by three military commanders, Andromachus, Menedemus and Caranus. It was an unfortunate arrangement; Pharnuches, it seems, possessed little military knowledge, and in consequence his subordinates had no confidence in him. Alexander then spent the following twenty days in building the walls of his new frontier city of Alexandria Eschate (the 'Farthest', Khojend) on the left bank of the Jaxartes near its right-angle bend to the south of Tashkent.

While thus engaged, the Scythians gathered in increasing numbers on the right bank, shouted insults at their opponents, and dared Alexander to cross. This, we may be sure, did not induce him to leave them alone; besides, as he was determined to secure his north-eastern frontier, he decided to teach these nomadic horsemen a lesson they would not readily forget.

---

[1] In A.D. 535 Belisarius did much the same at the siege of Naples; he entered the city through an aqueduct.   [2] Arrian, IV, iii, 2–4.   [3] Ibid., IV, iii, 7.

The Jaxartes at Alexandria Eschate was not very wide; but in face of a numerous enemy who relied on the bow, its crossing was no easy problem. The skins were prepared and, according to Curtius, no less than 12,000 rafts were constructed in three days[1] – he does not say how this was done. The left bank was out of bow-shot, for we are told that the Scythian arrows fell into the river; but in mid-stream this would not be so, and what is now called 'fire superiority' would have to be faced. To overcome this, Alexander deployed his catapults, of which he must have had a considerable number, along the left bank to cover the passage of the river, and when all was ready, at a preconcerted signal a bombardment was opened on the Scythians.

Some of them [writes Arrian] were wounded by the missiles, and one was struck right through the wicker shield and breastplate and fell from his horse. The others, being alarmed at the discharge of the missiles from so great a distance, and at the death of their champion, retreated a little from the bank. But Alexander seeing them thrown into confusion by the effect of his missiles, began to cross the river with trumpets sounding, himself leading the way, and the rest of the army followed him. Having first got the archers and slingers across, he ordered them to sling and shoot at the Scythians, to prevent them approaching the phalanx of infantry stepping out of the water, until all his cavalry had passed over.[2]

Curtius' account is more detailed, and though as usual he over-dramatizes it, it is sufficiently realistic to be worth quoting:

Alexander, he writes, stationed on the prows of the rafts 'those who carried bucklers, with orders to sink upon their knees, in order that they might be safer against the shots of arrows. Behind these stood those who worked the hurling-engines, surrounded both on each side and in front by armed men. The rest, who were placed behind the artillery, armed with shields in testudo-formation, defended the rowers, who were not protected by corselets. The same order was observed also on those rafts which carried the cavalry. The greater part of these let their horses swim astern, held by the reins. But the men who were carried on skins stuffed with straw were protected by the rafts that came between them and the foe.'

The rafts were somewhat like a line of amphibian tanks followed by unarmoured landing craft.

Next, he describes the dangers and terrors of the crossing.

[1] VII, viii, 7.   [2] IV, iv, 4-5.

The king himself [he writes] with a select band of troops was the first to cast off a raft and to order it to be directed against the opposite bank. To him the Scythians opposed ranks of horsemen moved up to the very margin of the bank that the rafts might not be able even to reach the land. Moreover, besides the sight of the army guarding the bank, great terror had seized those who were managing the rafts; for the steersmen could not direct their course, since they were driven (by the force of the current) in a slanting direction, and the soldiers, who kept their feet with difficulty and were worried by fear of being shaken overboard, threw into confusion the work of the boatmen. Although making every effort the soldiers could not even hurl their javelins, since they thought rather of keeping their footing without danger than of attacking the enemy. Their safety was the hurling-engines, from which bolts were hurled with effect against the enemy, who were crowded together and recklessly exposed themselves. The barbarians also poured such a great amount of arrows upon the rafts that there was hardly a single shield that was not pierced by many of their points. . . .[1]

Once the crossing had been made, Alexander's next problem was how to bring his enemy to bay. There could be no pursuit of the Scythians until he had smashed them, and to smash them he must compel them to attack him. Although before he crossed the river, Aristander, the soothsayer, had warned him that the omens were unpropitious and portended danger to him, his reply had been, 'that it was better for him to come to extreme danger than that, after having subdued almost the whole of Asia, he should be a laughing-stock to Scythians, as Darius, the father of Xerxes, had been in days of yore'.[2] And to induce them to attack him, he first sent forward a regiment of Greek mercenary cavalry and four squadrons of lancers, which undoubtedly were intended as bait, because the Scythians, when they saw how few they were, at once attacked them, 'riding round them in circles'.

Alexander next drew up his archers, Agrianians, and other light troops, under Balacrus, to form what would appear to have been a

[1] VII, ix, 2–8.

[2] Arrian, IV, iv, 3. This refers to the operations of Darius I after he had crossed the Danube in 512 B.C. To bring the Scythians to battle he sent a message to their king in which he inquired why he persisted in retiring before him. The king replied that he feared no man nor fled before any, and the reason he refused battle was that 'We Scythians have neither towns nor cultivated lands, which might induce us, through fear of their being taken or ravaged, to be in any hurry to fight with you' (Herodotus, IV, 126–7).

screen, and under cover of this force he led forward his cavalry. As soon as they came to close quarters, he ordered three regiments of Companion cavalry and all the mounted javelin-men to charge the Scythians, and the rest of the cavalry he led forward in column and made a rapid attack. 'Accordingly', writes Arrian 'the enemy were no longer able as before to wheel their cavalry force round in circles, for at one and the same time the cavalry and the light-armed infantry mixed with the horsemen, pressed upon them, and did not permit them to wheel round in safety.' [1] The Scythians then took to flight; 1,000 were killed, and 150 were captured.[2] Because of the excessive heat, and because Alexander was taken ill after drinking polluted water, the pursuit had to be abandoned.

Though Arrian's description of Alexander's tactics is obscure, with a little imagination it is possible to fathom what they probably were, and this is attempted in Diagram 19.

The Scythians were at (a) and Alexander at (b), and Alexander's aim was to bring on a battle. He threw forward a weak cavalry force (c), and the Scythians (d) at once began to circle round it. Now that he had drawn them in, his next problem was to destroy as many of them as he could. To do so, he sent forward a screen of light troops (e), and it may be assumed that its wings were thrown forward, so that the screen assumed the shape of a crescent. This would reduce the distance between the flanks of the light infantry and those of the advance cavalry. Next, Alexander advanced three regiments of Companion cavalry and the mounted javelin-men to charge the enemy. It is not known at what point, or points, they charged, but common sense dictates that it was at the flanks of the Scythians who were galloping about between the light infantry and the advanced cavalry. In the diagram, this force (f) is shown moving outwardly in two groups.

The result of these tactics was that the Scythians between the light infantry and the advanced cavalry were driven into a mob in the neighbourhood of (g). Then Alexander brought up his main force of cavalry (h), passed through the light infantry, charged the mob and slaughtered it. We are told that he killed no more than 1,000, a small number; therefore he did not defeat the whole Scythian army. The above tactics would seem to fit these results.

Whatever he did, it was something which greatly impressed the Scythians, for soon after the battle envoys were sent from their king

---

[1] IV, iv, 7.

[2] According to Curtius (VII, ix, 16) the Macedonian casualties were sixty horsemen and 100 foot soldiers killed, and 1,000 wounded.

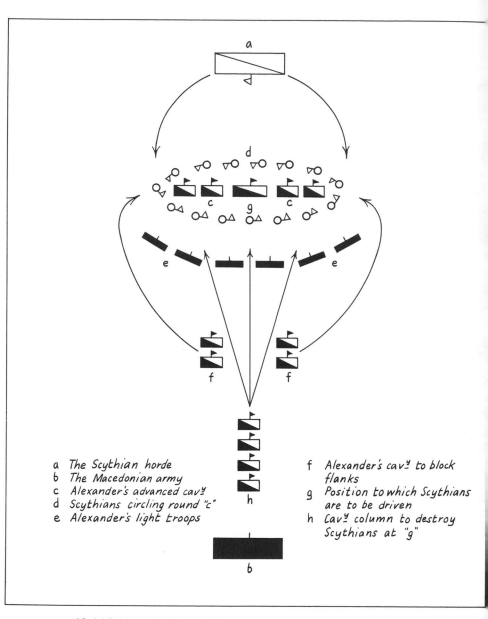

a — The Scythian horde
b — The Macedonian army
c — Alexander's advanced cav⁷
d — Scythians circling round "c"
e — Alexander's light troops

f — Alexander's cav⁷ to block flanks
g — Position to which Scythians are to be driven
h — Cav⁷ column to destroy Scythians at "g"

19 ALEXANDER'S TACTICS AGAINST THE SCYTHIANS

'to apologize for what had been done, and to state that it was not the act of the Scythian State, but of certain men who set out for plunder after the manner of freebooters'.[1]

Undoubtedly Alexander impressed upon the Scythians that, although their tactics had proved sound against the Persians, he could defeat them. His victory, though not great if measured by the numbers killed, was decisive if measured by its moral result – the defeat of their tactics rather than of themselves. If their method of fighting was useless, what could they do? Nothing, hence the envoys.

The tactics of this battle are full of interest, as they show the fertility of Alexander's mind when faced with a new tactical problem. For great battles he had many masters to turn to; for mountain warfare he had Xenophon; but for a battle on the plains against an enemy who possessed neither base, nor communications, nor organization, he had no predecessor in tactics, even the great Cyrus had been defeated by the Scythians.

In all his great battles, the organization of his enemy's army automatically created a decisive point, the brain of the organization – its command – to strike at, and in his mountain campaigns he could always strike at the villages of the hillmen, and so attack them economically; but nomads have no villages and no organization demanding a military brain. Against such an antagonist the only sure method is to compel him by ruse to mass in an area in which his mobility will be restricted, and when such cannot be found, then by manœuvring a hedge of moving men to fence him round and besiege him in the open. This Alexander almost certainly did; he grasped the conditions which had hitherto rendered the Scythians invincible, and because he so shrewdly penetrated them, he compelled them to do the very thing they did not want to do – enter a circle of trained, disciplined, and better-armed soldiers. They set out to circle round the Macedonians, then suddenly their imagined circumference became the centre of a hostile ring. Should this interpretation of Alexander's manœuvre be correct, then it is a model of its kind.

While Alexander was engaged with the Scythians, 150 miles to the south-west of him a very different campaign was fought, and although it has nothing directly to do with him, it is worth examination if only to illustrate how formidable nomadic horsemen could be when faced with an indifferently led army.

When Alexander was recapturing Cyropolis and the fortified posts, Spitamenes had laid siege to Maracanda, and Alexander had sent

[1] Arrian, IV, v, 1.

Pharnuches and three generals with 860 cavalry and 1,500 mercenary infantry to its relief. When Spitamenes learnt of their approach he raised the siege; Pharnuches, instead of occupying Maracanda, followed him. Meanwhile Spitamenes was joined by 600 Scythians, and when Pharnuches came up, Spitamenes resorted to the normal Scythian tactics, and surrounded his enemy with horse-archers. We read:

> When the forces of Pharnuches made a charge upon them, they easily escaped, since their horses were swifter and at the time more vigorous, while the cavalry of Andromachus had been exhausted by the incessant marching as well as by lack of fodder; and the Scythians pressed upon them with all their might whether they halted or retreated. Many of them were wounded by the arrows, and some were killed.[1]

As he did not know how to retaliate, Pharnuches formed his men into a square, and retreated to the river Polytimetus (Zarafshan) to seek protection of a woody glen which he hoped would make it difficult for the enemy to continue circling round him, and where his own infantry might be more usefully employed. But unfortunately his authority over his subordinates was so slight that Caranus, without informing Andromachus, pressed on with his cavalry to cross the river at a ford, and when the infantry saw this they took panic and followed him. Thereupon the Scythians 'dashed from all directions into the stream. Some pressed on after those who had already crossed and were retreating, others ranging themselves athwart pulled down into the river those who were trying to cross, others again from the flanks showered arrows at them, and others pressed on such as were just entering the river. Then the Macedonians, helpless every way, took refuge in a body on a small island in the river. The Scythians flocking round them, with Spitamenes' cavalry, in a circle, shot them all down; a few they took as prisoners, but killed all these also.'[2]

This disaster is reminiscent of innumerable similar events that sprinkle the pages of history; notably Carrhae (53 B.C.), Manzikert (1071), the Horns of Hattin (1187), and the Monongahela River (1755). All may be traced to the difficulty in developing mobility from a more or less static base, and though we are unable to tell how Alexander would have tackled this problem, it may be of interest to mention here that it was not insuperable. In the Seven Years War, against the

---

[1] Arrian, IV, v, 5.   [2] Ibid., IV, v, 8–9.

red Indians, Henry Bouquet, one of the most noted of small war leaders, solved it by the invention of an elastic square, a protective formation from which mobility could rapidly be developed.[1]

The concluding operations in the reduction of Sogdiana were very different from those against the Scythians. The plains had been won; Spitamenes was dead; it was mid-winter 328 B.C., and Alexander and the army rested at Nautaka. But four of the Sogdian barons, Oxyartes, Chorienes, Catanes, and Austanes were still in the field and the mountain strongholds of the first two were known as the Sogdian Rock and the Rock of Chorienes.

At the break of spring 327 B.C., Alexander set out against the first of these strongholds, and when he approached it, he found that it was precipitous on all sides; that a large number of Sogdians had sought refuge on its summit; that it was provisioned to stand a long siege, and that the deep snow made it difficult to approach, and at the same time provided its defenders with a plentiful supply of water.

At first he invited them to surrender on terms; but they jeered at this, and derisively bade him seek winged-soldiers to capture their stronghold for him, since they feared no other kind of men. He took them at their word and called for volunteers, skilled mountaineers, willing to scale the mountain. To the first man who gained its summit he offered an enormous award, and lesser awards for the second and third, and so on to the last man. According to Curtius, he said to them: 'Nature has placed nothing so high, that valour cannot overcome it. It is by trying what others have despaired of that we have Asia in our power.'[2]

Three hundred answered his call; they provided themselves with iron tent pegs and ropes, and because it was unguarded, they set out by night toward the most precipitous part of the stronghold. They drove the pegs into the crevices between the rocks, or into the ice, and by means of the ropes hauled each other up. After thirty had perished in the attempt, at the approach of dawn the rest reached the top of the mountain, from where, when it became light enough to see, they signalled with white flags to the camp below them that the ascent had been successfully accomplished.

When the signal was received, Alexander sent out a herald to shout to the Sogdian sentries to inform their leaders to surrender without

[1] See *An Historical Account of the Expedition against the Ohio Indians, in the year MDCCLXIV, under the command of Henry Bouquet, Esqre* (1766), pp. 40–8. Also *British Light Infantry in the Eighteenth Century*, J. F. C. Fuller (1925), pp. 106–10.
[2] VII, xi, 10.

further delay, since winged-men had been found and were in possession of the summit of the mountain. Then the herald pointed to its crest, whereupon 'the barbarians being alarmed by the unexpectedness of the sight, and suspecting that the men who were occupying the peaks were more numerous than they really were, and that they were completely armed, surrendered'.[1]

Then followed the episode of the marriage of Roxane, and the voluntary submission of her father, Oxyartes, because Alexander had respected her honour.

The occupation of the Rock of Chorienes was a more difficult task. Arrian attributes to it a height of twenty stades, and a circumference of sixty. It was sheer on all sides, and there was but one difficult way up it, so narrow that its ascent could only be made in single file. Further, a deep ravine encircled the mountain, so deep that in order to assault the Rock from level ground, it was first necessary for 'anyone desiring to bring the army against the rock . . . to do much filling up of the ravine'. Undeterred by this, Alexander ordered pine trees to be felled, so that ladders might be made to enable his men to descend into the ravine; and to expedite the work, he divided the army into two shifts, so that it could be carried on continuously by day and night. Yet in spite of this the task was so slow, that we are told it was advanced by no more than twenty cubits (about thirty feet) by day and less by night. It is described as follows:

> First descending into the ravine they fixed the stakes into the narrowest part of the ravine; the stakes being just as far apart from one another as was proper to give the necessary strength and to bear safely the load piled upon them. They then fixed upon the stakes hurdles of willow and osiers in bridge fashion; then binding these closely together they heaped earth upon them, so that the approach for the troops to the rock might be on the level.[2]

As Mr Robson points out in his translation of Arrian's *Anabasis*, this is difficult to understand. Why was not the ravine filled in, and why were so many workers needed? Robson's suggestion is that the ravine was not filled in, but bridged 'in a rude cantilever fashion', and covered with earth, and 'that the completed structure was thus both bridge and causeway'.

At first [Arrian writes] the tribesmen laughed at these attempts as if quite hopeless; but when at length arrows began to find the

[1] Arrian, IV, xix, 4.   [2] Ibid., IV, xxi, 5.

range of the rock and they proved unable from above to dislodge the Macedonians who had made screens against the missiles, so that they worked beneath them unharmed, Chorienes was aghast at the achievement and sent a herald to Alexander begging him to send Oxyartes to him.[1]

Alexander did so, and Chorienes, persuaded by Oxyartes to surrender, came down from his stronghold to his enemy's camp, where he was courteously received by the king, who not only entrusted the Rock to his safe-keeping, but 'made him governor of all he had ruled before.'

The Swat Campaign[2]

After Alexander had subdued the Aspasians in Bajaur, with difficulty the army crossed the Guraeus river (Panjkora) and entered Swat, which was inhabited by a prosperous and warlike people, known to the Greeks as the Assacenians. According to Arrian, they could put into the field 2,000 horsemen, over 30,000 infantry and thirty elephants, and they were preparing to challenge Alexander's advance. But on his approach they lost heart and sought refuge in their fortified villages, the largest of which was Massaga,[3] whose inhabitants had obtained the service of 7,000 mercenaries from beyond the Indus, and emboldened by their presence they determined to resist him.

Alexander marched on Massaga, and when the tribesmen watched him pitch his camp in its vicinity, so confident were they of their mercenaries that they did not wait to be attacked, but boldly advanced against him. So as to draw them away from their walls and rout them in the open, Alexander ordered his men to fall back toward a hill about a mile distant from the camping ground. This so encouraged the Assacenians, who imagined that he was afraid to meet them, that they rushed forward in a disorderly mob; but when they had approached to within bow-shot, Alexander ordered his army to face about. The mounted javelin-men, Agrianians and archers at once dashed forward to the attack, to be followed by Alexander and the phalanx. Surprised by this unexpected action, the Assacenians took panic, and losing some 200 in killed they fled back to their city. In this engagement Alexander was slightly wounded in the ankle by an arrow.

[1] Ibid., IV, xxi, 6.   [2] See Map 5.
[3] Curtius (VIII, x, 22–5) calls this town Mazagae, and Strabo (XV, i, 27) Masoga. The former says it occupied a strong position, and was surrounded by a wall of stone and sun-dried brick thirty-five stades in length. Sir Aurel Stein (see his *On Alexander's Track to the Indus*, 1929, p. 44) considers that it was probably located in Lower Swat.

Next day, Alexander brought up his siege engines and battered down a section of the city wall; but the Indians put up so gallant a fight that when the Macedonians attempted to carry the breach they were driven back; Alexander then withdrew the storming party. On the morrow 'a wooden tower was drawn up to the walls, from which the archers shot at the Indians, and missiles were hurled from the military engines which repulsed them to a great distance';[1] not even then could the breach be stormed.

On the third day the phalanx was brought up, and a bridge, such as had been used at Tyre, was lowered by means of an engine on to the wall near the breach; but when a party of hypaspists rushed on to it, it broke under their weight, and they were thrown to the ground. The tribesmen raised a shout, and from the wall shot arrows and hurled stones at the unfortunate hypaspists, while others poured out of gates near by and struck at them when in confusion on the ground. The survivors and wounded were rescued by Alcetas and his battalion of the phalanx, then Alexander recalled the storming party to camp.

On the fourth day another engine and bridge were brought up to the wall; but by now the Indians were disheartened by the loss of their chief, killed by a catapult bolt on the previous day, and they sent to Alexander to ask for a truce. Alexander agreed, because, as Arrian writes, 'He was glad to preserve the lives of brave men; so he came to terms with the Indian mercenaries on this condition, that they should be admitted into the ranks with the rest of his army and serve as his soldiers.' [2] The mercenaries then came out of Massaga with their arms and encamped on a hill near the Macedonian camp. But when Alexander learnt – presumably through his spies – that, because they were loth to take up arms against kindred Indians, they intended under cover of darkness to slip away and escape over the Indus to their homes, he surrounded the hill during the night and slaughtered them. Deprived as Massaga then was of its chief defenders, it was easily taken by assault. In the siege Alexander lost no more than twenty-five men.

Because Alexander surmised that the occupation of Massaga would strike terror throughout the land, he sent Coenus to Bazira, whose inhabitants he expected would surrender to him; at the same time he sent Alcetas, Attalus and Demetrius to Ora with instructions to block-

---

[1] Arrian, IV, xxvi, 5. 'The remarkable transport feat', writes Stein, 'involved in carrying this ancient artillery and siege train through the mountains, all the way from the Kabul river if not from the Hindukush, is a matter well worthy of the attention of the modern military student interested in these regions' (op. cit., p. 45).

[2] Arrian, IV, xxvii, 3.

ade it until he could arrive. At Ora a sortie was made on Alcetas, which was easily repulsed; but the inhabitants of Bazira, who trusted in the impregnability of their fortress, which stood on a precipitous mountain and was well fortified, showed no signs of capitulation.

Alexander then set out for Bazira, but on his way he received news that Abisares, rajah of Hazara, was about to assist Ora.[1] He ordered Coenus to fortify a position suitable as an eventual base of operations against Bazira, leave part of his force there to watch its garrison, and with the remainder to join him before Ora, toward which he himself set out. When Coenus had fallen back from Bazira, the tribesmen came down from their stronghold and made a sally against him; they were beaten back at a loss of 500 killed, and withdrew to their lair. A few days later Alexander carried Ora by assault, and when the tribesmen at Bazira heard of it, in despair they abandoned Bazira in the night, and with neighbouring tribesmen fled to the rock fortress of Aornus. With the capture of Ora Alexander's operations in the Swat valley were brought to a triumphant conclusion.

Once the valley was in his hands, he fortified and garrisoned Massaga, Ora and Bazira; then marched to the Indus, and found that sixteen miles above Attock, at Ohind, it had been bridged by Hephaestion. Alexander appointed Nicanor satrap of the lands west of the Indus, and on the capitulation of Peucelaitis (Charsadda), capital of Gandhara, he garrisoned it under Philip, after which he marched to Embolina, which was two days' march from Aornus, where, since the fall of Ora, large numbers of tribesmen had congregated.

Alexander's strategy at this time has been examined by Stein in relation to the topography of the region and with reference to the position of his enemy. He points out that, as the tribesmen in Swat relied on assistance from Abisares from over the left bank of the Indus, they withdrew from the valley of the Swat river toward where its right bank faced Hazara. This, he writes, helps us 'to understand the sound strategic reasons which caused Alexander, before attacking Aornos, first to turn south to the Peshawar valley. Once he had consolidated his hold there and made his arrangements for crossing the Indus quite secure, he could safely move up to the right bank and attack the mountain retreat of the Swat fugitives from the south. He

---

[1] In 1926, when on a mission of exploration of the North-West Frontier of India, with confidence Sir Aurel Stein identified Bazira as the ancient stronghold marked by the ruins on Bir-kot hill – 'the Castle of Bir'. Curtius (VIII, x, 22) calls it 'Beira'. Ora, Stein considers, lay farther up the Swat valley, and in all probability it may be identified with Ude-gram, seven to eight miles north of Bir-kot (op. cit., pp. 46, 59, and 60).

thus avoided the entanglement of the mountainous region that would have attended and hampered direct pursuit from the Swat side. The fugitive host could be cut off from retreat to the east of the Indus and from such assistance as Abisares, the ruler on that side, might offer. Finally, when attacking Aornos from the south, Alexander could command all the advantages which the Indus valley and the fertile plains of the Peshawar valley would offer in respect of supplies and other resources.' [1]

In 1926, as related in the Strategical Narrative, Stein identified Aornus with the highland of Pir-sar, and because its capture was the most famous exploit of all Alexander's mountain campaigns, it is of importance to record what Stein has to say of it.

Some seventy-five miles north of Attock the Indus makes a semicircular bend eastward, and within it is a massif in which two ridges, Una-sar and Pir-sar, meet at right angles and form an inverted L (⌐). The former extends from west to east, and from its eastern extremity the latter stretches from north to south. Pir-sar, which rises 5,000 feet above the Indus, has a narrow level top, which extends at an average elevation of 7,100 feet for over one and a half miles; its eastern and western sides are very deep rocky slopes, and in places sheer cliffs. At its southern end is a conspicuous hillock, known as Kuz-sar, and at its northern a bold conical hill called Bar-sar, which rises to about 7,900 feet. Immediately to the west of Bar-sar is a deep and precipitous ravine, the Burimar-kandao; its bottom is approximately on the same level as the plateau of Pir-sar, and it separates Bar-sar from Una-sar. A shoulder of Bar-sar, called Mashlun, juts out at a height of about 450 feet above the bottom of the ravine, and behind it precipitous cliffs rise for another 350 feet or so higher to the summit of Bar-sar. [2]

This decription in no way contradicts Arrian's. 'The circuit of the rock', he writes, 'is said to be about 200 stades, and its height, where it is lowest, eleven stades (6,675 feet). There was only one ascent, which was artificial and difficult; on the summit of the rock there was an abundance of pure water . . . and there was also timber, and sufficient good arable land for 1,000 men to till.' [3]

At Embolina Craterus was left with part of the army to gather in supplies of corn and other things requisite to convert it into a base of operations, should the capture of Aornus demand a long siege. Then,

---

[1] Op. cit., pp. 123–4.   [2] Op. cit., pp. 129–33.

[3] IV, xxviii, 3. Diodorus (XVII, 85, 3) gives its circumference as 100 stades and its height as 16. Both he and Curtius (VIII, xl, 7) state that in the south the Indus came close up to its base.

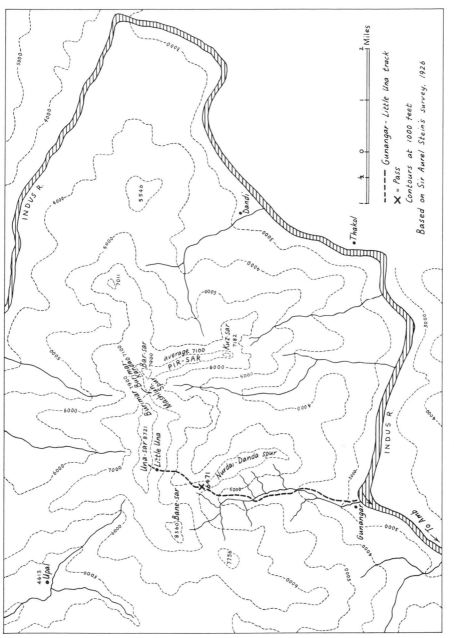

20 AORNUS (PIR-SAR) AND ENVIRONS

with the hypaspists, Agrianians, archers, the battalion of Coenus, the lighter-armed men of the phalanx, 200 of the Companion cavalry, and 100 horse-archers, Alexander set out for Aornus. In the evening he camped for the night, and on the next day came near to it, and encamped again.

There is only one full account of the siege of Aornus, that of Arrian in the XXIXth and XXXth chapters of book IV of his history. It is based on Ptolemy, who played a prominent part in the siege; but as Arrian had no maps or plans to guide him, his description lacks detail. So far as it is possible, this deficiency has been made good by Sir Aurel Stein, who brings Arrian's narrative into relationship with the topography of the area. Because of this, first will be given what Arrian has to say, and then the interpretation of Sir Aurel Stein.

When Alexander pitched his second camp after he had left Embolina, some of the neighbouring tribesmen deserted to him, and offered to lead him to a place from which the rock (Pir-sar) could best be captured. He accepted their service, and with some of them he sent out Ptolemy, in command of the Agrianians, other light-armed troops, and a picked body of hypaspists, to occupy it. He instructed Ptolemy that, as soon as he had got possession of the spot, he was to hold it with a strong force, and then by means of a fire signal inform him that it was held.

Ptolemy set out with the guides, and by way of a rough and difficult track he occupied the place, strengthened it with a ditch and stockade, and then made the fire signal. It was seen by Alexander who, on the following day, moved out of his camp with the army; but his advance was at once opposed by the tribesmen, and brought to a halt by the difficulties of the ground. When the tribesmen saw that he could advance no farther, they turned on Ptolemy and a severe engagement followed in which they attempted to pull down the stockade; they were beaten back, and withdrew at nightfall. So ended the first day.

After this failure, Alexander sent one of the deserters by night with a letter to Ptolemy, in which he instructed him that, as soon as he approached Ptolemy's position, Ptolemy was to attack the tribesmen who were opposing him, so that they might be attacked on both sides. At dawn he set out from the camp, but this time he followed 'the same incline by which Ptolemy had secretly ascended', because he reckoned 'that if he could force his way in this direction and join Ptolemy's force, the action would be a simple one'. We read that at midday a smart battle was fought with the tribesmen, but as detachment after detachment of Macedonians came up, early in the after-

A

PIR-SAR FROM THE NORTH

Shows Eastern (left) and Western (right) flanks of Pir-Sar. The wooded high ground immediately above A is Bar-Sar, and the Burimar-kandao is below it. The Indus can be seen in two places two-thirds up the photograph. Taken on April 25, 1957.

A   B

PIR-SAR FROM THE NORTH-WEST

Shows more fully the Western flank of Pir-Sar. Immediately below A is the Burimar-kandao **and**
the snowy ground above B is the eastern extremity of Burimar. The Indus can be seen in two **places**
two-thirds up the photograph. Taken on April 25, 1957.

noon the enemy was driven from the pass and a junction with Ptolemy was effected. We then read; 'As the whole army was now united, Alexander led it on against the rock itself. But the approach to it was still impracticable.' Thus ended the second day.

At dawn on the third day Alexander ordered each of his soldiers to cut 100 stakes, 'and when these had been cut he heaped up a great mound towards the rock, beginning from the top of the hill where they had encamped. From this mound he thought the arrows as well as the missiles launched from the military engines would be able to reach the defenders on the rock.' This task was pressed on with such energy that 'on the first day' the mound was advanced by no less than a stade (200 yards), 'and on the following day the slingers shooting at the Indians from the part already finished, assisted by the missiles which were hurled from the military engines, repulsed the sallies which they made against the men who were constructing the mound'. Three days later the mound almost spanned the gap between the contending forces, when 'a few of the Macedonians forcing their way occupied a small eminence which was on a level with the rock'. Without a moment's delay Alexander extended the mound, as he was desirous 'of connecting his artificial rampart with the eminence which the few men were now occupying for him'.

The Indians were amazed at the incredible boldness of the Macedonians who had seized the hillock, and when they saw that the mound was united with it, they sent a herald to Alexander to inform him that they were willing to surrender the rock if he would agree on a truce. Their design was to waste the day in parleying, and under cover of night to escape from their stronghold. But when Alexander discovered this – we are not told how – he drew in his investing patrols, so as to encourage them to withdraw. Then he waited until they began to do so, when with 700 hypaspists he set out 'to scale the rock at the part of it abandoned by the enemy'. He was 'the first to mount it, and the Macedonians, pulling each other up, followed'. At a signal they turned on the retreating tribesmen, slew many of them when in flight, while others in panic leapt down the precipices and perished.

'Thus', writes Arrian, 'the rock which had been inexpugnable to Heracles was occupied by Alexander.'

It at once becomes apparent how accurate Arrian's narrative is, when it is related to the topography of the region, which must have remained much as it was in Alexander's day. From the description of the stronghold, there can be no doubt whatsoever that Aornus is Pir-sar; but as Arrian makes no mention of the location of Alexander's camp, the reconstruction of the siege has to start from an unspecified point. But as by far the easiest route of approach to Pir-sar from the Peshawar valley leads up the right bank of the Indus to Amb, and thirty miles farther on reaches the present hamlet of Gunangar, at the western extremity of the eastward bend of the river, it would seem highly probable that, as the camp was two days' march from Embolina, which by some is held to be Amb, it was pitched at Gunangar.

Step into Alexander's shoes, and look at his problem as he must have viewed it. Because of the cliffs and precipitous slopes which flank the Pir-sar spur, it was impossible for him to assault the stronghold on its eastern, southern and western sides. In the north rose the Una-sar massif to a height of 8,721 feet ; therefore it dominated the average height of Pir-sar – 7,100 feet – by some 1,600 feet. There can be little doubt that the tribesmen, who offered themselves as guides, pointed Una-sar out to him, and told him that it was by way of Una-sar that Bar-sar, at the northern extremity of Pir-sa , could be reached, and as the guides were well acquainted with the locality, they are unlikely to have failed to inform him that Una-Sar was separated from Bar-sar by a deep ravine – the Burimar-kandao.

Alexander then sent out Ptolemy, and his guides led him by a difficult path, probably the one shown on the map leading northward up the nullah from Gunangar by way of the pass, marked 6,471 feet, to Little Una. In Stein's opinion, Little Una is 'the most likely site of Ptolemy's fortified encampment', because it is well-placed to guard the track leading up from the Indus, and therefore would help Alexander to reinforce Ptolemy. Further, it 'offers also', he writes, 'the advantage, at any rate today, of easier access to water, and by its situation it was less exposed to attack from the enemy's main position on Pir-sar'. This route is still in regular use.

When Alexander received Ptolemy's fire signal, he set out by the same track to join him, and his advance was obstructed by the tribesmen and delayed by the difficult nature of the ground. Stein suggests that from Pir-sar it would be easy for his enemy to collect on the Nurdai-Danda spur, and there the tribesmen 'could seriously interfere with the advance of the Macedonians up the valley, without risking a battle in the open'. Further, he adds: 'It was equally easy for them, when Alexander's advance up the valley had been brought to a standstill, to turn round and, moving higher up, to attack Ptolemy's detachment holding the fortified camp . . . . at or near Little Una.'

The attack on Ptolemy was beaten off, and during the night Alexander sent instructions to him by letter to attack the enemy in rear, while he attacked him in front. Stein suggests that the aim of this dual attack was to open the pass marked with the height of 6,471 feet, as no junction with Ptolemy was possible until it had been taken. Once the pass was carried, the rest was plain sailing; the forces of Alexander and Ptolemy linked up, and in the afternoon an advance was made on to the Burimar plateau. That it came to a standstill there is, writes Stein, 'fully explained by the great natural obstacle met beyond, the fosse of the Burimar ravine'.

As previously described, the bottom of the ravine lay some 800 feet below the steep rocky slopes of Bar-sar hill. These slopes could easily be defended from above, and could not be attacked with any chance of success, unless they were brought within range of missiles. From the top of Bar-sar to approximately the same level on the Burimar plateau is some 1,300 yards, and between the Mashlun shoulder of Bar-sar (Arrian's 'small eminence' or hillock) and a corresponding elevation on the slope below Burimar not less than 500 yards.

> It follows [writes Stein] that since the *ballistai* and *katapeltai* forming the Greek artillery of that period could throw stones and darts a distance of only some 300 yards, and slingers and bowmen their missiles not much farther, it was necessary to advance the position from which their 'fire' was to be discharged. This could be done here with effect only in a horizontal direction, for a descent into the ravine would not have increased the chance of commanding the higher slopes.[1]

It is to be regretted that Stein does not illustrate this with a sectional diagram of the ravine; had he done so, it would be possible to calculate approximately the height of the mound Alexander built. In the time at his disposal it cannot have been exceptionally high, and as we are told that, before he built it, he ordered each of his soldiers to cut 100 stakes, should this mean poles or the trunks of moderately young fir trees – a tree which abounds in this region – then it would seem probable that, what Arrian describes as a 'mound', was a crib-work erection which formed both a causeway and platform for the archers and catapults to shoot from. The speed with which it was built points to this, whereas to heap up a mound of stakes, as Arrian says was done, does

---

[1] The maximum range of the light catapult was probably 450 yards (see *supra*, p. 45). That in range the Greek bow exceeded it is unlikely because it was a less powerful weapon than the English long-bow, which had a range of 250 yards. Shakespeare mentions as a notable feat 280 and 290 yards (*King Henry IV*, part ii, act 3, scene 2).

not.[1] In addition, Stein points out that why the mound was advanced as much as 200 yards on the first day and less on the following three days 'is readily understood in view of the comparatively easy nature of the slope near the eastern edge of Burimar plateau. But it becomes steadily steeper and steeper as the bottom of the ravine is approached, and in consequence the rate of the daily advance necessarily decreased in proportion to the greater depth to be filled up. This explains why, even when on the fourth day a few Macedonians had forced their way to the small hillock on the opposite side, it was necessary, as Arrian tells us, to continue work on the mound in order to join the two.'

The small hill, mentioned by Arrian, which Stein identifies with Mashlun, which rises to a height of about 450 feet above the bottom of the Burimar-kandao, is about the same height above the flat portion of Pir-sar, and why Arrian says that it was on the same level as the rock 'is', writes Stein, 'easily understood, considering that a continuous slope passing Bar-sar connects Mashlun with the plateau portion of Pir-sar. That there still rose a steep height above the "small hillock",' he points out, 'is made perfectly clear by Arrian's narrative, where he describes the stiff climb which brought Alexander and his seven hundred to the top of the "Rock" after the mound had been joined to the hillock and while the defenders were abandoning Aornos.'[2]

When his survey of Pir-sar was finished, and Stein looked back on the tremendous difficulties that nature had opposed to Alexander, in admiration he writes:

I could only wonder that the story of Aornos should have escaped being treated altogether as a mythos. But then the whole tale of Alexander's triumphant achievements from the Mediterranean far into Central Asia and India is full of incidents testifying to such combined energy, skill, and boldness as would be sought rather in a divine hero of legend than in a mortal leader of men.[3]

This is to repeat what Arrian himself felt, when in the last chapter of his history, he wrote: 'it seems to me that a hero totally unlike any other human being could not have been born without the agency of the deity'.[4]

---

[1] That this extraordinary bridging operation could be carried out in the short time it was, must have demanded a considerable engineering train, in which felling axes, saws, other tools, and cordage were carried.

[2] For the above topographical facts, see *On Alexander's Track*, etc., ch. XX.

[3] Ibid., p. 154.   [4] VII, xxx, 2.

The Sangala Campaign[1]

After the battle of the Hydaspes, to avoid the scorching plains of Gujrat, Alexander marched northward into the foothills of Naoshera, a thickly wooded country where, Curtius writes, the air was cooler, 'for the shade tempers the force of the sun', and where water was abundant.[2] With difficulty and no small loss he crossed the swollen Chenab, which Ptolemy says was fifteen stades in width. There he left Coenus and his battalion to collect supplies, moved southward into the plains of Sialkot, and came to the Ravi. He crossed it more easily than he had the Chenab, and entered the land of the Cathaeans, who with the Malli, Oxydracae and other of the Aratta ('kingless') peoples were reputed to be the most warlike in the Punjab.[3] They were already in arms, because a short time before Porus and Abisares had marched against them; apparently, on Alexander's approach they abandoned their campaign so as to face him.

When he heard this, Alexander made two forced marches from the Ravi, and came to the city of Pimprana, which capitulated to him on terms. There he rested the army for one day, and then marched against Sangala, probably in the district of Amritsar, a great city, protected by a wall and in part by a shallow lake or marsh, in which the Cathaeans and kindred tribes had assembled in force. Immediately in front of the city was a hill, possibly the abandoned mound of earlier cities, which, according to Arrian, was not equally steep on all sides, and round it the Cathaeans had drawn up a laager of three concentric lines of wagons, in which they were encamped, or as Arrian describes it, 'were surrounded by a triple palisade of wagons'.[4] Apparently their aim was to let their enemy batter himself to pieces against the wagon lines, and then, when in disorder, to rush out and fall upon him. If so, their tactics closely resemble Ziska's in the Hussite wars.

When he drew near to Sangala, to cover the deployment of the army and impede the enemy if he should sally out from his laager before it was in order of battle, Alexander sent forward his horse-archers, and instructed them to ride along the front of the laager and shower their arrows at it, so as to pin down its occupants. Next, he drew up as his right wing the Royal Squadron and Cleitus' regiment with the hypaspists and Agrianians, and as his left wing Perdiccas with his cavalry regiment and the phalanx. The archers he divided into two

[1] See Map 5.   [2] IX, i, 11.
[3] Diodorus (XVII, 91, 3) says they practised suttee.   [4] V, xxii, 4.

groups, and posted one on each wing. We are told that, as he marshalled his army, the infantry and cavalry of the rearguard came up; of these, he divided the cavalry into two divisions, and sent one to each wing and the infantry he sent forward to reinforce the phalanx.

This deployment is far from clear, because Alexander's order of march is not given; but that it was a deployment from column of march is certain, because a rear guard is mentioned. What would appear to have happened is that, when Alexander set out on his march to Sangala, he expected to find the Cathaeans inside the city, and that, when he found them outside it, he at once sent forward his horse-archers, as we are told he did. Next, to protect their flanks, he drew up his leading troops in two mobile wings; then he built up the phalanx in the centre, and when the bulk of the cavalry came up, he reinforced the two wings.

When the deployment was completed he led the cavalry of the right wing toward the left of the laager, because he saw that the wagons there had not been so closely parked together, and when he neared it he was received with volleys of arrows, but the Cathaeans did not rush out upon him, as no doubt he hoped they would do. Because it was not practicable for the cavalry to attack the laager, Alexander galloped over to the phalanx, dismounted, and led it forward. With little difficulty it stormed the first line of wagons, but the second line put up a stout resistance, and only after severe fighting was it carried. The Cathaeans abandoned the third line, and fled into the city and shut themselves up in it. There is no record that Alexander attempted to follow them up; if he did not the probable reasons were that the capture of the laager had thrown his infantry into complete confusion, and that, as the laager would appear to have adjoined the city, the enemy could withdraw into it under the cover of the archers on its walls.

An interesting point in the tactics of this battle is the development of infantry shock power from cavalry protection. In the battle against the Scythians (see Diagram 19), the light infantry under Balacrus formed the base of action of the cavalry column marked (h). In the Sangala battle (see Diagram 21) the cavalry wings formed the base of the assault of the phalanx. Had the wagon laager been drawn up well away from the city, undoubtedly Alexander would have surrounded it with his cavalry; in the circumstances he could not do this, therefore the cavalry task was to protect the flanks of the phalanx. In both battles the tactical principles are the same: first to immobilize the enemy, next to secure the flanks of the attacking force, and lastly to assault.

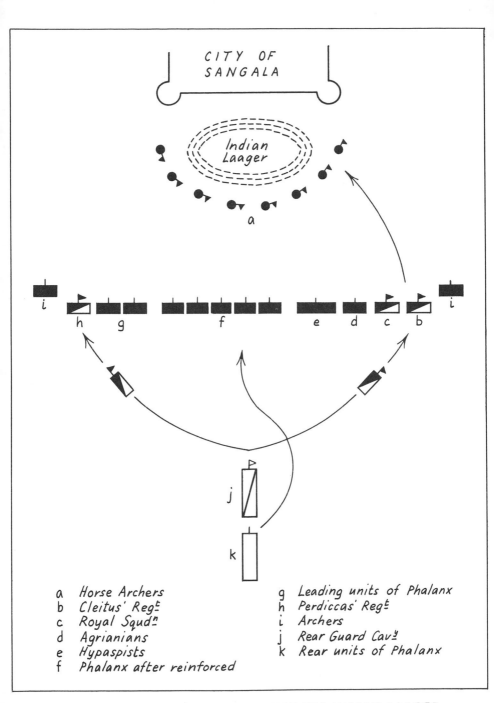

CITY OF
SANGALA

*Indian
Laager*

a

i h g f e d c b i

j

k

a	*Horse Archers*
b	*Cleitus' Reg^t*
c	*Royal Squd^n*
d	*Agrianians*
e	*Hypaspists*
f	*Phalanx after reinforced*
g	*Leading units of Phalanx*
h	*Perdiccas' Reg^t*
i	*Archers*
j	*Rear Guard Cav^y*
k	*Rear units of Phalanx*

21 ALEXANDER'S TACTICS AGAINST THE INDIAN LAAGER

When the Cathaeans had withdrawn, Alexander drew his infantry *en cordon* round the city, or rather around as much of it as he had men for, and opposite the unenclosed part, which included the shallow lake, he posted his cavalry. He did so because he conjectured that after their defeat the Cathaeans would attempt to abandon Sangala during the night. He was not mistaken, for Arrian writes that at the second watch they dropped down from the city wall, which shows that it cannot have been very high. Their attempt failed, and the foremost of them were cut down by the Macedonian cavalry.

Alexander then surrounded the city with a double stockade, except where it abutted on the lake, on the margins of which he posted strong guards. Next, he brought up his siege engines to batter down part of the wall, but before they were in position some of the Cathaeans deserted by night to him and informed him that the garrison intended that selfsame night to steal out of the city by way of the shallow lake, where there was a gap in the stockade. He ordered Ptolemy with the hypaspists, Agrianians and a body of archers to hold the gap and said to Ptolemy:

> So soon as you perceive them to be trying to force a way through here, you yourself will, with your army, prevent their going farther; and will at once bid a bugler to sound an alarm; and you, officers, on this signal, will each with his appointed forces make for the disturbance wherever the bugle calls you. Nor shall I myself be a laggard in this action.[1]

Ptolemy then, under cover of night, collected all the wagons he could and placed them in the expected path of the enemy, and also threw up earthworks between the lake and the city wall.

At the fourth watch,[2] as Alexander had been informed, the gates toward the lake were opened and the Cathaeans set out to withdraw. Then suddenly the bugle sounded and Ptolemy advanced against them; after he had killed 500 he drove the remainder back into the city. Soon after, by digging under the wall and placing scaling ladders against it, Sangala was taken by storm. Seventeen thousand Indians, we are told, were killed, and 70,000 captured, as well as 300 chariots and 500 cavalry horses. Arrian states that in the whole siege Alexander lost rather more than 100 men killed; but that the wounded 'were out of proportion to the slain, over 1,200'.[3]

[1] Arrian, V, xxiii, 7.
[2] The Greeks had only three watches, but Arrian is writing as a Roman.
[3] V, xxiv, 5. Not vastly so, as the normal proportion was ten wounded to one killed; in modern times four to one.

The Mallian Campaign[1]

When, in November 326 B.C., Alexander set out from Bucephala to sail down the Jhelum to the Arabian Sea, on his way he either reduced by force or received the submission of the tribes that inhabited its banks. But when he approached the lands of the Malli (Mahlavas) and Oxydracae (Ksudrakas), and learnt that they intended to oppose his advance, he pressed on with greater speed so that he might subdue them before they could mature their plans. By Arrian we are told that they were 'the most numerous and most warlike people . . . in that region',[2] and according to Curtius, they could put into the field 90,000 foot, 10,000 horse, and 900 chariots.[3] Further, Curtius informs us that usually they were at war between each other, but that on Alexander's approach they went into alliance to meet their common danger.[4]

The combatant strength attributed to them by Curtius and Diodorus is probably much exaggerated, but whatever it may have been, it was sufficient to cause consternation among Alexander's men, whose one idea was to get back to their homes with as little fighting as possible. This is understandable after ten years' constant campaigning, and because it becomes apparent in this campaign that their morale was not as high as it had been, it is worth quoting what Curtius has to say about it.

But when the Macedonians [he writes], who believed that they had already encountered every danger, knew that a fresh war with the most warlike nations of India still remained, they were struck with sudden fear, and began again to upbraid the king with mutinous language: that after being compelled to cross the Ganges and the regions beyond it, they had nevertheless not ended, but only shifted the war. They were exposed to unconquered nations in order that at the cost of their blood they might open a way for him to the Ocean. They were being dragged beyond the constellations of the sun and forced to approach places which Nature had withdrawn from the sight of mortals. For their new arms new enemies constantly appeared. Granted that they routed and put to flight all these, what reward awaited them? Gloom and darkness, and perpetual night brooding over an unplumbed sea, a deep teeming with

---

[1] See Map 5. [2] VI, iv, 3.
[3] IX, iv, 15. Diodorus says 80,000, 10,000, and 700 respectively.
[4] Curtius, IX, iv, 15, and Diodorus, XVII, 98, 1.

schools of savage sea-monsters, stagnant waters in which expiring Nature had met her end.[1]

Shorn of its rhetorical nonsense, the gist of this probably does reflect what was in the soldiers' minds.

Five days after it was learnt that the Malli and Oxydracae were preparing to oppose the passage of the army, the fleet reached the confluence of the Jhelum and Chenab, and had considerable difficulty in negotiating their turbulent cross-currents; once it had done so, Alexander ordered Nearchus to moor his ships along the right bank of the Chenab and repair those which had suffered damage. Next, he sent him with the fleet farther down the river; made an inroad into the territory of a tribe called by Curtius and Diodorus the Sibi, and marched to the spot reached by Nearchus, where he united the whole army. Then, in relation to the position of the Malli and the nature of the terrain, he decided on his plan of campaign.

The territory inhabited by the Malli extended north of the confluence of the Chenab and Ravi, and that of the Oxydracae lay to the east of the second of these rivers. But between Alexander's camp on the Chenab and the Ravi lay the Sandar-Bar, a waterless desert, and he therefore conjectured that the Malli would expect him to continue his advance as far as the junction of the Chenab and Ravi, and from there move up the Ravi against them. On this hypothesis he based his plan. To convince them that he intended to do what he assumed they expected, he sent Nearchus and the fleet to the confluence of the Chenab and Ravi, and instructed Craterus, after a three-day interval, to follow him along the right bank of the Chenab with Philip's contingent and one battalion of the phalanx. He then divided the rest of the army into three columns, one under himself and Perdiccas, and the other two respectively under Hephaestion and Ptolemy. His own he intended to lead across the Sandar-Bar, and surprise the Malli, presumably before the Oxydracae could unite with them. But as on his approach they might break away to the south – that is, down the Ravi – or double back westward – that is, toward the Chenab – to meet either of these contingencies Hephaestion's column was to advance in a southerly direction five days ahead of his own, and Ptolemy's was not to set out until three days after Alexander had. It is strange that no mention is made of the Oxydracae, because Alexander must have appreciated that an advance across the Sandar-Bar was more likely to drive the Malli in an easterly direction – that is, across the

[1] IX, iv, 16–18.

Ravi – than in a southerly or westerly one; in which case the columns of Hephaestion and Ptolemy would be useless. This is what occurred.

Alexander's column comprised the hypaspists, archers, Agrianians, Peithon's battalion of the phalanx, half the Companion cavalry and all the horse-archers, and with it he set out across the Sandar-Bar toward the Malli, whose settlements would appear to have been located on its eastern side. On the first day he advanced 100 stades (about twelve miles) to a water-hole, and there halted, fed and rested his men. He ordered every available vessel[1] to be filled with water, set out again, and during the remainder of the day and the following night covered 400 stades, and at daylight reached a city in which many of the Malli had congregated. Since it had never occurred to them that Alexander would attempt to cross the desert, they were unaware of his approach until he fell upon them. Those outside the city were indiscriminately butchered, and those within it cooped up by the Macedonian cavalry until the infantry arrived, or as Arrian describes it: 'He . . . made use of his cavalry in place of a stockade.'[2] When Perdiccas and the infantry came up, Alexander ordered him with a detachment to move on to another city in the neighbourhood and blockade it, but not to assault it until he joined him, as he did not want its inhabitants to scatter and carry the news of his arrival to the rest of the tribesmen. The first city and its citadel were carried in two assaults, and 2,000 of the Malli were slaughtered. Meanwhile Perdiccas reached the second city, but when he found it deserted, and heard that it had been abandoned only a few hours before, he pressed on after the fugitives, and massacred all except a few who sought safety in the marshes that bordered the river –presumbly the Ravi.

When his men had fed and rested until the first watch of the night, Alexander set out again, and we are told, after he had travelled 'a great distance throughout the night',[3] at daybreak he arrived at the Ravi. There he found that most of the Malli had crossed to the eastern side of the river – that is, into the lands of the Oxydracae – and when he came on those who were still crossing at a ford, he slew many of them before he reached the other bank and caught up with the fugitives, but most of them escaped to a strongly fortified position, which Peithon carried by assault. Next, Alexander marched against what Arrian calls 'the city of the Brahmans',[4] and when he reached it he

---

[1] The vessels were probably *mussuks*, goat-skin water sacks as carried by Indian bheesties.   [2] VI, vi, 3.   [3] Arrian, VI, vii, 1.
[4] It should be borne in mind that these so-called cities were probably much like many present-day Indian villages – conglomerations of mud-huts, the circumference of which formed a protective wall of no great height or thickness.

surrounded it with his infantry, who proceeded to undermine its wall. Its inhabitants then abandoned it and sought refuge in the citadel, but Alexander ordered its walls to be undermined and scaling ladders to be brought up.

Then occurred the first incident to point to a decline in Macedonian morale. When part of the curtain wall between two towers collapsed, and the scaling ladders were planted against the wall, it would appear that the storming party either hesitated or refused to mount them. The evidence for this is that 'Alexander first mounted the wall and all could see him holding it. Observing him, the rest of the Macedonians, feeling ashamed, mounted, one here, and one there.' [1] From this it is apparent that they must have refused or hesitated to carry out orders until he led the way. The Indians then fired their houses, and put up a desperate fight in which 5,000 of them were killed.

After one day's rest the advance was resumed: other cities met with were found abandoned; their inhabitants had fled into the desert. Peithon and Demetrius were then sent back to the Ravi, to march along it and slaughter all Malli found in hiding who refused to surrender, while Alexander led the rest of his column against the largest of the Mallian cities. It also was found abandoned, because the Malli, when they learnt of his approach, had re-crossed the Ravi, and to obstruct his passage they took up a defensive position on its western bank.

When this became known to Alexander, he at once advanced toward them with all his cavalry, and ordered the infantry to follow. 'When he reached the river and beheld the enemy drawn up on the opposite bank, he made no delay, but instantly, without resting from the journey, plunged into the ford with the cavalry alone.' [2] But when the Indians, stated by Arrian to be 50,000 strong, saw that he had cavalry alone they opposed him so vigorously that he broke off his attack and by deploying his cavalry *en cordon* around them, he pinned them to their position until his infantry came up. Soon after, the archers, Agrianians and other light troops began to arrive, and when in the distance the main body of the infantry was seen, the Indians lost heart, broke through the cavalry cordon, and in headlong flight made for a fortified city near by. Alexander followed them closely and slew a large number, drew his cavalry round the city until his infantry caught up, and as night was approaching he encamped under its walls.

The next day the army was divided into two attack columns, one under Alexander and the other under Perdiccas. But again, as they

---

[1] Arrian, VI, vii, 5–6.   [2] Ibid., VI, viii, 5.

approached, the Indians fell back from the city to its citadel. Alexander broke through a gate and entered the city ahead of Perdiccas, whose column, because its scaling ladders had been left behind, had considerable difficulty in surmounting the city wall.

Then followed another incident that points to a decline in Macedonian morale, and through which Alexander was nearly killed. In Arrian we read that because it appeared to Alexander 'that the Macedonians who were bringing up the ladders were malingering', he 'seized a ladder from one of those who bore them, and himself set it up against the wall, and gathering himself well under his shield mounted up'.[1] Then followed the Homeric fight described in Chapter 5 (p. 133) in which he was shot through the chest by an arrow,[2] and was rescued by Peucestas and Leonnatus. It was the climax of his conquest of India. A terrible slaughter followed, and for the time being the formal submissions of the Malli and Oxydracae brought the campaign to a close. All the columns were then united at the junction of the Ravi and the Chenab.

[1] Ibid., VI, viii, 3.

[2] According to Plutarch, this was Alexander's eighth and most dangerous wound. The other seven he lists as follows: In the Illyrian campaign he was wounded in the head by a stone and suffered a neck injury from a cudgel; at the Granicus a head wound from a dagger; at Issus a sword wound in the thigh; at Gaza an arrow wound in the ankle and a dislocated shoulder; at Maracanda a leg bone was split by an arrow; among the Aspasians an arrow wound in the shoulder; and among the Gandridae an arrow wound in the leg (*Moralia*, 'On the Fortune of Alexander', 327, 2).

9

ALEXANDER'S STATESMANSHIP

✺✺✺

As Captain-General

Since war, other than mere brigandage, is a political act and an instrument of policy, statesmanship and generalship are near akin, and although usually the responsibilities of conducting a war are divided between a government and its general, or in recent times its general staff, in Alexander they were united, because as king of Macedon and hegemon of the Hellenic League he combined in his person complete political and military authority. He could elaborate his own policy and develop his strategy in accordance with it, and had it not been for the genius he displayed as a statesman in his conduct of war, under no conceivable circumstances could his generalship have accomplished what it did. Accordingly, in this chapter and the next, under the headings of statesmanship and generalship, the intention is briefly to summarize and comment upon what has been recorded in the Strategical Narrative and the first three chapters of the Analysis.

Alexander was born in a revolutionary age in which the old city-state polity was growing senile, and when some of the greatest thinkers in history were concocting ideal political medicines to rejuvenate it. He was educated by one of the most renowned of these political physicians, and trained in the realistic military school of his father Philip, without comparison the most talented general of his day. Yet, when at the age of twenty the dagger of an assassin raised him to the throne, he stepped out along a path of his own choice, and began to develop a grand strategy – the product of statecraft and warcraft – which was to transcend the teachings of his master, eclipse the remarkable successes of his father, and set the civilized world spinning on a new political axis, undreamt of by the philosophers.

From Aristotle and his father he had learnt two lessons of inestimable value. The first was that Aristotle was supremely wrong to divide humanity into master and slave races, and assume that all except Greeks belonged to the latter. The second was that Philip was supremely right to appreciate that in war military force is not the sole weapon in the armoury of a general, or even the most puissant.

Though at times Alexander could be over-brutal to his enemies, he never fell into the error of holding them in contempt. He accepted that as human beings, though they varied in culture, they were endowed with the same virtues and vices to be found in his Greeks and Macedonians, and that anything more than transient success demanded this acknowledgement. Although he cannot have failed to realize that the machiavellian manœuvres so skilfully resorted to by his father could pay high dividends, he also must have understood that they were insecure capital investments, because they left the impression on the enemy's mind that he had been cheated out of victory by a trickster; that his opponent was morally inferior to himself. Similarly, after Chaeronea, his own reception by the Athenians must have made an indelible impression on him, and on this occasion he could not have failed to appreciate that his father's generous behaviour toward Athens achieved incomparably more than ruthlessness or craft.

The way he handled the desperate situation which faced him at the opening of his reign, and his behaviour toward the League of Corinth, reveal in him, in spite of his youth and inexperience, the qualities of a skilled statesman. Though the destruction of Thebes may appear to contradict this, because of the low repute of the Thebans it terrified rather than shocked the Greek conscience, and by many was looked upon as a just retribution for the extinction by Thebes of the autonomous cities of Plataea, Thespiae, Coroneia and Orchomenus after the battle of Leuctra. His lenient treatment of Athens, a city as culpable as Thebes, showed profound diplomatic sagacity, and, when his ardent temper is borne in mind, remarkable self-restraint. Not a few of his Macedonians must have urged him to adopt a more ruthless course, but he knew that Athens represented what was best in Greece, and that the preservation of her culture was of more value to him than her degradation. Throughout his life, and in spite of their constant intrigue against him, he never ceased to woo the Athenians, because Athens alone could crown his great work.

Even at this early period in his reign, it is probable that he looked upon the Hellenic League, crowning achievement of his father's life, as a temporary expedient, in which, as in its distant replicas – the League of Nations and the United Nations Organization – simulated fraternity was the cloak of self-interest, and theoretical political equality the mask of discord. Yet, as an instrument of policy, its value must have been as apparent to him as to its creator, his father, and by fostering its pretences it provided him with that semblance of legality without which it would have been nearly impossible for him to furnish the Greeks with an excuse to accept him as their supreme representative. Though, as a statesman, he appreciated that a war of revenge was of profound psychological value to stir up popular emotions, he was too clear-sighted to imagine that anything of permanent political value could be built on hatred. Nevertheless, he remained loyal to the principles of the League until the close of his reign, when with the least loss of face to to its members, he emasculated it by his deification.

Whatever may have been his actual aim when he crossed the Dardanelles, and the inclusion in his headquarters of historians, geographers, botanists, zoologists, metallurgists and other scientists suggests that it was not a limited one,[1] his first task was to liberate the ancient Greek cities of Asia Minor, which since the days of Cyrus had been subjected to Persia. It had, then, nothing to do with revenge which, presumably, was only to come into force after their liberation. But liberation in itself was no more than a political aim which, once attained, was bound to give birth to strategical consequences. These, as his subsequent actions indicate, were apparent to Alexander, and the primary one was that, in face of Persian wealth and naval superiority, the Greek homelands would never be secure until both flanks of the Aegean were firmly in Greek hands. Liberation was insufficient, and was likely to be ephemeral unless the liberated cities could guarantee the security of the eastern Aegean coast line. As they did not possess the power to do so, in turn their security would have to be guaranteed, and the only practical way to accomplish this was to advance the Aegean frontier eastward to the Halys. Thus, from the start of the campaign, the ideological aim of revenge was ousted by the strategical aim of security, with the result that Alexander was progressively drawn eastward until complete security could only be guaranteed by the conquest of the entire Persian empire.

As security fixed the as yet unseen goal, which was to draw Alexander to the river Beas, at the same time it revealed to him the political means without which he could not possibly have attained it. Although he came to the Asiatic Greek cities as a liberator, because he was a Macedonian, their citizens, who on the whole had been con-

[1] Although it is unknown how many of these men accompanied him when he set out, a number of them certainly did.

siderately treated by the Persians, are likely to have been doubtful whether a change of masters would benefit them. But when, after his victory on the Granicus, he set out to treat them as free allies, welcomed the restoration of their former democracies, exempted Ilium, Erythrae, and the Ionian and Aetolian cities in general from payment of tribute, beautified the temple of Athena at Ilium, ordered the restoration of Smyrna, and the rebuilding of Clazomenae, dedicated a temple to Athena at Priene, offered to restore the temple of Artemis at Ephesus, which had been burnt down in the year of his birth, and everywhere showed the greatest respect for Hellenic traditions, they saw him as not only a liberator, but a father who regarded them as his long-lost children.

This policy of conciliation was clearly premeditated, and it reveals that Alexander realized what so many statesmen forget: that the goodwill of the civil population is the moral basis of military power.[1] It follows from this that there are always two fronts in a war; an outer or physical front, the province of the general, and an inner, or psychological front, the province of the statesman. That on the former battles are fought with weapons, while on the latter they are fought with the ideas enshrined in the policy the statesman adopts towards the enemy's peoples. Should his policy be such that it progressively detaches them from their government – that is, subverts their loyalty – then increasingly will the moral foundations of the enemy's military power be undermined.[2]

The strategic importance of this cannot be overestimated, because without the establishment of an inner front it would have been impossible for Alexander, with the limited resources at his disposal, to have overcome the military power of Persia when related to the enormous extent of her empire. Without a friendly enemy population he would have had to garrison every city and province he occupied, as well as every mile of his communications, and the result would have been that, long before he could have reached the centre of his enemy's empire, his fighting forces would have been whittled to insignificance.

---

[1] Napoleon took note of this. At St Helena he said: 'What I particularly admire in Alexander is, not so much his campaigns, which are now difficult to reconstruct, but his political sense. . . . He possessed the art of winning the affection of the people. He was right to have Parmenion killed, because he was a blockhead who considered it wrong to abandon Greek customs. It was a great political act on Alexander's part to have gone to Ammon; thus he conquered Egypt' (*Mémoires écrits à Sainte-Hélène* (1822–25), Jany. 7, 1818, Gourgaud, vol. II, p. 435, and Montholon, vol. II, p. 246).

[2] Marshal Pilsudski calls the inner front 'that most dangerous of all fronts' (*L'Année 1920* (1929), p. 51).

This policy of conciliation was not confined to the Greek Asiatic cities. In Lydia, because Mithrines, the Persian garrison commander of Sardes, surrendered the city to him without a fight, he treated him with honour, and gave back to the Sardians and other Lydians the ancient laws they had been deprived of by Cyrus.

It was at Sardes that Alexander's wisdom as a statesman is seen in a collateral problem. As he advanced, in order progressively to establish peaceful and contented areas in his rear it was essential that Persian administration should not be destroyed, and his appointment after his victory on the Granicus of Calas as satrap of Hellespontine-Phrygia shows that he intended to maintain it. At Sardes, he safeguarded the administration by drastically curtailing the powers of the satrap he appointed; he deprived him of control over finance, taxation, and military command, a long over-due reform and which went far to curtail rebellion – the curse of the Persian satrapal system. As a further safeguard, the main fortresses in the empire, such as Sardes, Tyre, Gaza, Pelusium, Memphis and Babylon, were successively placed under Macedonian commandants directly responsible to Alexander.

But it must not be thought that he followed a uniform system of administration; he dealt with each city, district or province on its merits. In Caria, he appointed Ada, an Asiatic woman, as satrap, who after her death was followed by a Macedonian. In Phoenicia, except for Tyre, he maintained the city kings, and in Egypt he abolished the satrapy, remodelled the entire administration, and appointed an Egyptian as civil head. The practical reasons for this drastic change have already been mentioned; but even had they not held good, in a country over which he was not only recognized as king, but also regarded as a divinity, it would have been impolitic to continue the Persian administration – he had to efface the blasphemies perpetrated by Cambyses and Artaxerxes III. In brief, as an administrator, Alexander built on what existed, reformed and experimented with it as far as time permitted, and did not adhere to any system that failed to stand the test of practice.

As Lord of Asia

With his victory at Issus, Alexander's policy began to enter its second phase. Although he had been caught at a disadvantage in the Alexandretta defile, not only had Darius failed to exploit it, but his disgraceful flight in the middle of the battle must have convinced Alexander that he had nothing further to fear from him. Also, as is seen in the speech to his generals and allies, made immediately before he laid siege to Tyre, he rightly conjectured that Darius' defeat would force the withdrawal of the Phoenician and Cyprian fleets from the Aegean, and thereby deprive Agis of Sparta of Persian naval support. Because it added to the security of his home base, Issus went far to unshackle Alexander from the trammels of the League; whatever policy he might adopt towards it, he was assured that Antipater would be able to enforce it. It was immediately after Issus that, in his reply to Darius' first appeal to release his mother, wife and children, he first designated himself as 'Lord of Asia', and this shows that, although all Asia was as yet far from his, he realized that his victory had opened to him the road which, if he followed it, as he intended to do, must increasingly enhance his authority until it transcended his powers as hegemon of the League and king of Macedonia, and endowed him with the status of emperor.

At Memphis, his crowning and his consequent deification brought him a step farther toward this goal. Although to his followers his coronation is unlikely to have appeared to have been more than an act of submission by the Egyptians, so mystically-minded a man as Alexander must have seen in it a portent of the deepest significance, and whatever it may have been, it was of sufficient moment to persuade him to march several hundred miles across the Libyan desert to consult the god who had adopted him as his son. A few months later, he won his second great victory over Darius at Arbela and occupied Babylon, where his first act was to establish himself in the eyes of the Babylonians as the avenger of their gods.[1]

In Babylon he radically changed his policy. His earlier conquests were what may be described as the 'occupied provinces' of the Persian empire, those west of the Tigris in which, because the native populations were non-Iranian, he could successfully play the part of liberator. Eastward of them he was faced with the homelands of the Iranians, in which the people were loyal to the Persian monarchy and to whom the idea of liberation would be meaningless. The psychological war, which had garnered so profitable a political harvest, would prove ineffective

[1] As a political instrument polytheism is superior to monotheism. While the latter acknowledges but one god, and repudiates all other gods, and is therefore a non-co-operative and aggressive religion, the former enables its adherents to find counterparts of its own gods in the enemy's gods, and consequently, should they desire to do so, to enter into alliance with them. Because of this, at Tyre, at Memphis and at Babylon, Alexander was able without hypocrisy to sacrifice to the local gods, an enormous political advantage. Had he been a Christian or a Moslem, probably he would have destroyed the idols and thereby insulted their worshippers. To him an ideological religious war would have seemed blasphemy.

here, and Alexander would find himself up against a hard, instead of a soft inner front. He was some 1,500 miles from his base, and although he was unaware of this he still had well over 2,000 miles ahead of him before the whole of the Persian empire would be his. Thus far his policy of liberating the occupied provinces and conciliating their inhabitants had enabled him to keep his relatively small army intact; how long could he expect to keep it so in provinces in which the native population was loyal to Darius and could not be subverted? Also, should he suffer a defeat east of the Tigris, the whole of his rear, still only loosely organized, might blaze into revolt. And if the Iranian provinces proved hostile, he would have to leave strong garrisons as he advanced, and he had insufficient troops to do this. What, then, could he do?

His solution was remarkable. Because he could no longer win over the people, he decided to win over their leaders. Not by bribery – the Persian way – and not because he lacked the bullion to do so, but surely because, and there is no recorded instance that he ever resorted to bribing an enemy, as king of Macedonia and the chosen of Ammon, he thought it a degrading way to win over his opponents. His solution was to take advantage of the renown he had won and the degradation his victories had brought upon Darius to abandon the idea of ruling solely for and by means of his Macedonians, and to share his authority with his enemy. His appeal was to be no longer to the people, but to their satraps, in whose eyes Darius was utterly discredited. Would it not be more profitable for them to acknowledge him their king, and thereby retain their satrapies, than to remain loyal to a man who twice in battle had abandoned his army, and whose cowardice had uncrowned him? His appeal was to their self-interest.

How could this policy be inaugurated? His genius pointed out the means. Mazaeus, the former satrap of Syria, who so ably had commanded the right wing of the Persian army at Arbela, had sought refuge in Babylon, and on Alexander's approach he had met and welcomed his victor. In Aristotle's eyes Mazaeus was a barbarian, fit only to be treated as a slave. But ever since his remarkable conversation with the philosopher Psammon in Egypt, Alexander knew better, and because in his eyes courage was the highest of the virtues that marked out 'the noblest and the best', he offered the satrapy of Babylonia to Mazaeus, the man who a few weeks before had been his most formidable enemy.

This was a decision of sheer genius, unique in the history of war. Many generals have deserted to their enemy, many have been bribed by him, and many have been cajoled into entering his service; none so far had or was again to be appointed by his victor, almost on the field of battle, his trusted subordinate, in order to establish the only possible condition which could lead to a profitable victory: an alliance between victor and vanquished – that is, a victory which would establish, at least in theory, a peace in which the noblest and the best of both would jointly rule. Thus a policy of partnership[1] was to replace the policy of liberation, and as Alexander advanced, each satrap who followed the example of Mazaeus and surrendered without a fight, retained his satrapy, and for the time being Macedonians ceased to replace them.

To limit the dangers inherent in his policy, Alexander, as he had done in Lydia, removed military control from his Persian satraps, and placed it in Macedonian hands,[2] and he continued to appoint Persians until he had subdued Sogdiana, after which he reverted to Macedonians. The reason for this is obvious: the strategical value of these appointments then ceased; he was about to invade India, in which there were no Persian satraps to win over, so he either appointed Macedonians, or reshaped his policy by entering into alliance with the Indian rajahs, notably Taxiles and Porus. When he returned from India to find that several of his Persian satraps had taken advantage of his absence to abuse their powers, he deposed them; at the time of his death only three satrapies were left occupied by Persians. Though this shows that the appointment of Persians did not work as successfully from the administrative point of view as he had hoped, it should not hide the fact that, as a temporary measure, it did work from the strategical point of view. It enabled Alexander to keep his army intact until he entered India, as his policy of liberation had kept it intact until he arrived on the Tigris. After he crossed the Indus there can be little doubt that as he advanced eastward more and more of his men had to be employed on garrison and lines of communication duties, so that by the time he reached the Beas he had too few forces left to ensure a successful advance farther east. This situation undoubtedly would have arisen long before, had he not

[1] By the scholars Alexander's policy towards his Iranian subjects is frequently denoted as one of 'fusion', and sometimes it is held that the mass marriages he arranged at Susa point that his intention was to obliterate the differences between Greeks and Persians by a fusion of blood. Because Alexander must have been aware that the Persians outnumbered the Greeks by probably twenty to one, this is improbable. But to fuse, not through a mingling of blood, but through a partnership between the noblest and best of both peoples is an eminently wise and practical idea.

[2] Wilcken (*Alexander the Great*, p. 253) points out that, why special finance officers are not heard of in the eastern satrapies is 'possibly because the economy of these regions was based not on currency but on kind'.

resorted to his policies of liberation and partnership, and this is proof positive of their wisdom.

With the death of Darius the character of the war was changed. Until then Alexander had been a foreign conqueror; by right of the sword he had become the Great King, and although for obvious reasons he never adopted this title, it was clear to him that the Iranians were his subjects and no longer his enemies. 'It was not in harmony', writes Professor Wheeler, 'with Alexander's conception of a real and permanent conquest such as he desired, that a country should be held in subjugation by a foreign army. . . . It is in the formulation of this idea, rather than in feats of arms, that Alexander's first claim to greatness rests.'[1] His empire was to be neither Greek, nor Macedonian, nor Asiatic, it was to be Alexandrian. In its conception there are no traces of Aristotle's ideas, and it went far beyond those of Isocrates, who never dreamt of raising Asiatics to partnership with Greeks. It broke with the basic conceptions of the Hellenic world, and substituted for them a new world outlook.

After the death of Darius the policy of partnership, which thus far had been restricted to the maintenance of the satrapal system of administration and the appointment of Persian satraps and officials, was, in order to show respect to his new subjects, extended by Alexander to include the adoption of Persian court etiquette and the wearing of Persian apparel. These innovations antagonized many of Philip's old soldiers. They understood Alexander's action in adding Asia to his throne; but when they found that his intention was to deal with the Persians as he had dealt with the liberated Greeks of Asia Minor – that is, as allies – their resentment, which caused the tragic deaths of Philotas, Parmenion, Cleitus and Callisthenes, would certainly have wrecked the expedition of a less resolute leader. Blinded by their arrogance, they could not see that neither Greece nor Macedonia could provide sufficient men to fill the gaps in the army, let alone to supply the administration and furnish the ever-growing demand for garrison and lines of communication troops, and that without them their conquests could not he held. They belonged to the old world, and it would be wrong to blame them for their inability to accept the new, which was comprehensible to Alexander alone.

Besides the essential need of a mixed army, which soon after the death of Darius Alexander began to recruit, the two most powerful instruments in his partnership policy were the cities he built and the financial system he inaugurated. He realized that trade within his

---

[1] *Alexander the Great*, pp. 480 and 476.

empire was the greatest of mixers, because it brought all conditions of men into contact, and with the exchange of commodities went the exchange of ideas. Cities were the centres of trade, and because in the eastern Iranian half of his empire few existed, this deficiency had to be made good. He built cities – his Alexandrias – on the great trade routes, and except for Alexandria in Egypt, which was designed as an emporium, and Alexandretta, all his cities are to be found east of the Tigris. Tarn calls him 'one of the greatest city-builders of all time':[1] many of his cities still exist.

They had nothing directly to do with Hellenization, which was their by-product developed under his successors. Although Alexander's military settlements were designed for strategical and not for trading purposes, many of them grew into cities. They also formed part of his vast system of mixed colonization, and as usually they were garrisoned with mercenaries, they went far to absorb the exiles and unemployed, and so solved a problem that had been a curse to Greece since the Peloponnesian War. According to Strabo,[2] eight such settlements were founded in Bactria and Sogdiana; Justin[3] increases them to twelve; Polybius[4] says that 'a ring of Greek cities' (actually military settlements) was built around the fertile plains of Ecbatana to protect the royal studs from the neighbouring barbarians; and Curtius[5] informs us that Alexander built six in Margiane on the Oxus between Hyrcania and Bactria. There were many others, notably Kandahar, but they are either unnamed or their foundations uncertain.

It was to foster trade that Alexander established sea communications between India and Persia and ordered the construction of great harbours and dockyards at Babylon and Patala. He made the Tigris more navigable, improved the harbours of Clazomenae and Erythrae, and projected a 'new Phoenicia' on the coast of the Persian Gulf.

To facilitate the exchange of commodities, Alexander revolutionized finance. His conquests had placed in his hands some 200,000 talents of bullion, by far the greater part of which was unminted, because the traditional policy in the East has always been to hoard the precious metals as an insurance against future needs.[6] But Alexander's genius

---

[1] Ibid., vol. I, p. 132.   [2] XI, xi, 4.   [3] XI, v.   [4] X, 27.
[5] VII, x, 15.

[6] After the battle of Plassey, in 1757, when Clive seized the treasure of Bengal there was piled up before him 'after the usage of Indian princes', writes Macaulay, 'immense masses of coin, among which might not seldom be detected the florins, and byzants with which, before any European ship had turned the Cape of Good Hope, the Venetians purchased the stuffs and spices of the East' (*Essay on Clive* (edit. 1903), p. 53).

told him that if it were minted and placed in circulation, the wealth it would engender would be so great that the future could take care of itself. Soon after he seized the vast hoard in Persepolis, he established a financial civil service under Harpalus,[1] his imperial treasurer, and instructed him to convert the bullion into coinage and circulate it among the satrapies, so that by degrees the tribute collected in kind could be replaced by payments in coin. To establish a uniform currency, he reconciled 'the decimal coinage of Persia (1 gold daric = 20 silver sigoli) with the duodecimal of Philip II (1 gold stater, Attic standard = 24 silver drachmae, Phoenician standard)' by adopting the Attic standard and then reverting to a silver monometallism, 'thus making the stater = 20 silver drachmae, which, though lighter than sigoli, were accepted in Asia. He thus refrained from competing with Athens' coinage . . . but he demonetized the Persian gold, for as the hoarded treasures of Darius began to circulate gold fell below Philip's basic ratio, and the daric became bullion'.[2] This uniform coinage powerfully stimulated trade, and Wilcken mentions that in a short time Alexander's new tetradrachm was to have 'the highest value in the currencies of the world'.[3]

In addition, because the imperial treasury was also the king's privy purse, on his own initiative, by means of personal gifts, Alexander put vast sums of money into circulation. He gave 2,000 talents to the Thessalians and allies; 20,000 talents were issued to pay the army debts, and 15,000 for gold crowns for the generals; at the Susa mass-marriages generous dowries were given to eighty noble Persian women and 10,000 women of the people; 800 talents were allotted to Aristotle for research, and 10,000 to pay for Hephaestion's funeral. 'Of all the services which Alexander rendered to the ancient world', writes Professor Wright, 'the establishment of a plentiful currency was the greatest; and the expansion of trade that resulted from it gave Hellenistic civilization a material prosperity which the Hellenic never enjoyed'.[4] This was noted by Athenaeus in the second century A.D. He wrote: 'When Alexander carried off the treasures of Asia, "the sun of wealth with far-flung might", as Pindar has it, "verily rose".'[5]

Should Justin be correct when he states that at the time of Alexander's death the state treasure had been reduced to 50,000 talents,[6]

---

[1] 'His successor Artimenes introduced the first known scheme of insurance' (Tarn's *Alexander the Great*, vol. I, p. 129).   [2] Ibid., vol. 1, p. 130.
[3] *Alexander the Great*, p. 255.   [4] *Alexander the Great* (1934), p. 156.
[5] *Athenaeus, The Deipnosophistae*, trans. Charles Burton Gulick (1933), VI, 231e.
[6] XIII, i.

then, when seven years' tribute[1] is added to the 200,000 talents seized, Alexander must have put into circulation money to the value of some 250,000 talents during the last seven years of his reign.

After Alexander's death, the influence of his money economy is clearly to be traced in Greece and Egypt. In both countries (except in Athens, where at times extensive loans were raised) money economy had been restricted to petty usury. But under Alexander's successors banks began to spring up, and in Egypt were soon to be found in every village. Mr M. Cary writes that: 'To the Hellenistic banks we may probably attribute a considerable advance in the technique of payment by book entry in place of cash transfers'. Though the bankers did not make use of bills of exchange or cheques, 'they used banker's orders for the payment of debts on the spot or at a distance'. Further, Cary writes: 'The Hellenistic age marks a distinct stage in the progress from district economy to world economy.'[2] The influence of banks on trade was probably much the same as noted by Adam Smith in his *Wealth of Nations*. He says he had heard 'that the trade of the city of Glasgow doubled in about fifteen years after the first erection of the banks there; and that the trade of Scotland has more than quadrupled since the first erection of the two public banks in Edinburgh'.[3]

What Alexander's spending of the hoarded Persian bullion meant to the Hellenistic world may be appreciated by comparing it with a similar event – the unthawing of the frozen treasure of Hindustan by Robert Clive. Its effect was immediate and startling. Before 1757 the machinery for spinning cotton in England was almost as primitive as in India. Suddenly, all changed. In 1760 the flying shuttle appeared; in 1764 Hargreaves's spinning-jenny; in 1768 Cartwright's power-loom. 'But though these machines', writes Brooks Adams, 'served as outlets for the accelerating movement of the time, they did not cause the acceleration. In themselves inventions are passive, many of the most important having lain dormant for centuries, waiting for a sufficient store of force to have accumulated to set them working. That store must always take the shape of money, not hoarded, but in motion.'[4]

In Alexander's wars [writes Wilcken] the previous barriers between East and West were removed and in the next generation

---

[1] According to Herodotus (III, 95) the revenue of Darius I was 14,560 talents. Should this have held good under Alexander, then, between 330 and 324 B.C., the revenue paid to him would be a little over 100,000 talents. But, should Justin's estimate of the revenue – 30,000 talents (XIII, i) – be correct, then another 100,000 talents must be added. [2] *A History of the Greek World from 323 B.C. to 146 B.C.* (1932), pp. 301–2. [3] Cannan's edit. (1904), vol. I, p. 280. [4] *The Law of Civilization and Decay* (edit. 1921), p. 314.

thousands of Greek traders and artisans entered the new world, to seek their fortunes in the new Greek cities, which shot up out of the ground like mushrooms. In this way the two previously detached circles came more and more to coincide and form a single economic circle; and when the Western Mediterranean was attracted into the orbit of the great revolution that occurred in the East, there was finally created a world commerce, which embraced the whole inhabited world, and extended from Spain to India, and beyond through Central Asia to China. This development was completed only under the Roman Empire, but its basis was the conquest of Asia by Alexander.[1]

As Reconciler of Mankind

Although Alexander's conquest of the Persian empire, his new cities and financial reforms, were to lead to the rise of the Hellenistic kingdoms, and through the Roman empire which absorbed them, to lay the foundations of European culture and civilization, the remainder of his policy of partnership was largely ephemeral. Only over a long period of time and under a succession of leaders as able, or nearly so, as himself might they have borne fruit. But the spirit of nationality was too strong to permit them to take root in the span of a single life. At the close of his reign Alexander would seem to have suspected this, and to have seen that, unless his mixed empire were provided with a more permanent focal point than himself, on his death it would fall to pieces. That at the time of his death he had not named a successor was probably because he was still in the prime of life and had every reason to assume that he had many years before him in which to base his empire on lasting foundations.

In part, or in whole, many historians have accepted the plans which Diodorus[2] alleges Alexander gave to Craterus, when after the reconciliation at Opis the latter was sent back to Macedonia with the 10,000 discharged veterans, and on the strength of them have assumed that, had Alexander lived, he would have set out to conquer Carthage and the Mediterranean basin, and thereby establish his sovereignty over the entire known world of his day. Tarn does not accept this view; he considers that the plans cited by Diodorus were a latter-day forgery,[3] and because at the time of his death Alexander had not yet completed the conquest of the Persian empire – the great block of country from

---

[1] *Alexander the Great*, p. 284.   [2] XVIII, 4, 2–5.
[3] See *Alexander the Great*, vol. II, appx. 24.

Bithynia to the Caspian Sea was still unsubdued and had reverted to independence – he would have shown poor statesmanship had he planned to carry out what Diodorus suggests. It may be added that his hold on the Punjab was no more than nominal, and because he knew that thickly populated lands lay eastward of the Beas, surely he would have attempted to conquer them before contemplating the conquest of Carthage and the West. That he aimed at world dominion is in Tarn's opinion 'only the invention of a later day';[1] and if he had any plan, then reason suggests that what he had in mind at the time of his death was the conquest of the Caspian and Arabian Sea regions and the unification of his empire.

Two considerations point to a concern over unification; his personal position *vis-à-vis* his empire and the countries within his sphere of influence, and his prayer at Opis.

His personal position was extraordinarily complex. In Macedonia he was autocrat and a quasi-constitutional king; in Egypt, both autocrat and a god; in Asia, an autocrat but not a god; in Greece, a god but not an autocrat; and in India, a feudal overlord. Under him the Greek cities in Asia Minor were free allies; in Phoenicia, the kings were subject allies, and in Thessaly his leadership of the Thessalian League was no more than a life appointment. There were many other anomalies,[2] but these are sufficient to show that the consolidation of his empire demanded far more than partnership between Macedonians and Persians, and even could he have fused the two peoples – an impossible task – it would not, and could not, have unified the whole, because a common idea which, like a magnet, could draw all the parts together, would still have been wanting.

At bottom his problem was not so very different from that which later faced the primitive Christian Church. Its central ideas were enshrined in the Sermon on the Mount, which although in their completeness were beyond the power of man to attain, did establish a unified society in which spiritually all men were brothers – 'Where there is neither Greek nor Jew, circumcision nor uncircumcision, Barbarian, Scythian, bond nor free: but Christ is all, and in all.'[3]

Whether Alexander ever considered the anomalies of his leadership and the divergencies they were likely to cause, is not known. But it is known that immediately after his visit to the shrine of Ammon at Siwah, in his conversation with the philosopher Psammon, like St Paul on his way to Damascus, 'suddenly there shined round about him a light

---

[1] Ibid., vol. I, p. 122, and vol. II, appx. 24.
[2] See ibid., vol. I, p. 139. [3] *Colossians*, III, ii.

from heaven'.[1] It was that God was not only the ruler of mankind, but also the common father of mankind. Therefore all men were brothers, and consequently, Homonoia, which Tarn translates as 'a being of one mind together', or negatively, 'to live without quarrelling',[2] was the linchpin which, as it held each family together, could hold together his empire, a family of many races, in a state of peace. He had, then, to become the father as well as the ruler of his diverse peoples, and by assuming this status transcend the anomalies inherent in his position as their ruler.

It was this aspiration which he expressed in his prayer at Opis, and, according to Tarn, it had little to do with his so-called policy of fusion which was 'a material thing', but with an idea, 'an immaterial thing'.[3] It was firstly, that all men are brothers; and secondly, that he had 'a divine mission to be the harmonizer and reconciler of the world, to bring it to pass that all men, being brothers, should live together in Homonoia, in unity of heart and mind. . . . It was and was to remain a dream, but a dream greater than all his conquests'.[4]

The authority for this is to be found in Plutarch's 'On the Fortune of Alexander', in which to reinforce his argument that Alexander was 'a very great philosopher', he first turns to Zeno (335-263 B.C.), the founder of the Stoic philosophy, and writes that the one main principle in his *Republic* was: 'that all the inhabitants of this world of ours should not live differentiated by their respective rules of justice into separate cities and communities, but that we should consider all men to be of one community and one polity, and that we should have a common life and an order common to us all, even as a herd that feeds together and shares the pasturage of a common field. This Zeno wrote, giving shape to a dream or, as it were, shadowy picture of a well-ordered and philosophic commonwealth'.

After this Plutarch writes: 'but it was Alexander who gave effect to the idea'. And to support this, he next quotes or paraphrases what Eratosthenes[5] (c. 275–194 B.C.) had to say:

---

[1] *Acts*, IX, 3.

[2] *Alexander the Great*, vol. II, p. 400, and *Alexander the Great and the Unity of Mankind* (1933), p. 4.

[3] *Alexander the Great*, vol. II, p. 434.   [4] Ibid., vol. II, pp. 447–8.

[5] Although Plutarch does not refer to Eratosthenes by name, there is no doubt that he is his source, because Strabo (I, iv, 9) mentions that at the close of Eratosthenes' book 'Eratosthenes blames the system of those who would divide all mankind into Greeks and Barbarians, and likewise those who recommended Alexander to treat the Greeks as friends, but the Barbarians as enemies'; and that Alexander disregarded this advice, 'and patronized without distinction any man he considered to be deserving'.

For Alexander did not follow Aristotle's advice to treat the Greeks as if he were their leader, and other peoples as if he were their master; to have regard for the Greeks as for friends and kindred; but to conduct himself toward other peoples as though they were plants or animals; for to do so would have been to cumber his leadership with numerous battles and banishments and festering seditions. But, as he believed that he came as a heaven-sent governor to all, and as a mediator [Tarn's translation is 'reconciler'] for the whole world, those whom he could not persuade to unite with him, he conquered by force of arms, and he brought together into one body all men everywhere, uniting and mixing in one great loving-cup, as it were, men's lives, their characters, their marriages, their very habits of life.[1]

Tarn's conclusion is that Eratosthenes' account must go back to an 'eyewitness' of the feast at Opis, who actually saw the great crater on Alexander's table; that 'Eratosthenes used the metaphor of the loving-cup to illustrate the phrase "reconciler of the world"; that phrase then also belongs to, or depends on, the scene at Opis, and may ultimately go back to the same eyewitness; indeed it is conceivable (I will put it no higher) that Alexander used the occasion to proclaim his mission'.[2]

Although not all classical scholars accept this,[3] Tarn shows that, except for Alexander, there is no one known between his death and the date on which Zeno wrote his *Republic* (probably some years after 301 B.C.) from whom Zeno could have borrowed the idea that 'all mankind was one and all men were brothers', an idea which, through Stoicism, revolutionized the mental outlook of the Western World. From its birthday at Opis it lived on to fructify the Roman Empire, in which, Professor M. Rostovtzeff says: 'men began to realize that there is something higher than local and national interests, namely, the interest of all mankind',[4] and over which, at its close, Claudian (A.D. ?370–?404) pronounced his great eulogy:

'Tis she (Rome) alone who has received the conquered into her bosom and like a mother, not an empress, protected the human race

---

[1] Plutarch's *Moralia*, 'On the Fortune of Alexander', 329, 6.

[2] *Alexander the Great*, vol. II, p. 442.

[3] Wilcken holds that the prayer meant no more than 'the fraternization of Macedonians and Persians'. 'There is', he writes, 'no trace whatever of Alexander's treating all mankind as one brotherhood' (*Alexander the Great*, p. 221); and Ehrenberg writes that: 'an oecumenic unity was aspired to, not a unity of mankind; political organization, not world-wide fraternization, was intended; and the peoples were to be comprised in a worldwide empire, not to be dissolved into humanity at large' (*Alexander and the Greeks* (1938), p. 91).

[4] *A History of the Ancient World* (1926), p. 10.

with a common name, summoning those whom she has defeated to share her citizenship and drawing together distant races with bonds of affection. To her rule of peace we owe it that the world is our home, that we can live where we please, and that to visit Thule and explore its once dreaded wilds is but a sport; thanks to her all and sundry may drink the waters of the Rhone and quaff Orontes' stream, thanks to her we are all one people.[1]

Beyond the import of Alexander's prayer and what Eratosthenes has to record of his mission, there is nothing definite to indicate what, had he lived to a riper age, Alexander might or might not have done. Yet it is hard to believe that, instead of consolidating and unifying his empire, the winning of which had cost him so much blood and toil, after his return to Babylon he would have set out to conquer the lands bordering the Mediterranean. His genius does not warrant light acceptance of such a plan on his part. Whatever Plutarch's statement may be worth, it would seem to strike a truer key.

But Alexander [he writes] desired to render all upon earth subject to one law of reason and one form of government and to reveal all men as one people, and to this purpose he made himself conform. But if the deity that sent down Alexander's soul into the world of ours had not recalled him quickly, one law would govern all mankind, and they all would look towards one rule of justice as though towards a common source of light. . . . Therefore, in the first place, the very plan and design of Alexander's expedition commends the man as a philosopher in his purpose not to win for himself luxury and extravagant living, but to win for all men concord and peace and community of interests.[2]

---

[1] *Claudian*, trans. Maurice Platnauer (1956), 'On Stilicho's Consulship', III, 150–159.   [2] 'On the Fortune of Alexander', 330, 8D–9E.

10

ALEXANDER'S GENERALSHIP

※≪≪≪

As Genius

Although in war no two campaigns or battles are the same, and the talents of generals vary, one factor binds the Great Captains into a common brotherhood; it is their genius, and because genius is undefinable, comparison is the sole means by which to plumb its depths and measure its heights. To attempt so intricate a task is beyond the scope of this book, if only because it would demand a book of its own; yet something should be said on this mainspring of generalship, because it was Alexander's genius that gave soul to his army and astonishment to the world of his day. Shortly before the news reached Athens that Darius was dead, Aeschines, an Athenian onlooker, expressed this astonishment in a speech.

What is there [he asked] among the list of strange and unexpected events that has not occurred in our time? Our lives have transcended the limits of humanity; we are born to serve as a theme for incredible tales to posterity. Is not the Persian King – who dug through Athos and bridged the Hellespont, – who demanded earth and water from the Greeks, – who dared to proclaim himself in public epistles master of all mankind from the rising to the setting sun – is not *he* now struggling to the last, not for dominion over others, but for the safety of his own person? [1]

Napoleon, himself one of the select brotherhood, had no doubt that genius was the mainspring of generalship. On one occasion, when conversing with Montholon at St Helena, he said:

The personality (*présence*) of the general is indispensable, he is the head, he is the all of an army. The Gauls were not conquered by the

[1] *The Speeches of Aeschines*, trans. Charles Darwin Adams (1919), 'Against Ctesiphon', 132. The translation is Grote's.

Roman legions, but by Caesar. It was not before the Carthaginian soldiers that Rome was made to tremble, but before Hannibal. It was not the Macedonian phalanx which penetrated to India, but Alexander. It was not the French army which reached the Weser and the Inn, it was Turenne. Prussia was not defended for seven years against the three most formidable European powers by the Prussian soldiers, but by Frederick the Great.[1]

In a similar strain Robert Jackson[2] writes:

Of the conquerors and eminent military characters who have at different times astonished the world, Alexander the Great and Charles the Twelfth of Sweden are two of the most singular; the latter of whom was the most heroic and the most extraordinary man of whom history has left any record. An army which had Alexander or Charles in its eye was different from itself in its simple nature, it imbibed a share of their spirit, became insensible of danger, and heroic in the extreme.[3]

Further, Jackson points out that throughout the ages, attempts 'to move armies to their duty have rested either on fear of punishment' or, on what he calls, 'an impression of love', by which he means the soldier's affection. He adds:

The experiment has been made in instances without number; and it is found after all trials, that neither the pure fear nor pure love of a commander are sufficient to animate an army, strongly and consistently in the various conflicts of war. Fear and love are coverings; behind them must lurk the spirit of genius which cannot be fathomed; for, whether a commander be kind or severe, he cannot be great and prominent in the eye of the army, unless he be admired for something unknown. It is thus, that troops can only be properly animated by the superior and impenetrable genius of a commander whose character stands before the army as a mirror, fixing the regards while it is bright and impenetrable, losing its virtue when its surface is soiled or softened so as to receive an impression. That a commander be a mirror, capable of animating an army, he must be

---

[1] *Mémoires écrits à Sainte-Hélène*, Montholon (1823–5), vol. II, p. 90.
[2] Robert Jackson (1750–1827) was at one time Inspector-General of (British) Army Hospitals (see *Dictionary of National Biography*, vol. X). In 1804 he published a remarkable book entitled *A Systematic View on the Formation, Discipline, and Economy of Armies*, which on moral factors in war is far in advance of anything Clausewitz has to say on them. A second edition was published in 1824, and a third in 1845.   [3] *A Systematic View*, etc. (edit. 1804), p. 219.

impenetrable; but he cannot be impenetrable without possessing original genius. An original genius does not know its own powers; consequently it cannot be known or measured by others. It thus commands attention, and it gives a covering of protection, in reality or idea, which proves a security against the impression of fear.[1]

So all important does Jackson consider genius to be, that he returns to it on the last two pages of his book:

A genius paramount in force and originality [he writes], manifested in the character of a general, animates the operations of the army with one impulse. . . . It impresses an opinion of superiority on the mass: everyone views himself in the splendour of his commander, assimilates, in idea, with his excellence, and, being superior in opinion, soon becomes so in reality. Hence, it is not the dry mechanical wisdom of the plan of battle, so much as the animating spirit of the leader, which may be considered as the pledge of success in war. . . . It may be observed, in this place, that good officers abound among all nations who cultivate the art of war; the genuine military genius is of rare occurrence: no power of industry can produce it; and no one can define the path in which it moves. The genius which leads to conquest, like the genius of a poet, is original: it is a first impression, improved by study in the book of nature only. . . . The spirit which knows not to submit, which retires from no danger because it is formidable, is the soul of a soldier. The soldier fixes victory in his eye, as a passion rather than a reason. This forms what may be considered as genius – a paramount genius, which domineers and conquers and enslaves.[2]

Jackson has been quoted at length because he is the only military writer known to the author who has written on the genius of the Great Captains with profound understanding and insight. His analysis goes far to explain how and why it was that Alexander achieved what the people of his age, or of any age for that matter, could not even have dreamt to be within reach of the possible. No legendary hero accomplished so stupendous a task; hence the 'Romance' which was conjured forth from his name, and which swept over the Old World from Iceland to China.

[1] *A Systematic View*, etc. (edit. 1804), pp. 228–9.   [2] Ibid., pp. 346–7.

As Strategist

At the opening of the eighteenth century the word 'strategy' – 'the art of the general (*strategos*)' – was added to the military vocabulary to denote the methodical manœuvres, marches and counter-marches prevalent in the age of strictly limited wars. Today, in most dictionaries, it is defined as the science or art of projecting and directing military movements, and after the Napoleonic wars, which, unlike the wars of the twentieth century, were still simple enough to bear some resemblance to Alexander's, Clausewitz defined strategy as follows:

> Strategy is the employment of battle to gain the end in war; it must therefore give an aim to the whole military action, which must be in accordance with the object of the war; in other words, strategy forms the plan of the war, and to this end it links together the series of acts which are to lead to the final decision, that is to say, it makes the plan for the separate campaigns and regulates the combats to be fought in each.

He adds that at its highest point 'strategy borders on political science, or rather . . . the two become one'.[1]

Alexander was as fully aware as Clausewitz that strategy employs the battle to gain the end in war. But where he profoundly differs from him is in the definition of the end – that is, in the aim or object of the war. In Clausewitz's days the twentieth-century democratic conception that the object is to annihilate the enemy, not only militarily, but politically, economically and socially as well, had not yet fuddled man's mind. To Clausewitz war was a clash between armed forces which protected their respective civil populations; each contended for a political aim, and when one side gained a decisive victory, the vanquished automatically sued for peace, and the victor's political aim was gained in a negotiated treaty. But Alexander's aim was not to bring Darius to terms, it was to appropriate his empire, and, were his conquest to be of profit to him, he had not only to defeat the Persian army but win his acceptance in the eyes of the Persian peoples. There was no question of suing for peace, which after his crushing defeat at Issus Darius vainly attempted to do, nor of a negotiated treaty, because Alexander's aim was conquest, and at the minimum expenditure of force and the minimum dislocation and damage of the Persian empire: his policy limited and moderated his strategy.

[1] *On War*, vol. I, pp. 164, 167.

This limitation is noticed by Polybius in a citation he makes from a speech delivered by Alexander Isius concerning Philip V of Macedon (221–179 B.C.). The orator said that Philip avoided meeting his enemies face to face, and instead employed his time in burning and plundering cities.

> Yet [he added] former kings of Macedonia had not adopted this plan, but one exactly the reverse: for they were continually fighting with each other in the open field, but rarely destroyed and ruined cities. This was shown clearly by Alexander's war in Asia against King Darius; and again in the contentions between his successors ... they had been prompt to war against each other in the open field, and to do everything they could to conquer each other in arms, but had spared the cities, that they might rule them if they conquered, and be honoured by their subjects. But that a man should abandon war, and yet destroy that for which the war was undertaken, seemed an act of madness, and madness of a very violent sort.[1]

It was because Alexander's aim was conquest, and not vengeance or spoliation, that, according to Justin, when 'marching forward in quest of the enemy, he kept the soldiers from ravaging Asia, telling them that "they ought to spare their own property, and not destroy what they came to possess" '.[2] Wilcken points out that 'his extensive money gifts to his army were a compensation for the prohibition of plundering the conquered districts, which for political reasons he thought necessary'.[3] While the aim of his strategy was to win great battles, the aim of his policy was to pacify and not antagonize his enemy, so as to limit the number of battles he would have to fight. In idea it was not far removed from the policy which Themistocles recommended to the Athenians after Salamis: 'I have often myself witnessed occasions, and I have heard of many more from others where men who had been conquered by an enemy, having been driven quite to desperation, have renewed the fight, and retrieved their former disasters.'[4] The same advice was given by Jason of Pherae to the Thebans after Leuctra. 'It behoves you to reflect', he said, 'that the Lacedaemonians, if they be forced to relinquish the hope of life, will fight with desperation; and the divine powers, as it seems, often take delight in making the little great, and the great little.'[5]

[1] Polybius, XVIII, 3.   [2] Justin, XI, vi.
[3] *Alexander the Great*, p. 243.   [4] Herodotus, VIII, 109
[5] Xenophon's *Hellenics*, VI, iv, 23. Aeneas Tacticus (xxxviii, 1–5) says much the same thing: 'But he who acts in a harsh and savage manner, immediately after

It was because Alexander's aim was to achieve, as far as it was possible, a bloodless conquest, that he drew so distinct a line between the Persian army and the Persian peoples; the defeat of the army was his strategical aim; the winning over of the peoples his political aim. The first was the means to attain the second, because, as long as the Persian army held the field, there was no certain assurance that the people would willingly accept him. Alexander needed no telling that 'War is only a part of political intercourse, therefore by no means an independent thing in itself'.[1]

After he had defined strategy, Clausewitz turned to the more important strategical principles, and these are worth quoting because they show that, had Clausewitz enumerated them in the fourth century B.C., Alexander would have had little to learn from them; in fact he might have tendered the German military theorist some useful advice.

There are three principal objects [he writes] in carrying on war:

(*a*) To conquer and destroy the enemy's armed forces.

(*b*) To get possession of the material elements of aggression, and of the other sources of existence of the hostile army.

(*c*) To gain public opinion.[2]

The first object calls for no comment: to remember the battles of the Granicus, Issus, Arbela, and the Hydaspes is sufficient.

The second needs none either, because once Alexander had seized the Persian treasure at Susa and Persepolis, he deprived Darius of his most important means of recruiting another army, and it prevented Darius from fomenting rebellions in his enemy's rear by bribery. Gold and silver, and not 'principal towns, magazines and great fortresses', were the chief 'material elements' in Alexander's day.

The third object – public opinion – is, according to Clausewitz, 'ultimately gained by great victories, and by the possession of the enemy's capital'. Although in the eighteenth and nineteenth centuries the occupation of the enemy's capital more frequently than not

becoming master of a city ... makes other cities hostile, so that the war becomes laborious for him and victory difficult to attain ... For nothing makes men so brave as to fear of what ills they will suffer if they surrender.' And Rabelais (bk. I, chap. XLIII) makes Gargantua proffer the following words of wisdom to Gymnast: '... according to right military discipline, *you must never drive your enemy unto despair*. For that such a streigth doth multiply his force, and increase his courage, which was before broken and cast down. Neither is there any better help for men that are out of heart, toiled and spent, than *to hope for no favour at all*.'

[1] Clausewitz, *On War*, vol. III, p. 121.
[2] Ibid., vol. III, p. 209.

brought war to an end,[1] in classical times, except for Rome,[2] strictly speaking there were no capital cities; instead there were city-states, or royal residences, such as Babylon, Susa and Persepolis.[3] With the exception of war between two city-states, because the occupation of cities and royal residences did not bring war to an end, as has several times been pointed out in these pages, Alexander substituted the ultra-modern conception of subversion of the enemy's people. Russia is today the leading exponent of this.

Clausewitz next lays down five strategical principles.

The first, and in his opinion the most important, is: 'to employ *all* the forces which we can make available with the *utmost* energy'.

'The second is to concentrate our force . . . at the point where the decisive blows are to be struck, to run the risk even of being at a disadvantage at other points, in order to make sure of the result at the decisive point. The success at that point will compensate for all defeats at secondary points'.

'The third principle is: not to lose time. . . . By rapidity many measures of the enemy are nipped in the bud, and public opinion is gained in our favour'.

The fourth is surprise: '. . . it is the most powerful element of victory'.

And the last is: 'to follow up the success we gain with the utmost energy. The pursuit of the enemy when defeated is the only means of gathering up the fruits of victory.' [4]

After what we have recorded on Alexander's generalship, and because these principles will be discussed in the next section, it is unnecessary to point out here that the value of utmost energy, concentration at the decisive point, rapidity of movement, surprise and pursuit were as clearly apparent to Alexander as they were to Clausewitz.

In all strategical problems which embrace war, either in its entirety or in part, there are two outstanding strategical factors – the establishment of secure bases and secure communications. The first may be compared with the foundations of a house, they must be sufficiently substantial to bear the weight of the superstructure; the second is the scaffolding, which enables the builders to maintain contact with the

---

[1] Though the occupation of Paris in 1870 failed to do so, in 1940 it immediately led to the capitulation of France.

[2] Had Hannibal after the battle of Cannae (216 B.C.) occupied Rome, the probability is that he would have brought the second Carthaginian war to an end.

[3] The occupation of Athens by Xerxes in 480 B.C. did not bring war to an end, nor did Alexander's occupation of Babylon, Susa, and Persepolis.

[4] Ibid., vol. III, pp. 210-11.

ground (base), and progressively feed the masons with the materials they require. Should the foundations sink, the superstructure will be imperilled; should the scaffolding collapse, its erection cannot be continued until the scaffolding is restored.

When a war or campaign is compared with the superstructure, the importance of the base – its starting point – at once becomes apparent, and no general has understood this better than Alexander. First, he established a secure home base – that is, his initial or main base – by his Danubian campaign and the destruction of Thebes. The Danubian campaign was a strategical operation, the establishment of a secure northern frontier; the destruction of Thebes a political operation, the establishment of a quiescent inner front. They were complementary; one removed a danger that might have been exploited by anti-Macedonian factions within Greece, the other resulted in the paralysis of these factions, and thereby deprived the Thracian and Illyrian tribesmen of all hope of being able to take advantage of revolt within Greece. Together they secured the Macedonian home base throughout Alexander's reign.

Next, Alexander established his base of operations against Persia on the eastern coast of the Aegean, which, before he moved eastward, he secured by his victory on the Granicus. It did not secure the sea-link between his base of operations and his home base, because naval command was in his enemy's hands. That was why, because there was no Persian army west of the Halys which could impede his advance, his strategy was to strike at his enemy's naval bases, the more important of which lay in Phoenicia and Cyprus. This strategy is so clearly revealed in his speech to his generals immediately before the siege of Tyre, that it is worth reverting to it. With his home base in mind, it will be remembered that Alexander said: 'I am apprehensive lest, while we advance with our forces toward Babylon and in pursuit of Darius, the Persians should again conquer the maritime districts, and transfer the war into Greece.' The offer of non-belligerence made to him by the Tyrians was insufficient; it was imperative that Tyre and Egypt should be occupied, for then, as he said, 'no anxiety about Greece and our land will any longer remain'. He also saw that, when the Phoenician cities were threatened, the high probability was that the Phoenician fleets would come over to him and give him 'absolute sovereignty of the sea'. The aim of his strategy, then, was not only to deprive his enemy of his sea power, but simultaneously to acquire it and thereby win the command of the eastern Mediterranean, and secure his home base and his conquests in Asia Minor for good and all. Only then did he consider that he would be free to renew his land operations against Darius.

Again, when he reached Arbela, he abandoned his pursuit to strike at the 'material' base of his enemy's military power; first he occupied Babylon, and next seized the treasure stored at Susa and Persepolis. With that in his hands, he was in a position of strength such as the French would have been in if, in 1940, they had decisively defeated the Germans, and, instead of pursuing them, had occupied the Ruhr – the material base of the German fighting forces. Here again, it will be seen that Alexander's strategy led to the augmentation of his own power, not by destroying the foundations of his enemy's power, but by appropriating them. As the Persian fleet had passed into his hands, so did the Persian treasure. He became financial master of Asia, and Darius a bankrupt.

After the death of Darius his first action was not to pursue the usurper Bessus, but to secure his rear – his most advanced base – by subduing the tribesmen of the Elburz mountains. As soon as this had been done, he set out after Bessus; but directly he learnt of the revolt of Satibarzanes, he broke off the chase to re-establish his authority over his rear before he continued. In Sogdiana he followed an identical strategy. After the capture of Bessus, suddenly he found himself in an extraordinary predicament; the revolt of Spitamenes not only threatened his base at Maracanda, but deprived him of Cyropolis and his frontier posts on the Jaxartes. He was between two forest fires – which should he extinguish first? Should he turn on Spitamenes, the leader of the revolt? No, he must first secure his base of operations against him, and this meant the reoccupation of Cyropolis, and the defeat of the Scythians. Once this had been done his rear was secure, and he was free to deal with Spitamenes. Later, the same basic strategy was followed. When he had occupied the tribesmen's cities in the Swat valley, he did not march on their stronghold at Aornus, but moved southward into the Peshawar valley to establish a firm base of operations from which he could operate against Aornus without imperilling his communications. Soon after this he established his advanced base at Taxila before proceeding against Porus.

It is important to remember that the means Alexander used to make secure the more important bases, that covered extensive territories, were more political than military. Their administration was carefully organized, peaceful conditions were restored, trade was stimulated, and the garrisons left in them were police forces and colonists rather than armies of occupation. As his conquests extended, his empire progressively took form; he won his peace as he waged his war,[1] and bound the whole into one by means of his communications.

Strategy today is so intimately related to communications – road, rail, river, canal, sea and air – that it is difficult to picture a strategical problem in which there are no maps, and movements are limited to a few caravan routes and an unknown number of pack-ways and trails connecting village with village.[2] In Greece there were no made-up roads, except in the vicinity of important sanctuaries, and no road-construction is recorded during the reigns of Alexander and his successors.[3] But, as described in Chapter 4, since the days of Darius I a number of main roads had existed in the Persian empire, and it was possible to travel by road from Ephesus, on the Aegean, by way of Sardes, Babylon, Ecbatana and Bactra to Taxila. This great thoroughfare was the axis of Alexander's communications – a kind of trans-Siberian railway.

In addition to this road, and a number which branched from it, Alexander had the sea, and at the beginning of the war it was one of Antipater's tasks to keep open the passage of the Dardanelles. After the fall of Tyre, when the threat to the Aegean was eliminated, this responsibility was delegated to Philoxenes who, according to Plutarch, was appointed 'governor of the coast-line of Asia Minor',[4] or what would seem a more appropriate title – Base Commandant. His headquarters were at Ephesus – the western terminus of the axial road – and there he collected supplies and reinforcements coming from Macedonia and Greece, and when required dispatched them in convoys to Alexander. When Susa was occupied, Alexander placed Menes, son of Dionysius, in command of sea communications between Phoenicia and the west,[5] and when the Thessalians' service was terminated, he was instructed to arrange for their transit by sea from Syria to Euboea.[6] Finally toward the close of his reign, Alexander was engaged on open-

---

[1] In the Civil War in Spain (1936–9) General Franco did the same; directly a district was won it was placed on a peace footing.

[2] In recent times much the same difficulty faced the British command in the South African War of 1899–1902. Roads were no more than cart tracks, approximately shown on unreliable maps, and footpaths were known only to the local inhabitants. Only what may be called bee-line strategy was possible

[3] From an early date the Romans were aware of the importance of roads, but it was not until 312 B.C. that the earliest of the main roads, the Via Appia, which linked Rome and Capua, was built.

[4] Plutarch's *Moralia*, 'On the Fortune of Alexander', 333A.

[5] Arrian, III, xvi, 9.   [6] Ibid., III, xix, 6.

ing a sea-way from Patala on the Indus to Babylon on the Euphrates, to help him to hold India.

From west to east, with the axial road as its backbone, Alexander divided his land communications into sections, each under a responsible officer. The most westerly section included Asia Minor, and was allotted to Antigonus with his headquarters at Celaenae in Phrygia. East of it and to some undefined point eastward – possibly Meshed or Herat – came the next section, first under Parmenion and later under Cleander, with headquarters at Ecbatana. Then there was probably the Bactrian section, and possibly east of it the Indian, but of these sections nothing is known.

Although we have no details of the organization of Alexander's communications, because of the ease with which reinforcements constantly reached him, it is not difficult to supply them. Depots, at which supplies were collected from the surrounding country, and staging camps, each a day's march from the other, must either have been established or taken over from the Persians in each section along the axial road. Further, it would appear that the Persian postal relay system was retained and improved upon, because we are told by Plutarch that, when Alexander was at Samarkand, 'some people came bringing Greek fruit to the king from the sea-board'[1] – a distance of well over 3,000 miles. Incidentally, this fruit was the indirect cause of the death of Cleitus, because Alexander was so struck with its 'beauty and perfection' that he asked him to share some with him at the fatal supper.

In only one of his Asiatic campaigns did Alexander lose touch with his home base, and then only for twenty-four hours before the battle of Issus; only once is it recorded that his supply system broke down, and that was during his march across Gedrosia.[2] This is sufficient proof of the superb staff work of his headquarters.

His lack of maps was made good by what must have been a highly organized intelligence service. He always tried to obtain advance information about the country he decided to conquer, and there was nothing adventurous in his movements. Like Napoleon and Wellington, whenever possible he saw things for himself, and from his actions it may be judged that he held with Napoleon that, 'A general who has to see things through other people's eyes will never be able to command an army as it should be commanded.' And he could, with truth, have said with Wellington: 'The real reason why I succeeded . . . is

[1] Plutarch's 'Alexander', L.
[2] Due largely to Apollophanes, who failed to forward supplies.

because I was always on the spot. I saw everything, and did everything myself.' When this was not possible, as happened repeatedly, he stepped into his enemy's shoes, looked at the situation through his enemy's eyes, and fathomed his intentions. Although he was one of the most audacious generals in history, the risks he accepted were seldom left to chance; they were carefully weighed and calculated probabilities.

As Tactician

As a tactician, Alexander's greatest asset was the army he inherited from his father; without it, and in spite of his genius, his conquests would be inconceivable – it was an instrument that exactly suited his craft. Its composition has been dealt with in Chapter 2, here its organization will be briefly examined, because it was from its organization that Alexander was able to develop his tactics.

On the opening page of his great work *On War*, Clausewitz makes a very simple yet profound remark. It is, that 'War is nothing but a duel on an extensive scale', and he likens it to a struggle between two wrestlers; between two pugilists would be a more apt comparison. If so, then the primary elements of tactics are to be seen in their simplest form in a fight between two unarmed men. They are: to think, to guard, to move and to hit.

Before a bout opens, each man must consider how best to knock out his adversary, and though as the fight proceeds he may be compelled to modify his means, he must never abandon his aim. At the start he must assume a defensive attitude until he has measured up his opponent. Next, he must move under cover of his defence towards him, and lastly by foot-play, and still under cover of his defence, he must assume the offensive and attempt to knock him out. In military terms, the four primary tactical elements are: the aim or object, security, mobility and offensive power.

If the two pugilists are skilled in their art, they will recognize the value of three accentuating elements. They will economize their physical force, so as not to exhaust themselves prematurely; they will concentrate their blows against the decisive point selected, the left or right of their opponent's jaw, or his solar plexus, and throughout will attempt to surprise him – that is, take him off-guard, or do something which he does not expect, or cannot guard against. In military terms these accentuating elements are: economy of force, concentration of force, and surprise.

With this elementary picture in mind, Philip's tactical organization can be considered. It was threefold, not merely a phalanx with protective bodies of cavalry on its flanks, as was then customary, but a phalanx with two fighting arms, each of which was more mobile than the trunk, each of which could be used either to guard or to hit, and of which the right was the more powerful, because Philip decided to concentrate his punching-power in it. His army – whether intentionally, accidentally, or experimentally does not matter – was a gigantic pugilist, and in the hands of a skilled leader it could fight as such.

The only extraneous point worth making is that, although in the inter-city wars the punching had been done almost entirely by infantry, Philip decided that it should be done by cavalry; not only because cavalry was more mobile than infantry, and so could be concentrated more rapidly against the point of decision, but also because throughout history there has been something irresistible and terrifying in the cavalry charge, and the foot soldier has always dreaded being trampled by horsemen – hence the value of mounted over foot police. In other words, provided that cavalry could charge, the moral effect produced by the combination of two living creatures – man and horse – coupled with mobility, was greater than anything the foot soldier could produce.

In most military text books, more particularly in those known as *Field Service Regulations*, a list of the principles of war will be found. Five, as propounded by Clausewitz, have already been given. There are several versions of these so-called principles, but they are no more than pegs on which to hang our tactical thoughts. There is nothing irrevocable about them; sometimes they may be discarded with impunity; but as a study of military history will show, they should only be discarded after deep consideration. They are very important guides rather than principles, and in the writer's opinion the simplest and most useful are derived from the seven tactical elements mentioned above – aim or object, security, mobility, offensive power, economy of force, concentration of force, and surprise. Further, they are as applicable to strategy (operations in plan) as to tactics (operations in action), two terms which should never be separated by a bulkhead, because their components flow into each other and together constitute the art of war, which, incidentally, was cleverly defined by Captain Cochegrue when he said: 'In great battles, he endeavoured always to give blows without receiving them, which is, and always will be, the only problem to solve in war.' [1] It is illuminating to examine the military activities

[1] *Balzac's Droll Stories* (English trans. illustrated by Gustave Doré, 1874), 'The Devil's Heir', p. 111.

of Alexander by applying to them, in turn, the seven principles cited.

The Principle of the Maintenance of the Aim: 'To conquer is nothing, one must profit from one's success' – Napoleon.

The first point to note in all Alexander's tactical operations is, that they were invariably subordinated to the strategical aim of their respective campaigns. For example, when he acceded to the throne of Macedonia and when Greece was in turmoil, because he planned war with Persia, his strategical aim was to establish his authority as rapidly and peacefully as he could, and he did so with such lightning-like speed, that a display of tactical force was sufficient to attain it without bloodshed. Soon after this, when the Thebans revolted, because his aim was still the same, he offered terms of surrender; but when they refused them, to paralyse their allies he obliterated Thebes, and attained his aim at the cost of one city. Again, after his victory at Issus, he abandoned his pursuit and laid siege to Tyre in order to maintain his strategic aim, which was then the elimination of his enemy's naval power. After Arbela, again he sacrificed pursuit in order to occupy Babylon and seize Susa and Persepolis, because the treasure stored in these cities was the mainstay of Persian political and military power. In all his campaigns it was the same; his strategical aim was subordinated to his political aim, and his tactical aim to his strategical aim, and the result was systematic and methodical conquest.

In each of his four great battles his aim was to assault from a secure base and annihilate his enemy's power of resistance; his base was his order of battle which, except in the battle of the Hydaspes, he never varied. With the phalanx as his chest, his left arm was his left wing, which he used defensively; and his right arm his right wing, used offensively to break through the enemy's front, and thereby disrupt his organization. Penetration was his tactical means, and he held fast to it in all his great battles. At the Granicus, he broke through the Persian cavalry at the head of his Companion cavalry; at Issus, he broke through the Persian infantry, and at Arbela he broke through a gap in the Persian front. Only at the Hydaspes, his most skilfully fought battle, did he make use of his phalanx to deliver the knock-out blow, and that was because his cavalry horses would not face the Indian elephants.

During the heat of the battle he never lost sight of his tactical aim. At the Granicus, once he had effected a penetration, he turned on the Greek mercenary infantry; he did the same at Issus; at Arbela, first – as assumed – he came to the help of his hard-pressed right wing, and then – as is known – he set out to rescue his left wing, which was hard pressed by Mazaeus, that is, where the battle was still in doubt. At the sieges of Tyre, Gaza and Aornus, once he had made up his mind, the tenacity with which he held fast to his tactical aim is remarkable. But he was not a pigheaded general. When he decided to capture the island of Peuce in his Danubian campaign, and he found that it would be both costly and difficult, he substituted for its capture a more profitable operation; at the Persian Gates he did the same, and when in his campaign against the Malli, with cavalry alone he attacked the Indians who were holding the opposite bank of the Ravi, directly it became apparent to him that they intended to stand up to his assault, he broke off the engagement, surrounded them with his horsemen, and awaited the arrival of his infantry. Although he was always ready to attempt the seemingly impossible, he was just as ready to avoid the obviously unprofitable.

The Principle of Security: 'The whole art of war consists in a well-reasoned and extremely circumspect defensive, followed by rapid and audacious attack' – Napoleon.

Unfortunately, little has been recorded of the security measures adopted by Alexander while at rest, on the line of march, or in battle. Now and again it is recorded that he fortified his camp, ordered entrenchments to be dug, and picketed the road along which he marched, as he did in the Elburz mountains. On that occasion, Arrian writes, whenever he thought there was danger along the road, he posted pickets on its flanks to protect the marching troops from the hillmen on the heights above them.[1] Also, he frequently resorted to night movements to hide his intentions or to surprise his enemy, and notably so before the battles of Arbela and the Hydaspes and during the Persepolis campaign. The probable reason for the lack of information is that, unlike Julius Caesar, Alexander was not an entrenching general; the tactical conditions of his campaigns did not require him to be so, because the Persians seldom assumed the offensive, and the tribesmen he conquered did not indulge in night attacks.

In battle, the security of his army was guaranteed by its organization, coupled with its usual oblique approach. Its centre was impenetrable as long as the phalanx maintained its dressing, and its mobile wings, composed as they were of infantry and cavalry, were self-protective; they could adapt themselves to attack or defence as occasion demanded. Although reserves were hitherto unknown, at Issus Alexander is said to have held the Greek mercenaries in reserve, and

[1] Arrian, III, xxiii, 3. Compare 'crowning the heights' in present-day mountain warfare.

because at Arbela the Macedonian front was far outflanked by the Persian, to secure his front from an attack in flank and rear he drew up a second, or reserve, phalanx behind it, which, when the two wings on the flanks of the forward phalanx were drawn backward, enabled a hollow square to be formed, a formation which offered all-round defence. Yet it is strange that, neither at Issus nor Arbela, did he attempt to overcome the one great danger to his phalanx. It was that, due to its oblique approach and the speed of his assault on its right, it was liable to break in half, as it did in both these battles. To rectify this, all that was necessary was to withdraw one battalion of the phalanx and post it in rear of the centre of the others, so that, should a gap occur in the ranks in front, it could at once be filled by the battalion in rear.

Of the various protective means used by Alexander, the most interesting is his use of the catapult as field artillery. Though for long used as a siege weapon, until his campaign in Illyria it had never been brought into the field. It was then that for the first time in the history of war catapults were deployed to cover a river crossing, as again they were in the battle with the Scythians on the Jaxartes. Also, they were used with considerable effect to cover the assaults on Aornus and elsewhere. Wherever Alexander went his field artillery accompanied him, and after his death, in the hands of his successors it became a recognized arm in every well-organized army, and remained the artillery of the world until the introduction of cannon. Alexander has the distinction of being the first field gunner in history.

The Principle of Mobility: 'In the art of war, as in mechanics, velocity is the grand element between weight and force' – Napoleon.

Except for Napoleon, probably no other general appreciated as fully as Alexander the value of mobility in war. From the opening of his career until its close, speed dominated all his movements, and the result was that, by increasing the time at his disposal, in any given period he could proportionately accomplish more than his opponent.

In his first campaign his enemies were so completely paralysed by the rapidity of his advance that they were not allowed time enough to assemble their forces; in his advance on the Cilician Gates, although it was reported to Arsames, who held the pass, Arsames was so unhinged by his enemy's speed that he abandoned it. The dividends paid by speed, whether against an organized enemy on the plains, or hillmen in the mountains, were a long series of surprises, which enabled Alexander to accomplish with a fraction of his forces what at a slower pace might have demanded his whole army.

He was the first general in history to understand that the fruits of a great battle are to be gathered in the pursuit. At the battle of Arbela, directly he had assured himself of the safety of his left wing, he turned about his Companion cavalry, and in spite of their exhausted horses followed Darius, and pressed on to Arbela, thirty miles east of the battlefield. After his defeat of Ariobarzanes at the Persian Gates, in spite of a most fatiguing night march and the exertions of the battle, he pressed on to Persepolis, some eighty to 100 miles away, and reached it at dawn on the following morning. Also, in the heat of a Persian summer and in a region largely devoid of water, his pursuit of Darius was kept up for seven days at the average daily speed of either thirty or thirty-six miles. As Tarn observes: he taught the West a lesson his successors did not forget, 'that in warfare distance was no longer a prohibitive factor'.[1] Also he taught the West the advantage of marching in two divisions; one composed of a selected body of troops marching light, and the other of the slower moving troops and the impedimenta.

That the velocity of his movements on occasion led him into difficulties is understandable. It seems to have done so during his Illyrian campaign, when Glaucias came up on his rear, and it certainly did so at Issus, when he lost his communications and was surprised. But during his twelve years of campaigning the exceptions are so rare that they prove the rule that he who can move twice as fast as his opponent doubles his operative time and thereby halves it for his opponent. As a winner of time Alexander has few equals.

The Principle of the Offensive: 'In short, I think like Frederick, one should always be the first to attack' – Napoleon.

The reason why all the great captains were offensively-minded was not only because battle is the tactical aim in war but also because, as Moltke pointed out in his *Instructions for the Commanders of Large Formations*: 'The offensive knows what it wants', whereas 'the defensive is in a state of uncertainty'. In other words: the initiative is more readily gained by offensive than by defensive action; not only does it enable a general to develop his plan, select his point of attack, and surprise his adversary, but it exalts the spirit of his troops – as Frederick said: 'To conquer is to advance'. Though Napoleon was forced on the defensive at Leipzig, La Rothière and Arcis, he never once set out to fight a defensive battle; nor did Alexander, and all his offensive battles were successful.

What is remarkable about them is, that he overcame his several opponents by a tactics shaped to fit each occasion. Thus, with the

[1] *Hellenistic Military and Naval Developments*, p. 41.

same certainty with which he attacked his known opponents – Greek mercenaries or Persian cavalry – he overcame opponents who before he fought them were entirely unknown to him; the Scythians, Indian hillmen, and Porus with his elephants. In his many battles his tactical genius is apparent in the lightning-like speed with which he adapted his actions to novel circumstances; he never copied his former successes, and this was the main reason why success followed success.

Although in his great battles he relied on his Companion cavalry as his main offensive arm, he never brought it into action until he was certain that its assault would prove decisive. At the Granicus, because of the faulty deployment of the Persian cavalry, directly his feint against the Persian left began to tell, he charged instantly, and the battle was virtually won before the rest of his troops had crossed the river. At Issus he held back his assault until he had cleared his right flank, then in a headlong charge he burst through the Persian infantry; and at Arbela he fought a protracted defensive engagement with his right flank guard, which drew his enemy in and thereby created the opportunity for his decisive cavalry charge. When it came, in a flash he seized the initiative, and swept through the gap in the Persian front. The timing was perfect, and as Napoleon once said: 'The fate of a battle is a question of a single moment, a single thought . . . the decisive moment arrives, the moral spark is kindled, and the smallest reserve force settles the argument.' [1] And again: 'There is a moment in engagements when the least manœuvre is decisive and gives the victory; it is the one drop of water which makes the vessel run over.' [2] The last reserve in his right wing was his Company cavalry, and its assault was decisive, as was the assault of his phalanx at the battle of the Hydaspes.

The Principles of Economy and Concentration of Force: 'The art of war consists in bringing to bear with an inferior army a superiority of force at the point at which one attacks or is attacked' – Napoleon.

These two principles are closely related and their application is largely governed by the depth of the forces engaged. Today, it may run to many miles, with the bulk of the troops in reserve; because of this the battle is usually prolonged, and is decided by the reserves. Consequently, economy of force – the judicious expenditure of the reserves – is of vital importance. But when all troops are concentrated in the battle front, with no reserves in rear of them, economy of force is restricted to the troops immediately at hand, and in Alexander's day

---

[1] *Mémorial de Ste Hélène,* Las Cases (1823), vol. II, p. 15.
[2] *Correspondance de Napoléon 1er,* 'Précis des guerres de J. César', vol. XXXII, p. 27.

it was restricted to cavalry and light infantry because, when once engaged, the heavy infantry were unable to manœuvre. Few better examples of this restricted form of economy of force are to be found than his handling of the right flank guard at Arbela. By judiciously feeding his light cavalry, squadron by squadron, into the action, he progessively enticed his enemy to denude his left wing of its main cavalry forces, and so to create the fatal gap that led to his ruin. Another and equally notable example is to be seen at the battle of the Hydaspes. Because the elephants forbade Alexander his usual cavalry assault, he was compelled to rely on his phalanx to penetrate his enemy's front. But, in order to secure its advance, it was first necessary to draw in the whole of the Indian cavalry, to prevent it from attacking the phalanx in flank or rear. This he did by a most skilful economy of his own cavalry.

When Clausewitz wrote that 'the greatest possible number of troops should be brought into action at the decisive point',[1] he had in mind the battles of the Napoleonic wars, in which the depths of the contending armies were already considerable. But in battles of the classical age depths were seldom more than 100 paces, and frequently no more than that of a phalanx; so thin that, when a front was broken, it usually fell to pieces, and its men took to their heels. But to make certain of breaking a front, it was as necessary then as in Napoleon's day – and it still is necessary – to bring a superiority of force against the decisive point; but superior in quality rather than in quantity. Alexander did this by means of his superb Companion cavalry, coupled with his oblique order of approach, which automatically brought his offensive right wing opposite to the point in his enemy's front that he intended to penetrate, while his centre and left wing, though refused, were sufficiently close to the enemy's centre and right wing to threaten or hold them. Should the enemy attempt to overwhelm Alexander's left wing, which he could only do with cavalry, then he would have fewer cavalry to hold back Alexander's right wing. And should he concentrate the bulk of his cavalry against Alexander's right wing, he would risk penetration or envelopment of his own right wing by the Thessalian cavalry, who numerically were as powerful as the Companion cavalry and little inferior to them.

The only way out of this dilemma was to seize the initiative and attack first, and this Darius did at Arbela; he was frustrated by Alexander's application of the principle of economy of force. Coupled with the initiative, Alexander's oblique order of approach enabled him to

[1] *On War*, vol. I, p. 194.

concentrate a superiority of force against the decisive point, and at the same time, until he struck, economize – virtually hold in reserve – the rest of his army. First, the battering-ram assault, then '*tout le monde à la bataille*'. The assault preceded the general attack, a tactics which was reintroduced by the tank at the battle of Cambrai in 1917, and which characterizes so many of the tank offensives of the Second World War.

The Principle of Surprise: 'The art of war is no more than the art of augmenting the chances which are in our favour' – Napoleon.

According to Clausewitz, 'surprise lies at the foundation of all [military] undertakings without exception', and of the means at the disposal of the general it is the most effective in attaining either physical or moral superiority. 'Without it', he writes, 'the preponderance at the decisive point is not properly conceivable'.[1] But where is the decisive point?

Throughout the history of war its position has remained constant; it is the will of the commander as expressed in his plan, coupled with the will of his soldiers to carry it out. All other points of decision should be related to this ultimate goal, because they are no more than stepping-stones toward it. Therefore the question: 'Where should the decisive point be sought?' does not arise; the question is, 'How best can a preponderance of force be brought against the enemy's will?'

There are two answers to this question: to do something which the enemy cannot prevent, and to do something which he does not suspect. The first action may be compared to surprising a man with his eyes open, in the other, the man has his eyes shut. At the Granicus, Issus and Arbela, the Persians were the victims of the first of these modes of surprise, because they were unprepared to counter Alexander's great cavalry assaults; at the Persian Gates and the battle of the Hydaspes, Ariobarzanes and Porus respectively were victims because their eyes were shut. Though the battle of the Persian Gates was a rapidly improvised manœuvre, and the Hydaspes a methodically prepared operation, both were based on a common factor, the fixing of the enemy's attention, therefore of his will, in a direction other than the one in which surprise was to be sought. In all these surprisals, whether the approach was direct and visible, or indirect and invisible, Alexander paralysed the will of his enemy by shattering his plan. But it should be remembered that, in the warfare of his age, the will of the commanding general was far more his personal property than it is now,[2] when he

[1] *On War*, vol. I, p. 194.
[2] An example of this is the conquest of Peru by Pizarro and 183 men. The Inca power was so highly centralized that when Atahualpa was eliminated the whole country was rapidly subdued.

shares his responsibilities with his General Staff, and to a lesser extent with his subordinate commanders; therefore it was vastly more sensitive in Alexander's day.

As is to be expected, Alexander's small wars abound with surprisals, because – then as now – though tribesmen are adepts at ambushes and ruses, their lack of discipline and submission to authority make them particularly susceptible to surprisals. Alexander drew the Triballians into battle by a ruse; surprised the Getae by an unexpected crossing of the Danube; threw Glaucias off guard by a ceremonial parade; captured Pelion by an unlooked-for night attack; surprised the Uxian hillmen while asleep in their villages; re-took Cyropolis at an unsuspected point; lured the Scythians into battle by an inviting bait; captured the Sogdian Rock by scaling its most precipitous side; drew the Assacenians into battle by a feint withdrawal; and fell upon the Malli unexpectedly by crossing a waterless desert. Further, whenever it was possible, he attacked the hillmen during the winter months, when the snow kept them in their villages. The economy of force derived from these surprisals was enormous; without them his army would have rapidly melted away.

As Leader

Battles now are so vast, so complex, and so dependent on the handling of reserves, that a general-in-chief can no longer lead his army into action; he directs it from an elaborately organized headquarters, which may be 100 or more miles behind the battle front, and the leadership of his men is delegated, not to his more senior, but to his most junior officers.

In battles of the classical age the duties of the general and the subaltern coincided, and in consequence the personal leadership of the general-in-chief was of paramount importance. When Alexander took the field, he was both the thinking and fighting head of his army. In battle he invariably set his men an example of supreme personal bravery; on the line of march there was no toil that he did not share with them; in his sieges he laboured with them, and it was his presence among them that fired their imagination and awoke in them the mystical faith that led them to accept without question that there was nothing he would not dare, and nothing he could not do – to them, as to the priestess of Delphi, he was $ANIKHTO\Sigma$ – the Invincible. There are many examples of this in the preceding chapters; here, that side of his leadership which won the devotion of his officers and the affection of his men will be considered.

The Macedonian army cannot have been easy to lead, particularly because the prestige it had won under Philip divided its officers into two age-categories: the elder, who had shared his successes, and the younger – the boyhood companions of Alexander – who at the outset of the war still had their spurs to win. This division led to the growth of what may be called the Parmenion and Alexander factions: the stubborn-minded Philippians, and the more liberal-minded Alexandrians, men like Hephaestion, Nearchus and Ptolemy, who had been Alexander's playmates. Because of the constitution of the Macedonian monarchy, elimination of jealousies was no easy task. The monarchy was still partly of the heroic type, in which the idea of the kin survived. The king was the hereditary military chief of the Macedonian tribes; he was acknowledged by the assembly of the armed people – the army – and limited in power by the other 'kings', the heads of the aristocracy, who were his kin or companions. According to Macedonian usage, the army, not the king and his council, was the supreme court before which capital charges, such as murder or treason, were brought, as happened with Philotas. Alexander, though an autocrat, was not a despot who could do exactly as he liked.

In spite of this limitation of power, Alexander treated his followers impartially, and his attitude towards them was seldom one of suspicion. In Egypt, when it was alleged that Philotas was implicated in a somewhat similar conspiracy to the one which led to his death, because of the long friendship between them Alexander did not believe it to be possible; when word was brought to him by Ephialtes and Cissus that Harpalus had absconded with 5,000 talents, he threw them into prison, because he could not believe it of Harpalus, who had been a friend of his boyhood. Invariably, it would appear, he treated all his followers alike, and lavished honours and presents upon them so extravagantly, that his mother complained that he made them the equals of kings. But at all times he was their master, and when in India a quarrel arose between Craterus and Hephaestion, he publicly called Hephaestion a fool and a madman for not knowing that without his favour he was nothing, and in private he sharply reproved Craterus. 'Then he brought them together and reconciled them, taking an oath . . . that he loved them most of all men; but that if he heard of their quarrelling again, he would kill both, or at least the one who began the quarrel.' [1]

[1] Plutarch's 'Alexander', XLVII.

This was no idle threat, for he would not tolerate any infringement of his authority. 'For instance', writes Plutarch, 'when a certain Menander, one of his companions, who had been put in command of a garrison, refused to remain there, he put him to death.' [1] And, at the close of his reign in Babylon when Cassander, one of Antipater's sons, saw Persians doing obeisance to him, and burst out laughing, Alexander was so enraged that with both hands he clutched him by the hair and dashed his head against the wall.

And in general [writes Plutarch], as we are told, Cassander's spirit was deeply penetrated and imbued with a dreadful fear of Alexander, so that many years afterwards, when he was now king of Macedonia and master of Greece, as he was walking about and surveying the statues at Delphi, the sight of an image of Alexander smote him suddenly with a shuddering and trembling from which he could scarcely recover, and made his head swim. [2]

Whether on the battlefield or in camp, Alexander dominated his companions. Through his overmastering personality and his genius for war he won their trust and devotion, and many of them were outstanding personalities, among whom Cassander was not the least. [3] When it is remembered that the Macedonians were a truculent and semi-barbaric people, not a few of whose kings had perished by the knife, it redounds to Alexander's leadership that, in spite of his pro-Persian policy, which was so deeply resented by Philip's old veterans, he was able to carry out his conquests with so few internal dissensions as those recorded.

To his men he was not only their king but their comrade in arms, and on the battlefield one of them. Their devotion to him and reliance on him are touchingly described by Arrian in the scene which followed his wounding in the assault on the Mallian citadel. His extreme heroism, coupled with the hesitation of his men to mount the wall, must have awakened in them a sense of guilt and rage, which is to be seen in their indiscriminate slaughter of the unfortunate Malli and Oxydracae. When rumours spread through the camp that Alexander had succumbed to his wound, they were thrown into the depths of fear and despair; surrounded as they were by warlike tribes, without him how could they hope to return to their homes? Next, a rumour was

---

[1] Ibid., LVII.   [2] Ibid., LXXIV.

[3] He rebuilt Thebes, founded Cassandreia and Thessalonica (Salonika), was the slayer of Alexander's mother, son and widow, and had friends among the Peripatetics.

circulated that he was alive, but their despair was so great that they would not believe it, and as soon as his wound permitted, Alexander had himself carried to the river, placed on a boat and conveyed to the camp. But his soldiers still would not believe that he was alive until he raised his hand toward them, when a great shout burst from their lips. He was carried ashore and raised on to his horse, and when he dismounted at his tent and his men saw him walking, 'they all ran towards him from this side and that, some touching his hands, some his knees, some his garments; others just looked on him from near at hand, and with a blessing upon him went their way; some cast wreaths upon him, some such flowers as the country of India bare at that time'.[1]

This devotion was roused, not only by his heroism, but also by his daily concern in their welfare and happiness, and because of his deep understanding of how to stir their hearts. Before battle, he would ride down the ranks, and call aloud by name, not only the generals, but also those men who in previous battles had performed conspicuous deeds of valour; at such a moment to call a soldier by name is to electrify every soldier within hearing. After battle, his care for the wounded won the affection of all his men; 'and the dead he gathered together and gave them a splendid military funeral, the whole army marshalled in their finest battle array'. Then 'he praised all who, by his own personal witness, or by the agreed report of others, he knew had done valorous deeds in the battle; these men and all he honoured by a devotion suitable to their desert'.[2] At a prolonged halt, or after a notable success, he held games and festivals of all sorts to celebrate the prowess of his army.

What appealed to his men probably more than anything else, were his unexpected kindnesses toward them; such as when, after the capture of Halicarnassus, he sent his newly married men home to spend the winter with their families; the care with which he prepared the return journey of his Thessalians from Ecbatana; and when after the great reconciliation at Opis he not only rewarded his departing veterans in a princely way, but 'also ordained that the orphan children of those who had lost their lives in his service should receive their father's pay'.[3]

He never asked his men to do what he would not do himself. When, before he set out on his march to India, he found that the army train was cumbered with booty, he first ordered the contents of the wagons which belonged to him and his companions to be burnt. Also, he always placed the needs of his men before his own. When he

---

[1] Arrian, VI, xiii, 3.   [2] Ibid., II, xii, 1.
[3] Plutarch's 'Alexander', LXXI. Cf. Arrian, VII, xii, 2.

led his men on foot to set an example to them during the march through Gedrosia, he was distressed by thirst and some of the light-armed troops found a little water in a water-hole and carried it in a helmet to the king.

He received it [writes Arrian], and thanked those who had brought it; and taking it poured it out in the sight of all his troops; and at this action the whole army was so much heartened that you would have said that each and every man had drunk that water which Alexander thus poured out. This deed of Alexander's above all I commend most warmly as a proof both of his endurance and his excellence as a general.[1]

Incidents such as these bound his men to him with invisible and unbreakable moral ties. They endowed them with particles of his invincible will, and, under his leadership, they obliterated dangers, smoothed away adversities, and enabled him to lead them to what for them appeared to be the ends of the world.

[1] Arrian, VI, xxvi, 2–3. Plutarch ('Alexander', XLII) attributes this incident to the pursuit of Darius, and ends his account as follows: 'But when they beheld his self-control and loftiness of spirit, they shouted out to him to lead them forward boldly . . . declaring that they would not regard themselves as weary, or thirsty, or as mortals at all, so long as they had such a king.'

EPILOGUE
THE VALUE OF HISTORY

Throughout history wars have been unceasing; yet, strange to relate, statesmen, upon whom the main burden of the conduct of war falls, have paid only passing attention to the records of the past. That is why it is said that history repeats itself; it is the ignorance of history which does so, with the result that identical blunders recur in every age. 'It is history, and history alone', wrote Polybius over 2,000 years ago, 'which, without involving us in actual danger, will mature our judgement and prepare us to take right views, whatever may be the crisis or the posture of affairs.'[1] With one reservation this is undoubtedly true, and it is that, if the present is to profit from the past, only from a study of former periods in which the prevailing conditions resemble those of the present are profitable lessons likely to be found.

That the campaigns of Alexander can teach the present-day soldier much is self-evident, because war is an art which, whatever be the period in question, is based on the same principles, and only their application varies from date to date. But what is not so clear is: Can the age of Philip and Alexander teach the statesmen anything of profit?

Not a few historians have answered this question in the affirmative. In 1921, in his preface to *The Legacy of Greece* Sir Richard Livingstone wrote: 'if the twentieth century searched through the past for its nearest spiritual kin, it is in the fifth and following centuries before Christ that they would be found'. And more recently Professor Geoffrey Barraclough has pointed out:

If you believe that the study of history has any relevance to current events, then you will gain more, in the present world, by studying the life and times of Alexander the Great, or Caesar and the Roman revolution. And it is perhaps fundamentally important to get this fact firmly in our minds, because there could be no more serious mistake in current policy than to suppose that a return to a Europe similar to that of the nineteenth century can be effected, or to

[1] I, 35.

direct political action to the restoration of what is fondly called 'the traditional order'. [1]

In Chapter I striking resemblances are to be found between the conditions that prevailed in the fifth and fourth centuries before Christ and those that prevail in our present age. There is to be seen a dissolving civilization in which the city-states reduplicate the endless wars and discords of the national states of these days; the city-states as hidebound as the national states, and equally blind to the need to sacrifice some of their sovereignty in order to face the threat of being overwhelmed piecemeal by a foreign autocracy. Democracy was as emotional and therefore as irrational as it is now; demagogy was as prevalent; the Socialist Welfare State, in which unearned dividends are distributed among its members, was as well known; citizens were paid to attend their Assemblies as members of Parliament are now; and in Plato's Socratic archetypal city were all the refinements of Marxist-Leninism – the Guardians, or Party, the disenfranchised proletariat, the suppression of the individual, the prohibition of foreign travel, spies, secret police, censors and double-talk. It was Plato who wrote that he who endeavours 'to second the authorities in their work of repression, he is the great and perfect citizen'. Private armies, raised in the form of mercenary forces, may be compared with the Brown Shirts of Hitler, the Black Shirts of Mussolini, and the Red Cheka of Lenin.

Philip of Macedon exploited the inner front created by these discords, and Alexander improved upon his father's subversive warfare in his conquest of the Persian empire. Had they relied solely on military force, the certainty is that neither would have succeeded in attaining his respective aims. As the political and social conditions which prevailed during the twenty years between the two recent world wars resembled those which existed in the days of Philip and Alexander, could not the statesmen of these inter-war years have learnt a lesson of vital importance from these two great soldier-statesmen, a lesson which would have been of the highest value to them in the second of these world conflicts?

They certainly could have, had they realized that, if war is to be a profitable instrument of policy, policy must be shaped in accordance with existing political conditions. Their crucial error was that they failed to see that the First World War, like the Peloponnesian War in its day, had destroyed the political age which gave it birth; they did not

[1] *History in a Changing World* (1957), p. 217. In 1892 J. P. Mahaffy wrote much the same in his *Problems in Greek History* (p. 196): 'The history of Greece . . . is intensely modern – far more so than any mediaeval or than more recent history.'

realize that they were living in a new age, an age that demanded a very different war policy, which in its turn would demand different means to its attainment.

The profoundest political change the First World War gave rise to, or was followed by, was a series of catastrophic revolutions: the Austro-Hungarian empire vanished, the Russian was upheaved by Marxist Communism, the Italian by Fascism, the German by National Socialism, and in many other countries throughout the world Communist and Fascist movements of various shades took root and challenged nineteenth-century civilization. This meant that while in 1914, to all intents and purposes all belligerents had been firmly united nations, whose peoples staunchly supported their respective governments, in the next war, and more particularly in those countries in which revolutionary governments were established, there would exist reactionary inner fronts, and that these hostile factions would enable an enemy, who set out to cooperate with them, to attack these governments internally. Was this change recognized by the statesmen of 1939? Except in Soviet Russia, either not at all, or only superficially. How did this come about?

Hitler's political aim was to establish a German hegemony over Europe, and its attainment depended on the solution of two problems. The first was, how to conquer and annex the greater part of Russia in Europe, so that the Third Reich might become economically so powerful that it would dominate the rest of Europe? The second was, how to defeat Great Britain and France should they come to Russia's support?

In character these two problems were very different. Though the inner front in Great Britain was negligible, and in France composed mainly of people opposed to war and not necessarily disloyal to their country, in Russia the position was the reverse. Most of her western provinces, notably the Ukraine and Bielorussia (White Russia), inhabited by some forty million people, had been subjugated by the Russians, and because the vast majority of their inhabitants was antagonistic to the Soviet regime, the Russian inner front was immense. In 1939, Russia was still as Theodor Mommsen, nearly 100 years earlier, had described her, 'a dustbin held together by the rusty hoop of Tsardom'; fracture the hoop and the bin would fall to pieces. Hitler's western problem was essentially military, his eastern essentially political.

Hitler set out on sound Philippian lines to establish his hegemony; he created a new model army based on mobility, and immediately before he launched his war, he tricked Stalin into a faked alliance. Next, he overran Poland in twenty-seven days, and to show his good-will towards Russia he shared his plunder with her. Then he turned against the West, overran Denmark in one day, conquered Norway in twenty-three days, Holland in five, Belgium in eighteen, France in thirty-nine, Yugoslavia in twelve, and Greece in twenty-one. Philip could not have improved on this strategy, and had Hitler died on the day his Swastika flag was broken over the Acropolis, in the pages of history he might well have taken his place alongside the founder of the Macedonian hegemony. He lived on, but the Philippian light died within him, and that at the very moment when it was needed to illumine his Alexandrian task.

Some years before the war, in a conversation with Hermann Rauschning, Hitler is alleged to have said:

> The place of artillery preparation for frontal attack by infantry in trench warfare will in future be taken by revolutionary propaganda, to break down the enemy psychologically before the armies begin to function at all . . . How to achieve the moral break-down of the enemy before the war has started – that is the problem that interests me. Whoever has experienced war at the front will want to refrain from all avoidable bloodshed. . . . We shall not shrink from the plot-ting of revolutions. . . . The lessons of revolutions, these are the secret of the new strategy. I have learnt from the Bolsheviks. I do not hesitate to say so. One always learns more from one's enemies. Do you know the doctrine of the *coup d'état?* Study it. Then you will know our task. . . . I have made the doctrine of revolution the basis of my policy.[1]

This was sound Philippian strategy: Subvert your enemy from with-in, and when it is politically possible it is both easier and more profit-able than to attempt to crack his skull.

If this doctrine were true in preparing for war, it was doubly true when it was waged, and trebly true *vis-à-vis* Russia, because of her enormous inner front. France was down and out, and Great Britain for the time being impotent; that problem had been solved, and all that was needed to solve the other problem – how to conquer and annex the greater part of Russia in Europe – was for Hitler to put his revolutionary policy into operation. In other words, to enter into alliance with the subjugated peoples in Russia and destroy the Soviet

[1] *Hitler Speaks* (1939), pp. 19–21.

Imperium from within, as in his day Alexander had destroyed the Persian Imperium.

He was advised to adopt this course by Dr. Alfred Rosenberg, his expert on foreign affairs, a Baltic German well acquainted with internal conditions in Russia. He pointed out to Hitler that Russia 'has never been a national state, but a state of nationalities'; that the German problem was not to reconstruct the Russian empire, but to dissolve it; not to impose a new political system upon its subjugated peoples, but to recognize each nationality and foster each nation's independence. 'We should declare', he said, 'that we are not fighting the Russian people but the Bolshevik system', and that 'our fight will take place in the name of national self-determination of nations'.[1] In other words, Hitler should proclaim that his war aim was to liberate the subjugated peoples of western Russia; this was sound Alexandrian policy. But Hitler had become so intoxicated by his military successes that he abandoned all idea of relying on the revolutionary strategy he had expounded to Rauschning. He expected that Russia would collapse as France had done, in spite of the fact that the Russians had unlimited space to fall back in, as every former invader had learnt to his cost. Contemptuously he set Rosenberg's suggestions aside, and declared that: 'Our policy is to cut the gigantic cake with skill, so that it can be first mastered, secondly administered, and thirdly exploited . . . Naturally,' he said, 'the vast territories have to be pacified as soon as possible; this can best be achieved by shooting everybody who shows a wry face.'[2] Instead of offering the subjugated peoples their freedom, he set out to enslave them, and should they resist, to exterminate them.

In the initial stage of the invasion the Germans were everywhere welcomed by the common people as liberators; the Ukrainians looked upon Hitler as the saviour of Europe; the Bielorussians were eager to fight on the German side; whole regiments of Cossacks deserted to their enemy; and Georgians, Armenians, Turkomans, Tartars, and Usbeks, as well as Ukrainians, Bielorussians, and Cossacks, surrendered in droves. At Rostov, writes Erich Kern, 'all over the city there were people waiting on the streets ready to cheer and welcome us in. . . . Never before', writes Kern, 'had I seen such a sudden transformation. Of Bolshevism, there was no more. The enemy had gone . . . where-

---

[1] Abstracted from *Russian World Ambitions and World Peace*, R. Ilnytzky (1953), pp. 4–12.

[2] Ibid., pp. 12–15, citing Nuremberg Documents in evidence at the trial before the International Military Tribunal, Nuremberg, 1945–46.

ever we went now we met laughing and waving people. . . . The Soviet Empire was creaking at the joints.' [1]

Then came Himmler and his assassins, and 'by rousing the Russian people to a Napoleonic fervour', writes Kern, 'we enabled the Bolsheviks to achieve a political consolidation beyond their wildest dreams and provided their cause with the halo of a "patriotic war" '.[2] And Walter Görlitz writes: 'The fact that the destruction of Bolshevism began soon to mean simply an effort to decimate and enslave the Slav people was the most fatal of all the flaws in the whole campaign.' [3]

More than one historian has considered that Hitler's failure to occupy Moscow in 1941 was the turning point of the war; but the turning point lay in his policy. Had he assumed the role of a liberator instead of a butcher, the high probability is that he would have dissolved the Soviet Imperium long before the United States entered the war, and thereby have avoided the one thing he dreaded most – a fullscale war on two fronts. In spite of his military ineptitude, his crucial error was far more political than strategical: had he relied on counterrevolution instead of conquest, for him there probably would have been no turning point at all. He was decisively defeated, not by the Russians, but by his own stupidity.

In Germany, the revulsion against the National Socialist revolution of 1933 also created an extensive inner front, which embraced not only most of the civil population of over forty years of age, but also many highly placed civil servants and officers in the armed forces, including the Commander-in-chief, the Chief of the General Staff, and the Chief of the Counter-Intelligence Service. According to British intelligence sources, in 1939 opposition to Hitler had assumed such proportions that it might lead to a revolt and the downfall of National Socialism. When on September 3, 1939, the British and French governments proclaimed their aim to be the destruction of Hitler and Hitlerism, allied strategy was set to follow a revolutionary path. On the following day this was reinforced by the British Prime Minister, Mr Neville Chamberlain, who in a broadcast to the German people said: 'In this war we are not fighting against you the German people, for whom we have no bitter feeling, but against a tyrannous and foresworn régime.' To give effect to this, all that was necessary was to support all Germans opposed to Hitler, to promise them the best of terms should they succeed in his overthrow, and to help them in every possible way

---

[1] *Dance of Death* (English trans., 1948), pp. 86, 94, and 102. Kern was an N.C.O. in the *Leibstandarte Adolf Hitler*.　　[2] Ibid., p. 108.

[3] *The German General Staff* (English trans., 1953), p. 397.

to effect this on the inner front, while military operations were directed against Hitler on his outer front.

On May 10, 1940, Mr Winston Churchill succeeded Mr Chamberlain, and although he was the leading exponent of an ideological war against Germany, and when war was declared, had said in the House of Commons, 'We are fighting to save the whole world from the pestilence of Nazi tyranny', he at once scrapped Mr Chamberlain's policy of differentiating between pro- and anti-Hitler Germans, and set out to win the war solely by military means; a strategic contradiction, and the greatest allied blunder in the war.

Three days after he assumed the premiership, in an address in the House of Commons he said: 'You ask, What is our aim? I can answer in one word: Victory – victory at all costs, victory in spite of all terror; victory, however long and hard the road may be. . . . Come, then, let us go forward together with our united strength.' [1]

Although this clarion blast was received with vociferous acclamation, it was the negation of statesmanship in the conduct of any type of war, let alone an ideological war, because in war victory is no more than a means to an end; peace is the end, and should victory lead to a disastrous peace, then politically, the war will have been lost. Victory at all costs is strategic humbug.

A year later, because it was apparent to the British Government that Hitler's invasion of Russia was highly unpopular in Germany, and strongly resented by the German General Staff, it would be thought that no moment could be more propitious wherein to exert every means possible to win over and assist the ever-growing anti-Hitler factions in Germany. Then was the time to fortify that inner front, which the Gestapo and concentration camps attempted vainly to eliminate.

At 9 p.m. on the day Hitler invaded Russia, in a broadcast to the British peoples Mr Churchill said:

We have but one aim and one single irrevocable purpose. We are resolved to destroy Hitler and every vestige of the Nazi régime . . . We will never parley, we will never negotiate with Hitler or any of his gang . . . Any man or state who fights against Nazidom will have our aid. Any man or state who marches with Hitler is our foe . . . That is our policy. . . . It follows therefore that we shall give whatever help we can to Russia and the Russian people.[2]

[1] *The Second World War* (1949), vol. II, p. 24.
[2] Ibid., vol. III, p. 332.

Why, then, did not Mr Churchill act to the full on this forceful declaration? If every man who fought against Hitler was an allied friend, why did he not support with every possible means the anti-Hitler 'fifth column' in Germany, as Alexander would certainly have done in his place? The most likely answer would appear to be that he was so blinded by the fire and smoke of his warlike propaganda that he could not see the German inner front; because he could not see it, he committed the self-same blunder made by Hitler when he failed to differentiate between the pro- and anti-Stalinist peoples in the U.S.S.R.

In Germany this danger was clearly seen by Dr Goebbels, who had opposed Hitler's insane Russian policy; in his diary he wrote:

> If I were on the enemy side, I should from the very first day have adopted the slogan of fighting against Nazism, but not against the German people. That was how Chamberlain began on the first day of the war, but, thank God, the English did not pursue this line. . . . The German people must remain convinced – as indeed facts warrant – that this war strikes at their very lives and their national possibilities of development, and that they must fight it with their entire strength.[1]

Because of their blind policy, a malign retribution stalked the allied powers. On January 22, 1943, the leaders of the two main anti-Hitler factions – those who wanted to assassinate Hitler and those who wanted to subject him to the General Staff – met in Berlin to square their differences. Then, on the following day, before they had arrived at a decision, Roosevelt's and Churchill's proclamation of Unconditional Surrender was announced from Casablanca: 'a formula which', Görlitz declares, 'gave the death blow to any hopes that may have been entertained either by the "shadow government" or by the oppositional elements in the General Staff, that their enemies would negotiate with a "respectable" government'.[2]

What did these two fateful words imply? The answer is, because Hitler and all who supported him would not surrender in order to be exterminated, and because the cause of their opponents within Germany was hamstrung by the refusal of the Western Powers to recognize it, the entire population of Germany was to be driven in desperation to Hitler's support, as the population of Russia had been driven to Stalin's support. This meant that the war was to be prolonged indefinitely; that hundreds of thousands of killed and wounded were to be

[1] *The Goebbels Diaries* (1948), p. 102.   [2] *The German General Staff*, p. 430.

added to the casualty lists; that scores of German cities were to be obliterated; and that a strategic vacuum was to be created in eastern and central Europe, which could be filled by one power only – Soviet Russia.

Shortly after these fateful words were broadcast to a demented world, Stalin, the adept in revolutionary warfare, proclaimed that 'It would be ridiculous to identify Hitler's clique with the German people and the German state', and that it was a stupid lie and senseless slander 'to suggest, as the democratic press did, that the aim of the Red army was to exterminate the German people and the German state'. Yet, as each foreign country was overrun, he established in it a Communist puppet government, which called upon him to support it with the Red army in order to destroy its opponents. Thus it came about that, by the time the war ended, Stalin was able to establish his autocracy over Estonia, Latvia, Lithuania, part of Finland, Poland, eastern and central Germany, a third of Austria, Yugoslavia, Hungary, Rumania and Bulgaria; and immediately afterward in preparation for the Communist conquest of the world, he began to foster inner fronts in the countries of his allies.

When the war policies of the Western allies are compared with those of Philip of Macedon and his son Alexander, will it be said that the democratic statesmen of the twentieth century could not have learnt lessons of inestimable value from the history of the fourth century B.c.? Their ignorance of history was their Nemesis, and their war a Greek tragedy.

INDEX

Other DA CAPO titles of interest